WOMEN'S TRAVEL WRITINGS IN INDIA
1777–1854

WOMEN'S TRAVEL WRITINGS IN INDIA 1777–1854

Edited by
Éadaoin Agnew

Volume III

LONDON AND NEW YORK

First published 2020
by Routledge
2 Park Square, Milton Park, Abingdon, Oxon OX14 4RN

and by Routledge
52 Vanderbilt Avenue, New York, NY 10017

Routledge is an imprint of the Taylor & Francis Group, an informa business

© 2020 selection and editorial matter, Carl Thompson, Katrina O'Loughlin, Michael Gamer, Éadaoin Agnew and Betty Hagglund; individual owners retain copyright in their own material.

The right of Carl Thompson, Katrina O'Loughlin, Michael Gamer, Éadaoin Agnew and Betty Hagglund to be identified as the authors of the editorial material, and of the authors for their individual chapters, has been asserted in accordance with sections 77 and 78 of the Copyright, Designs and Patents Act 1988.

All rights reserved. No part of this book may be reprinted or reproduced or utilised in any form or by any electronic, mechanical, or other means, now known or hereafter invented, including photocopying and recording, or in any information storage or retrieval system, without permission in writing from the publishers.

Trademark notice: Product or corporate names may be trademarks or registered trademarks, and are used only for identification and explanation without intent to infringe.

British Library Cataloguing-in-Publication Data
A catalogue record for this book is available from the British Library

Library of Congress Cataloging-in-Publication Data
A catalog record for this book has been requested

ISBN: 978-1-138-20272-6 (Set)
eISBN: 978-1-315-47317-8 (Set)
ISBN: 978-1-138-20278-8 (Volume III)
eISBN: 978-1-315-47293-5 (Volume III)

Typeset in Times New Roman
by Apex CoVantage, LLC

Publisher's note
References within each chapter are as they appear in the original complete work

Printed in the United Kingdom
by Henry Ling Limited

CONTENTS

Introduction	1
Ann Deane, *A Tour through the Upper Provinces of Hindostan* (1823)	13
Julia Maitland, *Letters from Madras* (1846)	177
Textual variants	317

INTRODUCTION

Ann Deane (1770–1847) arrived in the subcontinent in 1799, and Julia Maitland (1808–1864) departed in 1839. During this forty-year period, Britain's relationship with India changed considerably; by 1818, almost the entirety of India, with the exception of the Punjab and Sindh, was under the direct or indirect control of the East India Company, with the Company's role now shifting from trade and the accumulation of wealth to what was in effect the imperial governance of its extensive territories. And yet, as Ashley L. Cohen states in her Introduction to *Lady Nugent's East India Journal* (2014), this is 'an era that is relatively underrepresented in British literature about colonial India'.[1] She explains that most travel accounts, in their various forms, focus either on the earlier decades of great territorial conquest (1770s and 1780s), or on the time around and after the First War of Indian Independence in 1857. Critical interest in the intervening period is similarly sparse, especially in relation to women's travel writing, despite the publication of a number of interesting texts.[2] To counter such absences, this volume brings together Deane's *A Tour through the Upper Provinces of Hindostan; Comprising a Period between the Years 1804 and 1814: with Remarks and Authentic Anecdotes* (1823) and Maitland's *Letters from Madras, During the Years 1836–1839* (first published in 1843 but reproduced here from the second edition of 1846). In doing so, it illustrates some important ideological shifts in Britain's imperial policies that took place at the start of the nineteenth century and that contributed to a later phase of colonial expansion; and it shows that women took part in contemporary debates and discourses relating to these issues. At the same time, by reading these two texts together, we can trace changes to the travel genre; in particular, we see here the transition from information-based travel books to the more personal and narrative forms of travel writing now familiar to modern readers. In women's writing, such developments were undoubtedly influenced by increasingly dominant gender discourses that separated the public and private spheres; however, they were also the result of broader generic expectations and Britain's changing attitude to India.

INTRODUCTION

Ann Deane

Ann Deane was the eldest daughter of John Deane, Esq., of Hartley Court, Berkshire, a magistrate and receiver for the county, and Sarah Ann Deane (d. 1818). She married her cousin Captain Charles Meredith Deane (1762–1815) of the 24th Light Dragoons in 1786, and they had two sons Charles (1791–1853) and John Bathurst (1797–1887). In 1799 the family sailed to India, leaving young Charles at home in accordance with the custom at the time; children from the age of six or seven were often schooled in Britain while their parents were stationed in India. Accordingly, when John Deane turned eight, his mother travelled with him to England and placed him in Bath Grammar School. She returned to India in 1804, joining her husband in Calcutta, whereupon they departed for Kanpur almost immediately. They only returned to the 'City of Palaces' later that year, once the Second Anglo-Maratha War (1803–1805) had drawn to a close. It is at this point that Deane's travel narrative begins without any acknowledgement of previous events. This omission of biographical information is in keeping with the rest of the text and, as a result, we know little about Ann or Charles Deane.

Instead of disclosing personal information, Deane's account of India chiefly focuses on external elements. She adopts a style of writing that Carl Thompson refers to as the 'autoptic principle'.[3] At its most simple, this formal strategy employs first-person verb forms, such as 'I saw', 'I went', 'I did', and largely excludes sentimental or emotional engagement. In this way, Deane's narrative mode insists upon her value as a trustworthy eyewitness; it places her firmly at the scene and asserts her objectivity. The prefatory advertisement further emphasizes this position by stating that the travelogue was written by 'a lady, who has witnessed all that she describes, and whose chief aim on the indulgence of the reader is authenticity' (p. 21). It also explains: 'The scenes she has endeavoured to pourtray, occurred in the order wherein they are here related: the reader must not therefore expect a finished and elaborate performance; but a plain, simple narrative of facts' (p. 21). Yet even the most apparently impartial travel account requires selection and organization, and Deane's travels had a very particular focus, being largely determined by her husband's work as a District Collector in areas recently procured or protected by the East India Company.

In March 1805, the Deanes set out from Calcutta travelling north-west through Patna, Buxar, Benares, Kanpur, and Agra in the modern state of Uttar Pradesh. Historically a major administrative centre for the Mughal Empire and the site of architectural wonders such as the Taj Mahal, Agra had recently come under Company control as a result of the British victory over the Marathas. The Deanes settled just outside the city in Sikandra in July 1805, and this became their base for several years although Deane's narrative gives no account of this period of residence, with the exception of some information regarding the tourist sites. Deane then resumes her narrative when she embarks on her next journey on 1 December 1808. She travels north to the Mughal capital Delhi, which had, like Agra, fallen to the British during the Second Anglo-Maratha War, and follows a circular route through other notable sites of recent acquisition, such as Meerut, Moradabad, Bareilly, and Fateghar, and back to the residence at Sikandra. Approximately six months later, in September 1809, Deane travels along the Ganges from Fateghar to Pusa near Patna and returns by land to Meerut in January 1810. After this, there is another narrative gap until April 1811 when she sets out on her final tour of the Bareilly district, previously Rohilkhand, which Nawab Saadat Ali Khan (c. 1752–1814) had ceded to the British in 1801 as payment for debts accrued during the Rohilla War (1773–1774). The Deanes spent two months in Jehanabad, near Pilibhit, and a month in Bareilly before arriving in Meerut in July 1811.

At this point, Deane closes the travelogue rather abruptly, giving no explanation and providing no narrative closure, although it would be another three years before she left India in 1814; her husband remained in India and died there a year later. Deane's departure was possibly due to escalating tensions between the British and the Maratha Empire, which culminated in the Third Anglo-Maratha War a few years later (1817–1818). Arguably this ongoing conflict and the complex political situation, together with Deane's personal loss, prevented the completion of her narrative, which was not published until 1823. By waiting until after the War, when there was a period of relative stability in the upper provinces, she perhaps felt more able to produce a reliable and useful account of British territories. And Deane undoubtedly intended for her text to be helpful, not least because she travelled through areas relatively unfamiliar to Western travellers. To this end she provides information about modes of transport and the viability of roads, as well as accounts of military stations, historical ruins, and royal residences. Deane also outlines the recent political history of the area, discussing conflicts such as the battles of Plassey (1757) and Buxar (1764), and often focusing on the despotic and capricious nature of the indigenous leaders who challenged Company rule, such as Mir Qasim (*d*.1777).[4]

In addition to the main narrative, the text includes two glossaries, one for the tour and one for the voyage out, and a 'Guide' intended for any 'young man' (p. 145) travelling to India, especially those employed by the King's troops or the East India Company. Here Deane sets out 'the correct distances of every station, and what their [sic] produce' (p. 143) without the broader historical, cultural, and political material. The separation of such factual information from the more descriptive elements of a travel account was not uncommon. It was also used, for example, by Anne Elwood in her *Narrative of a Journey Overland from England by the Continent of Europe, Egypt, and the Red Sea to India* (1830). This formal arrangement allowed for the inclusion of personal and literary modes of writing travel while maintaining a strong commitment to utility. Thus, while Deane maintains a largely impersonal and generally informative tone throughout, she occasionally digresses, in her main narrative, into subjective and what were at this date more typically feminine points of interest, such as information about domestic life on the road and in the camps, the types of servants required, the different forms of accommodation available, and the necessary arrangements for carrying food and for cooking. Deane also expresses considerable interest in the lives of Indian women, especially those in the upper echelons of society such as the renowned Begum Sumroo (c. 1753–1836) whom she met in Delhi in 1808. Begum Sumroo had risen from inauspicious beginnings to become the ruler of Sardhana and Deane recognizes this authority in gendered terms, writing: 'This woman has an uncommon share of natural abilities, with a strength of mind rarely met with, particularly in a female' (p. 94). She praises the Begum's military prowess and political position and eagerly accepts an invitation to accompany her to the Mughal Court at Delhi. Deane is undoubtedly interested in the Mughal Emperor Akbar II, but she takes advantage of her privileged access to the women's quarters and largely focuses her attention on the women of the court: the Queen, the Dowager Begum, and the princes' wives. In doing so, Deane caters to the persistent Western fascination with these secluded spaces, providing insight and information that was unavailable to her male peers.[5]

Deane's time among India's elites is short as her itinerary is subject to her husband's work in some of India's richest and most fertile areas. However, Deane also uses this to her advantage and writes extensively about the natural landscape. Information about India's flora and fauna was particularly valuable at this time. The recent wars had been costly and in the early decades of the nineteenth century India faced economic depression.[6] In light of this, both the Company and the British Government perceived the land as a probable source of development. To this end a Trigonometrical Survey of the subcontinent had been launched in 1802 and Colin Mackenzie (1754–1821) appointed as Surveyor General of India in 1815;[7] these endeavours were further extended by a network of investigators responsible for cataloguing every aspect of India's natural resources. Deane and her husband travel for a time with two such surveyors:

> These provinces having been newly conquered by the British army, had as yet paid no revenue to Government, who accordingly appointed two commissioners to survey them, and form an estimate of what they were capable of furnishing. I consider myself particularly fortunate in being of their party, since it afforded me a more perfect view of the manners and customs of the natives, and a better opportunity of seeing the country than was likely to occur again; indeed we visited some parts of it where Europeans had never been before.
>
> (p. 90)

This opportunity enabled Deane to pass on to a general readership valuable information about raw materials, plants, and trees, as well as the condition of the roads, the climates, and the landscape in the upper provinces, which she generally perceives in relation to productivity and utility. In doing so, she usually avoids the aestheticizing eye associated with later women travel writers in India such as Fanny Parks (1794–1875) and Emma Roberts (1794–1840).[8] Deane occasionally refers to picturesque or sublime scenes, but it is surely notable that the word 'cultivation', or some derivative of it, appears 35 times in *A Tour*; for example:

> [W]e struck across the country, driving through groves of mango and tamarind trees alternately, enlivened by cultivation of grain, through which meandered a deep pellucid stream called the *Rewah*, bounded by banks of the liveliest verdure.
>
> (p. 51)

In this way, her representations of India's landscape contribute to an 'imperial archive', to use Thomas Richards' term, even though she could not work directly for the East India Company or British Government.[9]

While Deane focuses largely on material aspects of the Indian landscape, she acknowledges an interest in British governance beyond its ability to generate increased revenue. Deane tells her readers that Charles, during his time as Collector, cleared the jungle around Bodgepoore and put the lands into a state of cultivation. She writes that now 'Indigo flourishes particularly well in this part of India' (p. 60). She also notes that this action freed the area from banditti who were too afraid to carry out their depredations in the open space. Her mention of the blue dye alongside assurances of new-found stability and safety was surely deliberate. Indigo was a highly profitable natural resource in great demand, and her comment indicates the economic potential of this recently secured area. But she also attends to an encroaching paternalism that found the desire for pure profit unpalatable and so sought to emphasize the benefits for the local community.

Deane predominantly perceives the Indian people in stereotypically religious terms. Muslims are apparently brave, while being treacherous and tyrannical; Hindus are caste-ridden, superstitious, and indolent, as manifested by sensationalized accounts of *sati* and the notorious hook ceremony. Nonetheless, she appears to support the East India Company's position on religious non-interference:

> It is a system of policy on the part of the English to protect, as far as is in their power, the religious ceremonies of both; since it is chiefly owing to these means that we keep our possessions in the country.
>
> (p. 62)

Deane is clearly aware of current debates around religious conversion, which were brought into focus by the East India Act of 1813, and its removal of the ban on missionary activity. But unlike Maitland some 20 years later, Deane sees conversion work as rather fruitless and maintains an illusion of British co-operation with, rather than coercion of, Indian customs and traditions.

In this regard, Deane's account reveals an enduring Orientalist admiration of India's upper echelons (understanding 'Orientalist' here in the sense outlined in the General Introduction: see Volume I, p. xiv). She delights in the pomp and circumstance of the Royal Palace at Delhi and is particularly impressed by the opulent adornments of the Empress. The Indians who receive her highest praise, however, have also willingly engaged with European culture. Deane takes care to mention that the Begum Sumroo only follows Muslim traditions with regard to food, and that she frequently entertained notable British figures, such as Lord Lake. Similarly, Deane celebrates the Nawab of Lucknow's adoption of Western ideas and compares him to an English nobleman.

Britain's persistent fascination with India's ruling classes is reflected in the largely positive reviews of Deane's text, which keenly point out her elite interactions. For example, *La Belle Assemblée or Bell's Court and Fashionable Magazine* especially enjoyed Deane's tales of the Nawab's lavish lifestyle.[10] In contrast, the *Gentleman's Magazine* preferred to mock the Nawab's erroneous assumption of British customs and his misuse of imported crockery.[11] Such disdain possibly reflects the decline of indigenous power and authority during this period; it is also indicative of the growing dominance, among many British commentators by the 1820s, of Anglicist over Orientalist attitudes. Both of the latter tendencies – the declining power of native elites and an increasingly dismissive attitude to Indians among the British – are even more emphatically on show in Julia Maitland's *Letters from Madras*, published over 20 years later. Somewhat paradoxically, however, Maitland seems both to evince yet also to lament and critique these developments.

Julia Maitland

Julia Maitland (*née* Barrett) was born in London to Henry Barrett (1756–1843) and his wife Charlotte, *née* Francis (1786–1870), the niece of the novelist Frances Burney. In 1836, Julia met and married James Thomas, a widower with three daughters and a judge in the Madras Presidency in India. They left for India almost immediately and arrived in Madras in December 1836 where they stayed for seven months before James Thomas was appointed Judge at Rajahmundry. They spent the next 18 months in this 'up country' station, with the exception of seasonal sojourns in Samuldavee by the coast. In 1839, Thomas received two new postings; the first took him to Cuddapah and Bellary, the second to Bangalore. At this time, Julia Thomas was advised to return home with their daughter Henrietta, who was sick, and their newborn son. Not long after she left, her husband died in India. Two years later, in 1842, Julia married the author and curate Charles Maitland (1815–1866).

Like Deane then, Maitland's journey was not undertaken independently; both women accompanied their husbands to India. However, unlike Deane, Maitland did not embark on further interior travels. Her experiences were limited to a few south Indian locations, and her published narrative largely describes her own daily life in these areas. As such, it is one of the earliest examples of a domesticating 'travel' account in India, a genre that developed as increasing numbers of British women journeyed to the subcontinent in order to facilitate the wider policies of racial difference and distance instigated by Lord Cornwallis's reforms of 1793. Subsequently, an upsurge in Protestant evangelicalism, a rise in utilitarian and reformist politics, and a pronounced sense of imperial superiority in the victorious aftermath of the Napoleonic Wars (1803–1815) produced an overarching ideal of 'Anglicizing' India through moral and social change. To help achieve this, English women were asked to fulfil their colonial duty by marrying English men, living in English bungalows, producing English children, and generally enacting the virtues of Victorian femininity in India.[12]

Like many British wives in the subcontinent, Maitland spends her days managing her home, attending social engagements, supporting her husband, learning languages, and pursuing various hobbies, such as entomology. These are largely recorded as leisurely pastimes, apparently entertaining rather than instructive; but such seemingly trivial pursuits also contributed to the broader sphere of imperial knowledge that underpinned British commercial and political interests in Indian.[13] Of particular note are the insect specimens Maitland collected and sent to the British Museum, which included five new species.[14] In addition to these activities, Maitland became involved in various philanthropic projects, which brought her into contact with local people. Her narrative focuses on these individuals, their social and religious differences, and her commitment to the 'improvement' of India through the civilizing properties of an English education, Christian morality, and British governance as propagated by imperial individuals.

This heightened sense of personal responsibility for empire is arguably reflected in the more subjective tone of Maitland's narrative, which allots far more space than Deane's journal to incidental or personal impressions and to amusing or whimsical reflections. Such subjectivism would become strongly associated with female travellers in the latter half of the nineteenth century; this stylistic shift has in turn often encouraged later readers to gloss over women's contribution to imperial projects, since their accounts seem so resolutely focused on personal and domestic details. Maitland's more personalized and entertaining style on the one hand reflects a broader generic tendency in travel writing in the 1830s and 1840s. These decades saw a dramatic upsurge in the publication of guidebooks in a recognizably modern form, produced by publishers like John Murray and Baedeker; and as guidebooks did away with the need to provide straightforward practical and historical information for travellers, more literary modes of travel writing began to prioritize the presentation in print of a distinctive authorial sensibility and style.[15] In the colonial setting of India, however, we may perhaps also read this stylistic tendency as reflective of the ostensibly reformed, and reformist, imperial attitudes emerging in this period. Arguably it signals a more benevolent narrator, who privileges personal engagement and responsibility over political and economic concerns.

With regard to this aspect of Maitland's narrative, we should also keep in mind Sara Mills's observation that such seemingly 'subjective' narrative forms and reflections were often discursive negotiations that did not necessarily preclude the pursuit and provision of authoritative knowledge.[16] In the early decades of the nineteenth century, for example, both men and women often used letters or journals (usually edited at some later date) to emphasize the authenticity and immediacy of their writing and to position the narrative self as an accurate and truthful observer.[17] Indeed Maitland is keen to assert the authoritative nature of her text, declaring that her narrative letters were 'printed verbatim from the originals' (p. 181) with the necessary omission of family details, such as full or correct names. For Claire Broome Saunders such claims to truthfulness often had a dual function: 'Truth in travel writing appears, paradoxically, as both an assertion of "masculine" objective rhetoric, and the apparently "authentic" utterance of such "feminine", domestic, private literature'.[18] Arguably then, Maitland's more personal style seeks to inscribe, rather than disguise, a certain authority. This is certainly the case when she writes about educational reform.

When Maitland arrives in Madras, she is immediately keen to engage with the local people. She expresses a desire to 'get into one of their native houses' (p. 206), and she frequently laments her British companions' – and indeed, her husband's! – lack of curiosity about the local people and criticizes their condescending attitude. She disparages the pervasive ennui and arrogance of Anglo-Indian society in Madras, stating a preference for Rajahmundry because she feels it is the 'real India' (p. 227). This is, of course, a problematic assertion but Maitland did have the opportunity to engage with many Indian people from various walks of life during her time there. For Maitland, these interactions were much more interesting than the obligations of a growing colonial society.

Over the course of Maitland's published narrative, one senses the author becoming more sharply critical of particular governing policies. The later letters include some angry denunciations of the East India Company's taxation system and its role in causing famines, and also of the flow of indentured labourers from India to Mauritius – something Maitland regards as slavery in all but name. Such attacks on contemporary colonialism, however, do not seem to have diminished Maitland's belief in Britain's 'civilizing' role in India. Nor did they encourage greater receptivity and understanding of Indian culture. She remained critical of many indigenous beliefs, traditions, and cultures. The Indian people's apparent ignorance and their seemingly stubborn attachment to traditional ideas about religion and science frustrate her, and she refers frequently to this as evidence of their uncivilized and unenlightened nature. As Indira Ghose explains, by the 1830s, 'evangelical notions that equated Indian culture with depravity had gained widespread currency'.[19] On occasion, Maitland also deploys a racialized – and racist – terminology, referring to 'brownies', 'blackies', and a 'nigger-looking child' (p. 223). This vocabulary arguably reflects the growing influence of contemporary race science, which postulated essential moral and intellectual differences between the races. Nonetheless, like many of her contemporaries, Maitland evidently believed that such racial characteristics could be overcome through education and reform. In thus seeking to transform Indian society, however, she was at odds with official Company policy. There was considerable discussion about the extent to which Britain could and should intervene in indigenous practices, especially given the long history of non-interference. But ultimately the Company, wary of alienating local communities, maintained that Indian religions must be respected, and insisted upon the continued presence of British officials at local religious events, a dictate that infuriated Maitland. She records in scathing and sarcastic tones several instances when colonial officers were required to facilitate religious feasts and celebrations, such as the festival at Trichinopoly where the troops had to stay in the sun for nine hours, 'firing salutes, and "showing respect" to Mohammed' (p. 254).

In 1837, such obligations prompted 203 East India Company employees to submit a request for exemption from compulsory attendance at indigenous religious events. The official Government response, as quoted by Maitland, stated: *'no salutes to idols be discontinued*, but all respect be paid to the native religions as heretofore' (p. 254). For Maitland, this policy went beyond mere respect and toleration and actively encouraged what she regarded as idolatrous and barbaric practices:

> I believe that if idolatry were merely tolerated and protected, the idol services would fall almost to nothing, from the indifference of the mass of the people; but our Christian Government not only support and encourage it, but force it down the people's throats.
>
> (p. 255)

Maitland was by no means alone in her outrage. She sympathetically notes that Sir Peregrine Maitland resigned from his position as Commander-in-Chief at Madras because he too disagreed with the current directives.

Despite Maitland's clear opposition to the government's policy of non-interference, she did not engage in explicit efforts to convert the Indian people to Christianity. Instead, she devoted her energy to educational projects, believing these would pave the way for religious change. She established a local school with her husband for male students of different castes and provided them with a predominantly English education. She then set up a reading room in the bazaar, stocked with reading material in a variety of languages: Gentoo, Hindi, Tamil, and English.[20] The success of this endeavour further encouraged her, and Maitland began to circulate endorsed reading materials in nearby villages. Eventually she also publicly called on her peers and the government to put in place a national schooling system as outlined in her open letter on 'Native Education'.

Maitland first published this short treatise in *The Spectator*, a daily newspaper in Madras, and subsequently included it in *Letters*. Here she set out – in a public forum – a clear model for the public funding of European schools throughout the subcontinent, providing costings and organizational structures, as well as ideological justifications for including religious education in the curriculum. She engaged directly with specific debates around religious conversion and India's anglicization, as outlined by the likes of Thomas Babington Macaulay in his oft-quoted *Minute on Indian Education* (1835), and it is possible to read Maitland's paper as a direct engagement with this earlier proposal. Macaulay had argued for the creation of an English-educated middle class of Indian men who would then act as civilizing forces by disseminating colonial cultural values in their local societies. Like Macaulay, Maitland believed that an English education would eventually displace indigenous beliefs; she writes: 'I fully believe that, if schools were set up all over the country, it would go far towards shaking their Heathenism, by putting truth into their heads, at any rate, instead of falsehood' (p. 232). It was a popular idea and there was much support for this model of education in the early decades of the nineteenth century. It was expressed in travelogues, such as that by Marianne Postans.[21] And it was documented in official papers by the likes of Alexander Ross and Sir Thomas Munro, the Governor of Madras, who had devised a comprehensive plan for governmental education in south India but died before he could implement it.[22] Consequently, as Maitland explains, there existed various independent projects, such as Andrew Bell's school, but there was no organized or standardized structure. She hoped to rectify this with her proposal, written at a timely moment.

Letters from Madras was published anonymously in 1843. Maitland's firsthand experiences of colonial policy meant that her narrative was received as a useful contribution to knowledge about India, especially by those who also opposed the East India Company's policies on religious toleration. *The Churchman's Companion*, for example, stated that Maitland gave 'a fearful picture of the Infidelity of the Indian Government' and included extracts from her narrative as proof of this problem.[23] Other reviewers flagged up the volume's entertaining style, praising Maitland for what one review termed 'her natural vivacity and smartness'.[24] Yet for most of these reviewers, it seems these literary or belle-lettristic qualities did not prevent Maitland's narrative also being regarded as a source of useful information. Thus the *Gentleman's Magazine* highlighted Maitland's 'very lively style' and 'dash of satirical observation' but also judged the book 'a good, and evidently a genuine account of the manners and society of India'.[25] Similarly, Elizabeth Eastlake writing anonymously in the *Quarterly Review* praised 'the sound domesticity that pervades this book', and described it as 'the very lightest work that has ever appeared from India' – but then immediately appended to the last comment, 'yet it tells us more of what everybody cares to know than any other'.[26] Apparently, a travelogue could be both diverting and educational, and Eastlake did not perceive these properties in terms of gender.

In the early decades of the nineteenth century, women like Deane and Maitland usually travelled and worked alongside their husbands. Their journeys and subsequent travel narratives thus usually arose from specific imperial purposes and roles, rather than individual whim or aspiration. In that sense, their subjectivities, and to some extent their gender, remained secondary to an overarching ideal: the provision of information about India. By the 1830s, however, changing literary tastes and an increasing sense of individual duty and colonial responsibility encouraged some imperial travellers to include a greater quotient of personal information. There was a greater demand for individual engagement and private lives, and the female traveller had a sufficiently strong sense of her own imperial duty to inscribe her experiences in the travel narrative. Maitland does not extend to the emotional reflections of other contemporary writers, such as Emily Eden or Lady Nugent, but she does move significantly beyond the far more objectivist reporting of Deane's narrative.[27] We see here a generic progression that is not entirely related to gender.

Notes

1 A. L. Cohen, 'Introduction', in *Lady Nugent's East India Journal: A Critical Edition* (Oxford: Oxford University Press, 2014), p. xxxi.
2 See for example: Maria Graham, *Journal of a Residence in India* (1812); Harriet Ashmore, *Narrative of a Three Months' March in India, and a Residence in the Dooab* (1841); Eliza Fay, *Original Letters from India, Containing a Narrative of a Journey through Egypt and the Author's Imprisonment at Calicut by Hyder Ally* (1817); Marianne Postans, *Western India, in 1838* (1839); A. L. Cohen (ed.), *Lady Nugent's East India Journal: A Critical Edition* (New Delhi: Oxford University Press, 2014).
3 C. Thompson, *Travel Writing* (Abingdon: Routledge, 2011), p. 65.
4 Deane relates various stories about Mir Qasim, see for example p. 55.
5 See J. Nair, 'Uncovering the Zenana: Visions of Indian Womanhood in Englishwomen's Writing, 1813–1940', *Journal of Women's History* 2:1 (1990), pp. 8–34; I. Ghose, *Women Travellers in Colonial India: The Power of the Female Gaze* (Oxford: Oxford University Press, 1998), Chapter 3: 'The Female Gaze: Encounters in the Zenana'.
6 B. D. Metcalf and T. R. Metcalf, *A Concise History of Modern India* (Cambridge: Cambridge University Press, [2001] 2013), p. 77.
7 For more on the surveying of India, see M. Edney, *Mapping an Empire: The Geographical Construction of British India, 1765–1843* (Chicago, IL: The University of Chicago Press, 1997).
8 See for example, Fanny Parks' *Wanderings of a Pilgrim in search of the Picturesque, During four and twenty years in the East; With Revelations of Life in the Zenana* (1850) and Emma Roberts' *Scenes and Characteristics of Hindostan, with Sketches of Anglo-Indian Society* (1835).
9 See T. Richards, *The Imperial Archive: Knowledge and the Fantasy of Empire* (London: Verso Books, 1993).
10 'Review', *La Belle Assemblée or Bell's Court and Fashionable Magazine* 29 (February 1824), pp. 77–8.
11 'Review of Tour through Hindostan', *Gentleman's Magazine: and Historical Chronicle* 94:1 (February 1824), pp. 144–5.
12 See É. Agnew, *Imperial Women Writers in Victorian India: Representing Colonial Life 1850–1910* (Cham: Palgrave Macmillan, 2017).
13 Agnew, *Imperial Women Writers*, pp. 105–35.

14 Maitland mentions that she sent new specimens to the British Museum, and she notes that there were five new species; see *Letters*, p. 289. The Natural History Museum in London has a record of the donation but no record of the specific specimens.
15 See C. Thompson, 'Nineteenth-Century Travel Writing', in N. Das and T. Youngs (eds), *The Cambridge History of Travel Writing* (Cambridge: Cambridge University Press, 2019), pp. 108–24, especially pp. 119–22.
16 S. Mills, *Discourses of Difference: An Analysis of Women's Travel Writing* (Manchester: Manchester University Press, 1991), p. 63.
17 See for example, M. Park, *The Life and Travels of Mungo Park* (London: J. W. Parker, 1838) which was based on his journal, and R. Heber, *Narrative of a Journey through the Upper Provinces of India* (London: J. Murray, 1828), which used the epistolary form.
18 C. Broome Saunders, 'Introduction', in *Women, Travel Writing, and Truth* (Abingdon: Routledge, 2014), p. 3.
19 I. Ghose, *Memsahibs Abroad: Writings by Women Travellers in Nineteenth-Century India* (New Delhi: Oxford University Press, 1998), p. 77.
20 J. Wang, 'Entry on Julia Maitland', *Oxford Dictionary of National Biography*, available at www.oxforddnb.com.ezproxy.kingston.ac.uk/view/10.1093/ref:odnb/9780198614128.001.0001/odnb-9780198614128-e-48645?rskey=b1xReC&result=1. Last accessed September 2018.
21 See M. Postans, *Western India, in 1838* (London: Saunders and Otley, 1839), p. 307.
22 See R. E. Frykenberg, 'Modern Education in South India 1784–1854: Its Roots and Its Role as a Vehicle of Integration under Company Raj', *The American Historical Review* 91:1 (1986), p. 42.
23 'Infidelity of the Indian Government' in *Churchman's Companion*, 30:2 (August 1847), p. 63.
24 *Monthly Review* 1 (New Series, 1843), p. 101.
25 *Gentleman's Magazine* (1843), p. 58.
26 E. Eastlake, 'Lady Travellers', *Quarterly Review* 76 (June 1845), pp. 53–74; these quotations, p. 60.
27 See E. Eden, *Up the Country* (London: Virago Press, [1866] 1983), p. 396, and Nugent, *East India Journal*, p. 333.

ANN DEANE,
A TOUR THROUGH THE UPPER PROVINCES OF HINDOSTAN (1823)

Ann Deane (1770–1847) travelled to India in 1799, accompanying her husband, Captain Charles Meredith Deane of the 24th Light Dragoons. The couple left behind their eldest son, Charles, so that he could be educated in England but took with them a younger child, John Bathurst Deane. Little is known of the first period of the Deanes' residence in India; however, in 1804 Ann returned to England to place John in school, then sailed back to India with Charles, now aged 14. She rejoined her husband at Calcutta, and then resided in India for another ten years. During this time she accompanied her husband – now employed by the East India Company as a District Collector – on several long tours of the Company's recently acquired northern provinces in Bengal, Bihar, and Uttar Pradesh. These tours subsequently became the focus of her published narrative, which elides the family's periods of more settled residence and instead records four main journeys taking in Patna, Buxar, Benares, Kanpur, and Agra (in 1805); Delhi, Meerut, Moradabad, Bareilly, and Fateghar (in 1808–1809); to Pusa along the Ganges and then back to Meerut by road (in late 1809); and finally through the Bareilly district (in 1811). Deane then remained in India a further three years, finally quitting the subcontinent in 1814; her departure was possibly due to escalating tensions between the East India Company and the Maratha Confederacy, which culminated in the Third Anglo-Maratha War of 1817–18. Charles Meredith Deane remained behind and died in India in 1815.

A Tour through the Upper Provinces of Hindostan; Comprising a Period between the Years 1804 and 1814: with Remarks and Authentic Anecdotes was published anonymously in 1823, nine years after Deane's return to Britain: it is not known why there was such a time lag between her return and the volume's appearance. The book was widely reviewed and generally received favourable – albeit clearly gendered – notices. Thus the *Literary Chronicle* rather neglected her political discussions but praised her instead for 'observations and occurrences as might be expected to be noticed by an intelligent female'.[1] Similarly, *The Gentleman's Magazine* praised Deane's prose, citing her adherence to the 'lively brilliance of prattlement, a subtle tact and delicacy which often distinguishes the sentiment of women'.[2] Indeed, despite Deane's inclusion of glossaries, maps, and a Guide designated for male travellers, the text was principally seen as amusing rather than instructive. *The Gentleman's Magazine* concluded:

> To invite women to read heavy books, would be like asking them to drag a garden-roller, or trundle a loaded wheelbarrow; but we fearlessly placed this interesting Tour before some of our female acquaintance; and they declared that they had found it as entertaining as a novel, and had skipped only the maps and letter-press guide. In truth, it is an uncommonly pleasing book.[3]

Perhaps due to this feminization which depoliticized Deane's text, there were no subsequent editions, and this is the first reissue of the volume.

Little is known of Deane's life back in Britain, and she did not publish any further books. She died in Bath in 1847.

Notes

1 'Review of *Tour through the Upper Provinces* by A. D.', Literary Chronicle 52 (1823), p. 819.
2 'Review of *Tour through the Upper Provinces* by A. D.', Gentleman's Magazine: and Historical Chronicle 135 (1824), p. 144.
3 Ibid., p. 145.

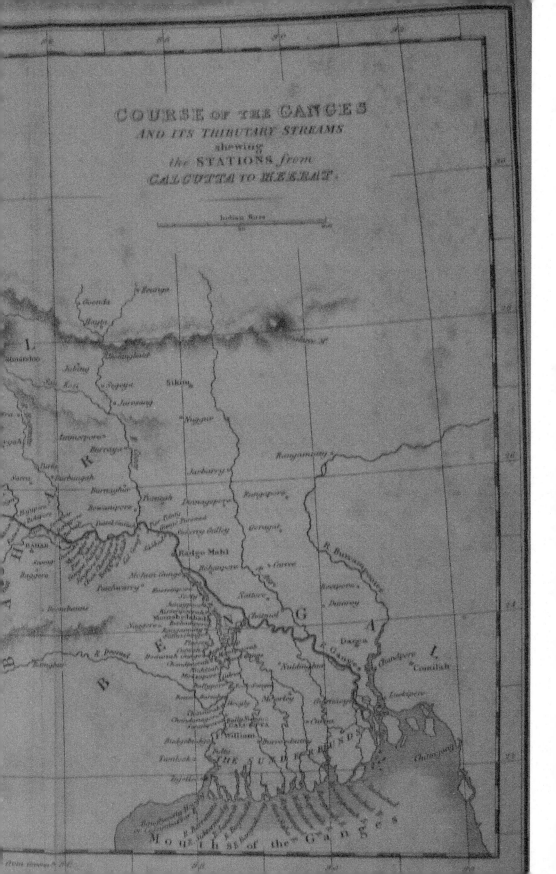

A

TOUR

THROUGH

THE UPPER PROVINCES

OF

𝔇indostan:

COMPRISING A PERIOD BETWEEN THE YEARS
1804 AND 1814:

WITH

REMARKS AND AUTHENTIC ANECDOTES.

TO WHICH IS ANNEXED,

A GUIDE UP THE RIVER GANGES,

WITH

A MAP FROM THE SOURCE TO THE MOUTH.

BY A. D.

LONDON:
PRINTED FOR C. & J. RIVINGTON,

ST. PAUL'S CHURCH-YARD,

AND WATERLOO-PLACE, PALL-MALL.

1823.

ADVERTISEMENT.

THE following pages were not originally intended for the public eye, nor may they perhaps be deemed worthy public attention. They are neither the production of a philosopher, nor of a man of genius; but of a lady, who has witnessed all that she describes, and whose chief claim on the indulgence of her reader is authenticity.

The scenes she has endeavoured to pourtray, occurred in the order wherein they are here related: the reader must not therefore expect a finished and elaborate performance; but a plain, simple narrative of facts, committed to writing while their impression was yet fresh on the mind of the author.

It may be objected, that this work has too much the manner of a mere journal; but the writer begs to state, that it was composed during her tour, and designed only for the future amusement of her friends.

CONTENTS.

CHAPTER I.

JOURNEY from Calcutta, in Bengal, to the western provinces of Hindostan—Description of the Missionary School at *Serampore*—The governor-general's country residence at *Barrackpore*—The cantonments, &c. . . 29

CHAPTER II.

Superstitious observances—Tatties, how made; the different kinds, and their use—Comocolly feathers—Deserted village—Opposite qualities of the tamarind tree, &c. &c. 33

CHAPTER III.

Description of a serai, or inn, of the country; also of Radge Mahl—The ridge of mountains—People who inhabit them—Obstinate adherence to ancient custom—A curious anecdote 38

CHAPTER IV.

Radge Mahl hills, palace, &c.—A peculiar kind of sheep and goats; also of fence against wild beasts—Description of a *tannah*, or pensioner's village—Ditto of the hill people, or inhabitants of these mountains—Singular mode of guarding against beasts of prey—Unfavourable prospect for missionaries, &c. 44

CHAPTER V.

Apathy of the Hindoos—Predestination—*Monghir*, its chalybeate springs—Curious birds, &c.—An extraordinary machine for crossing torrents—Mode of extracting wheat from the ears—Peculiar properties of the neem tree—Advice to travellers in a foreign country—Traffic on the Ganges—Weavers' looms—City of Patna—Massacre by Sumroo, a German, in the service of *Meer Kossim*, Subah (or chief) of Bengal. 49

CONTENTS.

CHAPTER VI.

PAGE

Curious mistake—Hindoo marriage ceremony—Unjustifiable revenge—power of parents over their children—*Danapore*, a military station; its productions—*Soane* pebbles—banditti 56

CHAPTER VII.

Fort of *Buxar*—Hair-breadth escape from a tiger—*Ghazipore*, a large military and civil station; soil, produce, &c.—City of *Benares*, disturbance at; the cause of it—Anecdote—Insolence of Mussulmen—Produce and manufactures—Important festivals, both Mussulman and Hindoo—Ingenious mode of attack by thieves—City of *Allahabad*, on the confluence of the rivers Ganges and Jumna 61

CHAPTER VIII.

Diamond mine—Medicinal gum—Cowardly nature and avaricious propensities of the natives—Difference between females of Mussulman and Hindoo persuasion, with respect to their occupations and pursuits—Arrival at *Cawnpore*, the largest military station in India—Journey to *Lucknow*, the capital of the province of Oude, and residence of its *Nawaab*—Reception at his court—His mode of evading the laws of his prophet, where they were not agreeable to him—Humorous anecdote—Bigotry of some Mussulmen, an instance of 68

CHAPTER IX.

Arrival at *Futty Ghur*, the residence of the commissioners for the upper, or ceded and conquered provinces—City of *Furrukabad;* its *Nawaab*, produce, &c. &c.—Accident by lightning—Country inundated in a few hours, by a storm—Cruelty of the Pindarees; description of them, mode of warfare, support, &c.; happy effects of their extermination—Extraordinary instances of sudden death—Extent of territory—Conduct of the natives in a state of desperation, equalled only by the Romans in former ages—of *Rajpoots*—Treachery of some native princes, during the war of 1816 and 1817—Siege of *Huttrass*—Description of the blowing up a magazine of Gun-powder—Escape of the Rajah—The *Jauts*, their origin, &c.—Plunder of *Agra*—Putting out the eyes of the Emperor Shaw Allum—Description of the palace at *Agra*—*Secundra*—Superb mausoleum of the Emperor *Acbar* 77

CHAPTER X.

Ferozabad—Native collector of revenue—Effects of intense heat—*Ettamaadpore*, description of—Tomb and garden-house of a rich Mussulman merchant

CONTENTS.

and his wife—Fort of Agra—Wonderful phenomenon—*Chokidars*, their use—Rash invasion of religious ceremonies—*Futtypoor Siccra*, splendid monument, palace, &c.—Description of the *Tadge* at *Agra*, built by the Emperor *Shaw Jehan* in memory of his favourite wife, supposed to be the most beautiful and chaste structure in the world—Verses written on it . .   84

CHAPTER XI.

Town of *Sarseney*—Mud forts—City of *Coel*—Substitute for yeast in rising bread—*Toddy*, its properties—Mats, from what made—Castor oil—Wretched state of the people—Grass jungle—Severe cold—Village inhabited by banditti—Field of battle in 1803, near Delhi—Arrival at Delhi—Reception by the resident at his palace—Memoirs of the *Begum Sumroo*—Palace of the reigning Emperor—Description of, reception by the royal family; their dresses, manners, customs, &c.—Grand entertainment by the Begum Sumroo 89

CHAPTER XII.

A party to view the *Kootub Minar* and wonderful brazen pillar—Tomb of *Suftur Jung, Humayoon*, &c.; also of the Emperors of *Delhi*—Extraordinary prohibition—Effects of priestcraft—Dancing girls—Recitation—Pantomime—Royal Baths, menagerie, and gardens—Singular ceremony—*Meerat*, a large cantonment, arrival there—Description of the country, city, &c. 100

CHAPTER XIII.

The *Begum Sumroo's* palace at *Sirdannah*, her troops, &c.—Fatal effects of cold—A Brahmin's conscience easily satisfied—Arrival at *Saharunpore*—Fancy beards, dress, and dexterity of the *Sieks*—Sale of children—Source of the river *Jumna*—Fortified palace belonging to the Rajah of *Hurdwaar*—Description of this extraordinary man—*Munglore*, the simplicity of its inhabitants, productions, &c.—Impenetrable hedge—The peacock held sacred—Caravan of merchants from *Cabul*—In what their merchandise consisted—First range of hills near the snowy mountains—Reception by the Rajah—Etiquette observed on the occasion—Description of the hall of audience—approach the mountains—beasts of prey—fall in with a party of Sieke Rajahs and their wives—*Hurdoar*, a celebrated bathing place; description of, name, from whence derived—Mode of establishing a village in Hindostan—Town of *Tunkal*, full of magnificent and costly palaces; the reason why—Pilgrims—Waterfalls—Curious method of fording a river—English shrubs and trees found on these mountains—Sagacity of elephants—Stupendous mountains—Grass, like reeds, fourteen feet high—A wild elephant kept at bay—Cross

CONTENTS.

a morass—Enter the *Rohillah* country—*Nugeebabad*, the first place where duties are levied by the British Government on Persian goods—Sugar-mills—Slaves from the hills—Excuse for bringing them down—Their general appearance 107

CHAPTER XIV.

Extraordinary instance of sagacity in a tigress—Town of *Nugeenah*, its manufactures, &c.—Town of *Daumpore*, its manufactures, &c.—A tree scented like mignionette—City of *Moradabad*, its inhabitants, situation, appearance, advantages, and manufactures—Villages in the Rohillah country, in what respect differing from those in the country of the *Douab*—Productions of the Rohillah country—*Bareilly*, a city of some celebrity in history, description of; its inhabitants, climate, manufactures, &c.—*Kutterah*, the scene of conflict between *Sujah Dowlah*, *Nawaab* of Lucknow, and *Haffiz Ramut*, chief of the Rohillahs—Origin of the Rohillah war—Trip to *Behrmundeo* through a thick forest—Food of the native inhabitants, their pursuits and resources—Temple of the deity they worship—Villages on the summit of these mountains—Gold dust—Traverse the snowy mountains—Plants of extraordinary beauty—Dreadful alarm—Dangerous enterprise—Fair held at *Bellary*—Humorous anecdote—All's well that ends well—A wild elephant near the camp—Means taken to frighten him away—A bullock carried off by a tiger—Climate of this terrific region—A band of robbers—Proper months in which to visit it, with any degree of safety—Jellalabad, city of—Crossed the river *Ram Gonga*—Attack by a wild buffalo 117

CHAPTER XV.

Trip down the country by water—Hints how to manage on these occasions—Loss of baggage—Boat in a storm—Ingenious mode of robbing boats—Quicksands—An annual fair for horses of a particular description—Arrival at *Poosa*—Raft of bamboos—Beautiful scenery—Committee—Climate of *Tirhoot*—A wonderful gay spectacle—Return by land to *Meerat*, near *Delhi*—*Palebothra* of the ancients—medals and coins—Fortified tower, the haunt of banditti—A sad accident—worse and worse—Interview with the Rajah of *Huttrass*—Wild hog—Visit from a native chief—Marching establishment for a European of any rank—A tiger hunt—Curious ceremony for young girls in this district 126

CHAPTER XVI.

Journey into the district of Bareilly towards Pilibete—Cross the Ganges—No trace of a road—A useful hint respecting water for drinking—Town of *Amroah*, for what celebrated—Instance of

CONTENTS.

	PAGE

faith, and the reliance some Hindoos place on the judgment of Europeans—An immense bed of sand—Perpendicular bridge—Sagacity of an elephant in the suite—Mephitic vapour, its consequences—Angels or devils—Attacked by banditti—Visit to the town of Pilibete; its productions—Description of a mosque there—Singular arrangement for medical attendance on the poor—Wild elephants, how to tame—Dock-yard—Return to *Bareilly*—Rainy season—Perilous situation—Tent overflowed—Conveyed on men's heads—Advantages of an eastern climate—Severe consequences of a chill—More calamities—Arrival at Meerat 135

A GUIDE UP THE RIVER GANGES, from Calcutta to Cawnpore, Futteh Ghur, Meerat, &c.; with the correct distances of every station, and what their produce 145

Vocabulary adapted to the Tour 154

Vocabulary adapted to the Voyage 155

A
TOUR THROUGH HINDOSTAN.

CHAPTER I.

AFTER a voyage of nearly five months from England, we reached that city of palaces, Calcutta[1] in Bengal;[2] but destined as we were to join the army in the upper provinces of Hindostan,[3] our stay in it was very short. After hiring boats, and making the necessary preparations for a three months' voyage up the river Ganges,[4] we started for the principal military Station, Khaanpore.[5]

At the expiration of the war, in 1804,[6] we revisited the Presidency,[7] leaving Khaanpore in a budgerow[8] on the 6th of November, and reached Calcutta on the 19th of the following month. The stream at this season runs six miles an hour.

In Calcutta we remained until the month of March, enjoying the splendid gaieties of the season, and then set forward by land on our return. Our tent equipage, conveyed on camels, was despatched a few days previous, that the cattle might be more fresh for the journey. It consisted of three tents, one used for sleeping, one for eating, and a smaller one, to answer the double purposes of butler's pantry, and as a shelter, in case of bad weather, for our servants; two palankeens,[9] each carried on the shoulders of four natives, called bearers;[10] with a machine of the same description, but inferior materials, named a dhooley,[11] (this latter contained crockery, cooking utensils, &c. &c.); three small waggons drawn by bullocks, for baggage, poultry, and stores.

The natives in general, but particularly the Hindoos, always prefer travelling on foot. Sheep to be killed for consumption on the road; and goats, for the purpose of furnishing milk, are driven on these occasions, and keep pace with the baggage. Their march is performed before sun-rise, at the rate of from twelve to fifteen miles a day.

We generally contrived to send forward half the establishment, so as to find breakfast ready, and every thing prepared for our reception. The camp bedsteads here are similar to those made use of in Europe, and are transported upon men's shoulders. The palankeen bearers have a tune, not unpleasing to the ear of those accustomed to it, which regulates their steps. Their usual rate of travelling is from three to three and a half miles an hour, which they perform with perfect ease to themselves, often indulging in jokes with their companions on the road; for they are witty fellows in *their* way.

I was once travelling with a young man, recently arrived in the country, who, being ignorant of their language, and rather of an impatient temper, had provided himself with a long whip, which he applied at intervals to the legs of the unfortunate natives who supported his palankeen. This treatment they bore with great magnanimity until it began to grow dark, when, arriving at a *bazaar*,[12] generally crowded about that time, they set him down and left him. My palankeen had proceeded nearly three miles before I missed him. Concluding that something untoward had occurred, I returned in search of him; and after a delay of more than two hours, with difficulty succeeded in procuring other bearers.

Barrackpore,[13] the first station we came to, is fourteen miles from Calcutta; the road broad and good, shaded on either side by lofty trees. It contains a number of good dwelling houses for English officers in the East India Company's service, attached to *Seapoy* corps.[14] These houses, which generally occupy the centre of a small garden, are raised from the ground by two or more steps, covered by a cement in imitation of white marble, and surrounded by a *veranda*. They form two lines, running parallel with the bank of the river *Ganges*, on which this Station stands. This river is here called the *Bhagaretti:* it does not assume the name of *Ganges* until beyond the influence of the tide, which reaches to a village called *Sook Saaghur*, a few miles higher.

At *Barrackpore* is also to be seen the superb country residence of the Governor General of India,[15] surrounded by a park and pleasure-grounds of considerable extent. Through these are a number of beautiful drives and walks, open to officers and their friends. A menagerie, a curious collection of wild beasts, a botanic garden, ponds well stored with fish, cascades, &c. are among the attractions of this princely domain. The Governor General's house is so situated as to command a view of three foreign settlements on the opposite shore, viz. *Chandanagore*,[16] formerly belonging to the French, *Chinsurah*[17] to the Dutch, and *Serampore*[18] to the Danes.

The houses at *Chandanagore* are detached from each other, with a crucifix attached to the top of each; they are, for the most part, enclosed within four melancholy walls, with large folding gates. The streets are characteristically dirty. A spacious esplanade, parallel to the river, extends along the front, and several handsome chapels are situated in the rear.

Chinsurah presents a handsome front to the river. There are some good houses in it, with gardens laid out in the ancient style of dull uniformity.

Serampore was a place of considerable traffic, when in possession of the Danes. Vessels of five and six hundred tons burthen find good anchorage before it. It is at this time chiefly inhabited by those whose finances will not enable them to reside in Calcutta, and by English Missionaries,[19] who have established schools for children of both sexes upon a very extensive scale. These Missionaries are permitted by Government to use their own printing press, and manufacture every thing necessary for the purposes of this laudable establishment.

Their library contains many valuable manuscripts in the oriental languages. Amongst the students, at this time, was a young Malay prince,[20] who had been sent from *Java*[21] by his father to be educated: he appeared a smart intelligent boy, about ten years of age; but I was sorry to find that they had not been able to eradicate that spirit of revenge so peculiar to his nation. Although scarcely a twelvemonth there, he could write and speak English admirably. The habitations of the girls and boys are separate, large, and commodious, while the greatest attention appeared to be paid to their health and morals. Large gardens and a play-ground are attached to each seminary, while a general appearance of cleanliness pervades the whole. All the little creatures were occupied, and all looked happy, to the number of one hundred girls, and a greater proportion of boys, chiefly under twelve years of age. The total expense per month for each child is forty rupees (five pounds) for a girl, including clothes, and thirty-two rupees (four pounds) for a boy. Their studies are not confined to any particular language or science: works of the best masters, different translations of the classics, plans for fortification, sketching, maps, etching, engraving on copper plates, engrossing, &c. are taught with equal skill. From these Missionaries, their wives, and families, every description of instruction emanates. In the printing-office were types in three-and-twenty different languages, besides English; in all of which, they were printing dictionaries, grammars, vocabularies, Bibles, &c. no one department interfering in the smallest degree with the other. It was really curious to see them making their own paper and types. Some of their books are sold by permission of Government for the benefit of the institution, but the principal part of them are disposed of by the missionaries themselves, gratuitously.

Serampore, with its white flat-roofed buildings, presents a magnificent front to the river; but on a nearer approach is found to abound in narrow streets ill paved, dirty, and offensive.

From *Barrackpore* we continued our journey in an open carriage, passed through several small villages, over ploughed fields and commons, without the smallest track to guide us, enquiring our way from one village to another. On the second day of our expedition, we learned that *Barrackpore*, not being in the direct road to the upper provinces, we had been obliged to cross the country in order to come into it at the village of *Amdunga;* whereas we ought, on leaving *Calcutta*, to have proceeded by way of *Dum-Dum*,[22] the principal Station for artillery. Had we done so, we should have found a good military road the whole way, besides having an opportunity of seeing the cantonment to which all cadets in the East India Company's service are sent on their first arrival in the country.

The following morning we pursued our way through a large village called *Jaggree* to *Hundunpore*, where fortunately our tents had been placed under the thick shade of an adjoining grove, or we should have found the heat exceedingly oppressive. The hot winds set in, in this part of the country, generally about the 15th of March, and it was now the 4th. A short distance from this place brought us to a causeway of considerable length, (scarcely wide enough to admit two carriages abreast of each other,) thrown across a morass,[23] and from the nature of the swamp apparently very insecure. There are no hedge-rows in this country, as there are in England, to separate property; but the natives make use of a land-mark, agreeably to ancient usage.

CHAPTER II.

THE villages in *Bengal* differ materially from those in the upper provinces of *Hindostan;* the huts of the former being composed of bamboos covered with matting, while those of the latter are uniformly built of mud, and thatched. Those of Bengal are generally found within groves of the bamboo plant, having small round granaries near them formed of the same materials, but raised a few feet from the ground upon blocks of wood, not unlike those that support our wheat ricks. The habitations of the natives in the upper provinces serve also as a receptacle for their grain; a deep hole is dug in the centre of each, lined with straw, wherein it is deposited, and by that means secured as well against the weather as against marauders, with whom these provinces abound.

Bengal differs as much in climate, manners, customs, and appearance of its inhabitants, as in the general face of the country. Here are no scorching winds in summer, or white frosts, with ponds frozen over, in the winter; but the burning sun, stagnant air, and heavy dews, are far more oppressive. Although these contribute to fertilize the ground, and to produce their boasted verdure, they are unwholesome, and frequently offensive. Our tent at sun-rise this morning was so completely wet with the dew that had fallen during the night, as to affect the clothes deposited on chairs within; and we were actually obliged to have them dried by a fire before they could be worn with safety.

Of their language and customs I shall say little; far abler pens than mine have already described them; I shall content myself with observing, that the *Bengalee* language[24] which *they* speak, is as little understood by the natives of the upper provinces, as the *Hindostanee* language[25] is by them; hence arises a difficulty in persuading servants of the one country to attend you to the other. There is, however, a still stronger reason for the people above *Patna*[26] objecting to a sojourn in *Bengal;* it is because, considering, as they do, the *Bengalees* to be of an inferior *caste,*[27] they are fearful of losing their own: for instance, if a man of inferior *caste* touches the food, or even utensil in which it is preparing, of a superior, it is contaminated, and no longer fit for use—all the cleansing in the world would be insufficient, in their opinions, to purify it. This leads to the common practice of each person cooking for himself, even among those of the highest rank; and even when this is not the case, they are extremely particular in having a cook of the same *caste* as they are themselves. Both Hindoos and Mussulmen are tenacious in this respect.[28] I remember a circumstance which occurred to me shortly after my arrival in the country, which astonished me not a little, and distressed me very much. It is the custom for boats going up or down the river to bring to for the night, and make fast to the bank, generally near some village where the boatmen may purchase food: this, they take the opportunity of dressing on small stoves formed at the time, of an adhesive kind of clay, of which these banks are formed. Round these they describe a circle, raised a few inches from the ground, the inside of which they smoothe with the hand until it has the appearance of being nicely plastered. The *dandies*,[29] as they are called, then place themselves round, to the number of three, four, and sometimes five in a party, with their legs tucked under them, and commence their attack upon the curry with all the eagerness of professed epicures. A number of these plans had been formed on the only level ground near our boat, and being ignorant at that time of their customs, I unfortunately stepped into one of the magic circles in my attempt to reach the high land. Our boatmen made no observation at the time; but on turning to view the prospect from above, I saw several of them employed in emptying the contents of their cooking pots into the river, and afterwards breaking the earthen vessels in which their food had been dressed. Upon enquiry of a person by me, who spoke a little English, what this meant, I learned to my surprise that *I* had caused the proceeding, by placing my unhallowed foot too near the stove and its circular enclosure. Laughable as it appeared to us, it was far from being so to them at the period I allude to; for as no village within a mile and a half could be found, these poor infatuated people were obliged to content themselves with parched grain. This grain, which resembles a large dried pea in a dark brown skin, is very abundant in India, and is used to feed horses as well as men. The natives are universally fond of it, and always carry a small quantity ready parched about them to chew at pleasure: with the boatmen, more particularly, who only get a hot meal before sunrise, and after sun-set, it is an essential article of food.

Although united by situation and laws, the Bengalees in no respect associate with the natives of the upper provinces. They are unlike also in appearance, the former being delicately shaped, of short stature, and of a very dark complexion; while the latter are, for the most part, tall, robust, and of a light copper colour. Indeed I have sometimes seen them, particularly the women, very little darker than the natives of France or Italy; and the higher you go up the country, the fairer the inhabitants become. This may probably be accounted for by the severity of their winter months; whereas, in Bengal, they may be said to have no winter at all, as far as respects cold, for it is never sufficiently felt to require a fire; and I remarked that there was not a single grate to be seen in Calcutta.

They differ in dress, perhaps, more than in any other particular. In Bengal they wear no turbans, merely their long black hair strained up round the head, and fastened in a knot at the top; a few yards of thin silk, of various colours, fastened round the waist, and loosely wrapped about the thighs, leaving the legs quite bare; a drapery of thin muslin, thrown carelessly across the shoulders, one end hanging in front, the other behind, completes their dress, as far as apparel is concerned. But a Bengalee gentleman has not completed his toilet until he has painted his face and arms. They have their beaux as well as other nations, who seldom appear without a wafer on their forehead, consisting of a white patch with a spot of bright scarlet in the centre, and a stripe of white paint down the middle of the nose.[30] These men universally wear ear-rings of the purest gold, and excellent workmanship.

This costume respects Hindoos only; such are the principal number of inhabitants in Bengal. Mussulmen, in every province, wear loose trowsers[31] made of satin,[32] dimity,[33] or calico,[34] according to the station of the wearer; their heads are shaved on the top, leaving only a row of hair round the poll and over the ears. They wear turbans of shawl or muslin,[35] with a dress of similar materials fitted to the shape; sleeves hanging over the hands, and skirts reaching to the ancles, with four or five yards of muslin or shawl about their loins. On occasions of unusual exertion, this part of the dress is bound tight, agreeable to the early custom of the East, alluded to in Scripture, "Gird up thy loins,"[36] &c. I have seen most superb and costly dresses of this description: one worn by His Highness the Nawaab of Lucknow,[37] was valued at two hundred and fifty pounds sterling. The dress was of *kinkob*,[38] or silk, brocaded with gold; the trowsers, a rich striped satin of various colours; the turban, as well as waistband, was of fine shawl, curiously wrought with flowers. The dress throughout was lined with scarlet shawl, and under it he wore another of delicate transparent muslin. His shoes, which curved from the toes back over the foot, and terminated in a point, were of scarlet velvet, embroidered with gold, silver, and pearls. These dresses do not reach higher than the collar-bones, leaving the throat exposed. The *Nawaab's* throat was, on this occasion, nearly obscured by three rows of immense pearls, the size of a hazel-nut, fastened round it like a stock. The jewels worn by the *Nawaab* of Lucknow are most of them public property, and descend with the office to the next successor.

The religion of the Hindoos, in Bengal, differs in many respects from that in the upper provinces, as do the form and attributes of the deities they worship, and the food on which they subsist. In Bengal, it consists chiefly of rice, paddy,[39] and fish; vegetables *are common to every description of natives.* In Hindostan they eat cakes by way of bread, made of a coarse kind of wheat flour called *otta*,[40] baked on an iron plate; parched grain, boiled *dhol*,[41] (a kind of vetch or field pea,) *kuddoo*, (an inferior kind of cucumber,) melons, &c.; to which, of late years, since the introduction of them by the English, may be added potatoes.[42] As strong liquors are prohibited by their religion, the inhabitants of Hindostan mix great quantities of spice, of various descriptions, with their food as a substitute: there is indeed a spirituous liquor which they extract from the berries of the *mowah*[43] tree, but their general beverage is pure water. The Bengalees appear to be characterized by a mixture of low cunning, cowardice, and dissimulation; while their more northern neighbours are manly, brave, and generous; but I do not mean to say that they will hesitate to use deception when it is necessary to carry a point. They are however, generally speaking, more trust-worthy when they *are* good, and rogues of a higher stamp when disposed to become so. Perhaps the difference of climate may have influence on their minds as well as bodies; for as in Bengal it is damp and enervating, so in the higher provinces it is dry and often bracing.

After this digression, we will pursue our journey from *Hundunpore* over a flat country thickly wooded, and abounding in stagnant pools. At the romantic Station of *Krishna-nugger*, or, as it is commonly called, *Krishna-ghur*, we remained two days, and found some agreeable English society. This place took its name from

Krishna,[44] the Apollo of the Hindoos, to whom is dedicated a very ancient temple built on this spot. It is one of those denominated in this country "civil Stations," on account of its containing an European judge, a collector of revenue, a surgeon, &c. with a company of seapoys, who are occasionally relieved by others from *Barrackpore*. The scenery about *Krishnaghur* is highly picturesque and beautiful: a fine clear river called the *Jellingy* runs in front of the station, over which is a ferry to the island of *Kossimbazar*.[45]

Having dispatched our camp equipage, we were prevailed upon to remain until the evening. We then travelled a distance of seventeen miles to our tents, not without risk of losing some of the attendants by tigers, with which this part of the country abounds. We were in an open carriage, with just sufficient light to distinguish the road, when one of these animals, growling in a bush near us, caused the horses to plunge violently forward. They quickly conveyed *us* out of danger, but left the *syces*, or grooms, who run with the horses and take care of them, the more exposed. Fear had fortunately quickened their pace also, and they escaped unhurt. Our alarms were however not destined to subside; for on reaching the tents we learned that one of the servants, going towards a pond for water, had seen a tiger, and only escaped him by plunging in and swimming to a village on the opposite side. Another agreeable piece of information was, that in crossing a field of high grass near the camp, they had discovered two asleep; it therefore became expedient to kindle fires around us without loss of time; but before this could be effected, we were in reality attacked, although by a less formidable enemy—a half-starved wolf darted amongst our sheep, and carried off a poor innocent lamb. I believe I have mentioned that it is necessary on a march to guard against the want of provisions, by driving the live stock for consumption with the baggage; for in those towns or villages that are inhabited only by Hindoos, nothing of the kind can be procured—they never eat any thing that has had life. Emboldened, as it should seem, by success, scarcely was all quiet in the camp before depredations of the same nature were repeated. Our people, enraged at their slumbers being thus disturbed, caught up the first offensive weapon within their reach; and in one instant my ears were assailed by the firing of guns, pistols, shouting, beating together brass pots, kettles, and, in short, a mixture of discordant sounds; yet so hungry were our foes, that all this was scarcely sufficient to alarm and drive them away. Sleep was entirely out of the question; for in this manner, with a few short intervals, passed the night. Never was the dawn of day more welcome than I found it now; and we took advantage of it to quit this horrid neighbourhood. It is said that misfortunes seldom come alone; so, indeed, it proved on this occasion; for at the next place we halted, no supplies whatever could be procured, either for servants or cattle—every village within reach seemed to have been abandoned to the brute creation.

From this place we travelled along a vile road over a flat country, chiefly pasture land, for several miles, and at length reached *Shoolbereah*,[46] an indigo factory in the possession of Monsieur *Savi*,[47] a Frenchman, by whom we were most hospitably entertained. The family consisted, besides his wife and himself, of a young widow, (their daughter,) her three children, a son, and another young widow, (their cousin,) both under twenty years of age; three ladies on a visit at the house, a Catholic priest, and four French gentlemen,[48] their neighbours, who had come over to pass the day: being Sunday, we found them just returned from mass. The venerable appearance of the priest, on his first approach, bespoke my respect; but the *hilarity*, not to say *levity*, of his conversation during breakfast, soon turned it to disgust. I found reason, while in this family, to regret my negligence in not having cultivated the French language; for, from want of practice, I was considerably at a loss, and particularly so, as none of them spoke English. They soon prepared, as is the custom with Catholics, to celebrate the Sabbath by singing and dancing. The house was large and commodious; so that, while the party in the saloon amused themselves with an organ, pianoforte, tamborine, &c. I retired to a distant apartment to steal an hour of repose, which, after the recent alarms I had experienced, and consequent want of sleep, had become highly desirable. About three o'clock I was informed that the dinner was ready, and was conducted into a handsomer room than any I had yet seen. We sat down, about sixteen in number, to a really elegant repast; after which the dancing re-commenced, and was continued until late at night. Nothing could exceed the wit and spirits of these lively French women: care appeared to leave no stamp on them. The daughter of Madame Savi one minute declared herself the most wretched of human beings, lamented, and even wept at the hardness of her fate; and almost in the same breath would laugh at a *bon mot*[49] that accidentally caught her ear. She was an interesting looking young creature, in weeds, not yet eighteen. It seemed as if she disdained to be conquered by grief; for once she caught my eyes as they were fixed upon her, and taking my hand, she exclaimed with a lively air, "Do not look at me when I am sad, only when I am gay." The other young widow, her cousin, had left off mourning "more than a month," she told us, and with it, as it appeared, all serious thoughts. Happy people, to be able so easily to overcome the most severe of all afflictions! I had been hitherto taught to believe that the Roman Catholic religion enveloped its votaries in superstition and despondency; but were I to judge by my experience of to-day, it would lead me to very opposite conclusions.

CHAPTER III.

OUR sleeping tent was pitched at *Placey*,[50] about two miles beyond this place, on our route to *Moorshedabad*;[51] and it was near one o'clock in the morning before we reached it. *Placey* was once a place of some importance, as the scene of Lord Clive's first victory over the *Bengalese*;[52] it is now an insignificant village, with very few inhabitants.

Our journey was resumed the next morning over a road which was almost the worst I ever travelled; deep ruts and high banks constantly impeded our progress, nor did the scenery present any thing to compensate for these inconveniences.

The next place we came to, of any consequence, was the well-known city of *Moorshedabad*, the residence of the *Nawaab* of *Bengal*.[53] He enjoys, however, little more than an empty title, having neither territory nor authority, but enjoying in their stead a pension from the East India Company. *Moorshedabad* is one of their principal civil stations; besides the usual complement of civil servants, such as judge, collector, assistant, registrar, and surgeon, it contains a court of appeal, consisting of three superior judges with their appendages. About two miles from this is the military station of *Berhampore*,[54] also on the banks of the Ganges; it is an elegant cantonment, surrounded by cultivation, and kept in the highest order; the bank is steep, sloping gradually down to the water's edge, and planted with grass, which is constantly mowed and watered, with a broad gravel walk or parade on the top. Supplies of every kind are to be met with here; also a manufactory of cotton stockings, softer, finer, and much cheaper than they are in England; likewise of leather gloves, in imitation of Limerick, and but little inferior; black silk handkerchiefs, silks of various colours in the piece, ribbons, &c. &c.

The first twenty miles, after leaving *Moorshedabad*, were exceedingly unpleasant on account of the road; not that the ruts were so deep as on the other side the city, but the road was worn so uneven, and was withal so stony, as to be almost dangerous. This is generally the case in the neighbourhood of large cities in India, where much traffic is carried on. It is necessary to inform the reader that there are no turnpikes in this country, and that the roads are repaired by Government; but so shamefully neglected did *this* appear, that near a considerable village named *Bamuneah*, one entire arch of a bridge, originally built of brick, had fallen in, (nor did this event appear of recent date,) and we were obliged to cross the stream over a temporary one of mud and bamboo, which sunk under the horses' feet at every step. The country about this place is much covered with clumps of bamboo, intermixed with corn-fields. These crops, which in some were ripe, in others half cut, and filled with reapers, gave it a cheerful appearance; but the fallen leaves of the bamboo plant, which have a strong offensive smell, would form in my opinion a great objection to residing there.

Our tents were next day pitched in a grove of fine *mango* trees, whose fruit, the most useful and delicious of any in India, possesses, in the different stages of its growth, very opposite qualities; when ripe, it is about the size of a magnum bonum plum, with a thick yellow rind, often found tinged on one side with a deep red colour, and particularly juicy; in the centre of each is a large oval stone, the shape of the mango; and you seldom meet with two in fifty of the same flavour— the predominant taste is either that of the pine-apple or the strawberry. They are ripe about June or July. So fond are the natives of this fruit, that while in season it is their principal food, and is considered both wholesome and nutritive where water is the only beverage; but I have known instances where even *one* glass of wine, taken at the same time, has produced a painful eruption on the skin not unlike the nettle-rash, attended by a considerable degree of fever, particularly when ripened (as is frequently the case) on straw, to bring them forward before those become ripe that are in the open air. When green, this fruit has a most grateful acid flavour: it makes an excellent pickle or preserve, a delicious tart, and much improves a curry, soused fish, &c. Mango trees are generally planted in groves by the road side, affording an agreeable shelter for the traveller from the heat of a noonday sun, where they have generally also the benefit of a well, more necessary to the inhabitants of this country even than their food. The leaves of the mango tree are as large as those of the walnut in England; indeed the fruit, when green, is not unlike a walnut in appearance; the branches spread considerably, and they grow to a great height.

The road, as we pursued our journey, grew rather worse than better; it ran along a high causeway for upwards of ten miles, of barely sufficient width for two carriages to pass each other, and was besides much cut up by vehicles of burthen. The ground on either side was cultivated with rice and paddy, and must in the rainy season be completely inundated, forming the only soil in which these grains are said to flourish.

The villages we had hitherto passed were few, and of mean appearance. On making this observation, I was told that no Hindoo, if he could possibly avoid it, would live any where but on the banks of the sacred river, (the Ganges,) wherein he might bathe at least twice in the twenty-four hours, as enjoined by his religion; indeed, I have observed that they no sooner arrive at the end of a journey, be it long or short, than they strip themselves and plunge into the river; and where no river is at hand, squat down by the side of a well, and throw water over themselves until they are completely drenched. This custom of so frequent ablution may appear, in the idea of an European, extremely inconvenient and troublesome. To obviate this, their dress, which I have before described, is peculiarly adapted. This custom of frequent ablution,[55] and the supposed religious nature of the ceremony, may also account for the immense population on the banks of the Ganges, in defiance of the torrents which frequently sweep whole villages away, leaving no trace behind.

The unpleasant causeway I have described brought us to a place called *Kummerah*, where the river opened majestically on our view; and we continued our journey along its banks until we approached the tents, which, to our dismay, were pitched upon a plain, without a single tree to shelter them. We of course expected to suffer considerably from the heat; but whether from the vicinity of the spot to the river, or from any other local cause, it is difficult to determine, the day proved much less oppressive than those which preceded it, when we encamped under a thick shade. The wind blew hot and fresh. We had provided ourselves with *tatties*[56]* at *Moorshedabad*, which being fixed at the windward entrance of the tent, and kept well watered on the outside, rendered us extremely comfortable.

This river is an arm only of the great Ganges, and was at this time nearly dry. We travelled chiefly on its bank; but whenever the road deviated, it led through cultivated lands surrounded by embankments—a necessary precaution against its overflow in the rainy season. The crops here are wonderfully luxuriant, and so indefatigable are the people in encouraging them, that they even till the few dry patches in the bed of the stream. The whole, at this time, appeared one cheerful moving scene—pedestrian travellers, and innumerable droves of cattle passing and re-passing; boats sailing down, while others were tracking up the magnificent *Ganges*, separated from us only by a low bank of sand about a quarter of a mile across, presenting a *coup d'œil*[57] of the most agreeable nature. But we soon found ourselves obliged to cross a bed of sand which separated two cuts of the river; this happening to be deep, considerably impeded our progress, while the ascents and descents were almost perpendicular. In one part we encountered a narrow, rapid stream, through which the united force of the party, assisted by the horse that drew it, was scarcely sufficient to push the carriage. On reaching the declivity we discovered another sand, of considerable breadth, to traverse before we could gain the ferry, this ferry being at the junction of three branches of the Ganges.

Our march to-day had been so retarded by the sands, that the sun was getting high, and my impatience great for the shelter of a tent; so, jumping into a small fishing-boat, as the delay in conveying our carriage into the other was likely to prove considerable, I made the best of my way on foot towards our encampment, traversing ploughed fields and banks of sand for nearly a mile. This brought me to the village of *Sooty*, on the main bank of the Ganges, where our tents were pitched, and in about an hour I was joined by the rest of the party; thus crossing

---

* *Tatties* are frames made of bamboo, resembling trelliswork, rather closer one way than the other, to fit a door or window. These frames being covered by the fibrous roots of a sweet-scented grass, called *kus kus*, are kept wet by a person on the outide throwing water upon them. There is an art, even in this; since by leaving any part of the *tatty* dry, the purpose of cooling the apartment is defeated. The hot wind, which generally blows strong from the westward, passing through these *tatties*, becomes cool, and conveys a refreshing scent like roses. I have frequently felt the house so cold from them, as to be under the necessity of wearing an additional garment, while out of it the atmosphere has been intolerably hot. Another kind of *tatty*, for light airs, such as blow from the East, is made from a low briary shrub of a lively green, found on sandy places, named *jowassy*, which is placed tightly on the frame, and may be renewed daily.

Strong westerly winds make a healthy season, as do those from the East the reverse.

that arm of the river that separates the island of *Cossimbazar* from the main land. From this island of *Cossimbazar* are brought those beautiful feathers, so highly esteemed by European ladies, called the *Comocolly*.* The birds on which they grow are a species of water-fowl, about the size of a gull, peculiar to this island. The plumage of the young birds is grey, of the old white. The feathers most in request are found under the wings, and are light as ether down: they are either worn in a plume, or formed into various shapes, such as muffs, tippets, &c.; and although very expensive in England, may in Calcutta be procured for a mere trifle.

Owing to a curious circumstance, we found the village of *Sooty* almost deserted: a robbery to a large amount had been lately committed there on some travelling merchants, and all the principal persons, including their chief, had been taken to the Judicial Court at *Moorshedabad* upon suspicion of being concerned in it. It is, as I afterwards learned, not an unusual thing for these *jemeendars*,[58] or head men of villages, to keep a number of subordinates to plunder when they have opportunity, and divide the spoil. It is in this particular that our government is so beneficial to the country in general, inasmuch as its activity and justice protects the property of individuals. Of this the natives are well aware; and, for the most part, gratefully acknowledge it.

We spent the night at *Sooty*, but were much disturbed by the howling of a small animal called the *pao;* by which it is affirmed that the tiger is always preceded when in search of prey.

The first village of any consequence that we passed through on the following morning was *Narungabad*, where there is a number of fine large trees, chiefly tamarinds,[59] and a good bazar. The properties of the tamarind tree are somewhat remarkable, being at once a bane and an antidote. It is a well-authenticated fact among the natives, that a person sleeping under one of these at night, invariably complains, on awakening, of pain in his limbs, weariness, shivering, and other indications of fever; which symptoms, by drinking plentifully of an infusion of its fruit, are generally removed.

Our journey was now chiefly across low lands, intersected by stagnant pools, on which were innumerable wild fowls, but principally ducks, precisely like those we have in England, and equally good in flavour. From hence, by a gradual ascent, we reached a plain of the finest turf, and drove on it for a considerable distance without the slightest impediment, tracing the boundary of a fine transparent stream, called the *Collah Pawnee Nullah*.† On this stream appeared more than fifty fishing boats preparing to cast their nets. The prospect altogether, aided by the fineness of the morning, (for there was a refreshing breeze,) rendered this ride truly delightful.

We found our tents pitched in an extensive grove of varied foliage, on a very romantic spot near the village of *Downapore;* but as every advantage has its

---

* The name of that part of the island where these birds are chiefly found.
† *Collah*, in Hindostanee, here means *dark; Pawnee*, water; *Nullah*, a stream.

contra, no drinkable water could be procured within half a mile; although this circumstance was immaterial, as far as regarded ourselves, still after a long march it was very fatiguing to our servants, who drank nothing but water.

The next morning, at day-break, we proceeded as usual, and accomplished the first twelve miles before breakfast. The country was woody, and for the most part cultivated, with the exception of a plain of considerable extent, indeed without any apparent boundary, which led to two streams, separated by a narrow bed of sand, whose banks were so exceedingly steep that we were literally under the necessity of scrambling up them; the only wonder was, that our carriage ever reached the top. The road on the following day was not only rough, but high in some places and low in others, bounded by the river on the right, and the *Radge Mah'l* hills,[60] at about two miles distant, on the left, leaving a space of highly cultivated land between.

A few miles before reaching *Radge Mah'l*,[61] we drove through the village of *Futteh Poor:* it contains an indigo factory, and a pretty large *serai*.[62]* This latter is a place of reception for travellers; it is in form a square, enclosed on each side by high brick walls, with large folding gates at the east and west entrances. The wall on the inside is lined with small sheds, or thatched hovels, each furnished with a bedstead of the rudest materials, called a *char-piah*,[63] such as are commonly used by the people of this country. It is a square frame, about five feet and a half long, covered by coarse twine strongly woven together, and supported by four pieces, or rather small blocks of wood, of about a foot and a half in height, without posts or tester. Fortunately, these people do not require the luxury of a bed; and in cold weather they carry their coverlid upon their backs. Curry and rice, cakes made of *otta*, (or coarse flour,) milk, and good water, may be procured in these *serais* for a trifling consideration, as also food and lodging for cattle. Gentlemen, when sending their horses to a distance, find them very convenient; but, in a general way, they are frequented only by those natives who travel without tents, or a sufficient guard to protect them. About two miles beyond this, we crossed a bridge built of red brick over the *Oodah Nullah*,[64] celebrated in the annals of this country as the scene of an obstinate battle between two of their strongest native powers. It was very sultry, and near nine o'clock before we reached *Radge Mah'l*, as it is commonly called; but properly speaking, *Rajah Ko Mahul*, signifying "the property of the Rajah."[65] On approaching this place, which is of considerable extent, the country assumes a woody appearance, while innumerable small hamlets, peeping through clumps of bamboo, render it extremely pleasing to the eye.

Radge Mah'l was formerly a place of great celebrity; it contained the best bazar in India, and was resorted to from the most distant provinces. Of all the arts and manufactures which rendered it celebrated when in its original grandeur, there remains only a manufacture of earthen-ware, and the art of carving on marble; of which material they make sundry small articles for sale. Here the eastern and western *dawks*,[66] or post, meet, and exchange bags, the inhabitants of the upper

---

* A party of the police are stationed in every *serai*.

provinces not choosing to go lower, and those of the lower provinces not wishing to proceed higher up the country. The remains of a magnificent palace[67] of the rajahs are still shown, but it is fast falling to decay. The whole town, shortly before our arrival there, had nearly been consumed by fire; fortunately for us, a baker and his house had escaped the conflagration, for he soon made us some excellent bread and hot rolls for breakfast next morning. The substitute for yeast, called toddy,[68] is met with here in great perfection; it exudes from the palm-tree, and makes much lighter bread, without any bitter taste.

At so great a distance from any European station, a baker is certainly a great convenience; and the man who, in this sequestered spot, devotes himself to the comfort and accommodation of travellers, certainly deserves greater encouragement than the casual reward of his labours. Two or three rupees a month, from Government, would keep up this establishment from generation to generation. The Hindoos will never, if they can avoid it, forsake the trade of their fathers; and are so exceedingly tenacious in this particular, that they are even scrupulous of improving upon it. I asked a baker once to make muffins, and offered to translate a receipt I had for them into Hindostanee, promising him at the same time a recommendation to all my acquaintance, which being pretty large, and at one of the principal military stations, must have been highly lucrative to him. He listened very patiently until I had finished my speech, when closing his hands in a suppliant posture, "Pardon me, Lady," said he, "but my father never made them, my grandfather never made them, and how can I presume to do it? My grandfather brought up sixteen children, my father fourteen children, without making *mufkeens*, and why should not I?" Such close reasoning as this I was by no means prepared to parry, so bowing assent, I dismissed him, and there the matter ended. The Hindoos are, beyond a doubt, the least enterprising people in the world.

Radge Mah'l is just eleven miles from our last encampment. We were pitched on the bank of the river, at its widest part; but having neither wind nor shade, we found the heat almost intolerable.

CHAPTER IV.

OUR route on the following day ran so near the edge of a precipice, that the smallest deviation might have proved fatal to us. A thick grass *jungle*, or underwood, and a range of mountains bounded our view on one side; on the other flowed the Ganges; while the bank on which we drove was narrow, and in many places much broken.

The sheep and goats of Bengal are remarkably small, the latter generally white, and are, when young, the prettiest little creatures imaginable. They thrive here in great abundance; but in consequence of the number of wolves and tigers with which this neighbourhood is infested, it is necessary to keep them closely guarded. Goat's milk, in India, is infinitely preferable, in tea, to that of cows, being much richer, and without any unpleasant taste.

Over a fine down, on which our tents were pitched, we drove three miles the following morning as on a soft green velvet, and passed a large village different from any I had yet seen. The huts were of straw, or long grass, neatly plaited together, supported on four bamboo poles, with fences round them of similar materials at a little distance, so constructed as to secure their different kinds of cattle at night from beasts of prey. This kind of elastic fence, by yielding to their spring, alarms them, and they invariably sneak off. Beyond this village lay a deep sand, covered by long grass and briars, through which, as might be expected, the road proved miserably bad. Considering this as a public way, leading to all the principal European stations on the banks of the Ganges, it appears somewhat extraordinary that it should be so entirely neglected, as the badness of the road must necessarily impede commerce, not only with the provinces, but also from the *Mharattah*[69] and other states. Within the distance of seventeen miles, no less than seven bridges appeared, almost dangerous to cross, for want of a little repair. To my observation on this subject may perhaps be replied, that Government is now making a new military road up the country another way. Very true; but can Government induce the natives to form villages on it, so great a distance from their sacred and favourite river? and if not, how are travellers, particularly natives, to procure supplies? They answer, The distance will be so much lessened. But who, in undertaking a journey of nearly a thousand miles, would not be glad to go a few miles more, in order to pass a pleasant day in some friendly habitation? In a multitude of counsellors, however, we are told, there is wisdom; I must of course conclude that every thing is arranged for the best. Great part of our way now lay through a *jungle*, full of tigers; but they rarely attack a human being in the day-time, particularly where cattle are so numerous as in Bengal. Our people observed one at a distance, sneaking off to a thicker covert.

Gunga Pursaad, the village we next came to, was close to the river, and of very mean appearance. Like *Radge Mah'l*, it had lately suffered by fire; nor is it surprising that such circumstances should frequently happen, when we consider of what materials their hovels are composed, and their carelessness in throwing away the lighted particles which they have been smoking.* Another circumstance which greatly tends to lessen our commiseration, is, their extreme apathy concerning each other; for if a man succeeds in rescuing his own property, he immediately marches off with it, regardless of the entreaties of his neighbour for assistance.

The natural indolence of these people is indeed very great; no plea but necessity induces them to move *at all*. They would like to sit and smoke the whole day long. "Better," say they, "to sit than stand; better to lay down than sit; better to sleep than either." If assailed by any sudden misfortune, they instantly lose all presence of mind, and run bawling about like so many mad creatures.

From *Gunga Pursaad*, by an almost perpendicular road, we ascended the mountains. On either side grew thick underwood, and the path was covered with loose stones. By slow degrees we approached the pass of *Telliah Gulley*, where we found the remains of two fortified gateways, which in former times had been forced and carried by a people called *The Jauts*.[†,70] On one side appeared an impenetrable wood, intersected by frightful chasms; on the other a tremendous precipice, on the edge of which lay a dismounted gun of large dimensions. This pass divides the province of Bengal from that of Bahar,[71] into which we now entered. Bahar is *now* considered one of the centre provinces of the East India Company's possessions in this direction. While I gazed on the mouldering remains of a fortified gateway, on the summit of this almost inaccessible mountain, whose turrets frowned in awful majesty on the thick wood beneath, I could almost fancy I heard the groans of some poor wretch confined within its walls. Silent, dreary, and forsaken, save by beasts of prey who prowled to quench their thirst at the mountain torrents, far from the haunts of men, was this terrific region! Nor was the descent on the other side less formidable: huge stones, over which, as before, we were obliged to scramble, perpetually impeded our progress; the poor horses could with difficulty keep upon their legs; and it required three or four men to hang on the back part of the carriage, in order to prevent its falling over, so steep was the declivity.

Just at this crisis our guide declared himself unable to proceed—he was so fatigued he could go no farther. His services were however indispensable: a little wine might have recruited him, but that he would not touch; at length, by promises of additional reward, he contrived to creep along. And now, what should present itself but a camel newly slain by a tiger! the blood was still flowing from its throat, and the creature scarcely cold. The scent of the tiger was very strong; and it was conjectured that, hearing us approach, the ferocious animal had left his prey. It was some time before the horses would proceed; and not one of them,

---

* The practice of smoking is universal throughout the eastern world.
† See Dow's Hist. of Hindostan.[72]

until a bandage had been placed over his eyes. I cannot say but I shuddered a little myself. A different scene however soon dissipated the horrors of the last: a beautiful and fertile valley opened on our view, bounded at the distance of about half a mile by a range of hills still higher than those we were about to quit; while an expansive lake, covered with a variety of wild fowl, and a table land of luxuriant turf, proved a pleasing reverse to the bold scenery of its neighbouring hills. A fine smooth road conducted us through this romantic spot, amid small bushes of odoriferous shrubs, and peacocks, feeding in the full security of solitude. From hence, ascending by a gradual and almost imperceptible ascent, we caught sight of another range of hills, which still separated us from the Ganges. The first rays of the rising sun were beginning to shed their lustre on the prospect. What heart so insensible as not to feel the Divine influence! to adore the great Creator, and to think with Milton, "These are thy works, Parent of good!"[73]

Our road lay through a thick *jungle*, interspersed with wild roses and creepers of singular beauty, differing both in shape and colour from any I had seen, although some of them bore a strong resemblance to various hot-house plants in England. About eight o'clock we reached the plain on which our tents were pitched; it happened to be near a little mean village, called *Palliah-poore*. This place was inhabited by invalid pensioners of the East India Company's regiments, who, when disabled in the service, have the option of retiring to *one* of the many villages set apart for that purpose, where a spot of ground is allotted to each individual, and a few rupees paid monthly to them by the superintendent, or visiting officer. This gratuity affords the seapoys an opportunity of sitting down comfortably with their families for the remainder of their days, and is a most admirable institution. Unfortunately for us, the pensioners of *Palliahpoore* happened to be Hindoos, who only keep sufficient supplies for their separate consumption, and having no *bazar*, our Mussulman servants came badly off. On these occasions, Hindoos have greatly the advantage; a little parched grain, and a draught of water occasionally, will support them for many days. It is computed that one rupee and a half (three shillings and nine-pence) will furnish a Hindoo with food and raiment for a month; whereas three rupees (seven shillings and sixpence) are barely sufficient for the maintenance of a Mussulman of the same rank and station, for the same space of time.

About half a mile from *Palliah-poore* is an indigo factory. The gentleman who resided there,[74] no sooner heard of our arrival, than, with that spirit of hospitality so general throughout India, he invited us to his house; which on our declining to accept, he sent his servants to our tents laden with fruit and vegetables. In the course of the day we were visited by some of the hill people, bearing earthen jars filled with the most delicious honey I ever tasted: it was perfectly white and transparent.

These are quite a distinct race of people;[75] they never quit their native hills but to exchange honey and wood for grain in the neighbouring villages, appear totally uncivilized, and speak a language peculiar to themselves. Their stature is short and thick, with skins nearly black; small black eyes, low foreheads, thick coarse black curly hair, on which neither men nor women wear any covering, and very little *clothing* at all. They are timid and inoffensive, as far as respects human beings, but very ferocious with beasts, against which they are armed with poisoned arrows, and clubs of such a size and weight, that a man not accustomed to them could scarcely wield them. The post-man, in traversing these wilds, is attended by a guide carrying a *tom tom*, or small drum, which he beats as he runs along, to alarm and disperse the savage animals that infest them; amongst others, the wild buffalo is not *the least* to be feared. I was present when one of these furious creatures attacked a gentleman on horseback, who only saved his life by the speed of the animal on which he rode.

Here, for the first time since leaving Calcutta, our people drew water from a *well;* hitherto they had been obliged to use that of the river, or some stagnant pool.

From *Palliah-poore* the road is rough and rather hilly, on a gravelly soil; it runs generally through a kind of brush-wood and briars; but near villages the country is well cultivated. Thus we continued travelling, at the base of a ridge of hills, until we reached the large and populous village of *Kol Gong*. The opposite side of the river, which we occasionally caught sight of, appeared covered with underwood, and, we were told, was full of game. I observed several herds of cattle, and that one of them had always a bell hung round his neck, to prevent the rest from straying.

The village of *Kol Gong* stands immediately under the hills, whose sides are covered with shrubs; and in front of it runs the Ganges. Many indigo planters, and officers retired from the Company's service, are settled here; some of them have built large houses in the European style, which gives it somewhat the appearance of England. Two most extraordinary rocks, of a pyramidal form, rear their monstrous heads about the middle of the river, nearly opposite to this place; they appear to have been formed by huge stones, piled one upon another to an immoderate height. On the pinnacle of each is the hut of a *fakeer*,[76] or mendicant priest—the one a Hindoo, the other a Mussulman. They have each a small boat, in which they ply for charity from those who pass up and down the river, which is here two miles across. It may not be unworthy remark, that although there is not the smallest appearance of soil, shrubs and even trees grow almost to the summit of these rocks; the circumference of which, at the base, is about a hundred and fifty yards: their size is nearly equal. There is no tradition in existence respecting their origin. Approach to them in the rainy season is extremely dangerous, and many boats are wrecked here.

On leaving *Kol Gong*, we quitted the vicinity of these awfully romantic mountains, and by a broad beaten track entered a flat and highly cultivated country. The only unpleasant circumstance was its being intersected by ravines, in which were frequently a good deal of water; in that case, our only resource was to cross them on temporary bridges of bamboo, covered with earth. In descending one of these ravines, our carriage was overturned; but the soil being sandy, it sustained no injury. We had fortunately quitted it before the accident happened. The farther we journied west of Calcutta, the hotter and stronger the wind became; but the nights were still cool; nor did the hot winds commence blowing in general until about nine o'clock, continuing from that time until sun-set.

The following morning we reached *Baugulpoor*,[77] a station for civilians, and a company or battalion of Hill Rangers.[78] Here we were entertained by the Judge and his Lady,[79] and were induced to remain some days. A singular circumstance occurred, in consequence of the arrival of some Missionaries, while we were at this place. These gentlemen had been holding forth in the bazar, and having gathered together a numerous assembly of the people, particularly remarked *one*, as being more attentive than the rest; (a corn factor, of respectable appearance;) when, going up to him, the Missionary asked if he had been convinced by the arguments he had heard in favour of the Christian religion? After a moment's hesitation, "What will you give me," said the native, "to become a Christian?"—"The blessings of our holy religion will reward you," replied the Missionary. "That will not do," returned the native; "but I'll tell you what—If you will give me a lac of rupees, and two English ladies for my wives, I'll consider of it." The Missionary was indignant; and, but for the timely interference of the Mayor,[80] matters might have taken a serious turn.

Baugul-poor is not immediately on the Ganges, but on the banks of a fine meandering stream proceeding from the hills, which runs into it a few miles below. This stream is narrow, deep, and beautifully picturesque. At each winding is seen a handsome residence, grounds tastefully laid out, and planted with a variety of trees; amongst which, the bamboo and cocoanut appeared particularly to flourish. It is celebrated for the manufacture of cloth, known in England by the name of *ginghams*,[81] generally made in stripes of pink or blue, and sometimes plain coloured; the white is little inferior, on a transient view, to the shawl of Cashmere.[82]

CHAPTER V.

FROM *Baugul-poor* we proceeded through a woody, populous, and highly cultivated country, somewhat intersected by ravines, and over bamboo bridges as before. The village near which we found our tents, had been latterly much annoyed by tigers, one of whom had, for several successive nights, carried off a human being. At length, become desperate, the inhabitants had formed a resolution to watch, and turn out in a body against their assailant: accordingly, armed with arrows, stones, loaded sticks, spears, and an old matchlock or two, they had sallied forth the night before, and we found them rejoicing over their vanquished enemy; and an enormous brute he was, measuring four feet two inches high, ten feet one inch and a half long, and stout in proportion.

It may seem extraordinary to those who are unacquainted with the natural indolence of these people, that they should have suffered their relations and friends to be thus devoured, and remain so long inactive; but when informed that every Hindoo is a predestinarian,[83] and firmly believes in the transmigration of souls, their surprise will cease. A striking instance of this occurred to me, as I was sitting one day reading in our own bungalow at *Meerut*:[84] a kind of bustle in the verandah caused me to look up, when I perceived a large snake, of the species called by the natives *cóprah capell*,[85] or hooded snake, advancing towards me. Starting from my seat, I called to some palankeen bearers, who were looking on, to kill him. With the greatest composure, one of them asked if that was my hookam? (order.) "To be sure it is," I exclaimed. (The reptile meanwhile spreading his hood, and looking very fierce.) When approaching the snake, he made a profound *salaam*,[86] and muttering, *Maaf kurro*, (forgive,) with a stick he knocked him on the head, and despatched him in a moment. A very slight blow is sufficient on this part to destroy them. It is singular, that when one snake has been destroyed, another is sure to come: our people consequently watched, and in a few days killed its partner. To so great an extent do the Hindoos carry their superstitious ceremonies, that they even *salaam* to their tools of a morning before they begin to use them, and the same when they have finished their day's work, alleging as a reason, that it is to them they are indebted for subsistence. I verily believe this is the only species of gratitude they are acquainted with.

The road continued broad and good, bounded by a bank and hedge on either side, a circumstance rather unusual in this country, where the only land-mark, generally speaking, is a ridge of earth. Removing a neighbour's land-mark, is the source of more quarrelling and bloodshed than any other cause. You frequently hear of whole villages turning out against each other to revenge a dispute of this kind, and many lives are sacrificed. Until I knew that this was a common practice, I often wondered at hearing so much firing of matchlocks,[87] particularly in the territory belonging to the Nawaab of *Lucknow*, and other native princes. Although an additional reason may be applicable in these places, which is, that they are most insatiable landlords, and obliged to collect their revenue by force of arms.

About fourteen miles farther on, we caught sight of a range of hills running parallel with *Monghir*,[88] a place of great celebrity for the chalybeate springs,[89] both hot and cold, in its vicinity. These are found in five wells, close to each other. The water in one of them is so hot, that having dipped a glass full, you are glad to relinquish the hold.

The surrounding country is mountainous, with this small chalybeate stream meandering through it, which in its course turns vegetation black. The water itself has no unpleasant taste, and is perfectly transparent. A friend of mine brought some of it in bottles to England, and, by way of experiment, took several back to India; which, on opening, were found excellent to the taste, and sparkling like Champaigne.

These springs are about a hundred yards inland from the Ganges, and are guarded by *Brahmans*,[90] who levy considerable contributions from those who for their health frequent them. They are only four miles distant from the town of *Monghier*. This is a large populous place on the banks of the Ganges; it is a station for invalid Seapoys, who amuse themselves and increase their incomes by the manufacture of different articles—such as household furniture; iron, tin, and brass utensils, of various descriptions; bellows neatly studded with brass nails, (an article much in request to the north-west of *Monghier* in the cold season,) straw hats and bonnets, leather hunting caps, umbrellas, and toys for children. A great variety of birds of beautiful plumage are also offered here for sale, and cages neatly executed. These birds are of the smaller species, and few of them sing in a domesticated state; neither do they live long out of their native hills. I purchased one, rather less than a thrush, delicately formed; its plumage of a light green colour, with a black pointed beak, an orange-colour top-knot, the throat covered by a fine black down, with a bright purple patch in the centre. This bird is called the *huryah*.* It was either of too delicate a nature to bear a change of climate, or we had not discovered the proper food to nourish it, for it soon shared the general fate, and survived its departure from *Monghier* only a fortnight.

The ebony they bring from the hills to this place, in order to convert into furniture, is a fine-grained wood, and bears a beautiful polish. The town itself stands in a fertile valley, with the river Ganges winding in its front. It contains a pretty strong fort,[91] situated on an eminence, and a number of good brick houses. That of the General, or commanding officer, was an excellent one, built in the European style within the walls of the fort, but commanding an extensive prospect. While at this place I witnessed a most disgusting, but, I am sorry to say, common occurrence among these bigoted people. The ceremony[92] commenced by loud shouting,

---

* Huryah is green in Hindostanee.

accompanied with what they miscall music, alias, a combination of barbarous sounds produced from different instruments; and an immense concourse of Hindoos, who soon ranged themselves round a wooden pole of about twenty feet high, fixed upright in the ground. On the top of this pole, in an horizontal position, were placed three very long bamboos, from which were quickly suspended three men, (brahmins,) by means of large iron hooks passed through the fleshy part of their backs, immediately under the shoulder. These hooks were affixed to rings of the same metal fastened to the bamboo. In this manner they hung for fifteen minutes, swinging round with wonderful velocity. In order to prevent the flesh from tearing through by the weight of the body, a breadth of cloth was tied round the waist, and made fast also to the hook.

We were informed that this was an annual and voluntary penance, by which the objects became almost deified, and generally collected a sufficient sum of money to support them the remainder of their lives. What will not avarice, combined with superstition, effect? I was naturally desirous to know if these misguided beings were not much exhausted by loss of blood, which I concluded must flow from their wounds. The man to whom I applied for information, smiled, and told me that those who make up their minds to perform this penance, determine on it at least six months before hand, and consequently have their backs prepared for it by boring, just as for an ear-ring, first introducing a small ring, and so gradually increasing its size, until it became what we had witnessed. "The part," added he, "by constant friction, soon becomes callous; and what appears to *us* so shocking an operation, is by *them* scarcely felt." Mark here the cunning of the priest, who, to account for no blood appearing, (they having been kept in ignorance of the preparation,) instructs the people, that these men being saints, their blood is too precious to be spilled!

After remaining two days at *Monghier*, we continued our route along the waterside. The road was tolerable in itself, but unpleasant from being extremely narrow, and bounded by a high bank on either side; soon, however, after passing one or two insignificant villages, we struck across the country, driving through groves of mango and tamarind trees alternately, enlivened by cultivation of grain, through which meandered a deep pellucid stream called the *Rewah*, bounded by banks of the liveliest verdure. Not far from this delightful spot, we observed a number of women and children collecting the berries that fell from a large tree (under which they had assembled with baskets) called the *mowah tree*. From these berries the Hindoos extract an ardent spirit, of which they are extremely fond. They are the size and colour of a white gooseberry, without seeds—sweet, juicy, and scarcely any flavour.

We crossed the *Rewah Nullah* at the ferry, but not in a boat, the stream being too rapid: a substitute for one however appeared in the shape of a square wooden frame, just large enough to hold one person sitting cross-legged, with four wooden legs of about a foot long; the frame being fastened together over the top by plaited twine, similar to the *charpiah* before described, only more firm, so as not to sink in the middle with any weight. To each leg of this machine was affixed a round, hollow, earthen pot, with the mouth downwards; while a man to each conducted it through the water with one hand, and swam with the other, to the opposite shore. Not that we landed *opposite* to the place where we embarked; for no sooner had I attained the middle of the stream, than with the rapidity of lightning I was whirled a mile lower down; indeed, it appeared quite uncertain where any of us should land; and scarcely could be imagined a more ridiculous scene than our carriages, baggage, &c. presented. A considerable time elapsed before they could be collected again.

A custom prevails in these provinces of having oxen to tread their corn, which reminds me of that passage in the law of Moses, wherein he says, "Thou shalt not muzzle the ox that treadeth out the corn."[93] Unlike the Jewish lawgiver, the natives here think it quite necessary; for you see none that are not muzzled.* The prospect varied to-day with each succeeding hour: in some parts were seen hands innumerable reaping the corn, while in others large herds of cattle appeared regaling in the most luxuriant pasture.†

The immense mountains we had lately traversed, now by degrees receded from our view, and an open country lay before us. After travelling about eighteen miles, we reached a village completely inland, called *Barayah*, stored with every requisite for travellers. Our tents were not so agreeably placed as we could have wished, having only a single tree to cover them, and that not of sufficient magnitude to afford much shelter, although of a species called the *neem*,[94] which often grows to a great height, and spreads considerably. This description of tree somewhat resembles the *beech* of England, as to size and general appearance; but its leaves are differently formed, these being long, narrow, and regularly jagged to the point. It flourishes all over the interior of Hindostan, but is seldom found near the coast. The leaves of this tree have the peculiar property of healing flesh-wounds when applied cold; and as a hot poultice, are equally beneficial in maturing an inflammation, and producing suppuration. When divested of the bark, the wood possesses a smell which is so offensive to snakes, that they will not approach it; for which reason, when in tents, we made a practice of laying branches round the feet of our beds, particularly on a sandy soil, where these reptiles are chiefly found. I have frequently seen them lured from their holes by the sound of a small pipe, not unlike a shepherd's reed, and kept at bay by a stick newly cut from the neem tree; during which, a person from behind has contrived to despatch him by a blow on the head—(the only vital part.)

---

* There are no corn mills in this country. The operation of grinding it is performed by placing two flat circular stones upon each other, with a stake through the centre, and a handle on the top, which is turned by one woman, while another supplies the machine with grain. Both women sit cross-legged on the ground, which is plaistered with a kind of clay made with cow-dung, forming a hard dry floor, so that the meal is preserved perfectly free from dirt. This method of grinding corn elucidates that portion of Scripture mentioned in Matt. xxiv. 41, "Two women," &c.

† The oxen of Hindostan have all humps upon their shoulders: it is a fleshy substance, about the size of a moderate round of beef. When salted, these humps are most excellent eating; being regularly streaked, fat and lean.

To compensate for the want of shade, we were placed at *Barayah* close to a well of most excellent water; which is a circumstance of some importance in this climate, but particularly so during the hot winds, when so much is required to wet the *tatties*. There are several manufactories at *Barayah;* the largest of them is of coarse cloth, on account of the East India Company.

On quitting this place, the following day we drove principally through groves of mango, whose boughs were bending under the weight of ripe fruit, passed many populous villages, and halted at *Derriah-poore*. Clumps of bamboo became less frequent as we journied towards the West: they are plants that require constant moisture, and consequently are seen most flourishing in the province of Bengal. I observed also that the goats here were of a much larger size, and that an infinite number of small grey squirrels, striped with black, having long bushy tails, were domiciliated in all the villages; but saw none of the colour we are accustomed to find in England.

About midnight, so tremendous a storm of thunder, lightning, and rain, came on, as threatened to carry away the tent; it literally poured down in torrents. I had scarcely time to hurry on my clothes before the water rushed through our tent like a rapid river, which continued for near an hour, and so damaged the tent equipage, that the march of our baggage was delayed until morning,* which deprived us of many comforts on our next encamping ground.

I would advise travellers to arm themselves with patience before they leave home, and not be dismayed, although the path be sometimes rugged, reflecting that the occasional deprivation of an indulgence never fails to enhance its value. What reconciled me in a great measure to waiting three hours for my breakfast, was, the delightful spot our *avant couriér*[95] had selected for us to spend the day on. It was a verdant turf close to the Ganges, shaded by trees, with an extensive prospect on either side. The air had been cooled by the storm of the preceding night, and every herb breathed fragrance. About a hundred yards from us stood a small romantic cottage belonging to the superintending officer of an invalid station† at about half a mile distant, called *Moor Ko Choky*. Sitting at my writing-desk, I counted above sixty sail of vessels laden with merchandize, sailing down, or tracking up, this beautiful river: the traffic on it is scarcely credible to those who have not witnessed it.

The next morning we proceeded twenty miles farther, and found another cottage belonging to the same officer. The old man in whose charge it had been left, invited us to occupy it: it was delightfully cool, and we passed a most agreeable day.

The country in this direction is well wooded, although covered by cultivation. It abounds in large populous villages, through which runs an exceedingly good road, enlivened by occasional views of the Ganges. Some long shady lanes through

---

* All the tents not in use, and heavy baggage, cattle, &c. start at night, to be ready on the next encamping ground.

† These villages for Seapoy pensioners are called *tannahs*.[96]

which we passed, reminded me forcibly of my native country. This place is called *Umal Golah*, rather too long a march from *Moor Ko Choky*, as we did not reach it until nine o'clock, when the heat had become quite oppressive. It would have been better had we known it to have halted at a place called *Bar*, through which we passed, about eight miles short of our present encampment.

This district of *Bahar* is by far the most populous and flourishing of any I have seen. It is, in fact, the granary of the upper provinces, although, properly speaking, not one of them, having been classed with *Benares*[97] as the centre ones.

Both the upper and centre provinces are under the jurisdiction of the same commissioners. The lower ones have an establishment of their own, under the immediate superintendance of the Governor General, who resides there.

Our road from *Umal Golah* was by no means agreeable, from its running so near the water's edge; while the bank was, in many places, so broken as to render remaining in the carriage quite unsafe. By alternate riding and walking, therefore, we pursued our way to the village of *Bicket-poore*, about twelve miles farther, and found our encampment under the shade of some fine large trees, about a hundred yards inland. The bazar is a good one, but the well-water all bad.

For the last two days the wind had blown strong from the eastward, and rendered the atmosphere so cool that we had no occasion for tatties, and could enjoy the delightful prospect around us.

A most friendly invitation met us here from one of the Judges of the Court of Appeal at Patna,[98] from whence we were only ten miles distant; and another from the superintending surgeon.[99] These attentions are always accompanied by a present of fruit and vegetables, which are not to be purchased on the road.

In *Bicket-poore* and its vicinity, table and other linen is manufactured, for which *Patna* has been famed from time immemorial. The weavers' looms are placed under large groves of trees, the ground being kept as clean as the floor of any dwelling-house—not a single leaf is suffered to remain on it. These looms are upon the simplest plan imaginable, and worked with shuttles. They are erected in the morning, and taken away in the evening. This part of *Bahar* is particularly famous for cocoa-nut and palm-trees; from the latter they make excellent matting to cover the floors of houses.

The road (as is customary when running by the side of the river) is bad, leading through deep ravines to *Futtuah*, a very large place, inhabited only by weavers; in consequence of which there is no encamping ground, and we were obliged to send our tents sixteen miles farther on, through Patna, to a place called *Bankipore*,[100] where the Company's civil servants reside. From the eastern to the western gate of *Patna* is seven measured miles, in one continued street of shops. The inhabitants are all either Hindoos or Mussulmen. *Patna* is supposed to be, next to *Benares*, the richest place in India. I never saw a place so full of children—early of a morning you might almost walk upon their heads. Making this observation to a gentleman present, "A Mussulman," said he, "is so desirous that his possessions should descend to his posterity, as frequently to avail himself of a law which empowers a man (in case his wife does not produce a child within some given period) to repudiate her, and marry another; for 'A barren woman,' say they, 'is abandoned of God; and a man who has no progeny, can never go to heaven.' "[101]

The city of Patna and its dependencies came into possession of the English in the year 1764.[102] It was governed at that time by* *Meer Kossim Khan*,[103] Subah (or chief) of Bengal, with a German as his General-in-Chief, named *Sumroo*, (or Sombre,)[104] husband to the Begum of that name,[105] of whom I shall have occasion to speak as I proceed.

After sundry engagements at *Moorshedabad, Patna*, &c. &c., and contesting all the passes over the mountains, even to the gates of *Monghier*, Meer Kossim Khan was driven into that fortress,[106] where he sustained a siege of nine days, and then capitulated. Previous to this occurrence, Sumroo, with a barbarity almost unparalleled, invited some English gentlemen then at *Patna* to dine with him; and in a moment of conviviality, while seated round his table, he caused them to be massacred.[107,†] This outrage, however, was not long unrevenged: Major Adams, of the Company's service, with the Seapoys under his command, in four months from this period completed the conquest of Bengal, driving *Meer Kossim* and his followers to seek refuge with *Sujah Dowlah*, then Emperor of *Delhi*.[108]

---

* Meer signifies a prince.
† Since this period no Englishman has resided within the gates of Patna.

CHAPTER VI.

HAVING many friends at *Bankipore*, we were prevailed upon to remain there some days, which afforded me an opportunity of witnessing some ceremonies of the natives which I had not before seen, and of learning an incident so truly characteristic of the apathy of a Hindoo, that I cannot avoid mentioning it here.

A malefactor having committed some crime for which he was sentenced to be hanged, received the awful fiat with so much coolness, that the Judge was disposed to believe the man had not understood him, and accordingly caused it to be repeated by one of the native counsellors. The man replied, that he understood the Judge very well. "You are to be hanged tomorrow," repeated the barrister. "*Saheb ko koosi,*" "as the gentleman pleases," returned the culprit, and followed his conductor out of court, apparently unconcerned. A few days elapsed before the sentence could be put in execution; and when brought forth, as they supposed, to suffer the punishment of his crime, there appeared quite a different person. This being reported to the Judge, he was ordered to be brought before him, and it was discovered that the other had given this man three rupees to be hanged in his place. The former one had of course made his escape; and, strange as it may appear, the substitute was afraid of being discharged, lest he might insist upon his refunding the three rupees, which he had spent, he said, on metais, cakes of which they are particularly fond, made of sugar and flour.

Another instance, though of a less serious nature, occurred in the person of a palankeen bearer in our service, who asked leave to go to his village and be married. This was the only time of the year they do marry. His master told him that he could not spare him immediately, but that, before the marrying season was over, he should go. "*A, eha Saheb,*" "very well, Sir," replied the bearer, "next year will do as well." Hence it may be concluded that parties in this country do not *always* marry from attachment; in fact, girls are betrothed by their parents before they attain their seventh birthday,[109] without regard to difference of age in the man—being of the same *caste* is quite sufficient. When all arrangements are made, the bride elect, decked out in all her finery, is introduced to her intended husband, and then retires to feast with the females of both families; while the males regale separately for two or three days, or as long as the parents of the girl can afford it.* They then return to their several occupations; and she is allotted an apartment in her father's house, out of which she must not stir again unveiled. About three years after this ceremony, she is supposed capable of managing a family, and the husband returns to claim her. The head man of the village is then applied to, who draws up the marriage contract, which he signs himself, and several other

---

* The males and females of families never eat together.

witnesses. They send cardamum seeds, as notices of invitation, (or cloves, if they are rich,) to all the persons they wish to see, notifying by a special messenger the day the marriage is to take place. These tokens are sent three days previous to the grand entertainment; but a smaller one is provided on the two former days, when none but very intimate friends are expected. On the second day, the women (all except the bride, and any sister or relative that she may have under seven years of age) go in procession to the house of the bridegroom, and tinge his head and the palms of his hands with *mindy*,[110] a sweet-smelling shrub, which, when bruised and mixed with water, produces a beautiful red colour. After this operation he adorns his person by putting on a yellow turban and waistband, with a pair of yellow cloth shoes, and mounting a horse or poney as gaily caparisoned as himself, returns with some of his own friends at the head of the procession, when, as I before mentioned, the parties regale themselves—the men on the outside of the house, under an awning erected for the occasion, the women within. Every member of the family to which she belongs, feels it incumbent upon them on this occasion to present some pledge of friendship. I have seen the daughter of a rich merchant, or of a banker, go off with two or three loaded waggons in her suite. The bridal party spend most part of their time in feasting, smoking, and parading the streets, accompanied by all sorts of noisy instruments, to the great annoyance of the more peaceable inhabitants, particularly at night. The bride is conveyed from her father's house in a kind of covered cart, with curtains drawn closely round, (in which she contrives sometimes to make a small fracture just to peep through,) to that of her husband, attended by himself and his friends, some on horseback, some on foot, (but every one sports a little bit of yellow upon his person,) firing matchlocks, flourishing swords, and scampering round the bride's carriage with every demonstration of joy. Many other vehicles filled with company follow in her train, and the ceremony concludes with a wedding supper. The practice of using *mindy* is not confined to marriage ceremonies: no woman in Hindostan considers herself dressed without it. They rub it inside their hands and fingers, as well as at the roots of their nails, both of fingers and toes; while to heighten the brilliancy of their eyes, they describe a black line close to the edge of the lid with a powder mixed in water, called *Soolmah:* this they perform by dipping a small wooden bodkin into the mixture, and drawing it gently along the eye-lash when the eye is closed.

This must have been an ancient custom in the East, for it is spoken of in the second book of Kings, "She put her eyes in painting."[111] They also consider long hair as one of their principal ornaments, cutting it only when the moon is in the increase; and it cannot be denied that these women have the finest hair of any in the world; perhaps the quantity of oil which they daily apply to the roots, may be an additional reason for its being so extremely soft and luxuriant.

The Hindoos are uniformly tenacious in whatever respects ancient custom, but particularly so in regard to the difference of *caste*. A young Hindoo girl, of superior beauty, had by chance been seen and admired by a youth of the same religion, but of inferior *caste*. Knowing the latter to be an insurmountable barrier to the parents' consent, he at length prevailed on her to elope with and marry him in his own village. Her family soon discovered their retreat, and contrived by a stratagem to get her again in their power. Accordingly, her mother was despatched to negociate the pretended reconciliation, and prevail on her to return, in order that the marriage might be properly celebrated at her father's house. The poor girl, delighted at the prospect of so fortunate an issue, readily accompanied her mother, and was received by her father and brother with open arms. When three days had elapsed, and no marriage feast been proclaimed, she began to suspect the treachery, and determined on seizing the first opportunity of returning to the husband she had chosen. A favourable one seemed to present itself; but she had not been gone long, before she was overtaken by her brother, who affected to sympathise with, and offered to see her safe home. The road lay through an unfrequented path, which taking advantage of, he drew his sword,* and severed her head from the body. She was found the next morning weltering in her blood. The father and brother were immediately apprehended, and, wonderful to relate, not only confessed the crime, but exulted in the accomplishment of it: nor was it in the power of the Judge to punish them; for, unhappily, the Mahometan law,[112] by which natives of every description are tried, is so arbitrary as to invest parents with unlimited authority over their children, even to the depriving them of life; and it being proved in evidence that the son only obeyed his father's orders, they were both acquitted.

The Hindoos are the original inhabitants, and by far the largest population in this country, although the sovereigns and chiefs are Mahometans, being descendants of those Tartar, Persian, or Arabic princes, that formerly conquered and gave laws to Hindostan.[113] The Brahmins however remain despotic in all points that regard religion and superstitious ceremonies. These men worship bulls, peacocks, &c. Monkeys are also held sacred by them; and a vegetable called *toolsey*,[114] with many other things that I do not at this moment recollect. They do not eat any thing that is not prepared by one of their own *caste*, and commonly dress their own food. To kill a Brahmin is one of the five sins for which, according to their creed, there is no expiation. There are a variety of *castes*, or tribes; but the order of pre-eminence is indisputably fixed. An Hindoo of *inferior caste* would not presume to adopt the customs of a *superior;* severe punishment, and even death, would be the consequence. A Hindoo, or any other persuasion, may, on payment of a fine, and submitting to some trifling ceremonies, become a Mussulman†; but no one can become a Hindoo:[115] he must actually be born of Hindoo parents, or he cannot embrace their religion.

The Hindoos are the only cultivators of the soil; and although now *peaceful* cultivators of it, they have not laid aside their ancient custom of taking into the field their sword and shield. They are merchants also, and bankers; consequently, *Patna* being a mercantile place, its principal inhabitants are Hindoos.

---

* The meanest peasant in these provinces wears a sword.
† Mussulmen are forbidden by their religion to take interest for money, they therefore seldom engage in trade.

On quitting *Bankipore* we travelled on a fine level road, for about eight miles in a straight line, to *Danapore*,[116] the military station of this district for infantry regiments. Here are excellent barracks for nearly four thousand men, and good accommodation at a little distance for their officers. *Danapore* shows an extensive front to the Ganges, on whose bank it stands. It contains a capital bazar, and a number of good mechanics, by whom furniture and carriages, in the European style, are neatly executed. Leather is also cured and dressed here in a superior style. Their boots, shoes, harness, &c. are equal to those brought from England. Some English shop-keepers have settled at this place; but the natives imitate so well, that, I am told, my countrymen do not find the business answer. Wax candles are better made here than anywhere, and are indeed most excellent; in short, either here or at *Patna*, every thing for ornamenting house or person may be procured for money.

From hence we proceeded to *Moneah*,[117] distant only eight miles. This was formerly a station for cavalry; but since the acquisition of territory in the western, or upper provinces, it has been evacuated, and bears at this time no trace of a cantonment. The village of *Moneah* consists of one street a mile and a half in length; beyond which are many religious buildings of considerable antiquity, all in good repair. In the centre of each enclosure is a deep square pond, enclosed by brick walls, not higher than the footpath, with steps down the four sides, ornamented by figures carved in stone.

The evening of our arrival happened to be a festival, so that we had the pleasure to see these temples decorated with flowers, brilliantly illuminated, and thronged with people. Their musical instruments do not in general produce agreeable sounds to an English ear; but really, on this occasion, they were rather pleasing than otherwise. We found here such fine pasture for the cattle, that we halted the next day to indulge them. I also remarked some fine *peeple trees*,[118] the branches and leaves of which form the principal food for elephants.

We now crossed a wide navigable river, called the *Soane*,[119] famous for beautiful pebbles and the salubrity of its water, and took up our abode for a few days at the house of the Judge at *Arrah*,[120] whose Lady had been many years collecting these stones, and had a very valuable assortment: they bear a high polish, and vary considerably as to colour. The most curious and admired are pure milky white, with a small green weed in the centre of each, as distinctly traced as if it had been done with a pencil. She kindly presented me with a set, and we parted reluctantly on both sides. *Arrah* is a notorious place for snakes.

Our next encampment was at *Moraad Gunge*. The road to it is remarkably good, and beautifully diversified with trees. We passed through long vistas of different kinds, completely sheltered from the sun. This is a plentiful country for geese, and no less famous for banditti, who often surprise the sleeping traveller with a drawn sword, sharpened at either edge, flourishing over him. They seldom attack armed persons, their chief object being to obtain plunder, with which they are off like lightning; and the detection of them is very difficult.

Bodgepoore, the next place we came to, is one of the least civilized we had met with, and we might be truly said to have quitted the haunts of tigers, and entered the more ferocious ones of men. Scarcely had we retired for the night, before an alarm of thieves was given; but our people being upon the alert, it soon subsided. A short time afterwards an immense cavalcade, on foot as well as on horseback, and in vehicles of different descriptions, passed by, which we understood to be a wedding party conducting the bride, daughter to a rich merchant of *Patna*, to her future habitation, and that the wealth with them was considerable. All was again quiet, but not destined to remain so; for presently we heard the report of fire-arms, and concluding that the new-married couple were attacked, most of our servants instantly followed their master in the direction whence the sounds proceeded, and fortunately arrived in time to save the property, but too late, alas! to prevent bloodshed—two of their attendants were already cut down, never to rise again in this world. The *banditti*,[121] or *dakoities*,[122] as they are called, upon perceiving so strong a reinforcement made off, vowing vengeance against all parties. These robbers are pretty accurately conjectured to be in the pay of a rajah who resides there. Some years ago, before the country was cleared of underwood and thicket, no person could pass that road without being attacked; but on the appointment of Mr. Deane to the collectorship[123] of *Arrah*,[124] he caused the *jungle* to be cleared away, and the lands put in a state of cultivation; so that having no shelter, they were afraid to continue their depredations, which are not any thing like so frequent as they were before.

Indigo flourishes particularly well in this part of India.

CHAPTER VII.

THE next morning we reached *Buxar*[125] to breakfast, and were most hospitably received by the Colonel Commandant and his family,[126] who reside in the fort. Seven ladies and four gentlemen assembled at this meal—a disproportion very unusual in this country. The battle of *Buxar*, with the reduction of its fort, makes no inconsiderable figure in history. Some monuments of the English officers that fell before it still remain. It is now a station for invalid pensioners of the Company's European regiments. From the eminence on which it stands, being not more than a hundred yards from the Ganges, the windings of that river are seen in great perfection: the vast extent of country it commands, altogether forming a most delightful prospect.

Soon after breakfast, a servant of the Colonel's came running in to say that a tiger had been seen in a patch of sugar-cane near the village, and that many people were gone out after him; elephants and horses were immediately ordered to be got ready, and our gentlemen sallied forth. About an hour after, a clergyman,[127] one of the party, returned, more pale if possible than Hamlet's ghost.[128] He had seen the tiger, been thrown from his horse, and scrambled back he knew not how. We could scarcely pity him, for he had mounted in spite of all remonstrance. Every one told him how dangerous it was to pursue a tiger in any other mode than on an elephant: but he had "a remarkably steady horse, who would start at nothing, and gallop away from any thing:" the latter proved true; for he galloped away from his master, and was not heard of until the evening. The other gentlemen succeeded in killing the tiger, who received nineteen rifle balls before he fell.

On the first of May we bid adieu to our friends at *Buxar*, and crossed the Ganges to *Mahomedabad*, a town about twelve miles from the opposite shore. The road to it was pretty fair; many large groves of mango and tamarind trees appeared near it; in one of the former they had pitched our tents. A canal runs through the town, navigable only in the winter season, but at all times containing a sufficient quantity of water for the purposes of irrigation. The distance from hence to *Ghazipore*[129] is nearly the same, and a delightful drive it is, being chiefly between rows of large trees on a broad level road.

Although solicited by the Judge of *Ghazipore*[130] to take up our abode at his house, we preferred pitching the tents on a plain between the military and civil stations, that we might be near our friends at both. On the day of our arrival we dined with the General in command,[131] and the day following with the Judge of the district.[132] The heat of *Ghazipore* at this season is beyond description: the soil is a deep sand, which when thoroughly heated continues so for a length of time; while the country is flat, and every where covered with buildings. It certainly felt many degrees hotter here than at *Buxar*. *Ghazipore* is famous for the manufacture of cloth, particularly of the kinds used for shirts and bedlinen, which, besides being beautifully fine, are very durable. Otta of roses,[133] and rose-water also, are produced here in great perfection; indeed the country round *Ghazipore* is one complete rose garden.

On the morning of the 4th we quitted *Ghazipore*, and reached the village of *Niah Serai*, where a patch of fine large mango trees afforded us ample shelter: near them was a well with plenty of water, pure to the eye, but extremely nauseous to the taste; from which we judged it to possess some chalybeate properties.

From hence we continued our route to *Sidepoore*, or rather a few miles beyond it. As the morning proved remarkably cool for the season, and the road good, we did not halt there, but proceeded to cross a ferry over the river *Goomty*,* so called from its numerous windings. This stream is fortunately narrow, for the boats are mere nut-shells, and badly constructed. Our tent was close to the opposite shore. From this place to *Chobipore* we drove the next morning, chiefly through ravines, and within a short distance of the Ganges the whole way. Four years ago this road was almost impassable; it has lately undergone a complete repair, and is now comparatively good.

From *Chobipore* to *Benares* is a beautiful drive on an excellent road, between avenues of trees the whole way. We reached the house of a friend to breakfast, and remained there until the 10th, dining the first and last days with him, and the intermediate ones with the General commanding,[134] and the Chief Judge of the Court of Appeal.[135]

Benares is one of the largest cities in India, and perhaps the richest. It extends five miles along the bank of the river, and three miles inland. It has never been completely conquered by the Mahometans; between whom and their Hindoo neighbours no good understanding prevails. It requires no little vigilance on the part of the British Government to keep them tolerably civil to each other. Half the city is inhabited by Hindoos, the other half by Mussulmen, as perfectly distinct as if the division were marked by a line; yet, during their festivals, it is the most difficult thing in the world to prevent their interfering with each other. This is the only place in which so rooted an enmity appears, and it is kept alive by the Hindoos boasting that this, their most sacred city, was never conquered. It is a system of policy on the part of the English to protect, as far as is in their power, the religious ceremonies of both; since it is chiefly owing to these means that we keep our possessions in the country.[136] *Benares* is particularly reverenced by the Hindoos, as they have a tradition that their principal deity sprung from thence. At particular seasons of the year it is the resort of pilgrims from all parts of the eastern world. The Hindoos, its ancient inhabitants, were attacked, and for a short time overpowered, by the Emperor *Aurungzebe;*[137] but by degrees regained their footing, and are at this time the greater proportion of its inhabitants. This prince, in order

---

* The Goomty swarms with otters.

to evince his triumph, caused the places of Hindoo worship to be only *partially* destroyed, and *Musjeeds*,[138] or Mussulman ones, to be erected on the same scite. This pitiful act has been the source of much discontent, and even bloodshed. In the month of November, 1809,[139] so serious a dispute arose in consequence, that it became necessary to send for troops from *Ghazipore* to assist those stationed at *Benares*, to prevent a general massacre; and it is highly probable that while a vestige of these ancient buildings remain, their animosity will not subside. There is always praying going on, of one kind or other—the streets are overrun by their different priests. When the Brahmins wish to assemble a congregation, or at the usual hour of prayer, they mount to the top of one of the minarets and blow a horn; and this happens two or three times a day; while Mussulmen go about tingling a little bell.

You may always know when a Mahometan is becoming desperate or enraged, by his turban being pulled over the left temple, leaving the other side exposed. On this signal, those of his friends who are inclined to support him, arm themselves, rally round, and soon the affray commences. "Go, set thy turban straight," is a kind of defiance, expressive also of contempt, which they are a good deal in the habit of using to each other. This puts me in mind of an old saying, "Do you cock your hat at me?"—"Sir, I cock my hat."[140]

There are a set of people (Mussulmen) at this place called *bankas*,[141] or prize-fighters, who are often extremely troublesome. An English gentleman was met, a short time since, by one of these on a narrow tracking path by the side of the river, where there was barely room to pass: neither seemed disposed to turn out of a straight line; but putting on a very fierce look, the Mussulman pulled the turban over his left eyebrow, and drew his sword, muttering *kaufur*, which means infidel. The gentleman had nothing else for it, than to make a dart past, and push his opponent down the bank; but his life would have paid the forfeit of this temerity, if he had not quickly escaped to his boat, and shoved off.

This place is justly celebrated for the beauty of its manufactures, particularly of gauzes, (white and coloured,) either spotted, sprigged, or striped, with silver or gold, worn by natives of rank as turbans; also a kind of stuff for dresses, called *kinkob*: this is composed of different coloured silks, brocaded with gold or silver sprigs, forming a valuable and superb texture. In the houses of great men, you frequently see cushions (the only seats they use) covered with it. Ivory is turned here with great taste, particularly chess men, a game of which natives of rank are generally fond. It is likewise a good place to purchase pearls, diamonds, and other precious stones, as well as shawls, there being a number of merchants residing here who trade largely in these articles; sandal wood, boxes, children's toys most beautifully executed, &c. &c. They also excel in the art of dyeing, their colours are remarkably fine.

Mahometans have four important periods in the year.[142] First, the birth of Mahomet,[143] which continues seven days, when every Mussulman that can afford it kills a goat to regale his friends.

The second is the fast of the *Ramzaan,* or *Ramdaan,*[144] *(Lent,)* commencing on the first of September, and including the period of thirty days, in which time Mahomet is said to have travelled from *Mecca*[145] to *Medina.*[146] During this season his followers are required to abstain from animal food. A strict observer will not smoke tobacco, or drink water, from sun-rise to sun-set, or omit attending prayers at the mosque at noon, where every one mutters his own; and when the *moollah* (priest) thinks they have had sufficient time, he begins. Every Mussulman, when he prays, sets his face towards *Mecca,* first standing, then sitting on his heels, bending his body forward at intervals, so that his forehead may touch the ground at each obeisance. The Ramzaan ends by a grand feasting.

The third is the commencement of their new year,[147] computed by the lunar month, when the property of every man is estimated, and a tenth of it collected to support the poor. On this occasion they cleanse, thoroughly repair, and beautify their dwellings.

A fourth is called the *Moharum,* to commemorate the deaths of *Hussan* and *Houssein,*[148] two brothers, who were killed on the plains of *Kerbela,*[149] near *Mecca,* in endeavouring to defend each other. It commences on the 10th of October, and lasts ten days; during which the Mahometans wear green turbans, their mourning colour, as is yellow that of rejoicing. During this period they march in procession through the streets, following a decorated bier[150] containing two coffins, round which they occasionally discharge fire-arms to denote the cause, flourishing drawn swords, &c. It is extremely dangerous for a person of a different persuasion to touch any part of this paraphernalia; for those who accompany it are worked up to such a pitch of fanaticism, that they would not hesitate to sacrifice him on the spot. It is really lamentable to see with what vehemence they beat their breasts, crying out, "Houssein, Hussan, Hussan, Houssein," until they are so bruised, and hoarse that you can scarcely hear them. Several of these biers are seen in different parts of the town, which in the evening are surrounded by lamps. The people watch them to prevent their being extinguished. *Houssein* was the son of *Ali,* and married *Fatima,* the daughter of *Mahomet. Ali* was *Mahomet's* nephew.

This mournful scene is immediately succeeded by a festival of the Hindoos, sacred to the *God of Wealth.*[151] It is the beginning of *their* year, and answers by our computation to a period between the 15th of October and the 15th of November, as the moon happens to be, commencing on the tenth day after the full moon. On this occasion they illuminate their houses and temples; dress in their best apparel, covered with wreaths of flowers; parading the streets with music, fireworks, &c.; and indulging in every species of dissipation. Previous to this festival the Hindoos whitewash their houses, merchants take an account of their stock, and settle their yearly accounts; when their treasure chests, covered with silk and flowers, are carried triumphantly before them.

On the 10th of May, the wind blowing intolerably hot, we bid adieu to *Benares,* making a march of sixteen miles to a large town called *Tumunshabad;* and the next day proceeded to *Gopee Gunge,* where I purchased some carpets equal to those made at Wilton, in Wiltshire.[152] This place is twenty miles from our last encampment. From hence to *Sidabad* the road was very indifferent, particularly for the last eight miles, which being in the dominions of the *Nawaab of Oude*, whose seat of government is at *Lucknow*, some distance from it, had been totally neglected; and so dangerous is this part of the country considered on account of thieves who murder as well as plunder, that we made *one* long march, instead of two short ones, to get out of it, although met at *Sidabad* by two armed horsemen, sent by the Judge of Allahabad[153] for our protection; but "a burnt child dreads the fire,"[154] and we had on a former occasion owed our lives to stratagem at this very place. The attacking party creep into the camp upon their hands and knees, armed with two-edged knives, quite naked, and oiled all over to prevent being caught; and often come in such numbers, that it is impossible to escape them.

We now entered a ferry-boat, in order to cross over to *Allahabad*,[155] which is situate on the opposite bank of the *Ganges*. Not without difficulty was this desirable end accomplished; for about midway, a bank of sand had lately made its appearance, extending at least a quarter of a mile over. This it was necessary to pass, and reembark, as we were told, on the other side of it. This bank being a quicksand, I was advised to keep moving while the horse was putting into the carriage; and even in that short space of time he sunk considerably above the fetlock joint, which so alarmed him, that the moment we were seated he plunged forward, darting carriage and all into the opposite stream. Fortunately for us, it proved fordable; but the force of the stream carried us much lower down than we intended to have gone. For above fifteen minutes we were in this perilous situation. To say that I had no fears, would be deviating from the truth—I certainly did feel considerably alarmed, but endeavoured to suppress it, that I might not confuse my charioteer. The water was one instant running through the carriage, the next, one wheel was upon a bank of sand, and then we sunk altogether in a hole. The horse was powerful, and he had a skilful driver; so that, with the aid of Providence, we at length landed in safety. An almost perpendicular bank of three or four feet, to ascend, was nothing after the danger we had passed; and the horse did not seem less sensible than ourselves of our escape, for with one plunge he drew the carriage upon even ground. Here we met the Judge's chariot, which conveyed us to his house about three miles farther. *Allahabad* was formerly a fortified city, with a strong fortress and palace, built by the Emperor *Acbar*[156] at the confluence of the rivers *Jumna* and *Ganges;* but having for some years been neglected, it was rapidly falling to decay, until repaired and garrisoned by the British Government. A considerable revenue is derived at this place from the *Mahrattas*, who come at particular seasons of the year to perform their ablutions.[157] The new city is a mile and a half inland. Fish is particularly fine here, and in great abundance.

During our stay at *Allahabad*, it was understood that a Hindoo woman had signified her intention to end her existence on the funeral pile of her husband.[158] The Judge, with whom we were on a visit, sent for her father, and endeavoured to prevail on him to dissuade her. He said he had done all he could; but she was firmly determined upon it. The Judge then sent for her, but talked with as little success; she was bent upon immortalizing her name, and, as she said, of showing her family the way to heaven. In short, the day was fixed, and a gentleman who was present gave me a description of this horrid ceremony. An immense concourse of people having assembled, her approach was announced by the blowing of horns and beating of drums: next came a number of *Brahmins*, bearing lighted torches, and singing some appropriate stanzas to inspire this victim of credulity, who followed, attended by her relations and friends, all bearing torches but herself. She was richly dressed, having her hands, neck, and feet, covered with ornaments. The dead body of her husband was carried on a bier immediately before her. It was then placed upon the funeral pile, the priests forming a circle round. The father and mother having led the young woman within the circle, left her there, and retired among the crowd. Music, or rather discordant sounds, struck up, and the *Brahmins* again sung, while she marched slowly round the pile; when, divesting herself of her ornaments, with wonderful presence of mind, she distributed them to her weeping friends; then, exchanging her veil of white muslin for one of crimson, she was presented with a lighted torch, (the *Brahmins* meantime exhorting her by songs and gestures to be firm,) and again marched round the pile. She stopped a few moments, *salaamed* to all she knew, then putting the torch into the hand of her father, she calmly ascended the funeral pile, and seated herself by the side of her husband, amid the shouts and plaudits of the multitude. Her father, he believed, set fire to the pile; but a number of torches were instantly applied, drums beating, trumpets sounding, horns blowing, and guns firing, so that all was at once a scene of confusion and noise, sufficient to have drowned her cries if she had uttered any. Among other things, he observed that they threw a quantity of oil, salt, and dry straw, to increase the fury of the flame; and in less than ten minutes, nothing remained but ashes. What rendered this sacrifice the more unnatural, was, his being an old man, and she a young woman; but then he was a Brahmin! and it is considered incumbent on the widow of a Brahmin to pay this respect to his remains, or become an outcast from her family for ever. These unfortunate women are taught to believe that, by this single act, they expiate not only their own, but the sins of all their family, and that their souls fly instantly to Paradise. In some instances, I was told that the priests are obliged to assist their exhortations by copious draughts of opium, which first intoxicates, then stupifies their victim. The British Government in India are doing all they can to prevent the barbarous custom, by not suffering it to take place within reach of their troops; but the deluded natives find means to evade their vigilance.

The origin of this sacrifice is by some imputed to the extreme jealousy of the men, others to the conduct of the women themselves, who are uniformly skilled in the properties of herbs and drugs, and have not unfrequently been known to have recourse to them, on finding themselves mismatched in wedlock. Girls having no option, are often married to old decrepid men, who use them like slaves, and are so jealous, that when out of their sight they are invariably under lock and key.

Tradition indeed relates, that the circumstance of poisoning husbands was at one time so frequent, that the *Brahmins* established this mode of securing their own safety.

The day following I was attacked by inflammation on the lungs, which detained us here for several days. We then proceeded to *Konkerabad*, distant from *Allahabad* twenty-four miles; but, with the assistance of our friend's horses, we were enabled to accomplish it with great ease. Our pedestrian domestics made two marches of it—they were accordingly dispatched the day before. We drove next day to the house of a friend at *Kurrah*, twelve miles farther, where we remained two days.

Kurrah is a very ancient city, formerly carrying on considerable traffic in cloth, muslins, table-linen, &c. The remains of some magnificent mausoleums are still in existence. This, like most other Mussulman towns, is well supplied with poultry, eggs, milk, vegetables, and fruit, and every other requisite for travellers. Diamonds are found in this province; but they are not an article of commerce, on account of the great expense necessary to work the mines.

The heat of the weather had now become so great, that it was judged preferable to march in the evening instead of the morning; we consequently started about six o'clock on the 2nd of June, and pursued our journey as far as *Haut Gong*, a place of great antiquity, but rapidly falling to decay.

CHAPTER VIII.

HERE the remains only of spacious mansions are to be seen. The country is overgrown by a thick low jungle, (underwood,) through which the road lies—it is consequently very bad. A recent and partial storm of rain had fallen so heavily that we actually waded through mud for nearly fourteen miles. Two miles farther brought us to *Futtehpore*,[159] where we occupied the house of a Nawaab for two days, which gave us an opportunity of seeing the place. It is a large town full of inhabitants, chiefly Mussulmen, some of whom were very attentive in showing the beauties and curiosities of it, and, amongst others, a jail that had lately been built by Government, where the prisoners supported themselves by working at the loom. This is a great punishment to the generality of them, who would otherwise sit with their *hookahs*[160] in their mouths, listening to a twice told tale, and smoking until they fell asleep. It happened to be Friday (their Sabbath) when we were there, so the looms were not at work; but the plan pursued is most excellent. Whatever a man can earn beyond what is necessary for his support, forms a fund, which is given to him when the term of his probation is expired, in order that distress may not be pleaded as an excuse for crime.

Between *Haut Gong* and *Futtehpore* is a village, famous for turning wooden utensils; we purchased some that were extremely neat. The country is flat and low; the surface of it is a fine white sand, in many places overrun with a small prickly bush, in others with a broad-leafed shrub, called *dok*, from which exudes a gum that produces an elegant varnish for the painter, and a valuable article in medicine.

As the moon was not expected to rise until a late hour, we commenced our journey this evening by torch light. About eight o'clock we came to a spot where, the guide told us, seven native travellers had been murdered ten nights before, and the perpetrators had not yet been apprehended. This account led me to scrutinize the countenance of the narrator, for, as it is customary to take guides from one village to another, they are sometimes conjectured to be a party concerned in these transactions; I could discover, however, nothing but vacancy in his. It is lamentable to find instances of cruelty and avarice so common. So great is the thirst of gain in this country, that for a single rupee they have been known to deprive a fellow-creature of existence; and were they not by nature cowardly, they would be a most formidable people to live amongst. But, strange as it may appear, there is an awe about a European that they cannot overcome, unless he be asleep, and then he takes care to be well guarded.

Murder, by the Mahometan law, is in many cases no crime. I have been astonished to read, in some of our periodical publications, a character of these people so different to what they deserve. In a late philanthropic magazine, it was truly laughable to peruse lines setting forth their "mildness," "beneficence," "patience under oppression," &c. &c.; and with respect to Mahometans, there are not a more dissolute set of people in the universe, both men and women—the former being, almost without exception, treacherous and tyrannical; the latter cunning and deceitful, preserving towards their superiors the outward appearance of respect, while they are secretly planning to defraud him. Thus the servant, who daily plunders your property, never approaches but in an attitude of submission, putting his hands together, and touching his forehead with eyes cast on the ground. Their women are adepts in blandishments: instructed in them from their infancy, they rival every other nation, possessing a servility withal that gives them unbounded influence over their European protectors, (infinitely more, I am told, than the most accomplished female of his own nation can attain,) whose pockets they fleece to support an indigent admirer, or itinerant *fakeer*. I have known men who, although in other respects sensible men, and of a decisive character, to have been in the hands of these women as clay in the hands of the potter, perhaps even more easily moulded. I speak of Mahometans, for Hindoo women never live with any but their own *caste*, and are more respectable in every point of view. *Their* mode of life differs little from that of the wives of labourers and mechanics in Europe. They are not, like the Mussulmans, confined to the *zenanah*,[161] but assist their husbands in his occupation, draw water from the well for household purposes, and dress his food; while the others do nothing but adorn their persons, study deception, and smoke their *hookahs*. A man, by the Mahometan law, is allowed four wives; and he cannot imagine a greater luxury than being stretched on a *charpiah*, with a hookah in his mouth, listening to an old *fakeer* who relates Persian stories, with one or two of these women to fan and *champoo*[162] him.

Both Hindoo and Mussulman are equally fond of money: they will quit the kindest master in the world for a few additional rupees. I do not mean to assert that this rule has no exceptions, for I believe there may be many; some, indeed, have come within my own immediate observation—I speak only of the generality. I have known Hindoo servants so attached to their masters, as never to quit the bed-side when they have been ill, except to eat their necessary food; but such instances are very rare.

The occupations of servants in this country are so distinct, that it is necessary to have some of each religion in your establishment, and even some of no *caste* at all; for neither Mussulman nor Hindoo will sweep the house. Kitchens are always at a distance from the dwelling-house, or *bungalow*,[163] on account of the effluvia. This prevents the master or mistress from attending so much to the interior management of it, as they perhaps otherwise would do; a *khansommah* therefore, or house steward, is considered necessary, who takes complete charge of every thing in this department, even to the hiring a cook and helper. The *khansommah* is also answerable for all the plate, china, glass, and table-linen, and has authority over all the Mussulman servants. The person who fills this situation is generally a man of respectability, and of some property; he gets much higher wages than any of the others—seldom less than thirty, sometimes fifty rupees a month. Two *kismutdars* are the usual proportion to each gentleman or lady, to wait on them at table, either at home or abroad; and there is an established custom amongst them, not to wait on any other person, unless particularly ordered so to do. The dress of all Mussulmen is made alike, the colour and quality varying according to the taste or wealth of the wearer. White muslin, with plain-coloured turbans and waistbands, is the usual dress of this description of people. They never allow their wives to take service, unless driven to it by necessity.

These *gentlemen kismutdars* being much too fine to clean knives or plates, that service devolves on a *masauljie,* who also carries a lantern, and fetches things from the *bazar*. This is the most useful servant about the house; for not being of a high *caste*, he does many things that the others would refuse: he never makes his appearance within the bungalow, but when called for. The *kismutdars* stand behind your chair, and hand you every thing but liquids, which being cooled in ice or saltpetre nine months out of the twelve, is the business of the *abdar*, or butler. The first appearance of the *kismutdars* is with the breakfast, a pretty substantial meal, consisting of fish, boiled rice, hot rolls, an omelette, chicken *kooftas*,[164] (made like forcemeat, and fried in small cakes, very nice and dry,) boiled eggs, cold ham or tongue, potted meats, orange marmalade, toasted bread, a small loaf or two, butter in silver vases, (surrounded with ice to keep it cool,) plenty of fruit, and in the centre of the table either a silver bowl filled with milk, or a glass vase with flowers. The coffee apparatus is placed at one end of the table, served out by one of the *kismutdars;* the tea-things at the other, by the *khansomer*. Urns are not made use of, on account of their heating the room; (the tea-pot is taken outside to be filled;) neither are tea-boards ever seen in India. After this, you see no more of the *kismutdars* until one or two o'clock, unless they are called for, when they bring in a meal called *tiffin*,[165] which may be explained by an early dinner, containing all the delicacies of the season. For this meal invitations are seldom sent, but every body is welcomed to it who happens to arrive at the time. About three o'clock the party separate, take each a book, and repose on couches until sun-set. From two o'clock until six is considered the hottest part of the day, during which the natives uniformly sleep. At six, it is customary to dress and take a ride (or attend parade, if in the army) until dark, and then return to dinner; after which, few people take any thing more than a dish of tea or coffee. Suppers are not general in India.

I must now speak of the rest of a gentleman's establishment, viz. eight or ten (which is called a *set*) bearers to carry his palankeen; an *hircarah*, or running footman, to go before it with a spear; a *sirdar*, or head bearer, and his assistant, who also act as valets, clean the furniture, make the beds, and take charge of the linen. Under these are one or two tailors, (a *dirjee*,) who sit cross-legged in the *verandah*, and some sweepers of the house. But I have not yet mentioned the whole complement of servants necessary to form an establishment, as most gentlemen have their own farm-yard, and kill their own mutton.

A *bhery-wallah* is therefore necessary to take care of the sheep and goats.

A *moorgy-wallah* for the poultry.

A *soor-wallah* for the pigs.

A *gorry-wan* for the bullocks.
A *mahawat* to take care of, and drive the elephant.
A *sur-wan* for the camels.
A *syce* and grass-cutter to each horse.
A carpenter to repair fractures.
Two or three gardeners.
And a *clashie* to pitch tents, and flog them all when necessary.

After these come the women servants, and washerman's family. Where there are no children, *one* ayah[166] and her assistant are sufficient; but it is usual for each child to have a separate servant: and all that I have enumerated live in huts on your premises, placed in some obscure corner where they cannot be seen. The grounds are generally extensive, and seldom without inequalities, particularly on the banks of the Ganges, so that they are easily concealed.

The idea one has of a tailor in England, by no means answers the description of a *dirjee* in India. They are, properly speaking, *sempsters*, or as *sempstress* in the female, so *sempster* in the male. They make up no gentlemen's clothes, except they be of cotton; but are exceedingly expert in making ladies' dresses, especially from a copy, which they imitate with the greatest exactness. I once knew of a ridiculous circumstance that happened in this way. Gentlemen in India, during the hot season, wear fine white jackets, made of shirt cloth. One of these being a little torn at the elbow, was given to the *dirjee* to repair, and he put a small patch upon it: a short time afterwards, the gentleman, to whom it belonged, wished to have some new ones made, and this being inadvertently given for a pattern, all the new ones appeared with precisely the same patch on each elbow.

But to continue my journal. The road from *Futteh-poore* to *Kalian-poore* is sandy, and particularly distressing to the eyes from being so very white. The soil, indeed, seems every where to be impregnated with alkali. The saltpetre produced in this country is a source of great wealth to the Honourable the East India Company. The road from *Kalian-poore* to the village of *Sersowl* is as bad as a road can be.

Scarcely were the torches illumined, (about an hour after we started,) than one of the springs of our carriage gave way: my charioteer however contrived, by means of a pocket handkerchief and a piece of rope, (we found in the seat,) to fasten the two parts together. With this contrivance we were getting on tolerably well, every moment flattering ourselves that the road might mend, or, at all events, hoping that it would carry us on to the next village, where we could get it properly repaired; when, what should appear but a rapid stream, with a steep bank on either side. I confess I viewed it in absolute dismay. Our carriage now so unsafe, all other conveyances far behind, and with no other light than torches, it was really an appalling sight; but *necessity*, we are told, has no law; so down we went, splashed through the water after our sable guides, and happily reached the opposite shore without a ducking. The next evening brought us to *Khanpore*,[167] having in three months safely completed a journey of eight hundred miles in the same open carriage, and a most delightful journey it was. Our cattle and servants, as may be supposed, required a little rest, which determined us to remain a few days in this cantonment. It is the principal depôt for the Bengal army,[168] containing seldom less than ten thousand troops, including a regiment of His Majesty's Light Dragoons,[169] and one or two of infantry, besides the Company's artillery, with Seapoy corps, both cavalry and infantry, officered by European gentlemen. It is likewise the head-quarters of the army, the Commander-in-Chief[170] residing there. An invitation to a dinner, ball, and supper, at the Judges,[171] was the consequence of this delay—we sat down, a hundred and ten persons, at table. A friend of ours, who at this time commanded the troops at Lucknow,[172] being anxious to see us before we proceeded to the frontier, as we were now within a night's run (fifty miles) of Lucknow, we availed ourselves of the opportunity; and as the most expeditious mode of reaching it, proposed travelling by *dak*,[173] that is, in palankeens, with relays of bearers every ten miles. No sooner did the Nawaab *Sadut Alli*[174] hear of our intention, than, with that attention to British subjects for which he was justly famed, he sent his own post chariot and four to meet us. I cannot say that we were perfect strangers, having on a former occasion spent a month in one of his palaces.

The city of Lucknow, excepting the Nawaab's palaces, is neither so large nor so splendid in appearance as that of *Benares; his* premises are of course superb, and his stud exceeded both in quality and number that of any other potentate. His table, to which all the English of any rank were welcome, had in every respect the appearance of a nobleman's in England; and no nobleman of any country could possess greater suavity of manners, or more genuine politeness. At the time I am speaking of, he was about fifty years of age; his figure tall, athletic, and commanding, with features expressive, and rather handsome; his complexion by no means dark for a native, and his eyes a fine hazel. On his table were always three distinct dinners—one at the upper end, by an English cook; at the lower end, by a French cook; and in the centre, (where *he* always sat,) by a Hindostanee cook. Hogmeat, wine, and turkeys, being forbidden by the prophet Mahomet, he allowed himself the latitude of selecting substitutes; accordingly, a bottle of cherry brandy was placed on the table by him, from which he pledged his European guests, and called it English syrup; while the hams on his table (which all came from England) he called English venison, and therefore ate with impunity. He was certainly not a Mussulman at heart; for I have frequently heard him ridicule their prejudices. He passed his early years in Calcutta, chiefly in English society, and had unconsciously imbibed many English ideas. He is styled the Grand Vizier,[175] and was placed by our Government upon the throne, to which by birth he was entitled, but by usurpation he had nearly lost. He travelled to Lucknow as an English gentleman, incog. in a palankeen, and just got within the city gates in time to prevent them from being closed against him. He was a staunch ally to the British Government; of which he gave convincing proof when the army under General Lord Lake[176] was preparing to take the field against the Mahrattas. Being in want of carriage cattle, he voluntarily furnished six hundred camels, five hundred horses as an addition to the dragoon regiments, a hundred and fifty elephants, and a thousand bullocks, besides baggage-waggons innumerable. In the second campaign also, when the officers and men were seven months' pay in arrears, he advanced Government twelve lacs of rupees, for eighteen months, without any interest. No man could have behaved more handsomely, and very few would have been half so liberal. He understood the English language perfectly, and wrote it correctly, but could not pronounce the words. Knowing my predilection for poetry, he presented me with the following specimen, in manuscript, written by

LEBITT BEN RABIAL, ALAMARY,[177]
A Native of Yemen, and contemporary with Mahomet.

"On the Return of a Person, after a long Absence, to a Place where he had spent his earliest Years.

"Those dear abodes that once contained the fair,
   Amidst Mitatus' wilds I seek in vain;
Nor towns, nor tents, nor cottages are there,
   But scattered ruins, and a silent plain.

The proud canals that once Kayana graced,
   Their course neglected, and their waters gone,
Among the levelled sands are dimly traced,
   Like moss-grown letters on a mouldering stone.

Kayana, say, how many a tedious year
   Its hallowed circle o'er our heads hath rolled,
Since to my vows thy tender maids gave ear,
   And fondly listened to the tale I told?

How oft since then, the star of spring, that pours
   A never-failing stream, hath drenched thy head;
How oft, the summer's cloud, in copious showers,
   Or gentle drops, its genial influence shed?

How oft since then, the hovering mist of morn
   Hath caused thy looks with glittering gems to glow;
How oft hath eve her dewy treasures borne,
   To fall responsive to the breeze below!

The matted thistles, bending to the gale,
   Now clothe those meadows, once with verdure gay.
Amidst the windings of that lonely vale,
   The teeming antelope and ostrich stray.

The large-eyed mother of the herd, that flies
   Man's noisy haunts, here finds a sure retreat,
Here tends her clustering young, till age supplies
   Strength to their limbs, and swiftness to their feet.

Save where the swelling stream hath swept those walls,
   And given their deep foundations to the light,
As the re-touching pencil that recalls
   A long-lost picture to the raptured sight.

Save where the rains have washed the gathered sand,
   And bared the scanty fragments to our view,
As the dust sprinkled on a punctured hand,
   Bids the faint tints resume their azure hue.

No mossy record of those once loved seats,
   Points out the mansion to enquiring eyes;
No tottering wall in echoing sounds repeats
   Our mournful questions, and our bursting sighs.

Yet midst those ruined heaps, that naked plain,
   Can faithful memory former scenes restore,
Recall the busy throng, the jocund train,
   And picture all that charmed us there before.

Nor shall my heart the fatal morn forget,
   That bore thy maidens from these seats so dear.
I see, I see the crowding litters yet,
   And yet the tent poles rattle in my ear;

I see thy nymphs with timid steps ascend,
   The streamers wave in all their painted pride,
The folding curtains every fold extend,*
   And vainly strive the charms within to hide.

What graceful forms those envious folds enclose!
   What melting glances through those curtains play!
Sure Weiras' antelopes, or Judah's roes,
   Through yonder veils their sportive young survey!

The band moved on—to trace their steps I strove;
   I saw them urge the camel's hastening flight,
Till the white vapour, like a rising grove,
   Snatched them for ever from my aching sight.

Nor since that morn have I Nawarra seen;
   The bands are burst that held us once so fast;
Memory but tells me that such things have been,
   And sad reflection adds, that they are past."

---

* Those carriages that contain women are always surrounded by curtains.

The original of this was beautifully written in Persian, not as *we* write with a pen, but with a sort of straight smooth reed,[178] about the same size, similarly cut, and admirably adapted for the purpose. The Persians always commence an epistle by an *Aliph*,[179] (the first letter in the Alphabet,) in order to signify the beginning; and write from the right hand to the left, or, as we should call it, backwards. They fold the paper narrow, and placing it on the palm of their hand, write with great facility.

A still more curious specimen of eastern phraseology than this, was sent to me once by a native gentleman, who had promised during my absence to visit my little boy, then a baby. It ran as follows: –

"To the Begum[180]—of exalted rank, source of radiance and dignity, may her good fortunes be perpetual!!

"After representing to the Presence illumining the world, that our fervent wishes for the honour of kissing the footsteps of her who is the ornament of the Sultanas of the East, are constant and never-ceasing; her slave begs to make known to the Illustrious Perception, that he this morning, when about two watches of the day were passed, agreeable to the commands resembling fate, presented himself at the threshold of the *Doulet Khannah*," (Palace of Riches,) "now darkened by the absence of its brightest luminary; and having made known his desire, was admitted to the honour of beholding the radiant countenance of the infant, resembling in beauty the moon of fourteen days, when with inexpressible joy he perceived that the rose-bud, (in whose presence the flowers of the garden blush,) fanned by the zephyrs[181] of health, was expanding with a grace far beyond his feeble powers of description. Having made the most minute enquiries respecting all matters fitting for him to be informed of, your slave learned that the infant, and the two cypress-shaped damsels attendant on the threshold, pass their days in uninterrupted tranquility. The fawn-eyed nymph,* whose beaming beauty fills with envy the splendid empress of the night; whose voice makes the plaintive bird of a thousand notes" (nightingale) "hang his head in despair; she whose fragrant looks cause to dissolve in sorrow the less odoriferous amber; with a grace which would have covered with blushes the lovely *Leila*, and made more frantic the enamoured *Mujnoon*,[182] begged her humble assurance of eternal obedience.

"Thus much it was fitting this slave should represent;—what further trouble shall he presume to give?

"May the sun of felicity and wealth be ever luminous.†"

---

* The fawn-eyed nymph was the chief nurse.
† The above is a literal translation.

While we were at Lucknow, a quantity of Worcestershire china[183] arrived, that had been sent to the *Nawaab* from England. He was as impatient to open it, as a child would be with a new plaything; and immediately gave orders for invitations to be sent to the whole settlement for a breakfast, *a la fourchette*,[184] next morning. Tables were accordingly spread for upwards of a hundred persons, including his ministers and officers of state. Nothing could be more splendid than the general appearance of this entertainment; but our dismay may be more easily imagined than described, on discovering that his servants had mistaken certain utensils for milk bowls, and had actually placed about twenty of them, filled with that beverage, along the centre of the table. The consequence was, the English part of the company declined taking any; upon which the *Nawaab* innocently remarked, "I thought that the English were fond of milk." Some of them had much difficulty to keep their countenances.

I cannot say that I regretted leaving this noisy city; for being just at the new moon, the natives had began, as is their custom, when not restrained by martial law, to blow horns about the streets, fire muskets, pistols, let off fire-works, &c. which was formerly the practice of the Jews on any festival or subject of rejoicing. In this country, the moment they perceive the new moon, all prostrate themselves on the earth, and offer up a prayer of thanksgiving; after which the uproar commences. In a military cantonment they are somewhat checked by watch setting, and patroles to keep the peace; here they are encouraged in it, and make a tremendous noise, both when the moon is new, and also when at the full. On either of these occurrences, the Mahometan as well as Hindoo religion enjoins their followers to bathe; and I have known some religious persons plunge breast high in the Ganges at twelve o'clock at at night, even in the coldest weather. After remaining a few moments in prayer, just at the instant the moon is supposed to be at the full, they make an offering of rice and flowers, which are gently placed upon the water, and float down the stream. It is a pretty sight to see these wreaths floating down at the rate of six miles an hour, with a number of small lamps attached to them.

It is not from seeing *much*, but in reflecting on what we *do* see, that we gather instruction and amusement for our declining years.

CHAPTER IX.

FROM Lucknow, instead of returning to *Khanpore*, we proceeded across the country to *Futty-ghur*,[185] where our camp equipage was ordered to meet us. It is the residence of the Commissioners for the ceded, conquered, and centre provinces, and is termed a *Sudder* Station,[186] from containing a complete establishment of the Honourable the East India Company's civil servants, with only one regiment of Seapoys, a company of artillery, and the Commissioners' body-guard. It stands on the bank of the Ganges, about three miles from the large city of *Furrukabad*,[187] which is inhabited only by natives, and is a great mart for trade. *Furrukabad* is one of the best places in India to purchase Cashmere shawls, and a fine description of cloth for neckcloths, called chandelly, which is brought from the Mahratta country,[188] and is like Scotch cambric,[189] only infinitely finer and more soft. The natives here, work well in gold or silver, and are ingenious mechanics. The principal part of the inhabitants at *Furrukabad* are Mussulmen. The Nawaab, bearing the title of the city, resides within it.[190]

Having devoted a few days to our friends at *Futty-ghur*, and despatched our tent equipage, on the evening of the 26th of June we were preparing to follow them in palankeens, when the clouds gathering portended an approaching storm, and we were much importuned to defer our intended journey until the morrow. I cannot say but that I felt well disposed to acquiesce; but my companion, who was the farthest in the world from being either self-willed or obstinate, appeared so bent upon starting that evening, that I could no longer oppose it; and the event proved him to be right.

Alas! the family we quitted,[191] little thought that, ere the morning dawned, they should not have a roof to shelter them. Weak-sighted mortals as we are, we know not what an hour may bring forth! We saw the conflagration; and had I not yielded mine to better judgment, should all have perished in it. Scarcely were we out of the cantonment, before our friend's house was struck by lightning; and so rapid were the flames, that in a few hours it was level with the ground. The table, round which we had all been sitting, was the first thing shivered to pieces. Fortunately the family, who had attended us to our palankeens, did not return to that apartment; and, happily, no lives were lost.

About this time is generally the commencement of the rainy season, when storms of this description are prevalent, often violent, but of short duration. The country between *Futty-ghur* and *Agra*[192] is tolerably well cultivated, abounds in groves of fine mango and tamarind trees, and is plentifully supplied with well-water. From *Futty-ghur* to *Mynpoorie*[193] we went in one night, and there found our tents. It is a beautiful spot, surrounded by groves of various description, some of them impervious to the sun's rays; and the country, far as the eye could reach, teeming with cultivation. The next morning's trip we made on an elephant; a heavy storm of rain that had fallen during the night so inundated the country, (which here lies flat for many miles,) that the only means of discovering the road was by observing where the water lay the deepest, so that we seemed to be passing along a canal. Our way for many miles of the journey lay across an extensive plain, which now presented one vast sheet of water, without even shrub or tree to relieve the eye. It occurred to my mind, that the spectacle Noah must have witnessed when he took refuge in the ark,[194] was not much unlike it. Thus we travelled slowly on, the next fourteen miles, to *Shekoabad*,[195] where our people had found a high dry spot to pitch the tents; and we were very comfortable, for the rain, as is frequently the case at this season, had been partial; not half so much had fallen *here*, as *we* had had. After these storms, the sun seems to acquire additional power: so great was the heat to-day, that one of our camels died upon the road.

Before *Agra* came into possession of the English, *Shekoabad* was a frontier station, occupied only by a regiment of Seapoys, and two or three troops of native cavalry. These troops being suddenly called away on duty, the station was attacked and plundered by a party of Mahratta horse, or probably *Pindarees*,[196] who put all the males (a few invalid soldiers) to death, and captured all the females. Amongst the latter was the wife of an officer, and her two children: one of these, being an infant, they inhumanly massacred; the other was about six years of age, and having gold ear-rings on, the barbarians literally tore them from her ears, and placing her behind one of them, while the distracted mother was guarded by another, they were conveyed to a fort in the Mahratta country, and there confined until an exorbitant ransom could be raised to liberate them.

These *Pindarees* are a race of wandering marauders, who, from a small banditti, have increased within the last few years to a considerable military force. Incapable of entering into bands of amity with any settled state, they supported themselves by plunder, and were in the habit of exercising the most atrocious cruelties, sparing neither sex nor age, and destroying what they were unable to carry away. Thus they came suddenly upon the peaceful cultivators of the soil, while their numbers and warlike accoutrements rendered them altogether irresistible. Having by this means acquired large territorial possessions, always on the alert, they were prepared to assist any native power who might think proper to employ them. Indeed it is a well-known fact, that the armies of *Scindia* and *Holkar* were of this description. Emboldened by success, they at length openly attacked the villages which the English had taken under their protection. Our late successful operations, under the command of the Marquis of Hastings, have overthrown, if not totally annihilated, this formidable enemy;[197] and since the war of 1818,[198] the river Indus[199] has become our frontier, while security and comfort have succeeded to the terror and misery formerly the lot of the inhabitants of these regions. Multitudes have already emerged from the hills, into which necessity had driven them, and now re-occupy their native villages. The ploughshare is again employed to turn a soil which for many seasons has lain undisturbed, save by the hoofs of predatory cavalry. Such exertions on the part of the British Government in India have immortalized us as a nation; I wish I could add, without any individual sufferings; but, alas! although successful as to the main object, we have to lament the loss of many a brave soldier, not so much from the actual chances of war, as from harassing and fatiguing marches in an unhealthy country. I am assured by an eye witness of the dreadful scene, that in one day's march of fourteen miles, out of eighteen thousand souls, which the camp was estimated to contain, between seven and eight thousand were left dead upon the road. The same correspondent adds, "The number of native servants and camp followers who lost their lives upon this occasion is incalculable. None of us," he continues, "had above one or two servants out of twenty, who were able to exert themselves; and so suddenly were they attacked, that no man could flatter himself he might not be a corpse before the next hour."[200] Several young men in the troop he commanded, singing and joking as they rode along, apparently in excellent health, would request permission to fall out of the ranks; they were so ill that they could not sit upon their horses; when, throwing themselves upon the ground, they were dead before the column had all passed. We have however the consolation of reflecting, that the war was not provoked by motives of ambition, or a desire of accumulating wealth, but entered into actually in self-defence.

Although in viewing the vast extent of territory over which our conquests have been spread, and considering that in less than a century (from a small factory on the coast) we have become sovereigns of a mighty empire; that the population of India is not less than 100,000,000, and spread over a continent of more than 1,000,000 square miles; that the dominion of this kingdom extends over more than one third of this extent, and over nearly two-fifths of that population; it may perhaps be said that we have increased our possessions by gradual encroachments to what they now are. I can only state, from unquestionable authority, that the war of 1818 was not of this description.

The *Pindarees*, at the commencement of it, consisted of from 30,000 to 40,000 regular and irregular horse, receiving continual re-inforcements, and, from want of organization, incapable of being attacked by disciplined troops. They were a collection from the remnant of former wars; the refuse of disbanded armies; the rallying standard of all discontented, untractable spirits, of the restless and ambitious; rapid and decisive in their movements, they were generally successful in escaping pursuit, and only to be defeated when surprised. They provoked the war by a series of outrages, such as no government could hear of and not resent. In 1812 they made an irruption into *Bengal*, plundering villages, and carrying away the peaceful inhabitants into slavery; in 1813, into *Bombay;* in 1816, accompanied by circumstances of unparalleled atrocity, into *Madras*,[201] at which period instances occurred where a whole female population precipitated themselves into wells to escape falling into their hands, while fathers and husbands buried themselves in the flaming ruins of their miserable dwellings. *Scindia, Holkar*,[202] and *Ameer Khan*,[203] took this opportunity of entering the lists against us; but for a considerable time we had no reason to expect hostility from the *Peishwa*,[204] a power so important, that all others sunk as nothing in the comparison. An attack of

Holkar on our troops was the signal for general action, the result of which proved the complete defeat of our enemies. *Holkar* was soon obliged to surrender all the territory he possessed south of *Santa-poora;* and the campaign was carrying on most successfully, when the *Peishwa,* long a treacherous friend, now became an open enemy, and stood the acknowledged head of the *Mahratta* powers. From that moment our arms were of necessity directed against him—he was driven from his capital, and finally reduced from the "exile of a wanderer, to the bondage of a captive." He is now in confinement at *Benares*. The Rajah of *Nagpore*,[205] with whom we had signed a treaty of peace in 1813,[206] also turned traitor, although indebted to us for his throne. *He* was repelled with similar courage and success.

Our army at this time consisted of 90,000 men—of these 10,000 only were English; and although the native troops found many of their relatives, and much of their property in the neighbouring territory of the *Peishwa*, such was their fidelity to their employers, that, defying his threats, they carried frequent proofs to their European officers of his attempts to corrupt their loyalty.

In the whole twenty-eight actions that were fought, the superior management of the British arms was conspicuous; and between the months of November and June, twenty forts (some of them deemed impregnable) were taken and dismantled. The frontier that then remained to be defended by the British force, extended nearly two thousand five hundred miles. One of these reputed impregnable forts was *Huttrass*, near *Agra*, in possession of a *Jaut* chief named *Diah Ram*,[207] a Hindoo prince of ancient family.

The *Jauts* are, properly speaking, cultivators of the soil, but have long been famed for their warlike achievements. Their origin has been variously represented: some believe them to have been *Rajpoots*,[208] a race of people whose only occupation was war; and from turning agriculturists, that they lost the name of *Rajpoot*, and were afterwards known by the name of *Jauts*. However this may be, it cannot be denied that they are the most skilful husbandmen in Hindostan, invariably quit the plough at the call of danger, and prove, if they ever did belong to the sect of *Rajpoots*, that they are not degenerated. The character of the *Rajpoots* for heroism in former times, when the distinction of *caste* was much more religiously observed than it is at present, is well known.

Diah Ram was related to the Rajah of *Burtpore*,[209] and was secretly in alliance with other states who were hostile to the British Government. He gained his territory by conquest, but was afterwards deprived of it by the *Mahrattas*, and reinstated by the British Government.

Previous to our going to war with the *Mahrattas*, this Rajah entered into a treaty offensive and defensive with *us*, which he afterwards broke by assisting *Holkar*, a Mahratta chief. On the subjection of the latter, a fresh treaty was made with him, wherein it was stipulated that he should pay ninety thousand rupees into our treasury, adopt our system of police, disband his troops, and cease to coin money. This treaty was no sooner signed than broken. He continued the coinage, was irregular in the payment of his tribute, strengthened his fort, which became the receptacle of all the disaffected, and, to crown his perfidy, when four of our police officers had been murdered in his district, he gave shelter to the perpetrators, and refused to give them up to justice.

At the time our troops attacked his fort at *Huttrass*, it was defended by five hundred pieces of artillery, with an outer fort, in which were twenty immense bastions, surrounded by a ditch ninety feet broad, seventy-five feet deep, and containing six feet of water.

The town is a rectangular work, about seven hundred and fifty yards from the fort. In form, it is nearly square, five hundred by four hundred and eighty yards, with nine circular bastions, and a pretty deep ditch.

The attack was made upon the fort at half-past eleven o'clock at night, March 2, 1817. On the preceding evening all our batteries were advanced within a hundred yards of the glacis, and by sun-rise next morning we had forty-three pieces of heavy cannon ready to bear upon it. The general[210] who commanded, gave the Rajah until nine o'clock, to decide whether he would stand a siege or surrender. He chose the former. Accordingly, at the hour appointed, all our batteries opened, and kept up an incessant firing until five o'clock the next evening; at which time one of the shells fell upon his principal magazine, containing six thousand maunds* of gunpowder, and caused a terrible explosion. It was the most awful and beautiful scene that could be imagined. The earth trembled as if shaken by an earthquake. This was immediately followed by a stunning crash, which even deadened the sound of our batteries. The fort was instantly enveloped in a thick black cloud, which gradually rose in the form of a regular and beautiful tree, growing rapidly yet majestically out of the ground, at the same time preserving its exact proportions.

The panic caused by this occurrence it is impossible to describe, each party supposing that the other had sprung a mine—all was, for a moment, silent horror and breathless expectation! The firing, which had been kept up without intermission for eight hours, ceased as if by magic. Every one seemed transfixed to the spot, too much astonished to speak; for, lo! they were in total darkness! which continued for more than eleven minutes. This so sudden change, from a fine clear sky, with the sun shining forth in all his splendour, to impenetrable darkness, was sufficient to strike the firmest mind with dread. The darkness subsided by degrees, and our people soon discovered what had been the cause; upon which our batteries again opened with redoubled vigour, the *Rajah's* answering them feebly, and only now and then, from which it appeared evident that there was much confusion within the fort. We kept it up, however, until eleven o'clock, when the *Rajah*, being fairly burnt out, contrived with two hundred of his best horsemen to effect his escape. They were all, as we afterwards learned, himself not excepted, clad in chain armour. The destruction occasioned by the explosion of the magazine in the fort was dreadful; scarcely a man or animal within but was wounded by it, and the greater part of the buildings were laid in ruins. The *Rajah* and his party made

---

* A maund is eighty pounds weight.

a dart through a picquet of the 8th Dragoons, and a regiment of *Rohillah*[211] horsemen, whose swords made no impression. During the night there had been just sufficient moonlight to distinguish the fort, over which our shells were seen to mount in air, then rolling over each other like so many balls of fire, eight or nine at a time, they sank majestically down. It was afterwards understood that *Diah Ram* had taken refuge with the *Burtpore Rajah,* another *Jaut* chief, to whom he was nearly related. The unfortunate failure of our troops in their several attacks on this *Rajah* of *Burtpore*[212] doubtless inspired others with courage to oppose us, and perhaps in some measure caused that obstinate resistance which we every where met with.

The *Rajah* of *Burtpore,* although very old, was a most formidable enemy. He is since dead. The *Jauts* have repeatedly revolted against the Mogul government,[213] the seat of which is *Delhi;* and although the whole force of the empire has at times been turned against them, they have so bravely defended their strong holds, that they have always been allowed to capitulate on the most favourable terms.

Within the last century, taking advantage of the anarchy which at length overthrew the throne of *Delhi** they issued forth in great force, subdued the province of *Agra,* where they demolished all the magnificent structures which the Mussulmen, with great taste, and at an enormous expense, had erected, and carried away plunder to an immense amount.[214] The ceilings of the royal residence were at that time covered with sheets of pure gold, or of the finest silver curiously embossed. These all became the spoil of the conquering *Jauts.* The *Tadge*[215] alone (that wonderful and most elegant production of art) escaped destruction; but the chandelier which was suspended from the principal dome, by ingots of silver, was soon deprived of its elevated situation. Many of the precious stones that were inlaid in the marble fret-work were rudely torn out, and much of the alabaster screen was mutilated. But their fury chiefly turned against the tomb of the Emperor Acbar, which is situated at a place called *Secundra,* about five miles from *Agra.*[216] It stands within a square enclosed by four brick walls, extending half a mile on either side: these walls are thirty feet high and eight feet thick. Within this enclosure was formerly a garden, planted in avenues of trees, principally orange, lemon, and citron trees, which flourish well in this district. In the centre of this garden stands the tomb, on a platform of stone, to which you ascend by many steps. A colonnade of arches, five and twenty feet high, and thirty deep, enclose the building. The interior, which contains the cenotaph, is entirely of white marble, beautifully inlaid, and was formerly richly ornamented. Many inscriptions of the *Koraan*[217] still remain, although many more have been defaced. The four gateways, East, West, North, and South, composed of red granite, and white marble, with sentences of

---

* Leaving only the shadow of royalty in the person of an old blind king, named *Shaw Allum,*[218] whose eyes were put out by one of his subjects,[219] who was the head of a faction. He was reinstated on the throne by General Lord Lake, about the end of the year 1803, and died at an advanced age, being succeeded by his son the present Emperor. These Sovereigns, from having ruled the whole of the Mogul Empire with despotic sway, are now reduced to the government of a single province.

the *Koraan* engraven on them, are very magnificent; and the minarets, which are immensely high, are faced with white marble. But it is impossible to do justice to these superb buildings by description—it is necessary to see them, in order to form a just estimate of their peculiar beauty and magnificence.

From *Agra* and its vicinity, flushed with conquest, the emboldened *Jauts* pushed on through the adjoining district of *Ally Ghur*,[220] in which are the three strong forts now belonging to *Bhagwaut Singh, Diah Ram*, &c.[221] In that of *Ally Ghur*, near the city of *Coel*, they placed a formidable garrison:[222] it afterwards stood a siege, and fell before British valour. This fort was taken, after an obstinate resistance, by the army commanded by General Lord Lake in person, August 1804.[223] Notorious for their rapacity and tyrannical dispositions, it is not to be wondered at, that wherever they go, the *Jauts* are both dreaded and detested, or that the former defenceless inhabitants should feel the utmost joy whenever released from their state of bondage, to feel the influence of British lenity and justice.

The *Jauts* are brave soldiers and good cultivators; but in order to make good subjects, they must be divested of all power.

I have been led by this subject to an unconscionable distance, and will therefore return with all speed to *Shekoabad*, from whence the digression took place.

CHAPTER X.

Ferozabad,[224] the next place we came to, is a large town, under the direction of a *Teseeldar*,[225] or native collector of revenue, and an establishment of Police. We found the former quite a polished gentleman, who having spent great part of his life in *Calcutta* among Europeans, had adopted, as nearly as was consistent with the Mahometan religion, their manners and mode of living. He not only waited upon us, as is customary, upon our arrival, but sent fruit, vegetables, and two excellent dishes of curry. What makes this dish so much better here than in England, is a soft and slightly acidulated curd they put into it, called *dhye*,[226] which gives it a beautiful bright colour and piquant flavour. A few slices of unripe mango is also a great improvement.

From *Ferozabad*, in consequence of no rain having fallen there, the immense plain we had to cross bore the appearance of a complete sandy desert, on which we were in some danger of being smothered; for a high wind blew the sand directly in our faces. Nothing could be more uncomfortable; even the horses betrayed symptoms of unwillingness to brave it. The heat on this day's march was so excessive, that the gig horse, who drew us the last ten miles, was no sooner unharnessed than he dropped down and expired.

At *Ettamaadpore*,[227] to which place we proceeded the next day, we met the collector of the district,[228] who happened to be there in tents, and spent the day with him.

From this place to *Agra*, (ten miles only,) it being considered unsafe to travel without a guard, we were escorted by four of the collector's armed horsemen; but when we arrived on the bank of the *Jumna*,[229] and were preparing to cross the ferry to *Agra*, we met some friends coming to pass the day at a garden house near at hand, and they prevailed on us to join the party. It was built by a man named *Ettamaad Dowlut*, meaning Ettamaad the Rich,*,[230] and is now under the care of the judge of the district. His burial place, or tomb, denominated also a mausoleum, with that of his wife, stands in the centre of the garden. The walls and pavement, of white marble, are elegantly inlaid with cornelian of different colours, porphyry, granite, &c. It is a square building, terminating in a dome, curiously and beautifully painted with flowers, and Mosaic. It stands on an elevated platform of white marble, having at each corner a lofty minaret of the same materials. The whole is surrounded by a marble railing. Under the dome, and immediately over the bodies, are two blocks of highly polished yellow marble, beautifully carved; and round both is an elegant net-work of white marble, inlaid with stones of different

---

* For the history of this native, which is somewhat singular, see "Dow's History of Hindostan."

colours. This man could boast of no pedigree, and not having any immediate successor, his estates became the property of the existing government, and *ours*, eventually, by right of conquest. In this country the Great Mogul, or, as he is now termed, Emperor of *Delhi*,[231] is the nominal proprietor of *all* the landed property, and takes upon himself to dispose of it to whom he pleases. Those who hold lands under his government are obliged, at their decease, to bequeath the property to him, when he distributes to the family of the deceased what portion of it he thinks proper. Every thing appears to be carried on in the same despotic way, from the Emperor down to the meanest of his subjects, where they have any power at all.

The premises of *Ettamaad Dowlut* extend considerably beyond the river *Jumna;* the house itself is built on its bank, and is the resort of many fishing parties from *Agra* and *Secundra*. The fort of *Agra*[232] stands on the bank nearly opposite to it.

The road from our last halting place was dreary beyond measure: it lay through a deep ravine, or pass, only of sufficient breadth for one carriage to travel, and so extended for at least six miles. Unfortunately for us, a waggon had broken down in one part, and completely filled the space; we were consequently obliged to leave the carriage, and scramble up the almost perpendicular side of this ravine, or wait for hours in the sun until the waggon was in a state to move on again. Luckily we had only a mile to walk, for the heat was excessive.

Early on the following morning we crossed the *Jumna*, and proceeded to *Secundra* to breakfast. Here we found a regiment of dragoons, tolerably settled in bungalows that they had raised since their arrival there a few months before.

The most tremendous storm I ever witnessed occurred on the following day. About ten o'clock in the morning the sky began to lower; black rolling clouds seemed gathering over our heads, with now and then a violent gust of wind. The atmosphere meantime became tinged as by a distant fire, which in an instant was succeeded by total darkness, accompanied by dreadful peals of thunder. On the spot we happened to be, *there* were we obliged to remain: for at least twenty minutes I could not distinguish my own hand. It was really awful! The natives fled from their houses, and prostrated themselves on the ground, in momentary expectation of an earthquake. A gentleman walking in his garden, was obliged to remain there: he could not see the way to his house. From the commencement of this wonderful phenomenon, until the sun shone forth again, was full three hours. I never witnessed such a scene before, and sincerely hope I never may again.

Secundra was at this time much infested by parties of predatory horsemen,[233] who were so expert at their trade, that notwithstanding *chokidars* (armed watchmen) were kept on guard at every house and stable, they contrived to steal and carry off many valuable horses. They were even bold enough, at one time, to attack individuals by throwing spears at their palankeens; so that when any lady or gentleman went from home, the former was attended by matchlock men,* and the latter never failed to carry pistols with him.

---

* Men who carry a very long gun that is fired by means of a match, which they carry ready lighted.

A catastrophe still more serious than these incursions of the predatory horse had nearly taken place, owing to the rashness of a young officer in the regiment; and but for the very great presence of mind of the Judge, who dined that day in the cantonment, every European would have been put to death. It was the season of the *Moharum*,[234] when galloping along by one of their ornamented biers, he overthrew some of the lamps. The alarm was instantly given; people flocked in numbers to the spot, raised a hue and cry, and some attempted to stop him, but he eluded them and took refuge in the guard-room. They then proceeded in a body to the commanding officer's house, and demanded that he should be given up, threatening, in case of refusal, to get reinforcements from *Agra*, and destroy every European they could find. A servant of the Judge's, upon hearing this, and knowing what a desperate set of people they were, went with all speed to inform his master, who was dining at the regimental mess-room. The Judge immediately mounted his horse, and galloped into *Agra;* which having entered, he ordered the city gates to be shut, and not to be opened again without his permission upon pain of death. The commanding officer of *Secundra*[235] meantime made a pretence of searching for this young man, (whose friends had assisted him to quit the place in disguise,) until informed that he was safely out of their power. He could not, however, venture to rejoin his corps again, and very soon after left the country.

The scenery round *Agra* and *Secundra* is somewhat dreary, from the numberless ruins which meet the eye on every side: but there are many things worth seeing in the neighbourhood, particularly the *Tadge Mahl* at *Agra*, the fort and palace,[236] and the mausoleum of *Christie*[237] at *Futtypoor Siecra;*[238] also a monastery[239] founded for those of the Roman Catholic persuasion of any country or nation, by *Sumroo*,[240] the German general, whom I before made mention of as having caused the massacre of Europeans at Patna. In this monastery he was buried.[241] The Begum Sumroo,[242] his widow, keeps up the establishment, and has also added a nunnery.

The *Tadge Mahl*[243] at *Agra* requires a much abler pen than mine to describe it; and it is not in the power of any pen, in my opinion, to do it justice. It was built by the Emperor *Shaw Jehaan*,[244] in the year 1719,[245] (at which period he began his reign,) over the burial place of *Montaza Mhul*,[246] his favourite wife. To her, when on her death-bed, he promised that he would erect a monument which should surpass in beauty any thing of the kind in the known world, and be as superior as *she was* to the rest of her sex. He accordingly issued his royal mandate to his ministers to collect, at any expense, artificers from all quarters of the globe, as he was determined nothing should be spared to render this work perfect. In as short a time as could be expected, artificers arrived from England, France, Italy, Greece,[247] and all the oriental courts, and the building was immediately commenced upon. The plan was the Emperor's own; but it is said that the ornamental part was sketched by a Frenchman, and executed under his auspices by artists from Rome, particularly the pattern and inlaid work of precious stones on the skreen and *sarcophagus*.

This building stands in the centre of a large garden, on the banks of the river *Jumna*, with large minarets containing three octagon apartments, one above another, at the four corners, each being surrounded by a colonnade. They are composed of porphyry, granite, and white marble.

The interior of the *Tadge* is divided into several suits of apartments, being in form of a square, with the cenotaph in the centre, under the first story; of which there are three at each corner, surmounted by marble domes, making in the whole one large, and four small domes, with a small high minaret at each corner also of the square marble platform on which it stands, and to which you ascend by a flight of steps from the garden. The platform, or terrace, is enclosed by marble railing. I was shown some lines written on this elegant structure, which I will here transcribe, with the reply.

"*Inscribed to the* EMPEROR *who caused it to be erected.*

"Oh thou! whose great imperial mind could raise
   This splendid trophy to a woman's praise;
   If love, or grief, inspired the great design,
   No mortal joy or sorrow equalled thine.
   Sleep on secure; this monument shall stand
   (While desolation's wing sweeps o'er the land,
   By time and death in one wide ruin hurled)
   The last triumphant wonder of the world!"

"*On reading the above.*

"No eastern prince, for wealth or splendour famed,
No *mortal* hand, this beauteous temple framed.
In death's cold arms, as loved *Montaza* slept,
While sighs o'er *Jumna's* winding waters crept,
Tears such as angels shed, with fragrance filled,
Around her form in pearly drops distilled,
Of snowy whiteness—thus congealed they stand
A fairy fabric, boast of India's land."

The *Tadge Mahl* is justly reputed the most elegant and chaste structure that can be imagined. Its walls are faced and lined with the whitest marble; the tomb, and whole of the interior, including the skreen, being curiously inlaid with precious stones, not only in the *form* of flowers, but even in their different shades and colours. In one small carnation I counted forty-two different stones. These stones are principally agate, cornelian of infinite variety, lapis lazuli, onyx, garnet, turquoise, and the like.

The grand gateway at the entrance of the garden is proportionably magnificent, (there are three others, with six apartments over each,) being of sufficient depth to contain the Emperor's body-guard drawn up in state for him to pass through, and lofty in proportion.

The palace and royal baths within the fort are something of the same style, but the materials are much inferior to those in the Tadge. The ceilings of the apartments in the palace were originally cased with solid silver or gold, and are alone reputed to have cost eleven lacs of rupees.* In each state apartment was a chandelier, suspended by silver or gold chains to match the ceiling. All these the *Jauts* destroyed and carried away, when they overrun the district; since which time they have been only washed with gold or silver, in imitation of their former splendour. The beautiful carved work of the apartments they likewise destroyed, a few patches only remaining by which we can judge of what it has been.

* A lac of rupees is twelve thousand pounds.

CHAPTER XI.

THE tomb of *Christie* at *Futty-poor Siccra*[248] is about a day's journey westward of *Agra*. It stands upon an elevation of one hundred feet from the ground, having just as many stone steps to ascend before you reach the grand entrance. These steps extend along the whole front of the building. The gateway is a square building of red granite, with a flat roof, and a parapet on the four sides: the front of it is covered with Persian inscriptions, and carving of curious workmanship. To this roof you ascend by three hundred and sixty-five stone steps, on either side. Through the gateway is a spacious area, arcaded on all sides, and paved with white marble. In the centre of it stands the tomb of a holy man named *Christie:* it was erected to his memory by a merchant, who having risked a considerable property on board some vessels to a distant country, promised him, if his prayers for their safe return should prove successful, that he would cause a monument of this description to be built in token of his gratitude, and that the entrance to it should exceed in height any thing of the kind in Hindostan. The same tradition states, that from the time these vessels sailed until their return, was precisely three hundred and sixty-five days, which the number of steps are intended to commemorate.

The *sarcophagus* is enclosed within a square building of white marble, surrounded by fretwork of the same, and raised by several steps from the area, which marble steps extend the whole length of the building on either side.

The tomb itself is white marble, richly inlaid with mother of pearl, fastened by small gold nails; the whole being enclosed within curtains of silver gauze. The dome, which surmounts this building, is beautifully painted on the inside with emblematical devices, and passages from the *Koraan*. This place is constantly guarded by priests, who have a college near the spot founded by the same merchant, and an annual stipend to keep both in repair.*

From hence we proceeded, about a quarter of a mile farther, to a magnificent palace built by the Emperor *Acbar*,[249] now, alas! rapidly falling to decay. The scite of it covers above an acre of ground. The apartments we were shown as having belonged to *Tamoulah*,[250] the beloved of *Acbar*, (as she was emphatically termed,) are composed of red granite and alabaster. The walls are divided into compartments, on which are landscapes in sculpture delicately executed.

A structure contiguous to the palace[251] particularly attracted our attention, as having an immense pillar in the centre, stuck from top to bottom with elephants'

---

* In one of the apartments of this mausoleum was a trapdoor, which upon touching the spring flew up, and discovered a gradual descent of some hundred feet; at the bottom of which was stable room for a thousand horses, who in cases of emergency have been concealed there.

teeth, on which we were told the trophies used to be hung that the Emperor gained in battle. This pillar supported an octagon gallery round it, for the ladies of his family, so contrived as that they should see what was going on below without being seen. On four sides of this gallery, were passages leading to the apartments occupied by these ladies. To the Emperor himself, a kind of throne, on an elevation in the body of the building, was appropriated; the whole of the interior being finished with peculiar elegance.

From hence we traversed an extensive stone terrace, to a building I can only describe as the rotunda, where, during the hot season, the Emperor was accustomed to sleep. The approach to it, like most others, was by several stone steps surrounding the whole. The apartment on the ground floor was of considerable size: it used to be occupied by his body-guard, and was surrounded by three hundred and sixty-five stone pillars. The one over it, in like manner, by fifty-two, and the upper room by twelve; to which the ascent led by a handsome stone staircase, in good preservation. From this apartment we could distinguish the fort of *Bhurtpore*,[252] before which our army were five times repulsed, and it still remains in the possession of its Rajah. The avenue towards *Delhi*, through which the Emperor *Acbar* used to pass in his approach to this palace, contains seven high arched gateways, at that time guarded by a proportionate number of armed men. The perspective through these is the most correct and beautiful I have ever seen. *Agra* and its vicinity, in the direction of this place, is celebrated for oranges: we ate them here in great perfection, although the barbarous *Jauts* had left little vestige of a garden.

These provinces having been newly conquered by the British army,[253] had as yet paid no revenue to Government, who accordingly appointed two commissioners to survey them, and form an estimate of what they were capable of furnishing. I consider myself particularly fortunate in being of their party, since it afforded me a more perfect view of the manners and customs of the natives, and a better opportunity of seeing the country than was likely to occur again; indeed we visited some parts of it where Europeans had never been before.

On the 1st day of December, 1808, attended by a regiment of Seapoys and a numerous retinue, we travelled in the suite of the commissioners towards *Delhi*, the capital of the Mogul Empire. Our line of march, including cattle, baggage-waggons, and followers, extended more than a mile.

On quitting *Secundra* we crossed the river *Jumna*, opposite to an ancient hunting seat of the Emperor *Acbar*, at a village named *Madower*. In the rainy season the *Jumna* is here both wide and rapid, although during the hot winds it is nearly dry: its waters in the hot season are supposed to possess properties like those of the Nile,[254] that is, in producing cutaneous disorders, which, although extremely troublesome, do not affect the general health. The irritation caused by these watery pustules is sometimes excessive, only to be relieved by cooling medicine and a spare diet; yet I am inclined to believe, that by boiling the water before it is made use of, the ill effects of it might be in a great measure if not wholly prevented: precipitating small pieces of charcoal will also much assist the purification of it.

From *Madower* we drove through a cultivated country supplied with water by numerous wells, and thickly planted with trees. Among these the *baubool** tree[255] rose conspicuous. On either side the road were fields of the cotton plant,[256] which at a distance appeared like low shrubs bearing innumerable large white blossoms: the cotton was, at this season, just starting from the pod. From hence we made *Huttrass* in two marches. *Huttrass* is two-and-thirty miles from *Secundra*. After passing through two or three small villages we came to a level country richly cultivated, and saw the fort of *Sarseney*. This fort was resolutely defended by its Rajah, *Bhagwaut Sing*, in the year 1802, but laid siege to and taken by the troops under command of General, afterwards Lord Lake, by whom it was dismantled, and is now in a ruinous state. The town of *Sarseney* appears to have recovered itself from the ravages of war; but the natives of these provinces are so prone to pillage, that merchants are afraid to expose their goods for sale. We were told of a waggon-load of merchandise, consisting chiefly of bale goods, that was plundered near this place only a few days before; and four matchlock men, who travelled with it for protection, were murdered on the spot.

Near *Sarseney* we saw the remains of some beautiful gardens, containing several light pavilions of white marble. They consisted of one large apartment, surmounted by a cupola, and surrounded by a verandah. These pavilions were raised six or seven feet from the ground. The approach to them was by wide paved terraces, crossing each other at right angles, shaded by lofty trees, under which were fountains and beds of flowers. The town is completely commanded by the fort, which stands upon an eminence, and is now occupied by a native collector of revenue, called a *teseeldar*.

The city of *Coel*, which we entered towards evening, is a large populous place, surrounded by a high brick wall, and secured at each entrance by ponderous gates, with a number of armed men.

The general face of the country, from *Sarseney* to *Coel*, is one extensive plain, with here and there a few small bushes, or a cluster of miserable huts. It is not here, as in England, that the eye is regaled at intervals by the smiling appearance of a neat thatched cottage, through the luxuriant foliage of a spreading oak. Small forts built of mud supply their place; and these are to be seen in all directions. Just before we reached *Coel*, I observed a number of *toddy* trees, the sap of which is made use of instead of yeast to lighten bread; and, when fresh, is eagerly drank by the Hindoo natives, who are many of them fond of intoxicating liquors, an effect which this syrup speedily produces. There is another sort, called *bang*,[257] extracted from a herb of that name which is cultivated in most of their gardens. The cultivated parts of this district are almost overrun with a plant they call *palma christi*,[258] from which an oil with medicinal properties is extracted, known in England I believe by the title of castor oil.

---

* From the *baubool* wood is made the best kind of charcoal, (a fuel much used in Indian kitchens instead of coals,) and also the best and strongest tent pegs.

From hence we proceeded the following morning, on elephants, through an avenue of lime trees a mile in length, to the fort of *Alli Ghur*,[259] which was taken by assault in 1804 by General Lake. It is situated on an extensive plain, has been put into thorough repair by the British Government, and was, at the time I am speaking of, garrisoned by British troops.

About ten miles from *Coel*, on an artificial eminence, stands the picturesque village of *Purwah*. The soil in general appears sandy, and except near villages, completely uncultivated. The next place we passed was *Chourpoor*, or, in plain English, Thieves' Village; we were however fortunate enough to go unmolested, and shortly after came to a fortified place called *Meah-poor. Kourjah*, where we arrived to breakfast, is a large well-built town, of red brick dwellings, embosomed in trees; the soil richer than any we had seen before. It was a beautiful sight to observe in one field the young barley springing up, and in the next, either grain in sheaves, or ripe for cutting. Thus they contrive to have the harvest come in succession, so that neither time nor ground shall be lost.

The fort of *Kourjah* is completely dismantled, and the appearance of the inhabitants we saw extremely wretched. I rode through the principal street on an elephant, accompanied by one of the commissioners; and we were followed by hundreds of children, sent by their parents to beg, *coda ka wasti*, "for the love of God," a few pice* to buy otta.† The remains of some fine orchards are observable, but the ravages of war still more so. On leaving *Kourjah* we crossed a down, bounded only by the horizon, leaving on the left hand a large village well wooded, and at a short distance from it two mud forts. The level country continued; but soon we found ourselves encompassed by a grass jungle five-and-twenty feet high; the stems of it were like small reeds, that rebounded as we passed by with considerable force. The immense height of this grass (although the chief of our party were mounted on elephants) prevented our distinguishing any thing beyond the road we travelled. This led us into another thick jungle of brushwood, which continued many miles. Wells, containing in general excellent water, are found by the road-side, for the accommodation of travellers, every five or six miles throughout these provinces, in place of running streams, which are very rare. The natives have frequently two or more wells in a field, from which, by means of a bamboo lever, they draw water very expeditiously; and swinging round the buckets attached to each pole, throw it over the land with great facility. We felt the cold at this place (Secundrabad) very severe. Our tents were pitched on a plain of fine soft grass, beautifully embellished by trees forming with their united foliage an extensive shade. In the evening I rode on horseback with some of the gentlemen, while others took their guns, and were well repaid for their walk by meeting with excellent sport. They brought home several brace of partridge,

---

* Pice is the smallest copper coin, answering to the French liard, but of even smaller value.
† Otta-meal of the coarsest kind.

some pheasants, a peacock, and two or three hares. In the course of the night our people saw two leopards.

Our journey the following morning lay through a thick jungle of briars; the road was tolerably beaten, but intolerably dusty. The air continued extremely bleak. At the entrance of a wood we came to a good looking village, which, the guide told us, was inhabited by banditti; this was not very agreeable intelligence, considering that our encampment could not be many miles distant. On arriving at the tents, we found the head man of this village waiting to present the commissioners with Persian and other fruits; amongst which was a quantity of grapes, so large and highly flavoured, that I wished it were in my power to transport some of them to my friends in England. The pears and apples were equally fine, and the oranges much sweeter than in England, but they wanted that grateful flavour; which may, I think, be attributed to their being left on the tree *here* until they are ripe enough to fall off, whereas those imported into England from Lisbon[260] are gathered when only *half ripe*, and always retain some little acidity.

Our next march was to a place called *Sooragepore*, fifteen miles farther. The weather continuing very cold, I mounted my horse, and, accompanied by some of the gentlemen, rode about ten miles, when we unexpectedly encountered a deep stream, which we were obliged to cross in boats. Whether my horse was alarmed, or from what cause I know not, but he would not allow me to mount him again; so, after many fruitless attempts, I gave it up, and his groom led him the rest of the way. The practice in this country of a groom running with each horse is frequently found a convenience, and it certainly proved so, in this instance, to me. There was fortunately an elephant, with a *howdah** on its back, at no great distance behind, who proved more tractable, and on him I prosecuted my journey. A few miles farther brought us to a *serai*, or receptacle for travellers, of which I have before spoken. Near this *serai* stands the tomb of some Mussulman of rank: it is composed of three large domes, cased with marble; and at each corner of the platform are four minarets of the same material. We encamped on this day near the field of battle on the memorable 11th of September, 1803, when the British forces under Lord Lake conquered the Mahratta army,[261] (full treble their number,) and made them fly in all directions. The presence of mind and bravery of this distinguished general was never more conspicuous than on this occasion: the conquest of *Delhi*, and possession of the royal family, were the immediate consequences. This place is about five miles from *Delhi*, and is called *Putpore Gunge*. It is divided from *Delhi* by the river *Jumna*, which having crossed in boats that awaited our arrival, we met a

---

* A *howdah* is like the body of a gig, fixed on the back of the elephant by ropes and an iron chain: under it is a thick pad, to prevent its chafing his back. This pad is entirely covered with housings of broad cloth, generally scarlet, with a deep fringe all round, reaching half way down his legs. On one side, under the housing, is hung the ladder, by which you ascend and descend; for which purpose the elephant sinks on all fours. His rising again is rather alarming, as he does so by a sudden jerk; the fore feet first, the hinder ones rather more leisurely. They sometimes roar most terribly when they kneel down.

messenger from the resident,[262] to conduct us to his house, and soon after, himself and suite came out to meet us. Accordingly, remounting our elephants, (who had forded the stream,) we followed our conductors, and were soon after seated at an elegant breakfast, at the resident's palace, where a numerous party were expecting our arrival. Amongst these was the *Begum Sumroo*, widow to the general of that name before spoken of.* Since his death, which happened many years ago, she married Monsieur L'Oiseaux,[263] a French officer in the Mahratta service, under General Perron.[264] Being at that time in possession of a large territory that had been purchased with the riches amassed by Sumroo, and having regular organized troops in her service, she gave him the appointment of commander-in-chief. But either owing to the natural fickleness of her disposition, or that she found him difficult to manage, she soon took an inveterate dislike, and formed a project to get rid of him. Having won over the troops to her views, she caused a pretended revolt among them; when, agreeable to the arrangement she had made, they seized and carried her to a place of confinement. Her emissaries immediately conveyed the tidings of it to L'Oiseaux; (who was enjoying himself at one of his hunting seats;) and this account was quickly followed up by another, purporting that the Begum had destroyed herself by swallowing a large diamond ring that she usually wore on her finger. She foresaw the effect this intelligence would produce on the timid mind of the Frenchman, who immediately became so alarmed, that with a pistol he put an end to his existence. No sooner was the Begum informed of the event, than she quitted her prison, resumed the reins of government, and every thing again wore the face of peace. This woman has an uncommon share of natural abilities, with a strength of mind rarely met with, particularly in a female. The natives say that she was *born* a politician, has *allies* every where, and *friends* no where. Her own dominions and principal residence is at *Sirdanah*,[265] about twenty miles from *Meerat*, and a day's journey from *Delhi*. She adheres to the Mussulman mode of living, as far as respects food, but no farther. She has not the slightest fancy for the seclusion they impose; on the contrary, frequently entertaining large parties in a sumptuous manner, both at her palace in *Delhi* and at *Sirdanah*. During Lord Lake's sojourn at *Delhi*, he was her frequent guest.[266] They used frequently to sit down between twenty and thirty persons to dinner; and when the ladies of the party retired, she would remain smoking her hookah, for she made it a point never to leave her "pipe half smoked." This Princess has been frequently known to command her army in person on the field of battle; and on one occasion, during the reign of the Emperor *Shaw Allum*,[267] she is said to have saved the Mogul Empire by rallying and encouraging her troops, when those of the Emperor were flying before the enemy. In consequence of which, *Shaw Allum* immediately created her a Princess, or Begum, in her own right, to take rank next after the royal family. He also conferred on her the title of *Zaboolnissa*, which signifies "ornament of her

---

* On quitting *Meer Kossim*, at Patna, General Sumroo entered the Mahratta service, and was stationed at Agra, where he first saw the Begum, then a young and beautiful girl, whom he contrived to steal from her friends, married her, and educated her in the Romish faith.

sex." Her features are still handsome, although she is now advanced in years. She is a small woman, delicately formed, with beautiful hazel eyes; a nose somewhat inclined to the aquiline, a complexion very little darker than an Italian, with the finest turned hand and arm I ever beheld. Zophany,[268] the painter, when he saw her, pronounced it a perfect model. She is universally attentive and polite. A graceful dignity accompanies her most trivial actions; she *can be* even fascinating, when she has any point to carry. She condescendingly offered to introduce me to the royal family, which without hesitation I accepted, as my curiosity had been much excited, and, being a lady, I knew that I should be admitted into the private apartments. The following morning she gave a splendid breakfast to our party, and I afterwards accompanied her to the royal residence. We were received at the palace gates by several of the household, who escorted us across three or four courts paved with flat stone, until we came to one of white marble. Here we quitted our palankeens, and, with some of the Begum's suite, approached the hall of audience. In the centre of this apartment stood the *musnud*,[269] or throne: it was a square block of crystal, of immense value. Before this the Begum made a profound *salaam*, and motioned to me to do the same; indeed I had determined to follow her example on all points of etiquette during the visit. We then ascended a few marble steps that led into one of the passages to the zenanah, where we were informed His Majesty[270] expected us. Before this door, which was about twelve feet high, hung a curtain of scarlet broad cloth. The Begum now led the way, through crowds of eunuchs,[271] into a square enclosure paved with white marble, enclosed by colonnades of the same, under which were doors leading to the different apartments. Here we were met by the Queen Dowager, mother to the reigning Emperor,[272] an ugly, shrivelled old woman, whom the Begum embraced; which ceremony over, the attendants left us in her care. We followed this good lady across another court, similar to the one we had just quitted, except that it was covered by a carpet, at the edge of which the Begum left her shoes. I was preparing to do the same, when I heard some one say, in Persian, "It is not expected of the English lady;" or, which is a more literal translation, "The English lady is excused." On looking up I perceived the Emperor of Delhi, seated at the opposite side of this court under a colonnade, surrounded by his family, to the number, as I afterwards learned, of two hundred: all, except the Queen, were standing.

The throne on which the Emperor sat was raised about two feet from the ground: the ascent to it was by two small steps. The whole was covered with a Persian carpet, spreading a considerable distance on either side. The cushion on which he sat (cross-legged) was covered with crimson kinkob, brocaded with gold, a large tassel suspended from either corner. Three large round bolsters, covered with the same kind of silk, supported his back and arms. On a small square cushion before him stood a silver casket, about the size of a large tea-chest, which contained otta of roses and betel nut.[273] His dress was purple and gold kinkob, confined at the waist by a long white shawl. His turban was also of shawl, across the front of which he wore a broad band studded with precious stones. On the King's right hand, below the steps of the musnud, (throne,) sat the Queen.[274] She was distinguished by a tassel of pearls, fastened on the top of her head, and falling over the left temple. Her hair, as is customary with women in India, was parted over the forehead, smoothed back with rose oil, braided behind, and hanging down her back. A gold ring, of eight inches in circumference, with a large ruby between two pearls on it, hung from her nostrils, which were pierced for that purpose. This ring denoted that she was the head of the family, a custom that applies to the meanest of her subjects in a similar situation. Round her neck were two rows of very large pearls, and a number of other necklaces, some set with precious stones, others of pure gold, with which her arms, wrists, and ancles, were also decorated. These gold rings are so pure as to be quite malleable: they are made from the coin called gold mohar,[275] merely melted down without any adulteration, and are generally put on the wrists of infants soon after they are born, being occasionally re-melted, added to, and the size increased, as the child grows larger, unless meantime the parents should require their value to purchase food; in which case they substitute silver: all slaves wear iron ones.* Her Majesty's fingers and toes were covered with rings of ruby, emerald, and sapphire, and an onyx by way of talisman: cornelian and lapis lazuli[276] are exclusively worn by the men. Her dress was of scarlet shawl, with a deep border of gold all round, in shape not unlike a pelisse, with an enormous long waist. Her ornee, or veil, covering half the head, and falling in graceful folds below her feet, was of clear white muslin, with a gold border. She, like the Emperor, sat with her legs bent under her, and, like him, chewed betel nut all the time she was speaking. This lady is a Pitaan,†[277] and of a remarkably dark complexion, almost black, which contrasted with the whiteness of the pearls produced an extraordinary effect.

The Emperor, who is of Mogul extraction, of the house of Timoor, and a lineal descendant of the great Tamerlane,[278] is remarkably fair for an Indian. His eyes are large, dark hazel; a well-shaped nose, fresh colour in his cheeks; and he might certainly pass for a handsome man, if he were not disguised by a black bushy beard. His age *appeared* to be about fifty; the Empress not half that age. I afterwards heard that she had been in the suite of the former Queen, and was not of royal parentage.

---

* Their distrust of each other, and perhaps being frequently surprised and plundered by hostile powers, first led to the idea of carrying all their valuables about them; yet is the practice of loading their children with such articles not unfrequently productive of much misery, for, lured by the prospect of gain, these unhappy infants become the prey of some unprincipled being, who having stripped them, throw their bodies down a well, and they are no more heard of. Such occurrences are, I regret to say, too common in this country.

† The Pitaans are a race of people who inhabit the tract of country to the north-west of Hindostan. The Afghans, who inhabit a country north-west of Delhi, are also called Pitaans, and, as tradition states, are descended from Saul, King of Israel. They were at one time in possession of *Kabul,* but it was wrested from them by Timoor Shaw, and made a royal residence for the Great Moguls. He removed his throne from Candahar to Cabul, and the seat of government was afterwards transferred to *Delhi*.

The Dowager Begum, mother to the King, took her station rather in front of the throne, on his left-hand side: he immediately ordered her a seat.

When a Mussulman Emperor dies, all his wives and concubines, except the mother of the reigning monarch, are confined in a separate palace, maintained, and guarded at his expense, as long as they live; nor do they consider such confinement any hardship, being accustomed from their infancy to attach the idea of respectability to that of seclusion. It is perhaps the only state in which these women could be happy. The dress of the Queen mother was ruby-coloured satin, with a gold and silver border. Her ornee was of green shawl, bordered with gold. On her neck, ears, and wrists, she wore a profusion of pearls, besides a superb armlet composed of different precious stones.* Her fingers, which were seen just emerging from the sleeves of her dress, were covered with jewels. The sons, and near relatives of the family, stood behind the Dowager Begum, forming a half circle: his own and his sons' wives were on the opposite side, while the Emperor, being seated in the centre, the party formed a complete crescent. I was particularly struck with the wife of one of the princes, named *Jehanghier*:[279] she was a tall thin young woman, of light complexion, (a Mogulanee princess,) of rather pensive appearance, dressed entirely in white muslin, without an ornament of any kind. Her husband, it appeared, was a wild extravagant youth, in disgrace with the Emperor his father, and under temporary banishment from court, but petted and supplied with money by the Empress, (his mother,) whom His Majesty frequently addressed, in my hearing, by the title of "Mother of *Jehanghier*."

When we were admitted into the Royal Presence, the Begum Sumroo made three *salaams*, and I followed her example. This is called the *tusleem*, and only performed to crowned heads. In compliance with eastern custom, I then advanced towards the throne, and presented, on a clean white napkin, the usual offering of four gold mohurs, (eight pounds sterling,) which the Emperor accepted, and with a condescending smile handed over to the Empress. I then, agreeable to the lesson I had been taught, retreated backwards to the edge of the carpet, again making the tusleem. The same ceremony, with two gold mohurs, was repeated to Her Majesty; which she having graciously accepted, the same sum was presented to the Dowager; so that I paid rather dear for my curiosity. Having gone through the pantomime of again retreating backwards, (it not being the etiquette to turn our backs on royalty,) I regained my post, by sidling into the circle next to the Begum Sumroo. The Emperor immediately ordered a seat to be placed for me at the foot of the throne, which politeness, rather than inclination, induced me to accept; for I foresaw that a conversation with him would be the consequence; and so it proved. The first question he asked me was, "What relation are you, Lady, to the Royal Family of England?" I hesitated to reply. Thinking that I had not understood him, he asked the Begum if I did not understand Persian. She replied, she believed I did, a little. He then repeated his former question to her. She said, she did not

---

* Every Indian wears a talisman on the left arm, in addition to their other ornaments.

know. I still remained silent, affecting not to understand him, although wondering what could induce him to ask the question. Not wishing to lessen my own consequence, and still more averse to telling an untruth, (for I saw that he had an idea of my being so related,) I turned to the Begum, and addressed some observation to her in the Hindostanee language, which seemed to convince him that I could speak no other; and as that is not the language of the court, His Majesty's conference with me was but of short duration. As a particular mark of favour, he then took a betel nut from his casket, and cutting it into two pieces, sent half of it to me by his youngest son, *Murza Selim*,[280] a boy of about twelve years of age. I did not at all relish the idea of putting it into my mouth; but it would have been an affront if I had not; so I contrived, unperceived, to get it out again as quick as possible. His *hookah* was then brought, from which he took two or three whiffs, and sent it away. The Queen's was also placed before her; but as it is not etiquette to smoke in His Majesty's presence, unless he signifies his approbation, (which he omitted to do on the present occasion,) hers was also, after a few minutes, removed.

On our preparing to take leave, the Queen took from a small tray (in the hands of one of her attendants) a pair of green shawls, which she gracefully placed upon my shoulders, saying, "Jeta ro!" which means, "Live for ever!" I then tusleemed to the King, who returned it by a slight inclination of the head; and, retreating backwards, we were soon out of the Presence. I took this opportunity to inquire of the Begum Sumroo what His Majesty meant by asking me if I was related to the Royal Family of England? and what reason he had for supposing me related to them? From her reply, I discovered that this mistake had arisen from my having on a gold bandeau under my white lace veil, which owing to its weight had slipped over the left temple. This circumstance, added to the rich appearance of the bandeau, (it being of the Etruscan pattern of dead and shining gold, tastefully intermixed,) impressed His Majesty with the idea that I must be a branch of that illustrious family; a bandeau on the head being with them the insignia of royalty.*

At the palace gates the Begum and I separated, to dress for dinner; to which we afterwards sat down, at the resident's table, in number upwards of fifty persons. Contrary to the practice of women in this country, the Begum Sumroo always wears a turban, generally damson colour, which becomes her very much, and is put on with great taste. I had almost forgotten to mention a ceremony that struck me as being extremely ludicrous, which is, that of a man, with a long white beard, marching into the room while the party were at breakfast, and, without any preface, beginning to read as fast and loud as he was able, all the news of the day, from a paper in manuscript called the *Acbar;* in which was related every, the most minute circumstance respecting the Royal Family, somewhat resembling a bulletin, which I understood was the practice at this hour in the house of every great personage. The Emperor is, in like manner, entertained with anecdotes of the resident's family, the city news, &c. I could scarcely avoid smiling at the

---

* Of this circumstance I was at that time ignorant.

profound attention paid by the Begum to this man's nonsense. These readers are much respected by the natives, who sit for hours while they relate Persian tales, the ladies of the family listening at the same time behind a *purdah*.* Both men and women are the greatest gossips in the world; but so averse are they to exertion, that they prefer paying a person for talking or reading to them, to doing either themselves.

---

* A purdah is a curtain, generally quilted, which hangs before a door, to denote that it is a private apartment; and so sacred a barrier is it considered, that no person, except the principals of a family, presume to approach it.

CHAPTER XII.

A PARTY was proposed for the next day to view the curiosities with which this neighbourhood abounds. I accordingly accompanied General O—[281] on an elephant, the rest of the party following, some on elephants, some on horseback. We first proceeded to the *Kootub Minar*,[282] a kind of obelisk so named, about twelve miles from *Delhi*. The resident being of the party, we had, in addition to our own attendants, his bodyguard, forming altogether a grand cavalcade. General O— and myself attracted particular attention, from being mounted upon one of the royal elephants that the Emperor had been so polite as to order for my use during our sojourn in his capital. The animal was of course richly caparisoned, and with a silver howdah on his back looked very superb; but another still more potent reason was, the handfuls of silver which the General threw among the populace as we passed. They soon recognized him as their former Governor, and gave the strongest proof of his popularity by the shouts with which they followed us much beyond the city gates. The first object that attracted my attention after passing through the adjmere gate,[283] was the remains of a college founded by *Meer Dahn Alli Khan*,[284] in the reign of *Shaw Jehan*, which must have been magnificent. A little farther, on the left hand side, stood the Royal Observatory[285] amid piles of ruinous palaces, too numerous to describe, but affording the most striking proofs of the opulence of their former possessors. In little more than an hour we reached the superb mausoleum of *Sufter Jung*,[286] grandfather of the late *Sadut Alli*,[287] Grand Vizier, and Nawaab of Lucknow. This building, which in magnificence and elegance of structure exceeds any I have seen except the *Tadge* at *Agra*, stands on an elevated terrace of marble, erected upon another of stone, in the centre of a large garden, surrounded by four high brick walls, and is in the most perfect state of preservation. The garden is filled with odoriferous shrubs of every description. The entrance to it lies through an immense arched gateway, beautifully proportioned, forming a hollow square open to the dome, round whose tastefully carved fret-work roof, were several small apartments railed in towards the square. The approach to these was by a handsome stone staircase. After passing through two or three of these small rooms, we came to a spacious apartment which extended the whole length of the building; on the sides and ceilings of which were flowers delicately painted, and of brilliant colours, on a silver ground. The building itself is of stone.

From hence we proceeded to the *Kootub Minar*, and were not sorry to find tables spread in a fine large tent, with an elegant cold collation. After doing justice to this repast, we sallied forth on foot to examine this greatest of all curiosities. It is considered to have been erected upwards of two hundred years, but whether of Mussulman or Hindoo workmanship does not appear so clear, although generally supposed to be the latter. It is in form an obelisk, two hundred and thirty feet in height, with a base in proportion, lessening very considerably towards the top. The building is divided into four equal parts, with a railing of stone round the outside of each. Its walls are composed of red granite and white marble, in alternate triangular and semi-circular pieces. A circular staircase leads to the summit—a flat roof, surrounded by a parapet. Having ascended half its height, I was glad to retrace my steps, being completely fatigued; but some of the gentlemen who reached the top, were amply compensated for their trouble by the beautiful and extensive prospect that presented itself. Although the day was remarkably mild, and near the surface of the earth scarcely a breath of air was stirring, yet on the top of the *Kootub Minar* the wind was so high that the gentlemen with difficulty kept their feet. Our march from hence, to the tomb of *Kootub ud Deen*,[288] was frequently intercepted by fragments of ruins. The remains of this holy man are enclosed within a court about fourteen feet square, paved and surrounded with white marble: the enclosure is of net-work, ten feet high. The marble slab over the body, when the weather permits, is covered with scarlet cloth, measuring ten feet square, fringed with gold, and richly embroidered. This place is guarded day and night. Two *moolahs*[289] receive an annual stipend for reading a certain number of daily prayers over the cenotaph. This extraordinary man exacted a promise when dying, and made it binding to all his posterity, under forfeiture of a considerable sum of money, that no woman should be allowed to approach his remains; which being politely signified to us, we contented ourselves with looking through the skreen, for as *I* was the only lady of the party, the gentlemen did not choose to make any distinction. This worthy Mussulman, we concluded, must have been crossed in love. The priests, (who were no small gainers by the visit,) now produced some white muslin turbans, one of which they bound round each of our heads. Thus adorned, we marched through sundry passages and marble courts, until we came to the tombs of *Bahadar Shaw* and *Shaw Allum*, late Emperors of *Delhi*.[290] The latter was father, the former grandfather, to the present monarch. Their tombs are within one enclosure, in the centre of a square space, similar to that of *Kootub ud Deen*, only larger, defended also like his by marble net-work. These tombs were covered by one large canopy of scarlet and gold *kinkob*, fringed with gold. This was supported by six long silver poles, most richly embossed. The grave of *Shaw Allum*, last deceased, was covered with a pall of the same materials as the canopy: two fans, of peacocks' feathers, with silver handles, lay at his feet; while two priests read alternately passages from the Koran, which we were told is customary for twelve months after the decease of any potentate, a certain number of moolahs being paid by the family for this purpose. A kind of mass is performed; and during these twelve months the lamps round the tomb are not suffered to expire. We then passed under a gateway of considerable depth, the ceiling of which (a square of twenty feet) was sandal wood, beautifully and curiously carved. This led to a bridge of rude stone by the side of a cascade, twenty-five feet in height by five-and-forty broad, rushing from an artificial rock, and over rugged paths, until the stream meandered slowly through an enchanting valley. This spot seemed formed for meditation; and I truly regretted the short time I could devote to its beauties. Our guides now conducted us to the "wonderful brazen pillar."[291] This pillar is of solid brass, twenty feet high, and four feet in circumference. Tradition reports it to have been placed there by a Rajah named *Patowly*, the founder of *Delhi*;[292] to which he was induced by his superstitious reliance on a Brahmin, who told him, when he was about to lay the foundation of that city, that provided he placed his seat of government on the head of the serpent that supports the world, his throne and kingdom would last for ever. This pillar was accordingly struck, to ascertain the precise spot, under the superintendance of the Brahmin, who announced to the Rajah that he had been fortunate enough to find it. One of the courtiers, jealous of the increasing influence of this Brahmin, pretended to have dreamed that the place on which the pillar stood was not the head of the serpent, which *he alone*, in consequence of his nightly vision, had the power to point out. The Rajah immediately gave directions for the pillar to be taken up. The Brahmin appeared equally anxious that it should be; "for," said he, "if *I* am right, you will find it stained with brains and blood; but if it prove otherwise, sacrifice me, and pin your faith upon the courtier." The experiment ended, as might be supposed, to the confusion of the courtier and eternal honour of the Brahmin, who literally contrived that it should appear as he had predicted, covered with brains and blood. The Rajah in consequence loaded him with riches, and the people ever after looked up to him as a superior being. Such is the power of priestcraft!

We now remounted our elephants, and returned, by a circuitous route, towards *Delhi*, in order to view the mausoleum of *Humayoon*,[293] eldest son of *Timoor Shaw*,[294] and Governor of *Candahar*;[295] also father of the renowned *Acbar*.[296] This building is enclosed by a wall of immense height and thickness, forming a square of considerable extent. Two ponderous gates, studded and barred with iron, command the entrance. On an extensive terrace of white marble, raised on many steps, stands this superb sepulchre; the component parts of which are granite and marble, tastefully disposed, and delicately inlaid with silver. The first terrace is of stone, to which you ascend by seven steps; from thence to the marble one are about fourteen more. Under this terrace are thirty-two cells for mendicant *fakeers*, and round it is a net-work railing of granite. It has one large dome of white marble, and four smaller ones, supported on pillars of granite, which are covered with a roof of grey marble. The ornament on the top of the principal dome is plated with gold. The sarcophagus is of the purest white marble, with verses from the Koran inscribed on it in Persian characters. This stands in the centre of a spacious apartment open to the dome, lined throughout with white marble, and paved with the same material. Four large windows in the dome diffuse a solemn gleam of light, calculated to impress the mind with ideas equally awful and magnificent. This room measures seventy feet square. Attached to each corner of the building is a circular one, with a winding staircase, leading to small apartments which are open to the dome, except by a low railing. The *fakeer* in waiting directed our attention to a large round plate of silver in the centre of the dome, from which, he said, had been suspended a chandelier of the same precious metal, but which was stolen by the *Jauts* when they overrun this province. There was notwithstanding still so much left to admire, that we should probably have devoted more time to it, had we not been engaged to dine with the Begum Sumroo.

Humayoon being the eldest son of *Timoor Shaw*, ought, according to English ideas, to have succeeded him on the throne;[297] but primogeniture was not considered at that period in Hindostan—the reigning prince usually named his successor. The sons of *Timoor Shaw* were not all by one mother: his favourite wife, an intriguing clever woman, and the mother of *Shaw Zemaan*,[298] caused *him* to be seated on the throne. He formed an alliance with *Tippoo Sultaan*[299] to attack the British possessions in India. *Humayoon* rebelled against this brother, who accordingly caused him to be seized, and his eyes put out.[300] The rest of his days he passed in confinement; and, when dead, was buried here by his son *Acbar*, at whose expense this splendid monument was raised.

At the *Begum Sumroo's* palace[301] we found thirty persons of rank assembled, and a splendid banquet in the European style. This ended, she arose and threw over the shoulders of each of the ladies a wreath of flowers formed of a tuberose plant, united by narrow gold ribbon. No sooner was she re-seated, than strains of soft music were heard, and two folding doors of the saloon flew open as if by enchantment, discovering a number of young girls in the attitude of dancing a ballet, or, as it is here termed, a *notch*.[302] It appeared to me, however, little more than a display of attitudes; indeed their feet and ancles were so shackled by a large gold ring, of more than an inch in thickness, and bells strung round another, that springing off the ground must have been impracticable; in fact, their dancing consisted in jingling these bells in unison with the notes of the musical instruments, which were played by men educated for that purpose. To this music they give effect by appropriate motions of the hands, arms, and person, not forgetting that more expressive vehicle of the sentiments, *the eyes*. Their movements were by no means devoid of grace, particularly when accompanied by the voice, although the tones were, in my idea, extremely harsh, and frequently discordant. Seldom more than three girls perform at a time, and with the characters they change the figure. They performed a tale admirably; for by attending to the different gestures, it was as easily comprehended as if it had been recited. One, more superbly dressed than the others, came forward alone, to go through the motions of flying a kite, which she performed to admiration, and with peculiar grace. They pique themselves, I am told, on this art.

After breakfast, next morning, we accompanied the resident to view the royal baths and gardens. The baths are small apartments, *en suite*, having cupolas on the top of each, with one or more small sky-lights of painted glass. They are paved and lined with white marble, inlaid with cornelian, lapis lazuli, agate, &c. in elegant Mosaic patterns. The cold baths are supplied by fountains from the centre, fixed in a marble bason nearly the size of the room, with a bench all round the inside of it. The tepid and hot baths are rendered so by flues supplied from without. From hence we passed to the aviary, a long narrow apartment formed of the same materials, in which at this time were only a few singing birds for show. There was a larger, we were told, in the *Zenanah* garden, much better supplied. A paved terrace led from this place to the *menagerie*. Here we saw tigers, lynxes, leopards, hyænas, and monkeys of various description and sizes; but, to my surprise, no lions. These beasts were reposing under colonnades of marble, secured to a staple by long iron chains. I do not think they liked our intruding on their retirement, for with one accord, but by different modes, they loudly testified disapprobation. The keeper said they were frightened at seeing so many white faces. The royal gardens came next in rotation, but were scarcely deserving of the name: they had never recovered the depredation made by the general enemy, the *Jauts*. The only things worth notice in them were a few large trees, planted by the Emperor Aurungzebe *himself*, who was fond of gardening, and kept his gardens in great order. A number of wide paved walks crossed each other at right angles, and in the centre of them was a bason containing gold and silver fish; besides which were fountains playing upon beds of flowers, laid out in the Dutch style of tiresome uniformity. Small circular buildings, supported by pillars and faced with marble, terminated the principal walks.

The description of the royal apartments in the fort at *Agra*, will answer also for those at *Delhi*. Fluted pillars of white marble, with gilt cornices; pavement of the same, nearly covered with a Persian carpet; are the leading features of the latter, with a chandelier suspended from the centre of each room. The chandelier in the banqueting room at *Agra*, was, in the time of the Emperor *Acbar*, suspended by ingots of gold. I did not hear of any thing so splendid at *Delhi*, where, for want of chairs and tables, the palace appeared to me scarcely habitable. There is however in every room a cushion, (or place for one,) raised a little from the floor, for His Majesty; indeed, when we consider that no one would presume to sit in his presence, or even in an apartment usually occupied by him, all other articles of furniture would be superfluous. The Emperor's general residence is in the Zenanah: he seldom occupies the outer palace, but on state occasions.

In the evening I was introduced to the son of *Abdoulah Khan*,[303] of cherished memory, among the learned men of his country as one of the most liberal patrons of the fine arts, besides being an excellent, just, and good man. He was a native of *Cashmere*,[304] and chief of a province. He died in 1805.

We had now only to view the *Jumna Musjeed*,[305] or principal place of Mahometan worship in this city; for which purpose some of the party set forward immediately after breakfast. This stands in the middle of the city. The ascent to it is by a number of large, handsome, stone steps, on three sides of an immense square area, out of three principal streets. To this area you pass, on either side, through a double gateway, having apartments over it crowned by a parapet of cupolas. The area is arcaded on three sides—the fourth is the *musjeed*, or chapel, at one corner of which a saint is interred within an enclosure or skreen of marble net-work, covered by a superb canopy: near this no person is permitted to approach with shoes on. The large area is paved all over with white marble, having a square reservoir of water in the centre. This *musjeed* is surmounted by three marble domes, with gilt ornaments of a spiral form on the tops of each, and is supported at either end by a handsome minaret of granite three stories high, each story having a balcony round it with marble net-work railing, and on the top of each a dome, open all round, supported upon pillars of granite. A spiral staircase leads to the top. The ascent to the *musjeed* from the area was by seven steps of granite, to a terrace of marble twenty feet broad, on which it stood, extending the whole length of the front.

As it was not a Sabbath-day, or at the usual hour of prayer, we were permitted to make a minute inspection. There were neither seats, divisions, nor pews, within the building; nothing but a plain marble pavement, with a pulpit similar in shape to those in England, formed from a solid block of marble; the whole being enclosed by arches, and the roof also arched, with curious carved work in all directions.

Some Mussulmen were at their devotions within the saint's enclosure, and we of course did not disturb them. I knew a gentleman who was imprudent enough once to touch one of his servants with a walking-stick as he passed along, while the man was in the act of prayer, which was no sooner ended, than deliberately taking his sword, he made a cut at his master that had nearly proved fatal: it separated his cheek from the mouth to the ear.

These people are wonderfully tenacious where their religion is concerned; and it is no joke to trifle with them. Several were bawling out at the *musjeed*, as loud as they were able, the first verse of the Koran,[306] which runs thus:

" Praise be to God, the Lord of all creatures!
" The most merciful!
" King of the day of judgment!
" Thee do we worship.
" Of thee do we beg assistance.
" Direct us in the right way:
" In the way of those to whom thou hast been gracious;
" Not of those against whom thou art incensed,
" Nor of those who go astray."

This verse is repeated by all good Mussulmen when about to undertake any thing of consequence, particularly by the *Siads*,[307] or immediate descendants of Mahomet.

In the course of the day I received a message from the Empress, through the *Begum Sumroo*, inviting me to accompany her to a grand entertainment, proposed to be given in the palace on the marriage of one of the royal family. It was to commence on the following evening, and to last for three days. Not doubting my acceptance of it, the Begum said that a Hindostanee dress was preparing for me to appear in, which would be presented by the Empress herself. Unfortunately, it was not in my power to make use of it; for the commissioners having finished their business, had made arrangements for quitting *Delhi* that very day. On taking leave of the *Begum Sumroo*, she presented me with a handsome shawl.

We accordingly set forward as usual, and marched about fifteen miles before breakfast. On leaving the capital of the Mogul empire, we re-crossed the river *Jumna*, and passing over a sandy plain, arrived at the pretty neat town of *Shaw Derah*. This place is exceedingly populous, being the depôt of grain for the city of *Delhi*, and also a place of security for the cattle belonging to the royal family.

The village of *Furr uk Nugger*, where we pitched our tents, is on the banks of the *Bind Nullah*, which, although a deep river, did not appear to fertilize the soil around it, as the next morning's march presented only an uncultivated waste: no symptom of fertility was perceptible until quite the latter part of it, near a small indifferent village named *Moraad Gunge*, and here was little more than a few shrubs and stunted trees. This country has so frequently been the theatre of war, that it is now nearly laid waste.

At sun-rise the next morning I mounted my horse, and, in company with two of the gentlemen, rode the next sixteen miles into *Meratt*[308] to breakfast; soon after which we received the visits of the Judge, two Rajahs, and several officers of His Majesty's 17th regiment who were there encamped.[309] It was now the 18th of January, the weather most delightful. On the 19th I received visits from the ladies, and the commissioners gave a dinner party.

On the 21st we had a large party to breakfast, and I afterwards returned visits; in doing which I had an opportunity of witnessing a most curious ceremony, peculiar, as I was informed, to these provinces. A young girl appeared veiled from head to foot, with a cord tied round her waist, the end of which was held by a man apparently much older than herself, who walked three or four yards before her, to whom we were informed she was just married. My curiosity induced me to make farther inquiries, when I learned that it was customary in the sect to which she belonged, for the father, or nearest male relative of a bride, to bind a rope round her waist, tying the end of it round the wrist of the bridegroom, when he leads her home as his property, followed by a procession of relatives, friends, and acquaintance, as we then saw. This ceremony, it appears, is intended to be emblematic of their being tied together for life, and that her family resign all right and title to her. In the evening some of us went out on elephants with the dogs, who put up three hyænas, whom we chased for a considerable time, but never could get within gunshot of them. Our people brought in a tiger that had just been killed: his skin was so beautiful that I had it cured, in order to cover footstools with it.

On the 24th I rode out coursing with some of the gentlemen of our party, and found so many hares that we were puzzled which to follow.

CHAPTER XIII.

On the following day the commissioners quitted *Meratt*, and halted a few hours at *Sirdanah*, a palace belonging to the Begum Sumroo, where she generally resides. We were escorted over the estate by her colonel commandant, a respectable old gentleman of the name of Peton, a Frenchman[310] by birth, but resident at her court for many years. She has a regular cantonment here for her troops, and a strong fort containing some good houses, which are inhabited by the officers and their families. Her soldiers are tall, stout men, with light complexions, hooked noses, and strongly marked features, being principally Rajpoots, who are the best soldiers, but much addicted to chewing opium, generally proud, and often insolent. Their uniform is a dress of dark blue broad cloth, reaching to the feet, with scarlet turbans and waistbands. Her park of artillery seemed also in excellent order: most of the large guns stood in a line in front of the palace gates. She paid us the compliment of ordering a salute to be fired, and apologized for not being there to meet us, on account of the entertainment at the palace, which had detained her at *Delhi*. We saw a number of fine horses in her stables, and an English coach that had been lately built for her in Calcutta, which was to be drawn by four of them, with two postilions. I had afterwards the pleasure of accompanying her in it. The carriage was painted a bright yellow, with silver mouldings, lined with violet-coloured satin, embroidered all over with silver stars. The window frames of solid silver; the lace and hangings silver ribbon, wove in a pattern, and very substantial, with silver bullion tassels. The wheels were dark blue, to match the lining. The postilions wore scarlet jackets and caps, almost covered with silver lace. She has several fine gardens full of fruit trees. The branches of the orange, lemon, and citron trees, at *that* time, fairly bent under their luxurious load.

The surrounding country is highly cultivated, presenting a most cheerful prospect. This is part of what is called the *Dooab*,[311] in consequence of its being fertilized by two principal rivers, viz. the *Ganges* and *Jumna*. *Doo* is Persian for *two*, and *aab* for water.* It is particularly pleasing to the eye, being well wooded and thickly planted with villages, wearing symptoms of great prosperity. In the course of thirteen miles, we passed through five of them.

From hence to *Katowly* nothing occurred worth mentioning. Like most other large towns, it is enclosed by a high brick wall, with four entrances, East, West, North, and South, secured by as many ponderous gates, studded and barred with iron, having a number of armed men at each of them.

---

* Applicable to all the districts west of Allahabad.

On the 28th we proceeded on our journey, and felt the cold uncommonly severe. The morning was fine, clear, and frosty, which produced wonderful effects on the breakfast table. Our road was over a sandy plain, with frequent inequalities, which, if they had not been heaps of loose sand, I should have called *hills*. This continued for six miles, and distressed our carriage cattle exceedingly. After that, we came upon an extensive down which commanded a good prospect. As I before mentioned, part of the tent equipage, crockery, &c. are sent forward at night to be ready on the next encamping ground in the morning. In consequence of the intense cold of the preceding night, two of the bearers were found dead upon the road. Nor was this the only fatal accident that happened: a bullock in one of the waggons was shot, by the carelessness of a man of the Seapoy guard, and died upon the spot.

A short distance from *Muzzuffer Nuggur*,[312] (the place of our destination,) we passed a handsome town called *Owlah*, built *entirely* of brick, which is rather unusual, as in general by far the greater proportion of houses in this country are of cob.* All brick houses in Hindostan have flat roofs with a low railing all round, where the inhabitants sit smoking their hookahs of an evening, listening to a relater of Persian tales, or a reciter of poetry, such as the *Shah Naumeh*,[313] &c.

About midway on our march the following morning, we were intercepted by a branch of the river *Hindon*,[314] which having forded on elephants, we returned to our carriages, and drove through groves of mango trees the rest of the way. After breakfast I accompanied some of the gentlemen on a shooting excursion, when we discovered a beautiful shrubbery surrounding the hut of a *Brahmin fakeer*, close by the side of a fine large lake, on which were innumerable wild fowl, of whom he was the protector. We found means, however, with a few rupees, to satisfy his conscience with respect to their being killed. This place is fifteen miles from *Muzzuffer Nugger*, which town is above a mile in length.

From this place the country was for the most part level, and cultivated down to the road side. We remarked several flights of wild pigeons on our journey, started a tiger cat and a brace of quail, and saw some romantic views.

I mounted my horse next morning with the intention of riding to *Saharunpore*;[315] but three miles beyond our encampment, we came to a river which we were obliged to ford on elephants, but re-mounted our horses on the other side, and reached *Saharunpore* to breakfast. Shortly after our arrival, the judge[316] paid us a visit, and invited the party to dine with him. I forgot to mention, that the judge and collector of every district always accompanied the commissioners to the boundary of it. The climate is considered colder here, than in any part of India. From the judge's house (which stood on an eminence within the fort) we could easily distinguish three distinct ranges of hills, covered with snow, which

---

* Cob is a mixture of mud, sand, and straw, with a portion of cow dung.

never entirely melts. *Saharunpore* lies low, and in the rainy season is considered extremely unhealthy, owing to the number of streams by which it is surrounded, bringing down putrid matter from the hills; consequently, fevers and agues are at this time very prevalent. The town is large, and built chiefly of brick. Near it we were shown a garden, the property of Government, well stocked with fruit and vegetables, but that was all—it had certainly no beauty to boast, in the year 1809. This was a frontier station to the *Sieke* country;[317] and it was now thought advisable to assemble an army at a place called *Cheelconnah*, (about seven miles from hence,) in order to check the encroaching spirit of *Runjeet Sing*,[318] their leader. Accustomed from their infancy to carry arms, both the Sieks and Mahrattas are expert in the use of them, particularly the matchlock, which they fire at a mark on full gallop, and seldom miss their aim. The higher classes of these men wear their beards long, and bushy up to the eyes, and are extremely fanciful in the colour of them, sometimes tinging them with lilac, pink, light blue, yellow, and even scarlet. I saw one man whose beard was white, edged with purple. Mahometans in general only wear mustachios. The dresses of the Sieks we saw, were made of silk, wadded with cotton, reaching to their feet; the sleeves entirely obscuring the hands, and edged with a broad gold or silver lace all round the skirts. These dresses are made to fit the shape; the skirt to wrap across the front, and fasten by strings on one side; their throat being always exposed.* Over this, they wear a long shawl, bound tight round the waist; a turban on their heads; and in cold weather, when they go out of doors, two square shawls, one plain, the other sprigged, envelope turban, face, and shoulders, leaving the smallest possible aperture, just that they may see their way: shawl socks, and shoes trimmed up at the points, either embroidered on scarlet or yellow cloth, or made of scarlet or yellow leather. Mussulmen are fond of gay colours, and have not the same objection to wearing any thing made of leather as the Hindoos have. The principal traffic among the natives here seems to be in slaves. Children are brought down annually from the hills for sale. I saw two, apparently about four and five years old, that had been purchased by a native lady for twenty-five rupees—(one pound eleven shillings and three-pence each.) I was horror-struck at the idea, and very far from thinking, at that time, that any circumstances could induce *me* to purchase a human being like a horse or any other animal; therefore let no one say what he will not do, for we are all, more or less, the creatures of circumstance.

Some of our party made a digression from *Saharunpore* towards *Fizabad*,[319] in order to examine the source of the *Jumna*. They experienced much difficulty on account of the roughness of the road, over which the cattle could not travel; so they were obliged to dismount, and pursue their researches on foot. At length

---

* Seapoys wear three rows of very large white stone beads, tight round theirs, which at a distance has the appearance of a stock.

they discovered what they sought; it was a pure stream, flowing rapidly through a narrow pass over a bed of large stones.

From this place, which our party quitted on the 3rd of January, we proceeded to *Munglore*, a fortified palace belonging to *Ramdial Sing*, Rajah of *Hurdoar*.[320] In so doing, we passed a large well-built town named *Jubrarah*, the residence of his eldest son, who came out to receive us at his castle gate. A more ruffian-like figure I never beheld: he measured, I was told, seven feet in height; and I can answer for it, that he was stout even beyond proportion. We did not quit our carriages upon this occasion; but he paid us the compliment of mounting his horse, and with his numerous retinue attending, or rather escorting us to his father's palace. Here we found the gates thrown open, and the old Rajah waiting to receive us with a silver salver in his hand, about the size of a common plate, piled up with gold mohars, which he first presented to the commissioners, and on their declining it to me, when, agreeable to etiquette, I made my salaam and declined it also. The same ceremony having been gone through to one or two others, he affected to appear much chagrined, and gave it to one of his servants, who carried it away. We now followed him into his castle. He was a fac simile of *Blue Beard*,[321] scimitar and all, that one reads of having murdered so many wives. Equally gigantic as his son, he possessed a stentorian voice that made one tremble. I verily thought that we had entered the country of the Brobdignags.[322] The Rajah's dress was no less singular than the rest of his appearance; and, to crown all, he had on a pair of bright yellow jack-boots.[323]

Munglore is a place of some consequence in the manufacturing line, besides being on the high road from Cashmere to our provinces. Persian goods of every description *must* pass this place. The town is large, and built entirely of brick, which the Rajah causes to be refreshed once a year, to make them look like new. The inhabitants weave cloth, print chintz, &c. They all forsook their houses on our approach, and followed us with loud shouting. I was told it was occasioned by seeing *me*, the only English lady they had ever seen; and my being on horseback astonished them still more. Their women, when travelling, have thick curtains drawn round the carriage, so as to elude the most vigilant inspection.

Munglore is surrounded by fine large timber trees; and the enclosures to the fields are all of prickly pear, a plant frequently met with in hothouses in England, and which forms an impenetrable fence. The inhabitants are all Hindoos. They esteem the peacock a sacred bird: we observed numbers of them walking quite tame about the streets.

While taking the air on an elephant in the evening, I fell in with a caravan of merchants from *Cabul*,[324] who at first stared at me as if they had seen an ourang-outang; but I desired one of my attendants to explain to them that we had a large encampment not far off, and if they would go there, they would be able to dispose of a great many things. They made no objection, and accordingly we all proceeded together. Their cargo consisted of beautiful Persian cats, birds, dried fruits, sheep with ponderous tails like those at the Cape of Good Hope,[325] and goats, from whose wool the Cashmere shawls are made. These animals were considerably larger and higher than those of Europe; their coats thick, black, and apparently coarse, until examined, when close to the skin is discovered that fine soft wool, the manufacture of which is held in such estimation for shawls. A couple of these goats were purchased in our camp for thirty rupees[*]

From hence we continued our journey to *Jualapore,* a village immediately at the foot of the Tibett mountains. Previous to reaching it, we came to a place named *Landowra,*[326] another palace belonging to the Rajah of *Hurdwaar,* who had gone forward to receive us. We soon descried him towering above his satellites, with an offering of gold mohars on a napkin; when, (agreeably to custom on such occasions,) descending from our elephants, we touched the gold mohars with the tips of three fingers of the right hand, and made a *salaam;* upon which, one of his servants took them away as before. It is merely a form in the person offering, to denote that he acknowledges himself an inferior. He then conducted us through a large paved court, and up several stone steps, into the palace, where we were surprised to find chairs placed round a large brazier filled with charcoal. As soon as we were seated, several servants entered with wooden trays of about two feet long and a foot and a half broad; on some of which were shawls, pieces of kinkob, muslin, &c.; on others, Persian fruits, fresh and preserved,—sweet cakes, biscuits, and otta of roses. About five-and-twenty of these trays were placed at our feet; while in the court before the palace were paraded several Persian and Arab horses, richly caparisoned, with silver chains about their necks, and pendant ornaments of value. From this superabundance of good things it was necessary, in order to avoid giving offence, to take something. I took a small square handkerchief, and one or two of the gentlemen a Persian sword of no great value. The horses had their walk only to be admired; after which they were quietly replaced in the stable; and mounting our elephants, we bade this good gentleman adieu.

Native chiefs are magnificent, and even profuse in their presents to Europeans. We might have given all we saw in charge of our servants, to take away, if we had wished it, and he would have been highly gratified, as he would have considered himself entitled to expect from us double its value in return, and would not have suffered much time to elapse without asking some favour. I once accepted a Persian cat, and in a few days after received a request from the *Bibbee Saheb*[327] to send her a pair of white shawls.

---

[*] Most shawls are exported unwashed, and fresh from the loom. They are better washed and packed at *Umrutseer*[328] than at *Cashmere,* where they are manufactured. Sixteen thousand looms are supposed to be in constant motion there, each of them giving employment to three men, whose wages are about three pice a day. It is calculated that eighty thousand shawls are disposed of annually. The wool from *Tibett*[329] and Tartary[330] is the best, because the goat which produces it thrives better there: twenty-four pounds weight of it sells at Cashmere, if of the best sort, for twenty rupees; an inferior and harsher kind may be procured for half the money. The wool is spun by women, and afterwards coloured. When the shawl is made, it is carried to the custom-house and stamped, and a duty paid agreeable to its texture—one fifth of the value. The persons employed sit on a bench at the frame, sometimes four people at each frame; but if the shawl is a plain one, only two. A fine shawl, with a pattern all over it, takes nearly a year in making. The borders are worked with wooden needles, having a separate needle for each colour. There is a head man who superintends and describes the pattern. The rough side of the shawl is uppermost while manufacturing.

Travelling over a vile road to *Paharpore*, we gradually approached the mountains, and reached *Juallapore* to a late breakfast. This being the entrance of the *Moradabad* district,[331] we were met by its judge and collector[332] with their separate suite. *Juallapore* is eighteen miles from *Munglore:* the last nine miles was through an inhospitable-looking jungle, where tigers are said to abound. We saw plenty of florican, the black-spotted feathered partridge, hog deer, &c. Where the latter are found, there are always tigers.

The following morning some of our party, myself among the number, made an excursion to the celebrated bathing-place of *Hurdoar*,[333] where we fell in with a party of *Sieks* of high rank: they consisted of the *Ranee Mutaab Kour*, wife of Rajah Rungeet Sing;[334] Rajah *Sahib Sing*, of *Patialah*, and his wife;[335] Rajahs *Bodge Sing*[336] and *Burgwaan Sing*.[337] These people paid us every mark of respect and politeness: they were attended by a numerous retinue.

The town of *Hurdoar* is on a bank of the Ganges, about eight miles from *Juallapore:* it is built chiefly of stone, and stands at the foot of an immense range of mountains covered with luxuriant verdure. The Ganges here divides into several limpid streams, which, after running for several miles over a bed of large smooth stones, unite in *one*, which measures twelve hundred yards across. Its source is near *Punniallee*, on the south-east side of *Hemallah*.

The name *Hurdoar*[338] is composed from *Hur*, the name of a Hindoo saint, (who made this his place of ablution, and eventually his residence,) and *doar*, which in the Shanscrit[339] language means a door; by which the natives understood that the way or door to this saint's favour, was by frequenting the place that he had named and patronized. As he had a high character for sanctity, and was withal a shrewd, clever man, it soon became a place of great celebrity, and continues so to the present time. There is an annual fair[340] held here to commemorate the anniversary of this man's birth, at which it is computed there assemble no fewer than a million of souls.* The extent of ground occupied by these, in one continued throng, is generally from three to four *koss*.† The grand bathing-day takes place on or about the 11th of April, dependant however on the state of the moon‡.

Tunkal is a town about three miles from *Hurdoar*, where five elegant houses have been built in the oriental style, with a profusion of Hindoo emblems and decorations, said to have cost thirty thousand rupees each. Two of them belong to

---

* The surest way of founding a village in this country is by setting down a *fakeer* on the spot, who immediately builds a mud hut, hoists a small red flag upon a pole, and the following year appears a populous village.

† A koss is about one mile and a half English.

‡ A pilgrimage to Mecca is also considered necessary to constitute the character of a *good* Mussulman, and is considered highly meritorious. These pilgrims support themselves chiefly by alms on the journey; and you not unfrequently see the most emaciated objects lying dead by the road side, particularly in a thinly inhabited country, as in the new road from Calcutta to the upper provinces of Hindostan. I counted five myself on that road, who appeared lying flat on their faces, with scarcely any clothing on them, and the bones almost starting through the skin. There is an institution at Mecca for pilgrims, provided for by the will of *Ahmed Shah;*[341] so that while they *remain there*, they are very well off.

rich bankers at *Naugreedabad;* one to Rajah *Nyn Sing*,[342] who lives in the neighbourhood of Muratt; one to *Goorah Khan;*[343] and one to *Ramdial Sing*, Rajah of Hurdoar. They were all built within the last seven years. Hindoos always plaister the inside of their houses with cow-dung, which old women and children are constantly employed picking up. They make it into flat cakes with their hands, and stick them on the outer walls of cottages to dry: they then pile them up, under shelter, for use. The walls and terraces, when perfectly finished, have the appearance of stucco, without any unpleasant smell at all. A general officer in the Company's service brought to England, some years ago, a Hindoo lady as his wife, and left her in handsome lodgings, in London, while he went to visit his friends in Scotland. The first thing she did, after he was gone, was to purchase a cow, and have her brought into the drawing-room. The hostess expostulated; but the general's lady assured her that if any damage was done, it should all be paid for, and she was pacified; but when, a few days afterwards, the housemaid told her mistress that all the cleaning in the world would never get the cow-dung off the gilt mouldings, she was petrified! concluding of course that the lady must be mad, she wrote off to the general by that evening's post.

Another common practice among Hindoos, is, that of exposing different kinds of grain on sheets, before their houses, to dry in the sun; so that the whole village looks like a bazaar.

The Brahmins who reside at *Hurdoar* persuade their followers, that by performing their ablutions, and making offerings to the *Ganges* at that place, they instantly become purified of their former sins. I hope I am not uncharitable; but could not help suspecting, that some of my party would not have been sorry to be so easily rid of theirs.

We saw here some pilgrims who had travelled all the way from *Juggernaut*,[344] in the bay of Bengal,[345] (some thousand miles,) to perform a penance. They were at this time just setting out on their return, laden with baskets full of small bottles filled with sanctified water, for the purification of those who were unable to come so far.

The road between *Juallapore* and *Tunkal* may be justly compared to those of the New Forest in Hampshire,[346] but still more beautiful from its vicinity to the mountains. After rambling about, (until we were tired,) viewing a number of descents by stone steps, with their appropriate decorations, that conducted votaries to the sacred stream, (each guarded by one or more fakeers,) we returned to our encampment infinitely gratified by the trip.

The commissioners being occupied by business, we did not quit *Juallapore* until the 12th, which afforded me an opportunity of viewing some waterfalls at *Angenny*, a place exactly opposite *Tunkal*, on the other side of the river. Six persons started on four elephants: three spare elephants having been pushed forward to sound the bed of the river, (as we proposed fording it,) and to clear the jungle on the other side. The stream where we crossed was about seven feet deep, rapid, and perfectly clear, so that we could distinguish a bottom of large round stones, which were so slippery that it was a service of danger to pass over them. The elephants trembled at every step, and supported each other by heeling to it, as ships do with a wind on their quarter. It must have been a curious spectacle from the opposite shore to see four elephants wedged like a wall together, with people on their backs, all stepping cautiously as if aware of danger. We crossed a little above the Falls, which are stated to extend for half a mile, and reach fairly across the river. Their descent in many places does not exceed eight or nine feet. We had a complete view of them from *Angenny*, and were delighted by the sound of dashing waters, and view of stupendous mountains clothed with the stately fir* and spreading bamboo, while the sweet warblers of the wood strained their harmonious throats to bid us welcome. Our advanced guard having shot some jungle cocks,† we had them broiled; and they proved a welcome addition (being young and finely flavoured) to the cold provisions we had brought. After regaling ourselves and resting the elephants, we re-mounted, in order to explore the country, and entered a bamboo jungle, the branches of which were so entwined that the spare elephants were absolutely necessary to force a passage for us. It was really wonderful to see with what dexterity these animals twisted off large branches with their trunks; or, at the instigation of their driver, tore up whole trees by the roots. After buffeting through in this way for about an hour, we came to a charming valley between two ridges of hills, whose summits seemed to touch the clouds. Trees and shrubs of various foliage adorned their almost perpendicular sides, while the meandering Ganges, in distant murmurs, died on the listening ear. Having made a circuit of some miles through this delightful country, we re-crossed the Ganges in boats, and reached our encampment before it grew dark.

The next morning was fixed on for pursuing our journey. I accompanied the judge of *Moradabad* (whose district we were just entering) on his elephant through thick grass jungles, higher than the animal on which we rode, although he measured fourteen feet. Our advanced party fell in with a wild elephant, from whom they defended themselves by collecting round a tree and firing at him, then setting up a hideous yell, which at length frightened him away.

For eighteen miles not the slightest trace of a road was perceptible; but the guides persisted that they were going right, and brought us to a village named *Kurranpore*. Here the inhabitants were so alarmed at seeing us, that they fled and hid themselves in a grass jungle. A little beyond this village is a *morass*, only rendered passable by loads of reed and bamboo that our people had spread the day before to form something like a road. The elephants did not seem at all inclined to cross it, nor do I think it was altogether safe, but fortunately no accident occurred.

Soon after this we reached a part of the Ganges where there is a ferry, and found excellent boats with platforms for the conveyance of our carriages and horses, waggons, bullocks, &c. &c. This place is named *Bhynee Ghattah*. Here we quitted what is termed the country of the *Doo-ab*, and entered that of the *Pungaab*,[347] or junction of five rivers, inhabited by a people called the *Rohillas*. The banks of

---

* This is the only place in Hindostan where the fir tree is found in perfection.
† Like English cocks and hens, only wild.

the Ganges, on the *Rohilcund*[348] side, are immensely steep; and the soil, a deep loose sand, which so considerably delayed the baggage, that many of the gentlemen's tents were not pitched until quite late at night. Our encampment extended two miles, over a plain that separated the villages of *Allum Serai* and *Nagul*. From hence we passed over a vile road through a jungle of brush-wood and low stumps, (called the dak shrub,) besides two or three streams knee-deep for the horses, to a place called *Nugeebabad*,[349] which is, being interpreted, "City of great Men." Our tents were pitched near the garden-house of *Sultan Khan*,[350] son of the Nawaab *Nugeeb ul Dowlah*,[351] whose tomb we visited in the course of the morning. It stands surrounded by trees that completely shade the building, and is encompassed by a brick wall. The tombs of him, and his favourite wife are united under a slab of stone, covered with a smooth white paste called *chunam*,[352] which bears a high polish, and at a distance looks like alabaster. They are raised considerably off the ground by a terrace of flag-stones. On three sides of this terrace are colonnades neatly painted with emblematical devices; the fourth is divided into three small apartments for devotion, terminating in as many cupolas. This is the first place, after leaving the Persian territory, where bales of shawl and other Persian merchandise are examined, and a duty levied on them by the East India Company. It is the abode of many merchants, who enrich themselves by purchasing wholesale, and retailing them into the provinces. Large plantations of sugar-cane were observable throughout this part of India, and mills for extracting the juice in order to make it into sugar, to be seen in every village. Those little neat baskets of split bamboo, in which pilgrims carry the Ganges water, are manufactured here, and find a brisk sale. I purchased some shawls and (under such circumstances that I could not avoid it) a slave boy! The circumstances were these:—A poor debilitated woman, with an infant in her arms, and this child, (about four years of age,) seated themselves at the door of our tent, and would not be removed. Thinking she was a beggar, I sent her a few *pice;*[353] upon which she said that she came to sell her child, and not to solicit *pice*, for they would do her no good. I then went out and remonstrated with her upon the cruelty of such an act; told her that if she did, there was not the smallest chance of her ever seeing him again—in short, said all I could to work upon her feelings as a mother, and endeavour to turn her from her purpose; but still she persevered, and implored me with tears to take him. She had a numerous family, she said, who must all starve unless she could get money by this means to pay the *bunyah*. The price she asked for the boy was thirty-six rupees, the half of which she owed for food. Her husband, she said, was a cripple, and could not work. I sent a person with her to ascertain the truth of this statement, and finding that the woman had not deceived me, I paid the money and received the boy. Some victuals that was placed before them they eagerly devoured. The child remained without a murmur, in hopes of another meal when hungry; and the mother departed happy, in the belief that her boy was provided for.

This traffic, so repugnant to English ideas, exists only near the hills, where the population is so great, and the means of providing for it so small, that unless purchasers could be found for the children, half of them must starve. This boy had quite the countenance of a Chinese Tartar,[354] with immense large eyes. The first thing I did was to have him bathed and clothed, for he was perfectly naked. He did not like being dressed at all, and for a long time took every opportunity of slipping himself out of it.

In the evening we mounted our elephant, and rode about a mile to inspect a large fort,[355] built of hewn stone, within which *Nugeeb ul Dowlah* had stood a siege by *Shaw Allum*, Emperor of *Delhi*, at that time denominated "The *Great Mogul*." This fort is at present untenanted, but is capable of being made a very strong intrenchment, large enough to contain a garrison of three thousand men, although for the actual defence of it perhaps five hundred might suffice. It is situated on an extensive plain, surrounded by a strong wall and two deep ditches, supplied from a reservoir within the fort.

CHAPTER XIV.

On the following day we halted at *Nugeenah*,[356] about fifteen miles from our last encampment. On the road we forded several small streams, one of which (the *Gongon*) is frequently impassable in the rainy season for many hours, being at that time both deep and rapid. We were told of a tiger that had been seen of late near this river, but he did not favour us with his appearance. A gentleman known to some of our party, had, in passing about two months before, the good fortune to kill one on this very spot. The small town of *Nugeena* contains eighteen thousand inhabitants: it is celebrated for the manufacture of blankets, and coloured glass. The *Nawaab's* residence is at *Arampore*,[357] which we passed close by. In the square space in front of the palace, we observed a number of his attendants—fair, handsome men, sitting or lounging upon *charpiahs*, with a degree of independence that surprised us. These *Rohillah* chiefs are not very partial to the English.[358]

From *Nugeenah* to *Dawmpore* (where we found our tents) is about fourteen miles. Our road lay over a level country, well wooded and watered, the cultivation in many parts reaching to the road side. *Dawmpore* is famous for the manufacture of pistols, swords, gun-barrels, and matchlocks.

From *Dawmpore*, by way of *Soharra* to *Saispore*, is, without any exception, the wildest fifteen miles of country I ever travelled: it is covered with bushes, the haunt of ferocious animals; through it runs a deep sandy road. The gentleman who was driving me in his curricle, told me that he had killed five tigers on the spot we then were, not more than a month before, and a most singular circumstance occurred. He had gone on to the village afterwards, where he had left his gig, in order to return home in it, when passing a bush where one of the tigers were found that he had shot, a tigress darted out and (what is very unusual) pursued him so swiftly, that notwithstanding he put his horse at speed, he had the greatest difficulty to escape her. The only reason he could imagine for her being so furious was, that it might have been one of her cubs which he had destroyed.

At a place called *Soondree*, about fourteen miles farther, the country appeared well cultivated, which is rather astonishing in such a neighbourhood, and the road tolerably good. We passed through two or three groves of the sweet-scented *bauble* tree,[359] whose odour resembles that of mignionette.

On the 21st we quitted *Soondree*, and reached the judge's house at *Moradabad*[360] to breakfast. The city of *Moradabad* stands in the centre of the most park-like country imaginable. Among the hills, not far from it, the apple, cherry, walnut, arbutus, and beech trees, flourish; and plenty of wild strawberries are found in the woods. The neighbouring gardens produce peaches, apples, strawberries, pine apples, and all sorts of vegetable in the highest perfection. The culture of potatoes[361] is particularly encouraged in this district, and succeeds remarkably well. In seasons when there is a scarcity of grain, (which frequently happens,) this vegetable may prove a most valuable substitute, and probably the introduction of it into India, be the means of saving many thousand lives. Although first cultivated by its European inhabitants, the natives are all fond of it, and eat it without scruple.

The houses at this place are in general large, and chiefly built of brick. The one in which the judge resides is a perfect palace; indeed it *was* formerly the palace of a Rohillah chief. It is surrounded by an out-work of embrasures, bastions, &c.; is situated outside the city, on a space sufficiently large to encamp an army; and was once attacked by the force under *Ameer Khan*,[362] (when united with *Holkar*, he threatened to exterminate the Europeans,) but gallantly and successfully defended by Mr. Leicester, at that time judge of the district, until troops arrived to his relief.

There are six principal squares, in which all the houses are of brick, and one square in the centre of the city, not only spacious, but magnificent. It has within it seventy gates, the whole being surrounded by a high brick wall. The streets, contrary to the plan usually pursued in this country, are wide. No manufacture is carried on here; but the inhabitants are celebrated as being excellent mechanics, particularly in the upholstering line. It is a station for one battalion of Seapoys, and a healthy situation at all seasons of the year. The river *Ram Gonga*[363] runs parallel with the north-east side of the city, and supplies the inhabitants with good water and plenty of excellent fish.

We remained here until the 28th, when the commissioners took their departure for *Futteh Ghur*.[364] We forded the *Gongon* in carriages, near the village of *Syfree*. Our road lay the whole way through fields of green barley or wheat, bounded on the right by groves of mango trees; while the left presented a pleasing and extensive prospect. A large estate, belonging to the principal *zemeendar*,[365] wore the semblance of great security and comfort. Passing along a fine hard road and level country, richly cultivated, we saw a place named *Ryepore*, near the large town of *Secrowly*, embosomed in gardens. Our tents were pitched on an extensive level of turf, surrounded by trees of various kinds. Villages in the *Rohillah* country[366] are in no instance surrounded by a wall, as in the districts of *Coel, Delhi, Meratt,* and *Agra;* (in fact, throughout the *Douab;*) neither have the Rohillas any fences to their fields. Sugar-cane, wheat, and barley, appear to be the chief productions of their country.

Neither the strength of our party, nor the sentries which at all times paraded before the doors of our tents, could at all times secure us from thieves; but we found a complete guard, at this place, in the person of a small terrier that had been fastened to one of the bed-posts. About the middle of the night, when all was quiet in the camp, (and the sentries, I suspect, asleep,) this little animal became very restless, then barked violently, and at length broke from his fastening, and made a dart towards the opposite wall of the tent. The glimmering light of the lamp discovered to me at the moment two large staring eyes, glaring frightfully round in search of plunder. The dog could not get at the man; but the alarm was given, and the intended thief secured: he had nothing on but a cummerbund*; yet in *that* were secreted two knives, sharpened at either edge. This place is named *Shoepore*.

---

* Cummerbund is a breadth of cloth wound round the loins.

From hence we continued our route over a fertile country, with occasional inequalities scarcely deserving the name of hills, to *Alli Gunge*. The cultivation reached the road on either side, interrupted only by occasional groves of the mango tree, through which we drove. On the other side *Alli Gunge*, the soil becomes sandy, and the face of the country assumes a totally different appearance. After crossing a small river, we entered what is called a *jow jungle*,[367] much resembling the birch wood in England, of which brooms are made. This continued for about three miles, and conducted us to the banks of the *Ram Gonga*, where ferryboats had been prepared, but, as it was then practicable, I preferred crossing it on my elephant. An elephant is the only animal, except a camel, that can ford this river, even when it is at the lowest. In the rainy season it would be impracticable to ford it at all, as it is then both deep and rapid.

From hence we drove in a curricle to *Barreilli*,[368] a city inhabited entirely by Mussulmen; it has been celebrated in history, and is still of considerable consequence. It stands on an extensive plain, bounded on every side by lofty trees. The soil is deep and sandy; the city itself irregularly built; and its inhabitants, chiefly *Rohillas*, are so very uncivil, (to give the mildest term to their demeanour,) that no European can enter it without the risk of being insulted. These people possess the pride of ancestry, in a preeminent degree. The city swarms with the insolent, proud descendants of *Haffiz Ramut*, chief of the *Rohillas:* he was killed in battle at this place by *Sujah Dowlah*, Nawaab of Lucknow, at the head of the forces belonging to the Emperor of Delhi, who, it is reported, owed his success on this occasion to the firmness of his English allies under the command of Colonel Champion.[369],* This circumstance is still fresh in the remembrance of the natives, whose veneration for their chief is very great; and their detestation of the English, from the part they took against him, proportionably so.

The city of *Bareilly* was founded by *Haffiz Ramut*;[370] and his remains are interred there, beneath a splendid monument erected to his memory. The inhabitants of this city are always ripe for rebellion, but are incapable of much resistance, having neither wall, nor ditch, to protect them. Among these are a few merchants who trade in drugs and timber, from the neighbouring hills, to whom the support of the English Government is of consequence. It is what is called a *Sudder* Station, having a court of circuit, a court of appeal, a judge of the district, collector, chaplain, surgeon, &c. with one battalion of Seapoys. In a court of circuit there are two judges, in a court of appeal three. The Seapoy cantonment is about a mile from the city. The houses of the civilians occupy an open space between the city and the cantonment: near them stands a fortified jail.

We passed nearly a month at *Bareilly*. It is almost the only place in India where the nights throughout the year are never oppressively hot. This place is famous for carpenters' work of all descriptions. They imitate the painting on China trunks, boxes, tables, &c. so well, that it is scarcely possible to distinguish them from

---

* See Hamilton's Account of the Rohillah War[371].

the original articles. Their chairs are beautifully varnished, and tastefully shaped. The *Bareilly* furniture is indeed justly estimated throughout the provinces, and produces a fund of wealth to the manufacturers. The facility with which they get timber from the hills, greatly assists their views. From hence to *Pilibete*,[372] which lies at the foot of those hills from whence the timber is brought, is only two days' journey. Being so near these hills, we were desirous of visiting the source of the *Gogra*,[373] which river takes its rise from thence; and accordingly, on the 1st of March, sent forward our camp equipage. The two first marches were unmarked by any particular occurrence: the country over which we travelled was flat and uninteresting; but on the third day we entered a beautiful and extensive forest of *sissoo* trees,[374] infested by every wild animal that the country produces, notwithstanding, the natives appeared to live in it without any visible means of defence. Curious to know the reason of such apparent apathy, I learned that they were all Predestinarians, and often saw their cattle and children carried off without an attempt to rescue them. "Their time is come," they say, "and if you should succeed in saving them from the threatened danger, another, still more terrible, is sure to be at hand."

The second day, in passing through this immense forest, we met travellers whose countenances bespoke them of a different race. They proved indeed to be inhabitants of the second, and third range of mountains, bringing their merchandize, chiefly drugs, to an annual fair, held about this time, at a village named *Bellary*, on the outskirts of the forest. *Assafœtida*[375] is a principal article of traffic, as it is a favourite ingredient in the cookery, both of Hindoo and Mussulman. It is a low bush, with long leaves, that are cut off near the stem, when a milky juice exudes, which hardens gradually, like opium, but loses its virtue, if left long exposed to the sun. The people I am speaking of, are of a bright copper colour; their stature is short and thick; they have broad faces, flat noses, small eyes, scarcely any beard, and no mustachios. They do not wear turbans like the natives of Hindostan, but fasten their hair in a bunch on the top of the head, with a long black bodkin. In appearance they strongly resemble those figures often seen on old china jars; and, living on the borders of Tartary, we may justly conclude them of Chinese extraction. Nothing could exceed the beautiful wild scenery of this day's march. We continued to ride through a thick forest, intersected by innumerable running streams, clear as the purest crystal, over which was occasionally thrown a tree in full foliage, to answer the purpose of a bridge. The approach to one of these streams was invariably marked by the feet of wild animals. On one part of our route, which lay along the edge of a steep precipice, we distinguished the footsteps of wild elephants, as if a drove had lately passed, and this appearance continued for more than a mile. Our guide informed us that a large male elephant had been occasionally seen, and was recognised, on this path, for many years; frequently attacking, and, of course, destroying, the unprotected traveller. As *we* were armed, and strongly guarded, I felt no apprehension, but could not avoid being anxious for the arrival of the servants that were to follow. Nature must surely have regarded with peculiar complacency this most enchanting spot. A rich valley, reposing beneath a majestic acclivity, covered with herds of cattle, grazing on its velvet pasture, under the shade of spreading branches, with here and there a cluster of peasants' huts, were its peculiar characteristics. All appeared tranquil as in the midst of the most civilized country, nor seemed to fear their lordly neighbours. Our breakfast tent was pitched a short distance beyond this, on the banks of the *Gogra*. The mountains, although in fact, at a great distance from us, appeared but just on the opposite shore, forming one of the finest landscapes I ever beheld. When the heat of the day had a little subsided, we sallied forth to enjoy the prospect, occasionally seating ourselves on a projecting rock. The moon was near the full, and arose from behind the mountains superlatively bright. To what sublimity of idea did their vast summits, illumined by her rays, give rise, while their more humble bases were veiled in obscurity!

Next morning, we pursued our way, and safely arrived at *Behrmundeo*. Our tents were pitched on a plain of the liveliest verdure. In front ran the *Gogra*, slowly meandering over its pebbly bed, bounded on the opposite shore by almost perpendicular mountains. The sides of these mountains clothed with trees of various foliage, many of them in full blossom, impregnating the air with the most exhilarating odours; while not more than a hundred yards from us, lay the forest, filled with game of every kind. The few native inhabitants of this country, are solely occupied in tending their herds and cutting wood.

The river supplies them with fish and wild fowl in abundance, both which they eat without scruple. Soon after breakfast, our Hindoo servants asked permission to pay their obeisance to the deity who is said to preside there. I confess my curiosity was raised to see a spot so celebrated: at sun-set, therefore, on the following evening, we repaired thither, when instead of a temple, as I expected, decorated with all the emblems of Hindoo superstition, I beheld only a pedestal of granite, about five feet high, with three rusty iron spikes of a foot long stuck into the top of it. These were ornamented with a few faded flowers and boughs, the pious offerings of our people, while at its base were seated three squalid unfortunate children of a mendicant *fakeer*, who, with mouths and eyes wide open, appeared like horrible fixtures to the place. Some *gentlemen*, we were told, had been at this place before, but never *any lady*. Finding so little attraction here, we walked along the sands, which as the river subsides, are left dry, and soon become hard, for a considerable distance. Large fragments of rock occasionally interrupted our progress. Near these were a cluster of deserted huts, that our guide informed us, were occupied at a particular season of the year, by the hill people, whose mountain dwellings, he pointed out to us, at an immense distance on the summits, and between the fissures of the opposite range. They came down, he said, to sift the sand for gold dust, lumps of which were frequently found there, as large as a common sized hazel-nut. This forms another part of their traffic with *Bellary*, the village before-mentioned, and on the approach of summer, these people return to their snowy dwellings. We now seemed to have reached the uttermost parts of the earth. Huge snow-capped mountains, frowning in awful majesty, formed an amphitheatre around us, from one of which (about the centre of this vast space) the river takes its rise. Not a human being to be seen or heard. It was stillness all.

Oh, had I but the pen of *Young*[376] or *Milton*[377] to describe it! The delightful reverie into which I had fallen, was at length interrupted by my companion, who having strayed some little distance, returned to point out to me amongst the varied foliage, that of the fir, oak, and ash. On returning to the tents, I mentioned having seen them, which induced some of the gentlemen of our party to ascend these mountains, and explore. I wished much to have accompanied them, but was persuaded to relinquish the attempt, as it could only be accomplished on foot, and, of course, with very great fatigue. Two only of the gentlemen reached the summit, and *they* passed the night in a hut that appeared not to have been long untenanted. After traversing a beautiful green sward, for about a quarter of a mile, along the bank of the river, they gradually ascended to the height of forty feet, and found themselves on a flat cultivated space. From hence they proceeded along a winding path, occasionally impeded by mountain rills, near which they observed innumerable plants of extraordinary beauty*; also the fern, ivy, and common dock-plant of England, and they had no doubt, from the nature of the soil, but that violets and primroses might have been found, had there been time to search for them. Sometimes they came to a beautiful valley interspersed with trees and huts, where the wild strawberry, raspberry, barberry, and hawthorn, flourished in abundance; at others, they were obliged to be assisted by their guides up perpendicular heights of six or seven feet. Near one of these, they were led to expect a mountain torrent of some magnitude, but were disappointed, from having missed the turn which would have led them to it; it proved to be four hours' walk beyond the village at which they halted for the night. Two beautifully picturesque valleys conducted them to an acclivity covered with the pine, fir, and mountain ash, intermixed with those trees which are peculiar to the more southern provinces. After toiling for four hours, over a path scarcely wide enough for one person, sometimes bordering on a precipice of tremendous depth; they reached the summit, on which they found a deserted village. The inhabitants, it was concluded, were gone to the fair at *Bellary*. A friend of ours, thinking it might prove a good speculation, ordered two or three hundred small caps of scarlet cloth to be sent there the following year, and exposed for sale. No sooner were these produced, than the hill people crowded round and evinced the strongest anxiety to possess them. So rapid was the exchange for drugs effected, and so clamorous did they become when all were nearly disposed of, that the vender was actually obliged, by stratagem, to make good his retreat.

But to rerurn to my narrative. These unsuspicious people, having left their habitations open, our gentlemen entered one of the huts, in order to take some refreshment and repose; but on calling for the provisions, what was their dismay to find that none were brought, although at least a dozen people had started with them. A bottle of brandy had been given to one of the guides, but by some accident he

---

* Some of them they brought to me, and I succeeded in propagating them, but they degenerated as well in colour as in size.

had broken it. In fact, neither cold meat nor brandy had arrived. They had then no other resource left, than to kindle a few sticks, in order to warm themselves, and determine to be as comfortable as circumstances would permit. So, dismissing the guides, and barricading the door with logs of wood, they sought shelter from hunger in the arms of Morpheus;[378] thus they might probably have remained some hours insensible to its attack, had not an alarm of a different nature occurred, which filled their minds at the moment, with a sentiment not very *unlike fear*. About midnight, the door of the hut was forcibly assailed, accompanied by voices who loudly demanded entrance. The wind had risen almost to a hurricane, and whistling through the interstices of their miserable dwelling, rendered quite unintelligible the language of the intruders. Having neglected to provide themselves either with fire-arms, or side-arms, they debated whether it would be more prudent rather to make the door more secure than to open it. One of the gentlemen, however, suggested that they might still be unable to defend themselves for any time; nor could they entertain the slightest hopes of succour from their guides, of whom it was most probable they should see no more; for, upon the least appearance of hostility, these men generally decamp. It was at length determined, that they should each take a log of wood in his hand, and boldly open the door; when, ridiculous to tell, instead of the abuse and blows they were prepared to parry, a party greeted them who had been sent by us with some good cheer. For we had learned after they were gone, that the provisions they intended to have taken with them, had been inadvertently left behind. No longer grumbling at the interruption to their slumbers, they seated themselves upon the ground, and never (as they afterwards assured me) made a more comfortable meal. These huts are composed of pieces from the rock, cemented together by clay, and thickly thatched. At dawn of day, our gentlemen began to descend, which they found as tedious, and more terrific than their labours on the preceding day. One of them had the curiosity to measure the height of the mountain, and found it from its base to the summit, exactly four thousand feet.*

The following day was passed in exploring the country in a contrary direction. Game of every description rose almost beneath our elephants' feet; amongst which were a great number of the black feathered partridge, equally as fine in flavour as beautiful in plumage; they are shaped like those of England, but rather larger: these and quails seemed to abound in the vallies where we were.

One night, while we remained here, a circumstance of rather an alarming nature occurred, but, providentially, was not succeeded by any serious consequence. The roar of a wild elephant near our camp, threw every thing into confusion, and we had reason to fear his nearer approach, as one of the female elephants that conveyed the tents was answering to his call, and all efforts to silence her were vain. It was supposed that she might, some time or other, have been used as a decoy

---

* The cattle bred in these hills are remarkably small, and nice eating; the meat being very fat, and the grain extremely fine. The bullocks in general are about the size of an English calf.

elephant, for our people were obliged to chain her round a large tree to prevent her running off, and also to kindle fires round the camp to keep him at a distance. But our perils were not destined to end here; as, before the fires were fairly lighted, a hungry tiger sprung on one of the bullocks and dragged him off. It was too dark to distinguish the tiger, but his growl could not be mistaken, which added to the screech of the elephants, made a most terrific concert. In vain did the gentlemen assure me, that the constant firing of musketry kept up by our attendants, would secure *us* from harm; I trembled at every joint, and most heartily wished myself any where else; nor were my fears dissipated until the return of day-light.

We next morning bid adieu to this haunt of our formidable enemies, and encamped about fourteen miles distant; where, free from shade, the sun was intensely hot, and the nights extremely cold. While taking our usual ramble one evening, we got intelligence of some neighbours that might have proved still more dangerous than those we had quitted. A party of five hundred *Mowattys*[379] had pitched their tents about a mile and a half from ours, and were reported to have plundered several villages in their route. These are a description of robbers, something like gypsies, and very desperate. As we were not ambitious of becoming acquainted with them, no time was lost in collecting our small forces, and striking the tents; or in taking speedy measures, as silently as possible, to decamp. We halted not again until we were entirely clear of the forest. The change of climate experienced now, was very great; not only the days, but nights, became oppressively hot under canvas; and although highly gratified by the trip, I was by no means sorry to find myself in a *bungalow* at *Bareilly*. March and April are the only months in which Europeans can visit *Behrmundeo* with safety. Before that time the weather is too cold, and afterwards, the water is so impregnated with melted snow, mixed with putrid leaves that are washed down from the hills, as to render it certain death to the traveller who attempts it. We just returned to *Bareilly* in time to eat ortolans[380] in perfection; they come in season with the hot winds, and are found in immense flights wherever there is a sandy space. These birds are about the size of larks, and when fried with crumbs of bread, are really delicious. At first, they are like little lumps of butter, and may be eaten bones and all; but towards the latter end of the season, they fall off amazingly, and are at all times so delicate that if you attempt to keep them alive, they are good for nothing; they are not killed with shot, but with a grain called *gram*.[381] Ortolans and mangoes are great delicacies during the hot season, and fortunately both are to be procured in abundance.

After remaining a short time at *Bareilly*, we proceeded towards Futty Ghur. In two marches we reached *Kutterah*,[382] the scene of battle between *Sujah Dowlah* and *Haffiz Ramut*, of whom I have before spoken. This town of *Kutterah* is large, populous, and in good repair. It was built by *Sujah Dowlah* to commemorate his victory over the *Rohillahs;* it is protected by a high brick wall, and secured by ponderous gates thickly barred with iron.* The wind having blown hard all night,

---

* Distant from *Bareilly* about thirty miles.

and still continuing to do so, I travelled in my palankeen. This country is more than usually diversified with hill and dale, which, with a variety of cultivation, afforded a most agreeable prospect; but we had the misfortune to find our tents pitched in an open space, without the shelter of a single tree, and the wind continuing to blow, raised the light sandy particles in such quantities as to render our situation, that day, by no means enviable. Added to this, none of the insignificant villages near us, afforded even fodder for our cattle. The country, from this place, continued level, and extremely fertile. We passed through the village of *Acbar*, and about four miles further, that of *Sianna*. Near the latter were some luxuriant *banyan* trees,[383] which formed an extensive shade, while clumps of bamboos in every direction, added much to the beauty of the scene. The wind had now considerably fallen, but the threatening aspect of the weather portended an approaching storm, it did not however deter me from mounting an elephant at this place, and we were fortunate enough to arrive at our encampment before the rain commenced, which soon afterwards fell in torrents, accompanied by heavy thunder, and some vivid flashes of lightning. The town of *Jellalabad*,[384] where we halted, is built upon an eminence, and contains a pretty strong fort. We found plenty of game in the neighbourhood, particularly hares, and the common brown feathered partridge. I saw also several foxes; these are the prettiest creatures imaginable, beautifully formed, and not much higher than a rabbit; the colour is the same as those in England.

The road from *Jellalabad* to *Umrutpore*[385] is very bad; I travelled it in an open carriage, at the imminent risk of my life. The prospect, however, is extremely beautiful, the country being checkered by groves of the *kudgua, mango*, and sweet-scented *banbool* trees.[386] About two miles after leaving *Jellalabad*, we recrossed the river *Ram Gonga*. As it was too deep to ford, we had recourse to boats. So thick a fog prevailed, that although the river is not broad, we could not distinguish the opposite side, and the cold dampness of the atmosphere was exceedingly unpleasant. About six miles farther, we crossed another stream of about three feet deep, beyond which, by a gradual ascent, we reached our tents at *Umrutpore*. This village stands upon a plain of considerable extent, as smooth as any bowling-green.

In the course of the journey to-day, a gentleman of the party being on horseback, was attacked by a wild buffalo, who, inflicting a wound with his horns on the flank of the horse, so frightened him, that he set off at speed, and by that means probably saved the life of his rider. I was fortunately on an elephant, of whom these animals are afraid. From *Umrutpore* to *Futty Ghur*, the distance is only eighteen miles; but the road is as bad as it can be, and passable; particularly the last two miles, which led through a thick *jow jungle* to the river Ganges. Here we crossed in boats so rudely constructed, that as the wind blew strong, and the stream was exceedingly rapid, I did not feel very comfortable.

Futty Ghur being the station appointed for the Commissioners to reside at, we left them there, and returned to the place from whence we had started, viz. *Secundra* near *Agra*.

CHAPTER XIX.[387]

AT *Secundra* we remained until the middle of September, 1809. At that time a committee was ordered to proceed to *Poosa*,[388] (below *Patna*,) where the East India Company had a *stud*, in order to select horses for the cavalry. Once more, then, I was to become a traveller, and destined to proceed in a contrary direction. We were to *march* as far as *Futty Ghur*, which stands on the banks of the Ganges, and thence go by water down the country.

Having in a former part of this narrative given a description of the road between *Futty Ghur* and *Secundra*, I shall pass over the present march, and commence my journal from the period of our embarkation at Futty Ghur on the 27th of September, 1809. Our boats having been prepared for the voyage, consisting of a *budgerow* to sleep in, a *pinnace*[389] to eat in, a boat fitted up as a kitchen; another for poultry, sheep, and stores; another for servants and baggage; and a sixth for the washing-boat and Hindoo servants; and being joined by the fleets of two other gentlemen, we set sail with a fair wind towards *Khawnpore*,[390] and arrived there on the 29th to dinner. The next day we sailed rapidly down the stream for twenty miles, and then came to for the night; on which occasion the boats were made fast to long wooden pegs, driven into the bank for that purpose. This gives the servants an opportunity of dressing their food on shore; besides which, shoals and quick-sands are so numerous in the Ganges, that it would be dangerous to move by night.

At day-break the next morning we again set sail, but had not proceeded far before our *budgerow* got aground, and it was six hours before she was under weigh again. This was by no means an agreeable situation on a river full of quick-sands. The weather was fortunately mild; and towards evening we reached a village named *Tickerry*, which being inhabited by Hindoos, furnished no supplies for our other servants. Having undergone much fatigue during the day, (for all hands are obliged to put a shoulder to the wheel in cases of emergency,) they preferred rest, and deprivation of a meal, to walking any distance in search of one. This circumstance, fortunately, does not often occur, as a man's strength in this country is estimated by the quantity of food that he eats. I have frequently known a palankeen bearer devour two *seers*[391] of boiled rice at a meal; and so proud are they of an enormous appetite, that they challenge each other to *eat*, as English clowns do to *fight*. *Kumjour wallah*, (a man of little strength,) is one of the most opprobrious epithets that can be used towards them; indeed, of so much importance do they consider a hearty meal, that while thus engaged you may summon a man in vain—he will not stir until he has finished it. Happily, the ceremony is a short one. They dress their victuals in earthen vessels, which are broken in pieces the moment that the contents are removed into brass ones; (out of which it is eaten;) and these are scowered with sand after every meal. Not a servant in the family, except the sweeper, would touch any thing from their master's table if they were starving; (in fact, Hindoos do not eat animal food at all;[392] and meat for Mussulmen must be prepared after the Jewish custom,[393] or they are forbidden by their law to eat of it:) so they betook themselves to their usual resource in such cases, composing themselves to sleep; some on the top of their boat, and others under an old sail on the bank. *Our* pinnace being the largest in the fleet, it was agreed that the party should assemble in it at breakfast and dinner. Of an evening, when the boats were made fast for the night, (which was generally the case about sun-set,) some of us walked or rode out until dinner was ready. The dinner hour here is eight in the evening.

The mornings began now to grow cool; and the party proceeded in high spirits, with a certainty that the weather would become pleasanter every day.

Finding ourselves near the town of *Jehanabad*,[394] which contains an excellent market, we came to there for the night considerably before our usual hour; but this frequently answers, as there may not be another good place to stop at when you wish to do so, the banks being often craggy and irregular, and no village within hail.

About noon the next day we came opposite to the ancient city of *Allahabad*, but the river had fallen so low that we could not approach it, we were consequently obliged to make for the opposite side of the river *Jumna*, where the water is always deep.

After procuring some necessary supplies by means of a small wherry[395] from *Allahabad*, we proceeded next day as usual; but no village being in sight at the hour for *legowing*,[396] our boats were made fast to a sand-bank in the middle of the river. Our voyage to-day was by no means agreeable; for the river was bounded on either side by high, and almost perpendicular banks. The wind blew strong from the eastward during the night, which being against the stream, caused a heavy swell, and annoyed us not a little; in fact, we were obliged to quit the position we had taken, and not without great difficulty gained the opposite shore. The river shortly after assumed the appearance of a sea, for which our boats were by no means calculated. Unfortunately for us, it soon increased to a gale of wind; during which, one of our baggage boats was upset, and the *budgerow* broke from her moorings, drifting with considerable rapidity towards a place in the Nawaab's country inhabited by thieves, whose chief support is from the plunder of boats, which they have a most ingenious mode of attacking without being seen. Accustomed to swimming and diving from their infancy, the water may almost be termed their natural element. When they perceive boats *legowed* for the night, and that the crews are retired to rest, they cover their heads with earthen pots, having two holes bored through them for eyes, and slipping into the river, float silently round until an opportunity offers of climbing upon deck, when making themselves masters of all property that is moveable, without disturbing any one, they swim off with it securely. So expert are they at this occupation, that a gentleman has frequently missed his writing desk in the morning, without the smallest appearance of any one having been there.

The next morning was cloudy, with a drizzling rain; but the wind proved fair, and we let go our anchorage. The river however winds so considerably here, that a fair wind one half hour is contrary the next, so that we made but little progress. The banks were still high, almost inaccessible: on their summits we observed several large villages. The weather had now become cool and pleasant. In the course of the day we saw a great many fishing boats, that amply supplied our table with delicious fish: one sort, called the *roe*, resembles the codfish we have in England. Mullet of all descriptions are very plentiful in this river. In a few hours the face of the country wore quite a different appearance: sloping banks clothed with verdure, villages disposed amid groves of trees, and whole families bathing and playing in the stream, succeeded to the barren craggy banks we had just left, and proved a most agreeable change.

About noon we arrived at *Mirzapore*,[397] a celebrated place for the manufacture of carpets, little, if at all inferior, to those of Turkey or Persia. *Mirzapore* is a station for civilians, that is to say, a judge, collector, registrar, assistants, &c. with one or two regiments of Seapoys. It is also a principal seat of customs.

The following morning, at an early hour, we passed the fort of *Chunar*,[398] which is considered one of the hottest places in India, and reached *Benares* about seven o'clock in the evening. Villages became daily more numerous, and ferryboats plied in abundance.

We passed this day two indigo factories, and the military station of *Ghazipore*, as likewise the fort and town of *Buxar*. From *Buxar* to *Chuperah*[399] the river winds considerably, and there are many quick-sands which, in the rainy season, render the navigation extremely dangerous. A gentleman, whose *budgerow* stuck on one of these, was obliged to walk backwards and forwards on it the whole night, knee-deep in water; for had he stopped but for one minute, he would have been swallowed up for ever. A boat from the shore, as soon as they could see him, put off to his assistance; but his own, with all the property it contained, was irretrievably lost. This part of the country is well cultivated, and rendered picturesque from the numerous villages and groves with which its banks abound.

The traffic on the *Ganges* is really wonderful: we passed in one day upwards of two hundred merchant vessels, laden with grain quite to the water's edge. About two o'clock a storm came on from the south-west, which nearly sunk our cooking boat, and obliged us to make fast to the nearest bank: it lasted without intermission for at least four hours. These storms are very common in the rainy season, which is called the south-west monsoon. It begins at *Khanpore* about the 20th of June, and continues until the end of October: in Bengal a month earlier. Heavy rolling clouds, from the south-west to the north-east point of the compass, announce its approach. The sky assumes a terrific aspect, and after some days of extreme heat, the rain comes down in torrents. The first shower or two, causes the earth to smoke and (such you can almost fancy to be the case) to hiss like water falling upon a hot plate of iron, but after that, the air becomes cool, and the whole atmosphere breathes perfume, carrying delightful fragrance on every breeze. This heavy rain does not continue, as in *Bengal*, to inundate the country for many weeks, giving to it the appearance of one large sheet of water, but is succeeded at intervals by fine reviving weather. The ravines which intersect the upper provinces carry off the superabundant water.

About ten o'clock the next morning we reached *Chuperah*, and finding it a cheap place for natives to purchase provisions, they were all permitted to go on shore. This delayed us so long, that we did not reach *Danapore* until the morning after. Here we crossed a small branch of the Ganges, (which by an accumulation of sand had been separated from the main river,) and continuing our course for ten miles farther, entered the river *Gunduk*, and soon reached *Soanepore*.[400] This village is situated on a promontory, between the two rivers *Gunduk* and *Ganges*. An annual fair is held here for those of the East India Company's stud-horses that turn out undersized, (or too low for the cavalry.) Here the cocoa-nut, bamboo, and tamarind trees, so beautifully intermix their foliage, that it may be justly termed a most luxuriant spot. We quitted the boats, and having despatched our camp equipage, mounted horses, and rode the first fourteen miles towards *Poosa*. We now came to a stream, which not being fordable, we were obliged to dismount, and cross it on a raft made of bamboos, fixed upon three canoes abreast of each other: an extensive lake now presented itself, covered with wild fowl. The surrounding country appeared populous, and consisted chiefly of pasture lands. Soon after crossing the narrow deep stream of which I have been speaking, we encamped under the spreading branches of a tree that afforded ample shelter for ourselves and cattle. The ground, as far as the eye could reach, was covered with the most lively verdure, interspersed with stately trees: here and there stood a hamlet, or cottage, neatly thatched, round which the stream meandered slowly, and the cattle browzed contentedly on its banks. After travelling the next morning in an open carriage for eighteen miles, on an execrable road, we arrived at *Poosa*. The superintendant at this time was a Mr. Moorcroft, who afterwards penetrated the third range of the Snowy Mountains, and published an ingenious work on the subject of his researches.[401] The pasture at *Poosa* is remarkably fine. The bamboo plant flourishes here in perfection, forming alike an admirable fence to their lands, and considerably adding to their beauty. A river called the *Choota Gunduk* fertilizes the soil. There appears however a strong objection to this place—I mean the climate—as is the case throughout the province of *Tirhoot*,[402] in which district, *Poosa* is situated: a cold, damp atmosphere, and constant fog in the winter; a hot, damp, close one, in the rains; (when very few escape the ravages of fever and ague;) and in the hot season a burning sun, without sufficient wind to cool, even by means of tatties, and yet too hot a one to live without them. The seasons in India are only divided into these three, of four months in each; but they are very different in the upper and lower provinces. The province of *Tirhoot* is favourable only for the growth of indigo and production of horses.

The superintendant's mansion stands alone: his nearest neighbour, with the exception of those attached to the establishment, lives twelve miles off. On the 4th of November we quitted *Poosa*, and crossed the Ganges by three separate ferry boats to *Patna*, being obliged to traverse beds of sand between each. From *Patna* we proceeded in carriages to *Danapore*, where we did not arrive until one o'clock, much fatigued, and almost starved. On the morning of the 12th, accompanied by a party from *Danapore*, we re-crossed the Ganges, in order to be present at the *Hadjepore* fair,[403] so called from a village inland, of that name, although the booths are erected and merchandize exposed at *Soanepore*, the village before mentioned as standing on a promontory at the junction of the rivers *Ganges*, and *Gunduk*, forming at this time the gayest scene imaginable. The surrounding scenery is very beautiful, being a continuation of woods along the bank of either river. Those who preferred living in their boats, sheltered by the spreading branches of luxuriant trees, made them fast to the shelving bank. On the present occasion, many were gaily decked with flags, and formed a line of above a mile in length. The noise of firing matchlocks, and the sounds of native music, proved to *our* ears exceedingly annoying. There is a fine race-course at this place, which was well attended, and the gentlemen had good sport. Instead of a ball as they have in England, this was a dinner for separate parties, provided by the same *traiteur*,[404] under the trees. The business of the Committee, and individual amusement, kept us here until the 28th, when we all returned to *Danapore*.

On the 3rd of December we turned our faces westward. Having before described the country between *Patna* and *Khanpore*, I shall only add, that we travelled it either on horseback or in an open carriage, and arrived there without accident on the 4th of January. Having passed a few days with our friends, we commenced our march towards *Meerat* by the way of *Chobipore*,[405] leaving *Futty Ghur* upon our right, and passed a fort belonging to the Rajah of *Tutteah*, before which Colonel Guthrie, of the Company's service, lost his life in 1804.[406] A little farther, on the same road, brought us to a place called *Canoge*,[407] where many curious coins have been dug up of as ancient date as Alexander's conquest,[408] and with his name upon them: how they came there has never been satisfactorily accounted for. The ruins are very extensive; and the natives make a great profit from these coins. They manufacture and dye red muslin for turbans in a superior manner at Canoge; also coarse cloths, checked muslins, rose water, otta of roses, &c. I observed also a number of gardens filled with poppies for producing opium, which they obtain by making an incision into the round part of the poppy, just below the flower. This is generally done in the evening, and before morning a sufficient quantity of opium exudes to take off. It appears like a clear dark gum, which hardens by exposure to the air.

Our route from hence lay through ravines for nearly fourteen miles. Scarcely could a space be found large enough to pitch our tents upon. We were much disturbed at night by wolves, which the sentries affirmed were the largest they had ever seen.

Next morning's march brought us near to a fortified place, reported to be the haunt of banditti. Our guide, by way of encouragement, informed us that a few days before a gentleman was robbed here, and two of his servants put to death. We had, however, the good fortune to pass the night unmolested, and proceeded as usual on the following day. A dreary road, over a bleak and sandy plain, much cut up by heavy loads, appeared before us. The wind blew exceedingly cold; and, to add to my discomfort, when about the centre of this dreary wild, one of the springs of our carriage snapped. Behold me, then, standing the picture of misery, shivering with cold, and sharply pressed by hunger, (for we had not yet breakfasted,) while they bound up, as well as circumstances would permit, the untimely fracture. Blacksmiths and carpenters are found in every village, so that the damage was easily repaired when we arrived there. Next morning the weather was so cold, that I preferred riding the first five or six miles on horseback; the carriage was consequently sent forward by one of the grooms, who having by some chance let go the reins, a spirited Arab mare, being in the shafts, set off at speed, overturned the gig, and almost killed the man. We received a present to-day from the Rajah of a wild hog that he had just killed; dressed some of it for dinner, and found it excellent, resembling both in appearance and flavour the most delicate veal. From hence we reached *Sarseney* to breakfast, which place having described in my journey from *Secundra* to *Hurdoar*, I shall here pass over; suffice it to say, that the town appeared more flourishing than at that period, and the fort exhibited more evident marks of decay. Its former Rajah, *Bagoin Sing*,[409] was so attached to the place from its having descended to him through a long line of ancestry, that he offered Government a large sum of money for the re-possession of it; but prudence forbids their acquiescence. He is one of those who are not to be trusted.

After marching the three successive days with little variation to the scene, and no remarkable incidents, we arrived near the fort of *Mala Ghur*, the residence of *Bahadar Khan*,[410] (a quiet, civil ally of the English Government,) and encamped close to his garden. *Bahadar Khan* himself was absent; but his brother, who lives with him, paid us a complimentary visit with a present of fruit and vegetables, and in the evening we walked with him over the gardens.

The next morning we drove through a beautiful country, over a fine hard road for about twelve miles, to *Galowty*, a village surrounded by clumps of trees and green fields. During this ride over a fine open plain, we started a herd of antelopes, which the dogs we had with us pursued for about half an hour full in our view, and afforded excellent sport. The antelopes at length eluded them by darting into a thicket. They are the most elegant animals in shape, as well as action, that I ever beheld.

The first four miles from *Galowty* led through fields of grain, chiefly barley; after which we entered a *dock jungle* that was extremely difficult to drive through on account of the stumps. This continued all the way to *Hauper*.

Hauper is a large town, situated on an eminence, with a brick wall all round it. It is a station for invalided Seapoys of the Mussulman persuasion, and a very refractory set they are. Their chief employment is drinking *bang*, (a spirituous liquor extracted from an herb somewhat resembling mint,) and smoking. An officer resides on the spot, but he cannot keep them out of mischief: they are always inclined to be insolent to strangers, and sometimes have been known to plunder them. Many fine large groves of the mango tree appeared about this place.

From *Hauper* we proceeded still through a *dock jungle* to *Ker Koondah*, a village as inhospitable as could be well imagined, and one in which little was to be got, and much apprehended. We did not however retire to rest until a very late hour, and kept the sentries upon the alert for the rest of the night, so that we escaped the usual fate of travellers at that place, (the loss of their property,) and arrived safely to dinner at *Meerat* next day.

Thus ended our trip from *Agra* to *Poosa*, and from *Poosa* to *Meerat*, a journey of sixteen hundred miles, performed chiefly in an open carriage. As it may perhaps amuse those who have not been in India, I annex a list of our establishment for the march.

Two palankeens.
Twenty-four bearers.
One sirdah, or head bearer, and his assistant.
Two elephants with their drivers, and two attendants. One of these carried a tent.
One gig.
Eight horses.
Eight grooms.
Eight grass cutters for the horses. Here it may not be amiss to mention, that the horses do not eat hay as in England, but the fibrous roots of grass well beaten, which requires a man for each horse to cut and prepare. These roots, and grain, (a kind of vetch,[411]) constitute the food of a horse in India.
One coachman.
Six clashies, or men to pitch tents.
Three tents, with two poles in each, and double walls: the space between the walls a passage of about five feet all round. These tents are twenty feet between the poles, about sixteen feet wide, and five-and-twenty feet high. Some of them have boarded floors and glass doors; but this is only in a standing encampment. They are lined throughout with chintz, carpeted, and have branch lights for candles fixed against the poles.
Twenty coolies—(people from the bazaar, at so much per diem, to carry furniture for the tents, which is all transported upon their heads.)
One washerman and his family.
One baker and his assistant.
One khansomer, or house steward.
Two footmen, or waiters.
Two tailors.
One masalgie, to clean knives and carry the lanthorn, go of errands, &c.
Two women servants.
One cook and assistant.
One sweeper to each tent.
Seventy sheep.
Thirty-five goats.
Two shepherds.
Nine camels.
Three camel drivers.

Fourteen bullocks.
Five waggons.
Seven drivers.
Twenty-four fowls, forty ducks, twelve geese, twelve rabbits, twelve turkeys.
Two men to take care of the poultry.

Besides the families of all these servants, with their horses, bullocks, and attendants, which may be computed upon an average of three to one.

As it is customary for every individual to draw water for himself from the wells, each of them are supplied with a brass pot, called a *lota:* it contains about a quart, and is shaped like two-thirds of a globe, with a rim round the top. Round this they tie a strong whip-cord, about the common depth of a well; and when travelling, each man fastens his *lota* round his waist; for they are much too cleanly to drink after one another.

Link-boys and guides are procured at every village; so indeed are coolies, should more be required on the journey. These are relieved at the next village by others, and so on. It is also customary to apply to the head man of that village to furnish a guard for the night, which guard is paid and discharged in the morning, except a robbery is perpetrated during the night, and then (unless by *dakoity,* as they are called) the man who furnishes the guard is answerable. He also presents a kid, or a couple of fowls to you, on your arrival.

We had not been long at *Meerat* before a party was proposed to go tiger hunting. As I had never witnessed the sport, I was prevailed upon to join them. Having procured five or six elephants that had been properly trained, some rifle and double-barrelled guns, &c. &c. the next morning at day-break we sallied forth. A native chief, with his hundred horsemen, and a numerous suite of attendants with spears and matchlocks, joined us. One of the boldest elephants was selected for me, as being the safest. A timid elephant, on these occasions, is considered dangerous, because when alarmed he starts off, regardless of any impediment that may lie in the way, frequently running under trees, and always making violent efforts to get quit of his load. It however not unfrequently happens that the means *we* think most likely to secure our safety, prove the cause of our destruction; so it had nearly happened to me. The elephant on which *I* was mounted, having by some chance got before the others in the jungle, smelt the tiger first, and instantly twisting his trunk round a bush that was before him, began tearing it up with all his might, roaring horribly all the time, when, to my utter dismay, up rose an enormous tiger. The party were there almost at the same instant. The tiger, alarmed (as they supposed) by the clatter of so many horses, probably aroused from sleep, made no resistance, but slunk off into a thicker covert. Nothing, however, could induce *my* elephant to move, as long as a single stem remained of the bush he had been crouched under, so that the party all pursued him, leaving me behind. I cannot say that I was much disturbed at the circumstance, for having seen a tiger alive, and in a wild state, I was satisfied; and after seeing him swim a small nullah, with his pursuers closely following, I returned quietly home. In a few hours the gentlemen came back. The tiger had shown wonderful sport, and had crossed another stream. At length, finding himself still closely pursued, he turned, made a spring upon one of the elephants, and for some moments hung by his fore-paws on the lower frame of the howdah. The gentleman who was on it immediately pointed his gun to the throat of the animal, which took effect: he let go his hold, when a volley from the party despatched him. He was a beautiful beast, stood nearly five feet high, with paws and legs beyond proportion large. It was supposed that, being gorged with food, he was asleep when *my* elephant roused him, and too lazy until enraged to offer battle. The claws of these animals are said to be poisonous; but I rather think the fatality lies in the jagged wound they inflict, which tearing away not only flesh, but sinews, is seldom known to heal, and generally proves fatal.

The next day I witnessed a sport of a different kind, being perfectly harmless, and I believe perfectly innocent. A number of young Hindoo girls, apparently about the age of six or seven years, most gaily dressed with scarlet muslin veils, &c. assembled round a pond. They were accompanied by a crowd of middle-aged women, whom I concluded to be their mothers, followed by a number of boys. On a signal from the women, these girls threw (each of them) something into the water; when the boys instantly plunged in, with sticks in their hands, and began battering most furiously what I now discovered to be dolls grotesquely dressed for the occasion. The girls it appeared, upon inquiry, being now of an age to be betrothed, the present ceremony denoted that they voluntarily threw away childish things, exemplifying that saying of St. Paul's, "When I was a man, I put away childish things,"[412] &c. As it was considered an ill omen if the doll did not immediately sink, the greatest anxiety was manifest in the countenance of each interested spectator; the boys meantime continuing to splash and halloo as long as any remained above water; after which, making their salaams to the pond, they all quietly retired.

CHAPTER XV.[413]

In the month of April in the following year, the commissioners were directed to make a further settlement of the *Bareilly* district. For this purpose they proceeded towards *Jehanabad*,[414] near *Pilibete;* and *we* joined them there, crossing the Ganges at *Ghurmoktasir Ghaut*,[415] about forty miles from *Meerat*. On landing at the village of *Tigree*, our dismay may be imagined, to find that there was no road for a carriage. Unfortunately, we had not brought any other conveyance: it was necessary therefore to make the attempt. After many hair-breadth escapes, (passing through a deep sand, covered with thorny brambles, without the slightest trace of human footsteps,) this was at length effected, and we reached the village of *Shawpore*. Here it was discovered that the water was so bad as not to be drinkable; and our people had neglected to bring any, prepared, as it generally is, either by a preparation of charcoal, or through a filtering stone; so that we were obliged to send six miles back to the Ganges in order to fetch some, and then wait two or three hours until it was purified. As I said before, patience is a great virtue, particularly in India!

We commenced our march the next morning as usual, about day-break, and soon crossed a stone bridge of considerable length, built across a morass. The vestiges of magnificence were perceptible in this structure; but time had proved a serious enemy—the pavement was much broken, and the parapet with its costly ornaments fallen away in large fragments. From this place to *Amrooah*,[416] which is about twenty miles, we traversed an open country much resembling Bagshot-heath,[417] and saw several herd of antelopes. Near this town are some very ancient Hindoo buildings, well worth the attention of an antiquary. This place is celebrated for a delicate kind of ware, like that invented, or rather brought to perfection, by Mr. Wedgewood:[418] the inhabitants make beautiful ornamental vases of it, pyramids, hookah stands, &c. chiefly white raised figures in groupes, from Grecian and ancient history,—and flowers, on a light grey or exquisite lilac ground.

From *Amrooah* we crossed a sandy plain of four miles long, without a hut, or even a shrub of any description to be seen. In general, these sandy plains are almost covered with wild melons; so kindly does Providence watch over the traveller, and those who seek their livelihood from afar! In this climate melons are particularly grateful, and conducive to health; not only the yellow solid melon, but the large green water melons, flourish abundantly in this arid and uncultivated soil.

This sandy plain conducted us into a vile road, with ruts so deep that the carriage was continually in danger of being overturned; and we were several times under the necessity of quitting it, in order to have it extricated. This unpleasant kind of travelling fortunately did not continue long—we had soon the pleasure of finding ourselves upon a fine hard down, with occasional clumps of trees. Our tents were pitched near a village called *Palkburrah*. The scene in front of us presented the cheering prospect of "valleys filled with wavy corn."[419] In the cool of the evening, while sitting at the door of the tent, a man, apparently in the situation of a farmer, came up to me, and respectfully making his salaam, entreated me to give him some medicine for his wife, who he informed me was extremely ill. I replied, that I was afraid of administering without seeing the patient; and asked if he could conduct me to her. With concern I learned that she lived seven miles off, and in a contrary direction to the road we were travelling. I then inquired if there were no Brahmin in his village who understood the properties of medicine? Yes, he said, there was, and she had consulted him; but had latterly got considerably worse, and had now no faith in his prescriptions. She had heard, he said, of our arrival there in the morning, and believing that the English knew every thing, she had requested him to come for our advice. I again repeated that it was impossible to prescribe with any prospect of success, unless I could see the patient. He said, if she thought herself equal to the journey, he would bring her into *Moradabad* next day, whither *we* also intended to go. I told him if he could accomplish *that*, I would consult one of our English physicians, who knew a great deal more about the matter than I did, and I was convinced would do every thing in his power for her. With this arrangement he appeared perfectly satisfied, and took his leave. I confess that I thought it very improbable we should hear any thing more of them; but, to my surprise, this poor woman was at *Moradabad* before us. She was sitting on the cart that had conveyed her thither. A faint smile illumined her pallid countenance as I approached her: she thanked me a thousand times for my condescension; (as she termed it;) expressed the greatest reliance on the English, who she seemed to think could do any thing they wished; and said she was sure she should soon get better now. It went to my heart to hear her talk so; for her complaint was a confirmed dropsy,[420] occasioned by poorness of blood. She was reduced, poor creature, almost to a skeleton. We immediately sent for the surgeon of the battalion, who was kind enough to receive her under his care, and promised to pay her case particular attention. Alas! assistance came too late—she survived only a month longer; but during that period I had the satisfaction of knowing that she had every possible attention paid her, and every thing done that could be to relieve her. I confess I felt deeply interested for this stranger; and my only consolation arose from the reflection, that I had done all in my power to save her. She was not more than two or three-and-twenty years of age. *Our* remedies often act with wonderful success upon these Hindoos, whose mode of living is so temperate, and their blood so pure, that you have only the complaint itself to combat. The constitution is naturally good; and if they *have* fever, it is soon conquered; besides which, they will take wine, or any thing, if given in the shape of medicine. A Mussulman, on the contrary, is so afraid of disobeying "the Prophet," that he would rather die than take any thing that is proscribed by the *Koraan*: an instance of the kind occurred in our own family. We were once travelling, when both Hindoo and Mussulmen servants were attacked by bilious fevers: the Hindoos were all restored to health by a few grains of calomel,[421] with a dose or two of Epsom salts,[422] and drinking plentifully of conjy*; whereas several of the Mussulmen died, because they did not know the preparation of calomel, and therefore would not take it.

Immediately on quitting *Moradabad* we forded a narrow stream, with a steep bank on either side, and crossed the river *Ram Gonga*. The bed of sand between these two streams is the deepest I ever passed: we were obliged to quit the carriage; and even *then*, the horse could scarcely drag it through. This sand extended nearly two miles; after which we came into a road so completely cut up by carriages of burthen, that a foot pace was all we could aspire to. I think I never was more tired of an expedition than of ours this morning. A little farther on we descried a stone bridge of one arch, over a rapid stream, so terrific in appearance from its immense height, that had it been practicable, I should have preferred wading through the water to passing over it. The road was paved with flat stones, and rose nearly perpendicular to the centre of the bridge, from whence the descent was equally abrupt; neither had it the smallest parapet or railing on either side. It really required great firmness of nerve to venture over in a carriage. After considerable fatigue we reached a village called *Moorah*, where our tents were pitched in a beautiful grove of mango trees, laden with green fruit. It was now the latter end of April. The fruit was then about the size of young apricots: they are delicious in tarts, and emit a most grateful odour.

From hence we travelled over an open country, with innumerable small hamlets, to *Kamora de Morah*, a village belonging to the Nawaab of *Rampoor*.[423] Our supplies at this place were scanty; but they were cheerfully furnished, which is not often the case in villages that belong to native chiefs. This country is much intersected by streams, some of which we forded, and over others found a rude kind of stone bridge, in many cases quite dangerous to pass. The climate is many degrees cooler in the *Moradabad* district than at *Meerat*. I found the nights at this season really cold.

We now travelled with cultivation on either side for seventeen miles, and encamped in a large grove composed of different sorts of trees—a thing very unusual in India, as they generally plant each sort separate. This variety of foliage may perhaps account for the different sorts of birds assembled in it, all straining their melodious throats at once. Of a grove composed of the mango only, the dove, and a small delicate creature called the mango bird,[424] seem to claim exclusive possession, while tamarind trees are covered by paroquets. The country here is very beautiful, being every where diversified by fields of corn, villages peeping through luxuriant groves, and rich pasture lands; but the roads so miserably bad that we expected the carriage every minute to overturn.

Halting at a village named *Ourourie*, near which runs a fine clear stream, we caught fish in abundance, particularly that named the *roe*, and found it by no means inferior to the codfish we eat in England.

---

* Conjy is rice boiled in water until dissolved, and taken in a liquid state.

From *Ourourie* we travelled over a plain, and were often delayed by being obliged to cross *nullahs*, whose banks were steep and rugged; we consequently performed this stage on an elephant, leaving the gig to be led slowly after us. The sagacity of the elephant is so great, that he always feels with one paw whether the ground will bear his weight before he trusts himself upon it; indeed I have heard it asserted, that they have even the power to smell the nature of the soil, and judge from thence whether it is firm or not. I have seen many instances myself of sagacity in these animals, but never any that struck me more forcibly than what daily occurred on this march. It is customary to feed elephants on cakes made of the coarser particles of wheat, after the flour has been separated from it. This is called *otta*, eaten also by the natives as bread, and sold in every bazaar. When our elephant arrived at her ground, after having (as usual) fastened her fore legs to a wooden peg fixed in the earth for that purpose, the *mahowat*, her driver, usually went away to purchase *otta**; upon which occasions he placed a child of his own, about two years of age, on a little straw between the elephant's legs, charging her to take care of the child until his return. Strange as it may appear, it is no less true, that so careful was the animal of her young charge, that during the father's absence, no one dared to approach her, not even a dog. On the man's return from the bazaar he loosed her feet, and mounted upon the neck, in order to take her to the river to drink and bathe, (which latter they delight in,) desiring her at the same time to give him the child. This she immediately did, by cautiously winding her trunk round the child's waist, and lifting him up within the father's reach. I have seen the same elephant take a piece of the cake that lay before her, and place it gently in the child's lap.

After travelling over as vile a road as could be met with, we reached the *Jehanabad*. This is a large town in the vicinity of *Pilibete*, where the commissioners having business, we remained for more than two months. In order to protect ourselves from the heat of the sun, (at this time excessive,) thatched roofs, supported on pillars of wood, were erected over our tents, which answered the purpose admirably. The party consisted of nine, myself and Mrs.—,[425] the only ladies. We found a kind of shed, sufficiently large to accommodate us all as a dining-room, and it was fitted up accordingly. We assembled about six in the evening, took a short ride before dinner, and passed our time delightfully. Being situated upon an eminence, *our saloon* commanded an extensive prospect. Immediately round us was a fine pasture land, ornamented by a number of small coppices, which gave it quite an English appearance; and beyond that, a diversity of hill and dale, extremely grateful to the eye. Going out one evening earlier than usual, we espied a man seated on a square of ground, measuring about six feet across, (a little raised,) surrounded by a fire made of a kind of peat, and himself besmeared, head and all, with ashes. A more deplorable object I never beheld. Upon inquiry,

---

* Otta, and the leaves of the peeple tree, are the usual food of elephants, who tear off large branches with their trunks, and load themselves.

we found that he sat thus, with his legs doubled under him, and his head bare, from sun-rise to sun-set, in pursuance of a vow; that he was a Brahmin, and this a voluntary penance—and a dreadful penance it must have been, for the fire was within his reach all the way round, and he kept constantly replenishing it. No one but a Hindoo, or one of *Don Juan's friends*,[426] could have supported it. I do really think that he must have washed himself with something, and so become fire-proof; otherwise, with the heat of the sun and fire together, he must surely have been melted; or perhaps his safety lay in having nothing to melt, for he was literally only skin and bone.

During our residence at this place we were visited by two gentlemen, who told us that they had been on a shooting party for about a month, and in that time had killed four-and-twenty tigers, one wild elephant, two wild buffaloes, and two bears. The skins of the latter were so fine, that I prevailed on them to spare one to me for trimmings.

This place, so inviting to walk in, was extremely dangerous on account of snakes, *centipedes*, and scorpions, with all which it abounds. Our servants complained also of the water, which they said was bad tasted, and unwholesome. It certainly had somewhat of an earthy flavour; but it was of little consequence to us—first, because we took the precaution to qualify it; and, secondly, that we had brought a good supply with us, and never drank any that had not been filtered or purified by a proportion of charcoal and alum. A much more serious objection to *us*, was, that the place was subject to blasts of mephitic vapour. One of these, rising from the valley, passed through the room in which we were sitting after dinner. There were at that time only six persons round the table—two on each side, and one at each end. The current of air of which I am speaking, was so partial as to affect only the gentleman and myself who sat on that side of the table. We were seized at the same moment by violent pain across the eyes, a sensation of extreme tension, and throbbing of the temples; giddiness, and sickness at the stomach. Nor were we free from acute pain in the head, for some hours after. The natives of *Jehanabad* seemed to feel a great dread of these visitations, by which, they told us, many had lost their lives; and we were given to understand, that they thought Mr.— and myself must either be angels or *diables* not to have suffered more. A few nights after this catastrophe, a band of desperate fellows attacked a village near, in which part of our retinue had taken up their abode: falling on its sleeping inhabitants, sword in hand, they plundered and cut down all who had the courage to oppose them. Our gentlemen, on hearing the tumult, ran with pistols to the spot, but too late to save the lives of many. Three servants of the party, besides a number of women and children, had already fallen a sacrifice to these barbarians. One poor little infant was cut to pieces in its mother's arms. Unfortunately, no prisoners were made; for hearing European voices, they immediately decamped, while the darkness of the night favoured their escape.

Being so near it, I took the opportunity to visit *Pilibete*, which appears to have been a place of some consequence. It is surrounded by a high brick wall, defended by ponderous gates. At the entrance of the town stands a handsome mosque, erected in memory of *Haffiz Ramut*.[427] The scite of this mosque is a square of considerable extent, at each corner of which is a solid minaret. Ascending a flight of steps sufficiently broad to give a just idea of the magnificent interior, we passed under an arched gateway into a spacious court paved with grey marble, having arcades of the same on either side. The central building was a solid square, entered by three arches from the front, surmounted by domes, with a small minaret at either corner. The inside of these domes are elegantly and tastefully painted to represent various flowers in their richest and most brilliant tints. A *mullick*,[428] whom we met in the town, gave us much intelligence respecting the place; and in the course of conversation I learned how the village apothecaries are remunerated for attendance on the poor. The head man of each village contracts with any Brahmin skilled in the use of drugs, to pay him eight annas (which is the half of a rupee) a year, for as many villages as are under his controul; and this *mullick* assured me that a native physician, (*hakime*,[429] as they are called,) then residing at *Pilibete*, by this mode alone realized a regular income of a hundred and fifty rupees per annum.

The town of *Pilibete* is celebrated for the manufacture of a strong coarse kind of cloth, made from hemp, which grows on the adjacent hills; and a very pure kind of lime called *chunam*, with which, buildings are faced to represent marble; and so complete is the deception, that even the touch scarcely convinces the inquirer that it is not marble. This district is full of wild elephants; numbers of them are caught annually in pits dug for that purpose. We saw a large male elephant brought in between two decoy ones, which are always females. They preserve their ascendancy by pushing him with great violence from one to the other, until the poor animal is so bewildered that he does not know which way to turn, and so becomes an easy conquest.

Pilibete is also a great mart for timber, which finds a ready sale at *Bareilly*. This accounts for the roads from hence to that city being so dreadfully cut up. They appear to cultivate *rice* and *paddy* at the foot of these hills, where the ground is occasionally overflowed. The etymology of the word *paddy*[430] is so extraordinary, that I cannot avoid mentioning it. The grain so named somewhat resembles rice, but more so tapioca. By the natives it is called *dahn;* but having originally been given to our troops in Bengal instead of money,—which *pay*, in the language of the country, is termed *poddy*,—it has, in the course of time, been converted into the word *paddy*, by which these fields are now almost as generally known as by their original name of *dahn*. Many subversions of the same kind have crept into the oriental languages, which often occasion ludicrous mistakes.

I observed here a few patches of the bamboo plant, which proved the springy nature of the soil. There is a noble dock-yard at this place, in which they were at this time building some trading vessels of large dimensions; while an immense number of people also found employment in the repair of a magnificent bridge of ancient structure, across the river *Ram Gonga*, which runs through the heart of the town.

About the middle of June we returned to *Bareilly*, and remained in a good bungalow until the 17th of July. This was the hottest season that had been known for years. The rain, which usually begins to fall about the 20th of June, did not commence until the 7th of July, and then it came down in torrents. Our party now separated—the commissioners for their residence at *Futty Ghur*, and we, to return to *Meerat*. The heavy rain that had fallen rendered the road so slippery, that at one place the poor horse which drew the gig was fairly tripped up, and lay for some seconds on his side, so much alarmed, that although a fine high-spirited Arab, he had not courage to move from this perilous situation; and was only relieved by being completely unharnessed. We had fortunately several attendants near, who dragged the carriage for about fifty yards into a more even road, which gave the horse time to recover himself, for he trembled like a human being. This incident delayed us so much, that it was near two o'clock in the day before we reached our tents at *Sickerry*. After being so long exposed to a scorching sun, I was delighted to see that they had pitched these tents under the shade of lofty trees by the side of a large pond. So cool and refreshing was it, that I thought with regret on the prospect of quitting it so soon. How many circumstances, trivial in themselves, serve to convince us that we know not what is best for us. About four o'clock the clouds foreboded an approaching storm; loud thunder rolled; the vivid lightning flashed; the angry waters would not be restrained—they burst their bounds, and in an instant our tent was overflowed. No remedy appeared but patience. I felt thankful that it happened before it grew dark, for the night multiplies all horrors; indeed I have observed, that in every misfortune some consolation may be derived, if persons would take the trouble to seek it; and I consoled myself also by thinking that it was too violent to last long—so, seating myself on a sofa *a la Turke*,[431] I quietly awaited the event. The storm abated in about an hour; but the atmosphere still retained so much humidity, that I awoke in the night with most excruciating pain in one of my ancles; and on attempting to rise next morning, I had the mortification to find that I could not stand—indeed, that I had nearly lost the use of my limbs. With some difficulty I was placed in my palankeen, and (as much by water as by land, for the whole country was overflowed) conveyed to our next encampment. My palankeen was borne the greatest part of the way upon the bearers' heads, instead of their shoulders; and the horse on which my husband rode by the side of it, swam with him in many places. I consoled myself with the conviction of the bearers being an amphibious kind of animal, who, if the water did not actually run into their mouths, would paddle their way through.

In the rainy season, unless the weather is cloudy, it is intensely hot; and there is sometimes a complete stagnation of air. The myriads of insects that swarmed around, were sufficient to tire the patience of Job[432] himself; when, to add to the miseries of this inauspicious journey, the bed and bedding came in completely drenched—it had been deposited in a pool of water. Nor had I in my travelling baskets one suit of dry linen. Exposure to the sun, however, soon extracted all moist particles, and rendered every thing as it was before. This is an advantage in an eastern clime, which in Europe you have not; but no remedy was at hand for my swollen foot, which, without any appearance of inflammation, had become exceedingly painful; I was consequently obliged to pursue the journey in my palankeen. This was not accomplished without sundry inconveniences: either the torches were extinguished on a barren heath by a powerful gust of wind, or one of the torch bearers was disabled by a thorn which had penetrated his foot; or, finally, the palankeen bearers fell down on the brink of a lake, &c. Once the two foremost men actually fell in, and the palankeen came down upon the ground; but they soon shook themselves, and resumed their position.

Thus, after perils by land and by water, we at length reached *Meerat;* and I made up my mind, that the rainy season was not the pleasantest for travellers. A short time after our arrival there, the inhabitants were alarmed by three separate shocks of an earthquake, which continued a few seconds each. It commenced by a noise, as of heavy waggons travelling rapidly on a paved road immediately under the house; birds that were in cages, flapping their wings, as if anxious to be free; doors opening, others shutting, without any person near them. I happened to be passing from one room to another, and was seized with such a sensation of giddiness in the head, and sickness at the stomach, that I was obliged to hold by a door-frame, still more unsteady than myself. In many places the earth opened, and several small huts were swallowed up; but, fortunately, the inhabitants had time to make their escape, and no lives were lost that I heard of. All this time the atmosphere was perfectly clear, and not a breath of air was stirring.

A

GUIDE

UP THE RIVER GANGES,

FROM

CALCUTTA TO CAWNPORE, FUTTEH GHUR,
MEERAT, &c.;

WITH

THE CORRECT DISTANCES OF EVERY STATION,
AND WHAT THEIR PRODUCE.

A GUIDE,

&c.

HAVING experienced both difficulty and delay, from ignorance of this navigation, and the different species of accommodation that each station offers to the voyager, the Author is led to believe that a correct statement of these particulars will not be unacceptable, particularly to those who, newly arrived in Bengal, may be under the necessity to make the voyage.

On his arrival in Calcutta, a young man is generally received into the house of some friend, or person to whom he brings an introduction; (a circumstance of great importance on his thus setting out in life;) but should he come unprovided with such recommendation, he is reduced to the necessity of resorting to a tavern; of which, although there are several in Calcutta, they are not considered a respectable residence, being for the most part dirty, unpleasantly situated, extravagant in their charges, and frequented chiefly by Europeans of the lowest class.

If in the King's service, a young man's first step is to wait upon the brigade-major to the King's troops, (who resides in Fort William,) and report the date of his arrival; from which day his pay and allowances commence. The brigade-major furnishing him with a certificate to this effect, *his* recommendation will enable a gentleman so applying to procure quarters in the fort—a subaltern officer two rooms, a captain four; but as these apartments are not furnished, such accommodation is only of use to those who are destined to remain there for some time.

If he happen to be an officer in the service of the East India Company, he should apply in a similar manner to the town-major, who will furnish him with the necessary certificates and instructions. He will perhaps learn from him that he is posted to a regiment in the upper provinces of Hindostan, to which he is directed to proceed by water, and that he will by proper application get his boat expenses paid. The mode of making this application, with the consequent preparations for the voyage, it is my intention, in as clear a manner as possible, to point out. He must, in the first place, after having procured his certificate, repair to the auditor-general's office, and produce it, stating the orders he may have received, and requesting his boat allowance to the place of his destination; the half of which will be immediately given him, and authority to draw for the remainder at a stated period.

There are but two kind of boats at the same time safe and commodious, and these are called, the one a pinnace, (or small cutter,) the other a budgerow. They are each drawn up the river by men called *dandies*, with another to guide the helm, named a *maunjie*.[433] They each contain a bed-room at the stern, a sitting-room in the centre, and an anti-room in front towards the deck, the whole being surrounded by Venetian blinds. They are hired at so many rupees a month, according to the number of oars: pinnaces, from one hundred and fifty to four hundred and twenty rupees a month; budgerows, from ninety-seven to one hundred and seventy-six. Baggage-boats to accompany the above, from twenty-two to ninety-seven rupees a month. To a budgerow carrying sixteen oars, at one hundred and fifty-seven rupees a month, a baggage-boat would be required at thirty-five, and a cooking-boat at twenty-two, which are of sufficient size to encounter any weather, and at the same time afford ample accommodation for servants, provisions, &c. The best mode of procuring these boats is by application to Messrs. Barber and Co. at the Old Fort Ghaut,[434] who will also furnish hands to navigate them, and become security for their not deserting, a circumstance by no means unusual on this voyage, which may perhaps be attributed to the custom of advancing the half of their wages to them before they start, in order, as they allege, to enable their families to procure subsistence during their absence. Besides the security given by Barber and Co., I should recommend that a clashee[435] be engaged as a servant to keep guard over, and expedite their movements on the voyage. This man will also be found useful in procuring supplies from the several bazaars *én passant*.[436] Some other preparations are also necessary, such as poultry, a few fat sheep, a couple of milch goats,[437] (whose milk in this country is free from any particular flavour, and in tea is infinitely preferable to cow's milk,) tea, sugar, a quantity of hard biscuits, bread, cheese, &c. This latter article is not manufactured in India, but may be procured in the China Bazaar[438] at Calcutta, fresh from England, at a moderate price, sometimes even under prime cost. The pine-apple shape is the best for keeping; and it should be kept in a common earthen jar, with a wet cloth tied over the mouth of it.

The voyage from Calcutta to Cawnpore is generally considered to occupy a space of three months; to Futteh Ghur a week longer; and to Ghur Moktasir Ghaut,[439] near Meerat, twenty days more.

Embarking from Calcutta during the months of March, April, or May, it will be necessary to surround the budgerow with tatties, or blinds, made on a bamboo frame to fit the windows, covered with the fibrous roots of a sweet-scented grass called cus cus,[440] which will last the voyage, and by being watered from the top of the budgerow, render the apartments cool and comfortable. Although these roots are firmly wove together, they by no means exclude the light. Of an evening, after the sun is set, they are removed entirely, and replaced in the morning. The hot wind seldom blows so violently as to require them, except from about nine o'clock in the morning until sun-set: the hottest time is from twelve o'clock until five in the afternoon. The clashee will procure these tatties, and is the proper person to superintend the watering them, &c. If you have palankeen bearers on board, they ought to assist.

A small book, called Hadley's Grammar,[441] (which can be purchased at any bookseller's in Calcutta,) is also a necessary appendage to prevent being imposed upon by the representation of any servant who may speak a little English, and thereby gain an ascendancy over his master to the prejudice of the rest. These men are frequently met with in Calcutta, and are always ready to serve a new comer; but they are generally people of low caste, and not to be depended upon.

Leaving Calcutta with the tide, you generally reach a place called *Bally Nuggur*[442] before it turns, unless indeed the wind blows strong against you. This place is inhabited entirely by natives. Here you cast anchor, and remain until the tide serves again; and having passed the Danish settlement of *Serampore*, the French one of *Chandanagore*, arrive at that of the Dutch called *Chinsurah*, where you encounter the second tide. You may indeed, if you are fortunate, reach a place called *Banse Bareah*, which is two hours farther; but here nothing is procurable except provision for natives. The boats are moored at sun-set, and unmoored at sunrise, it being dangerous on account of shoals to travel after dark. When you come too, for the night, (which it is adviseable on many accounts to do before sun-set,) the boatmen cook their victuals; which operation is performed on the shore by means of small stoves, formed from a loomy kind of earth of which these banks are composed. Their cooking utensils are not cumbersome: *one* large brass, or iron pot, serves to boil rice for all of the same caste, while each man carries his brass platter, and *lota*, of the same material, to drink out of.

It is usual to start the boats at day-break, but they manage it so quietly as not to disturb your repose.

Sook Sangor is the next place, and is about seven hours from *Banse Bareah*; from hence you may with ease reach *Ballypore* by sun-set. Milk may be procured at all these villages, and some kinds of vegetable; but no poultry or eggs, except where Mussulmen reside.

Start at day-break next morning, and in eight hours you reach *Culna*. From thence to *Mirzapore* is five hours farther, where you had better remain for the night, and may procure all sorts of provisions. This place contains many Europeans, and is celebrated for the manufacture of carpets, printed chintz, &c. Purchase *punkahs* here.

From *Mirzapore* to *Nuddeah* is seven hours; from *Nuddeah* to the entrance of the *Jalingy* river,[443] an hour and a half; from the *Jalingy* to *Stuart Gunge*, three hours.

From *Stuart Gunge* to a small village called *Meahpoorah*, six hours; and from thence to *Chandpoorah*, six hours. This latter is a miserably poor place; it is therefore better to stop at the first good bank for legowing upon after quitting *Chandpoorah*; of this, the mangy or captain of the crew will inform you. It is always desirable to keep him in good humour, by attending a little to his advice, as on him depends in a great measure both your expedition and comfort on the voyage.

From *Chandpoorah* to *Augur Deep* is ten hours good pulling, oftener twelve. The river between these places winds so much, that it takes nearly a day to arrive, where the distance in a straight line would not be above three miles.

From *Augur Deep* to *Dewarrah Gunge* is four hours; from *Dewarrah Gunge* to *Cutwah*, eight more.

From *Cutwah* to *Plassey* (the scene of Lord Clive's victory over the *Bengalees*, which first gave us footing in the country) is nine hours. This is a fine sporting country, but dangerous on account of tigers.

From *Plassey* to *Satan Gunge* is twelve hours; *Satan Gunge* to *Rangamutty*, four hours; *Rangamutty* to *Berhampore*,[444] eight hours. This is the nearest station to Calcutta which contains European soldiers, except the artillery cantonment of *Dum Dum;* but that is ten miles on the other side Calcutta, and inland. *Berhampore* contains besides a King's regiment of infantry, one or more battalions of seapoys, and is famous for sundry manufactures, which they bring to the boats for sale; such as stockings, silk handkerchiefs, &c. There are, besides, two shops kept by Englishmen, which are well supplied with articles from England of all description, sold at the average of a rupee for a shilling. The officers' barracks are about two hundred yards inland: they are handsome, and regularly built, forming a square, one side of which fronts the river. The bank on which they stand is high, sloping, and turfed to the water's edge, with here and there a flight of stone steps for the accommodation of passengers. The parade runs along the edge of it. This station is commanded by a general officer, to whom you are expected, through his brigade major, to report your arrival, and ask his orders; and in like manner report *progress*, as it is called, at every military station upon the river, and also to the adjutant of your regiment, wherever that may be.

From *Berhampore*, the city of *Moorshedabad* is about seven hours tracking, although by land the distance is only seven miles. The river at this place is low at all seasons, and the numerous boats *legowed* to its banks contribute to impede the voyager. The boat's crew provide themselves here, with rice for their voyage, it being very plentiful in this part; and the higher they proceed up the country, the more scarce, and consequently dearer it becomes. Sugar is also remarkably cheap at *Moorshedabad*.

A little beyond this city is the entrance of a small river called the *Kattaghan*, which it is adviseable to pass, and to fasten your boat on the opposite side, the inhabitants of *Moorshedabad* not being famed for honesty.

From hence to *Kissenpoorah* (a small village) it is six hours; from *Kissenpoorah* to *Jungypoor*,[445] six more. At the latter is a manufactory for silks, under the control of the commercial resident.

From *Jungypoor* to *Sooty* is six hours.

To *Kusseinpoor* six more.

From *Kusseinpoor* to *Mohun Gunge*, nine hours; and from hence to the entrance of the Ganges, three hours more.

Having now quitted the *Baugharetty* or *Cossimbazar* river, you proceed by the left bank of the Ganges, without seeing more than a few scattered huts, until sun-set.

From hence to *Radge Mahl* is seven hours. Here the ruin of a magnificent palace, formerly belonging to the Rajah, may be seen; and here, every day about noon, the postmen from East to West meet, and exchange their despatches, which affords the traveller an opportunity of communication either way. Bread, vegetables, kid, (which is a great delicacy in this country,) fowls, eggs, fruit, and charcoal, are found here in great abundance. The inhabitants sell also marble slabs to press paper, carved into various shapes. This is almost the widest part of the river, and in the rainy season has the appearance of an ocean.

From *Radge Mahl* to *Sickerry Gulley* is fourteen hours. This is a station for invalid seapoys, with a small bungalow belonging to the superintending officer of these establishments. This part of the country abounds with beasts of prey. *Radge Mahl* is the nearest approach that the river makes to that ridge of mountains which runs in a north-west direction from Calcutta, and are called the Radge Mahl hills.

From hence you quickly pass the small village of *Saabad*, and in two hours more that of *Gunga Pursaad*. Here it is adviseable to *legow* for the night, as you will not find so good a place for many miles. The finest honey in India is to be procured here, and very cheap. From *Gunga Pursaad* to *Sickerry Gully* is about five hours' tracking. This is a Hindoo village, and nothing to be got except milk.

The next village of any consequence is *Pier Ponty*, which you ought to reach in twelve hours.

From *Pier Ponty* to *Puttal Guttah* is a hard day's pull; but there is generally a breeze of wind near the hills, which carries the boat forward in opposition to the stream.

The next place is *Col Gong*, which you *may* reach about sun set on the following day. It contains a good bazaar, and the houses of several European officers of the Company's service who reside here upon their pensions, besides one or two indigo planters.

Move forward at day-break the following morning, about ten o'clock you will pass a *nullah;* and at three reach the populous village of *Bogglipore*. This is a station for seapoys commanded by European officers; a judge, collector, &c. A peculiar description of cloth is manufactured here, which takes its name from the place. It is adviseable to remain at *Bogglipore* for the night. The best ghaut to legow at, is called *Bibbee Gunge*.

Cast off the boats at day-break, and towards evening you will reach the village of *Chea Cheraigne*.

About ten the next morning you will pass the *Jinghira* Rock, about half-past one the Gurgut *Nullah*, and at sun-set find nothing but a patch of sand to legow upon; it is therefore adviseable to stop at the first good ground you meet with, after passing the *Nullah*.

The next place is *Pier Pahar*, where the stream runs so strong, that unless you have a breeze to stem it, you will not reach *Monghir* until seven or eight at night. At *Monghir* are some curious hot springs, and many other things worth seeing. It is a large station for invalid seapoys, commanded by a general officer. Birds of beautiful plumage are offered for sale, but they will not live away from their native hills.

Pass the end of two *nullahs*, and come to a village inhabited by seapoy pensioners, near *Soorage Gurrah*.

From *Soorage Gurrah* to *Bareah*, which is a good legowing place, may be done in about seven hours.

From *Bareah* to *Deriapore* (twenty koss from *Monghir*) will take the whole day: it is better to legow before you arrive there, as a koss or two beyond it, you will find nothing but sand.

Pass a bungalow at *Sennaar*, and come too at the village of *Bar*, about four koss farther, where, as there are Mussulmen inhabitants, many articles of consumption are procurable. The water about *Bar* is shallow, and the current rather strong.

About six miles from *Bar* is an indigo factory.

Pass *Bidapore*.

From *Bar* to *Patna* is full twenty-four hours.

From *Patna* to *Dinapore* about eight hours.

At *Seerpoor*, a little beyond *Dinapore*, the boat's crew lay in a stock of rice for the remainder of the voyage.

Pass the Soane River, which is famous for beautiful pebbles and fine clear water, to *Cheraigne, Wilton Gunge,* and *Chuprah.*

From *Chuprah* to *Revel Gunge* is three koss and a half, a good legowing place.

Pass the mouth of the *Deewah* River, and reach Berhampore Ghaut by sun-set.

Pass the village of *Berreah*, and come too for the night at a small place on the right, about two koss beyond it.

About eleven o'clock the next morning pass *Bulleah*, and reach the fort of *Buxar* in the evening. At Buxar it is necessary to wait on the commanding officer.

Pass the *Caramnassa* River to the village of *Chowra*.

From *Chowra* you proceed to *Arampore*, and from *Arampore* to *Ghazipore*, which is a large military station. Report your arrival to the commanding officer.

From *Ghazipore* you come to *Zemineah, Chursapore,* and to an indigo factory at *Danapoora*, in twelve hours.

From *Danapoora* you *may* reach Sidepoor in seven hours; to the end of the *Goomty,* (or winding river,) in two hours more; *Kytee*, in one hour; and *Kataroury*, in two hours. This place is a koss and a half (about three miles) from *Bulwar* Ghaut.

Move next morning at six o'clock, you will pass Bulwar Ghaut about nine; a small brick town named *Kylee*, about two; and reach *Radge Ghaut*, at *Benares*, in the evening, in good time to legow.

From *Benares* to opposite little *Mursapore* takes about three hours fair tracking; and to the cantonment at *Sultanpore*, (or chutah Calcutta,) nine hours more.

From *Sultanpore* to the fort at *Chunar*, six hours.

From *Chunar* to *Badsulah*, (on the other side the river,) ten hours.

From *Badsulah* to *Kutchwah Ghaut*, six hours.

From *Kutchwah Ghaut* to *Mirzapore*, seven hours.

From *Mirzapore* to *Jehangeerabad* is three hours.

From *Jehangeerabad* to *Bahaderpoorah*, five hours and a half.

From *Bahaderpoorah* to *Charracoar*, five hours.

From *Charracoar* to *Diggah*, (distant only ten koss in a straight line from *Mirzapore*,) five hours.

From *Diggah* to *Barrarie*, seven hours.
From *Barrarie* to *Tellah*, four hours.
From *Tellah* to *Sersah*, ten hours.
From *Sersah* to *Dumdumaye*, three hours.
From *Dumdumaye* to *Derah*, twelve hours.

From *Derah* to the fort at *Allahabad*, seven or eight hours, if the wind is not against you, and the water calm; but the stream in this part is very strong, and the river in many places very shallow; it is therefore adviseable to land on the *Jumna* side of the fort, and proceeding across the promontory in a palankeen, sending the boats round to a place called *Taylor Gunge*, which will take them nearly a day to accomplish. At *Allahabad* supplies of every description may be procured. Here it is necessary to wait upon the commanding officer in the fort, and report your name, rank, and destination.

From *Taylor Gunge* to *Ramohowdah*, (ten koss by land from *Allahabad*,) will take ten hours.

From *Ramohowdah* to *Jehanabad*, three hours.
From *Jehanabad* to *Acbarpore*, four hours.
From *Acbarpore* to *Konkerabad*, six hours and a half.
From *Konkerabad* to *Shaw Zadabad*, four hours.

From *Shaw Zadabad* to *Kurrah*, three hours. Muslin and cloth of the coarser kinds are manufactured here.

From *Kurrah* to *Mannickpore*, three hours and a half.
From *Mannickpore* to *Kerah Nugger*, six hours.
From *Kerah Nugger* to *Bunderpoor*, one hour and a half.
From *Bunderpoor* to *Nobusta* Ghaut, five hours and a half.
From *Nobusta* to *Ochree*, six hours and a half.

From *Ochree* to *Dalmow* the river is particularly shallow, and abounds in quick-sands; it is therefore almost impossible to say how long a budgerow will take tracking it, as the dandies are obliged to walk the greatest part of the distance up to their waists in water, and are frequently detained to push the boat off a sandbank. If no such impediment should occur, the usual time is about eight hours.

From *Dalmow* you pass the villages of *Kutterah, Garassen,* and *Singpore,* on the left; while on the right stand those of *Kosroopore, Hajipore,* and *Adempore.* Reach *Rowaadpore* from Dalmow in twelve hours.

Rowaadpore to *Buxar* and *Doreah Kerah*, in seven hours.

Doreah Kerah to Sooragepore, three hours.

Sooragepore to *Nuseeb Ghur*, ten hours. At the latter is a large brick house built by General Martine,[446] a Frenchman. He had another large house at Lucknow, and a fine estate near it called *Lac Peery*, which means a thousand trees. On this spot he erected a superb palace and tomb: the latter he soon after occupied. He was a man of low origin, great abilities, and made immense sums of money by various speculations. He came to India an adventurer, was formerly a general in the Mahratta service, but latterly a general merchant. His character was most eccentric: he caused two centinels of wood, the height and size of men, dressed in the uniform of a British artilleryman, to be placed on either side his tomb, where a lamp is kept constantly burning. He has directed by his will that the house at *Lac Peery* should be at the service of any European gentleman, or lady, to reside in for *one* month at a time, but no longer. It is in charge of the officer commanding at Lucknow. A large sum of money is also bequeathed to his native city of Lyons, in France. The origin of this man's fortune is said to have been collecting dead leaves, and selling them to the natives for fuel.

From *Nuseeb Ghur* to *Madarpore*, seven hours.

Madarpore to *Jaugemow*, three hours.

Jaugemow to the east end of *Cawnpore*, five hours.

Cawnpore is the largest military station, and depôt in the upper provinces, or indeed on this side of India. It is six miles in extent, and contains excellent accommodation for ten thousand troops.

From *Cawnpore* to *Betoor* takes twelve hours. This place is a station for civilians, who manage the revenue and judicial departments at Cawnpore, from which it is distant about twelve *koss*. It is celebrated by the Hindoos as one of their most ancient places of worship, and is therefore resorted to, at particular seasons of the year, by an immense concourse of people, who line the banks of the Ganges for many miles.

From *Betoor* to the village of *Dyepore* is about twelve hours. Here is a bungalow and an indigo factory.

Dyepore to the entrance of the *Ram Gonga* river, is twelve hours.

To *Singerampore*, twelve more.

Singerampore to *Futty Ghur*, twelve hours—that is, from sun-rise to sun-set.

From *Futty Ghur* it is about twenty days' tracking to *Ghur Moktasir Ghaut*, (the nearest point at which a boat can approach Meerat.) Pass many small villages, but no place worthy notice until you reach the large brick town of *Kurrah*, about the second or third day from *Futty Ghur*.

Remember to lay in a stock of supplies for one month before you leave *Futty Ghur*, as nothing more can be got until you arrive at Meerat.

From *Kurrah*, two or three hours brings you to *Sooragepore*, a small Hindoo village.

Sooragepore to *Budrowlee*, eight hours. This is capital legowing ground, except that the banks are low, and a number of alligators are generally to be seen upon them; a great variety of waterfowl frequent also this part of the river, particularly wild geese, in such flights as often to darken the atmosphere.

From *Budrowlee* you pass an uninteresting country to *Oolye Ghaut*, and from thence to *Heronpore*.

From *Heronpore* to *Kirkawara*, near which place much wheat is cultivated.

Kirkawara to *Ram Ghaut*, where there is a superb palace built by the *Rajah* of *Jyepoor*. Hindoos flock here in great numbers at stated periods of the year to make offerings to the Ganges, and perform ablutions. *Ram Ghaut* was formerly the resort of *Scindia* and the Mahratta chiefs. The palace is built upon a rising ground, about a hundred yards from the shore: it fronts the river—is surrounded by lofty trees. At the bottom of the garden is a flight of stone steps, upon an extensive scale, leading into the river. The town appears flourishing, and is built down to the water's edge.

A number of projecting banks impede the progress of the navigator until he reaches *Anopsheer*, which is considered about half way between *Futty Ghur* and *Meerat*.

The shores now assume a more pleasing prospect: luxuriant pasture, with numerous herds of cattle feeding on it, relieves the eye; and the adjacent country appears well wooded.

The village of *Ahar* contains some good brick houses, and a handsome *Ghaut;* but the river near it is very shallow.

At *Bussy Gusserat*, the next place of any consequence, there is capital legowing ground; and farther on, a village called *Sukerah Telah*, a great mart for trade.

To *Sukerah Telah* succeeds the village of *Poote*, where some Hindoo places of worship render the scene peculiarly picturesque. The most striking feature is a spacious flight of stone steps, highly ornamented, and shaded by trees down a sloping bank to the water's edge.

From this place to *Ghur Moktasir Ghaut*, is not more than a day's tracking.

Meerat lies about forty miles inland from *Ghur Moktasir Ghaut*.

VOCABULARY

ADAPTED TO THE TOUR.

Arampoore—*Aram* means ease, and *poore* a village.

Bungalow—is a cottage ornee.
Bunyah—a man who sells grain in a bazaar.

Charpiah—a bedstead without posts or tester.
Conjy—rice boiled in water.
Cummerbund—a breadth of cloth round the loins.

Dak—travelling post with relays of bearers.
Dakoity—banditti.
Deen—religion, or light.
Dock—a shrub with large leaves and thick stem.

Fakeer—a mendicant priest, either Mahometan or Hindoo.

Gold mohars—a gold coin, value two pounds English.

Jow jungle—underwood, brushwood.

VOCABULARY

ADAPTED TO THE VOYAGE.

Badul—thunder.
Bhallu—sand.
Bullow—call (any one.)

Chelli jow—Move quickly.

Daal—an oar.
Daal mokoof kur—Stop the oars.
Daal kench—Pull the oars.
Dandies—boatmen.
Douccra naar—another boat.

Geah—gone.
Goleah—the steersman.
Goon—rope fastened to the mast-head, by which they tow the boat.
Gungah—the Ganges.

Howah—wind.

Jeldi—quick.
Jure ko paunee—strong stream.

Kinnary—the shore.
Koldo—to open.
Kutchaar—a steep overhanging bank.

Legow—fasten.
Luggee—long bamboo poles used to push off the boat.
Lungur—an anchor.

Mastule—a mast.
Mhangy—captain of the boat's crew.

Naar—a boat.
Naar koldo—Unmoor the boat.
Nullah—a stream.

Owtah—coming.

Pankah—a muddy beach.
Paul—a sail.
Pawnee, bursna, lugga—It's going to rain.

Ro—Stay.

Soono—Do you hear?

Tiphaan—a storm.

THE END.

Editorial notes

Abbreviations

EIC   East India Company
Hobson-Jobson   H. Yule and A. C. Burnell, *Hobson-Jobson: The Anglo-Indian Dictionary* (Ware: Wordsworth, 1996)

Notes

1. *Calcutta*: Now Kolkata: a city in West Bengal. Calcutta was one of the three administrative centres of British India, the others being Madras (Chennai) and Bombay (Mumbai). Although located near to several Indian villages the town largely developed around the trading station established by the EIC in the seventeenth century, which was fortified in the early eighteenth century. In the latter part of the eighteenth century, Calcutta became known as the 'City of Palaces' because of the numerous palatial residences built there.
2. *Bengal*: A Presidency of British India (see note 7). The region is now divided between India (forming the modern Indian state of West Bengal) and Bangladesh.
3. *Hindostan*: Hindostan usually referred to the geographical area north of the Deccan, especially the area around the Ganges and the Yamuna rivers.
4. *Ganges*: The river that flows through India and Bangladesh, rising in the Himalayas and flowing into the Bay of Bengal. It is considered sacred by many Hindus.
5. *Khaanpore*: Now Kanpur: a city in Uttar Pradesh. Deane uses various spellings to denote this large military station. It gained notoriety during the First War of Indian Independence in 1857 when Nana Sahib (1824–1859) and his forces held the garrison under siege. After the British surrendered, Indian forces killed many of the British soldiers. Then, later at Bibi Ghar, they also killed around 200 British women and children.
6. *At the expiration of the war, of 1804*: The Second Anglo-Maratha War took place from 1803–1804, when the Scindias and Holkars, powerful Maratha dynasties, rebelled against the incumbent Peshwa, the leader of the Maratha Empire. At this time, the Peshwa was Baji Rao II (1775–1851). The EIC entered the war in support of the Peshwa and defeated the rebels, a victory that extended their control over central India. See also note 204.
7. *Presidency*: Administrative units organized and controlled by the British EIC.

8 *budgerow*: A long barge boat with big sails and living compartments. Prior to the construction of the railways, Europeans frequently used these boats to travel along the Ganges.
9 *palankeens*: Also palanquins: covered box-shaped carriages for single travellers, carried by two horizontal poles on the shoulders of four or six bearers.
10 *bearers*: Usually referred to a palanquin-carrier, but the term could also denote a domestic servant who looked after clothing, furniture, and ready money.
11 *dhooley*: Also doolie: another kind of covered carriage. It consisted of a chair suspended by a bamboo pole frame, which was carried by two or four men.
12 bazaar: A permanent market or street of shops.
13 Barrackpore: The British built a cantonment here in 1772, as an auxiliary station to Calcutta. It also became the site of the Governor-General's sprawling summer residence in 1801, when Richard Wellesley (1760–1842) appropriated the area and began work on an expansive estate. In the following paragraph, Deane mentions the residence with approval.
14 Seapoy *corps*: Also sepoy corps: an Indian branch of the British Indian Army.
15 *Governor General of India*: During Deane's time in India, there were four Governor-Generals. Richard Wellesley held the post from 1798–1805; he was followed by Charles Cornwallis, who took on the role for a brief period before he died, after which Sir George Barlow became acting Governor-General (1805–1807). Subsequently Gilbert Elliott-Murray-Kynynmound, Lord Minto, assumed the position 1807–1813; finally, Francis Edward Rawdon Hastings held the post from 1813–1823.
16 Chandanagore: Also Chandannagar and Chandernagore: At this time, Chandernagore was a French settlement but, between 1756–1816, Britain intermittently gained control of it.
17 Chinsurah: An unsettled area that passed between various European colonial powers. It was established by the Portuguese, and subsequently controlled by the Dutch. In 1825 it was ceded to the British in exchange for territory in Sumatra.
18 Serampore: From 1775–1845, this small Danish settlement was a hub of missionary activity, since it was exempt from the EIC's pre-1813 ban on missionary activity and religious conversion in British territories. See also note 19.
19 *English missionaries*: In the early nineteenth century, English Baptist missionaries, including Joshua Marshman (1768–1837), Hannah Marshman (1767–1847), William Ward (1769–1823), and William Carey (1761–1834), travelled to the Danish settlement of Serampore because they were unable to work as missionaries in British India. While there, they set up schools and colleges and established a religious printing press. Consequently, Serampore became an important centre for religious translation and publishing.
20 *a young Malay prince*: Not identified.
21 Java: An Indonesian island and the centre of the Dutch East Indies.
22 Dum Dum: A military cantonment north of Calcutta established in 1783, which became the headquarters of the Bengal Artillery until 1853. It was at the Artillery armoury there, in the early 1890s, that Captain Neville Bertie-Clay developed an expanding bullet that became known as the dum-dum.
23 *morass*: An area of boggy ground.
24 Bengalee *language*: Bengali: the language of Bangladesh and West Bengal.
25 Hindostanee *language*: The language spoken in northern India, derived principally from Hindi and Urdu.
26 Patna: Now the capital city of the state of Bihar, Patna was an important trading centre for the British from the seventeenth to nineteenth century. It was also the site of the infamous Patna Massacre in 1763 (see note 107), after which it came under British control, in 1764.
27 caste: A social and religious distinction in Indian society.

28 *Both Hindus and Mussulmen are tenacious in this respect*: Although Islam does not officially recognize caste, many Indian Muslim communities adopted this system of social stratification.
29 dandies: In this case, a boatman of the Ganges. However the Anglo-Indian dictionary *Hobson-Jobson* (1886) notes that it can also refer to a kind of ascetic who carries a staff. See *Hobson-Jobson*, p. 296.
30 *a white patch with a spot of bright scarlet in the centre, and a stripe of white paint down the middle of the nose*: Deane is presumably referring to the *tilak*, a Hindu mark usually worn on the forehead on auspicious occasions. It can also be worn on a daily basis, depending on the region. The colours and shape differ depending on the cultural tradition.
31 *trowsers*: Trousers, all made from local fabrics.
32 *satin*: A glossy material, usually made from silk.
33 *dimity*: A type of cotton, hard-wearing and woven with stripes or checks.
34 *calico*: Also a type of cotton, typically plain and unbleached. It became one of the most popular domestic textiles exported to England.
35 *muslin*: Another type of cotton, lightweight and weaved, that became a primary export.
36 *"Gird up thy loins"*: There are several references to 'girding up one's loins' (i.e. tying up a tunic) in the Bible. See, for example, 1 Kings 18:46: 'Then the hand of the LORD came upon Elijah; and he girded up his loins and ran ahead of Ahab to the entrance of Jezreel'.
37 *Nawaab of Lucknow*: Saadat Ali Khan II (c. 1752–1814) was the Nawab, or Mughal governor, of Lucknow and Awadh (1798–1814).
38 *kinkob*: A fine silk fabric embroidered with threads of gold or silver.
39 *paddy*: Rice in the husk, or before thrashing.
40 *otta*: A kind of coarse flour.
41 *dohl*: More commonly dhal: A dish made of lentils or other pulses, in this case pea.
42 *potatoes*: Although the Portuguese first introduced potatoes to the west coast of India in the seventeenth century, by the late eighteenth century, the British were planting them in the hills and plains of northern India.
43 mowah *tree*: *Madhuca indica*, a deciduous Indian tree. The green berries can be fermented and distilled into an alcoholic drink.
44 Krishna: A major Hindu deity and the eighth avatar of Vishnu. See also Maitland, Letter 17, note 272.
45 Kossimbazar: Also Cossimbazar, or Kasimbazar: A town in West Bengal. It was an important colonial commercial centre from the seventeenth to the nineteenth century.
46 Shoolbereah: Coolbariah in Bengal was the location of one of India's many indigo factories. There was a huge demand for the blue dye in Europe in the nineteenth century and Bengal was a major producer.
47 *Monsieur Savi*: Possibly John Angelo Savi (1765–1831), who established an indigo estate in Coolbariah 1780–1785. He was actually Italian but married to a Frenchwoman, Élizabeth De Corderan (1775–?) and had served in the French Navy.
48 *a young widow, (their daughter) . . . a Catholic priest, and four French gentlemen*: The individual identities of this party have not been identified.
49 *bon mot*: A 'good word' (French) or, as in this case, 'a witty remark'.
50 Placey: Also Plassey: a small village in Bengal and, as Deane goes on to acknowledge, the site of a famous battle in 1757 between Robert Clive (see note 52) and the Nawab of Bengal, Siraj-ud-Daulah (1733–1757). The British won and consolidated their presence and power in the area.
51 Moorshedabad: Also Murshidabad: a town in West Bengal. Previously the capital of Bengal during the Mughal Empire, it was taken by Major Adams (see note 64) in 1763.
52 *Lord Clive's first victory over the* Bengalese: Robert Clive, first Baron Clive of Plassey (1725–1774), was an army officer and administrator in the EIC. He defeated

Siraj-ud-Daulah at the Battle of Plassey in 1757 and appointed a seemingly more compliant nawab, Mir Jafar (c. 1691–1765) to secure British supremacy in Bengal.

53 *the residence of the* Nawaab *of* Bengal: As stated here, the Nawab of Bengal, Babar Ali Khan Bahadur, resided at Murshidabad. He was succeeded by his son Zain-ud Din Ali Khan in 1810. However, as Deane points out, in recent years, this role had become largely performative, with real power resting with the EIC.

54 Berhampore: Also Baharampur: a city in West Bengal that was fortified by the British after the Battle of Plassey in 1757 (see note 50). It became an important military station and it was the site of a major battle during the First War of Indian Independence in 1857.

55 *This custom of frequent ablution*: Deane refers to the ritual purifications of Hindus common in India. The rituals follow various forms but, as Deane notes, it is particularly auspicious to bathe the whole body in the sacred river of the Ganges.

56 tatties: Deane offers a lengthy description of the tatty in her footnote. In short, they were screens or mats made from the roots of a fragrant grass. They were placed in the openings of doors or windows and kept wet in order to produce evaporation and blow cold air throughout the house.

57 coup d'œil: 'Quick look' (French). It can also mean a 'brief survey'.

58 jemeendars: Also *zamindars* and *zemindars*: Indian landowners who were entitled to collect revenue from local farmers on behalf of the Government.

59 *tamarinds*: *Tamarindus indica* produces pod-like fruit which is used for making curries and pickles; the seeds can be used to make flour.

60 Radge Mah'l *hills*: A region located in Jharkhand, near Rajmahal, and inhabited by the Paharia people; it came under British control in 1765.

61 Radge Mah'l: Also Rajmahal: a city in the state of Jharkhand. It was the capital of Bengal 1592–1607, and 1639–1707.

62 serai: A building for the accommodation of travellers. See *Hobson-Jobson*, p. 811.

63 char-piah: Also *charpiah* or *charpoy*: a four-footed Indian bed.

64 *bridge built of red brick over the* Oodah Nullah: Major Thomas Adams (c. 1730–1764) of the EIC defeated Mir Qasim's army at Udhua Nullah in 1763. The British had appointed Mir Qasim as the Nawab of Bengal in 1760 when Mir Jafar, his father-in-law, proved too independent (see also note 103). However, Mir Qasim similarly resisted British control and conflict broke out.

65 *Rajah*: Originally meant 'king' but the British also used it to denote indigenous rulers.

66 dawks: A system of mail delivery, or passenger transportation, executed by relays of bearers stationed at intervals along a route.

67 *remains of a magnificent palace*: Deane refers to the remains of Shah Shuja's palace at Rajmahal. The second son of Emperor Shah Jahan and Empress Mumtaz Muhal, Shah Shujah (1616–1661) was governor of Bengal and Odisha between 1641 and 1661); see note 215.

68 toddy: The fermented sap of the palm used to produce palm wine. In India, it is also used for yeast in order to leaven bread.

69 *the* Mharattah: Now largely the state of Maharashtra and originally, the home of the Marathas, an ethnic group who originated from the Deccan plateau in central India. They grew in power as the Mughal Empire declined during the late seventeenth century, and they established their own considerable empire until they were finally defeated by the British during the Third Anglo-Maratha War (1817–1818).

70 The Jauts: The Jat or Jauts were an agricultural community originating in Rajasthan, the Punjab, and the North-Western provinces. As Deane mentions, some historians believe they were descendants of militant Rajputs; see, for example, W. Cooke, *Races of Northern India* (New Delhi: Cosmo Publications, 1973), p. 92. In any case,

the Jats were known for their rebellion against the Mughals in the late seventeenth century.
71 *Bahar*: Also Bihar: an Indian state known for its rich resources. It came under British control in 1764 after the Battle of Buxar. See note 125.
72 *Dow's History*: Alexander Dow (c. 1735–1779) was an Orientalist and officer in the EIC. His three-volume work, *The History of Hindostan* (London: T. Becket and P. A. De Hondt, 1768–1772), included a translation of a Persian history by Muhammad Kasim Ferishta alongside his own research. Widely reviewed and discussed in Britain, this volume shaped late eighteenth-century ideas about India and Indian people. In particular, Dow insisted that despotism had shaped the Mughal Empire.
73 *Milton, "These are thy works, Parent of good!"*: John Milton (1608–1674) was an English poet, best remembered for his Biblical epic *Paradise Lost* (1667). This quote is from Book 5, l.153: 'These are thy glorious works, Parent of Good'.
74 *The gentleman who resided there*: Not identified.
75 *These are quite a distinct race of people*: Deane may be referring to the Paharia tribe who occupied the hills around Rajmahal, Bhagalpur, and Kharagpur. The local people in this area had resisted British rule and attracted the attention of the EIC.
76 *fakeer*: Also fakir: in basic terms a beggar, but also a religious ascetic living on alms. The term originally referred to Muslims but, as seen here, it also applied to Hindu devotees.
77 *Baugulpoor*: Also Bhagalpur: an ancient city in Bihar mentioned in both the *Ramayana* and the *Mahabharata*.
78 *Hill Rangers*: The Bhagalpur Hill Rangers were an auxiliary force intended to pacify the Santal Parganas area in the 1780s. They were first organized by Augustus Cleveland (1754–1784), the city's first Collector and Magistrate, in 1780.
79 *The Judge and his Lady*: James Wintle (1781–?) was the Magistrate of Bhagalpur in 1805.
80 *the Mayor*: Not identified.
81 *ginghams*: A lightweight cotton yarn dyed before being woven. Along with muslin, calico, chintz, and dungaree, gingham was one of the primary textile exports from India to England.
82 *Cashmere*: A soft wool that originally came from the Kashmir goat.
83 *Predestinarian*: A person who believes that God foreordains all that will happen.
84 *Meerut*: An ancient city in the modern state of Uttar Pradesh. In 1803, the Marathas ceded this area to the British and Meerut became a garrison town.
85 cóprah capell: Deane is referring to either the Indian, or spectacled cobra (*Naja naja*) or the king cobra (*Ophiophagus hannah*). *Capella* means 'hooded' in Portuguese and refers to the ability of both species to flatten their necks so as to appear more threatening to predators.
86 *salaam*: A gesture of greeting in many Arabic and Muslim countries, typically consisting of a low bow of the head and body with hand or fingers touching the forehead.
87 *matchlocks*: A type of gun with a lock in which a cord or wick was placed to ignite the powder.
88 *Monghir*: Also Munger or Monghyr: a city in the state of Bihar, about four miles from the famous springs of Sita Kund, mentioned here by Deane. During Mir Qasim's reign (1760–1763), it was briefly the capital of Bengal.
89 *chalybeate springs*: Spring waters containing iron. From the seventeenth century, people believed they had healing properties.
90 *Brahmans*: Brahmins are members of the highest Hindu caste, traditionally the priestly caste; but, by the eighteenth century, they were widely employed in secular occupations.
91 *a pretty strong fort*: Munger's ancient fort was Mir Qasim's base during his conflict with the British in 1763–1764. See note 103.

92 *The ceremony*: The hook-swinging ceremony described by Deane in the following paragraphs has various names, such as *Charak* or *Churuk Puja*. The devotee is suspended from hooks passed through the body and attached to a long pole, apparently in order to satisfy Lord Shiva. It was the subject of many sensationalist accounts by nineteenth-century travellers, see for example F. Parks, *Wanderings of a Pilgrim in Search of the Picturesque, During Four and Twenty Years in the East: With Revelations of Life in the Zenana*, 2 vols (London: Pelham Richardson, 1850), vol. 1, p. 127.

93 *that passage in the law of Moses, wherein he says, "Thou shalt not muzzle the ox that treadeth out the corn"*: Deane quotes from Moses's speeches to the Israelites; see Deuteronomy 25:4: 'You shall not muzzle an ox while it treads out the grain'.

94 neem: The neem tree, *Meliaceae Azadirachta india*, grows all over India and, as Deane goes on to describe, the leaves, bark, fruit, and oil extracted from the seeds all apparently have medicinal properties.

95 avant couriér: 'advance runner' (French), i.e. a person running ahead, especially a member of the advance guard of an army.

96 *tannahs*: In addition to Deane's explanation, a *tannah* could also refer to a police station or a fortified post.

97 Benares: Also Varanasi: a city in Uttar Pradesh on the banks of the Ganges, and one of the seven sacred cities of Hinduism.

98 *one of the Judges of the Court of Appeal at Patna*: In Patna, in 1805, there were three Judges of the Court of Appeal and Circuit: Christopher Keating, James Edward Colebrooke, and John Rawlins.

99 *the superintending surgeon*: James Macnab was the surgeon in Patna in 1805.

100 Bankipore: Also Bankipur: an administrative centre for the EIC, now in the state of Bihar.

101 *"A barren woman ... can never go to heaven"*: It has not been possible to identify a source for this quotation. It seems that Deane is merely repeating inaccurate hearsay.

102 *The city of Patna and it dependencies came into possession of the English in the year 1764*: Patna officially came under Company rule after the Battle of Buxar in 1764. See note 125.

103 Meer Kossim Khan: Mir Qasim (d. 1777) was the Nawab of Bengal from 1760 to 1763. He was installed by the British when his father-in-law, Mir Jafar (1691–1765), refused to cooperate with Company demands. However, Mir Qasim soon became unhappy with various commercial advances made by the Company and conflict arose.

104 Sumroo, *(or Sombre)*: Walter Reinhardt Sombre (c. 1725–1778) is cited variously as French, German, Armenian, and Alsatian. Regardless of nationality, he served under both French and Indian leaders in the subcontinent, most notably Mir Qasim.

105 *husband to the Begum of that name*: Sumroo was married to Begum Sumroo or Samroo – original name: Zeb-un-Nissa (c. 1753–1836) – who became an infamous Indian icon and an independent ruler of Sardanah. See also note 263.

106 *Meer Kossim Khan was driven into that fortress*: Munger Fort (see note 91). Mir Qasim used Munger as his capital throughout his reign and strengthened the fort there. During the conflicts of 1763, he remained at the fort while his armies fought in the fields.

107 *he caused them to be massacred*: In 1763, Mir Qasim captured a group of British military officers and imprisoned them at Patna. Then, after the British victories at Munger and Udhua Nullah, the Nawab ordered their execution and this came to be known as the Patna Massacre. Various reports of the incident cite Walter Reinhardt Sombre (Sumroo) as the perpetrator of this violent act. See also note 104.

108 *Major Adams ... driving Meer Kossim and his followers to take refuge with* Sujah Dowlah, *then Emperor of* Delhi: Major Thomas Adams successfully recaptured Patna after the aforementioned massacre and drove Mir Qasim into exile. The Nawab then turned to Shujah ud-Daulah, Nawab of Awadh (1754–1775), and Shah Alam II

(1759–1806), Mughal Emperor, for support against the EIC. Consequently, and unsuccessfully, these indigenous leaders joined forces for the battle of Buxar in 1764.

109 *girls are betrothed by their parents before they attain their seventh birthday*: Child marriages were prevalent in India and an increasing source of concern for the British. As Deane notes, this tradition usually entailed a betrothal at a young age with marriage following the onset of puberty.

110 mindy: The tradition of *mehndi* is the art of producing designs on the body with a paste made from the leaves of the henna plant. It is typically applied to brides before the wedding. The term more commonly denotes the ceremonial artform, and not the shrub itself.

111 *second book of Kings, "She put her eyes in painting"*: See 2 Kings 9:30.

112 *Mahometan law*: Under the direction of Warren Hasting (1732–1818), the British codified a separate set of laws for Hindus and Muslims. 'Mahometan' is a contemporary synonym for 'Muslim'.

113 *The Hindoos are the original inhabitants . . . gave laws to Hindostan*: Deane paraphrases Charles Hamilton's account of the subcontinent here. See C. Hamilton, *An Historical Relation of the Origin, Progress, and Final Dissolution of the Rohilla Afghans in the Northern Provinces of Hindostan* (London: G. Kearsley, 1787), p. 2.

114 toolsey: Deane makes a slight error here as *toolsey*, or *tulsi*, is a type of basil considered sacred by Hindus. It is therefore a herb, not a vegetable.

115 *no one can become a Hindu*: Deane is mistaken here. It is possible to convert to Hinduism.

116 Danapore: Danapur: a military station in Bihar and the location of a sepoy uprising during the First War of Indian Independence in 1857.

117 Moneah: Maner or Maner Sharif: a village in the Patna district of Bihar.

118 peeple trees: Also known as the peepal and peepul tree: the *Moraceae Ficus religiosa* originated in the Himalayan foothills and is considered sacred by Hindus and Buddhists. As Deane mentions, the leaves feed elephants; but it also produces figs and nearly every part of the tree has medicinal properties.

119 *Soane*: Also Sone or Son: a tributary of the River Ganges.

120 *the Judge at* Arrah: Not identified.

121 banditti: *Banditti* were robbers, especially those belonging to a gang. In India they were also known as *dacoits*. See note 122.

122 dakoities: Also *dacoity*: a gang of armed robbers.

123 *collectorship*: The Collector of Revenues was the chief administrator of an Indian District. As the name suggests, their main duty was the collection of taxes but they also held magisterial powers.

124 Arrah: A city, now in the state of Bihar. During the First War of Indian Independence in 1857, it was the site of an eight-day siege at the fortified house of Richard Vicars Boyle (1822–1908), an Irish engineer.

125 Buxar: A city in the state of Bihar. As mentioned by Deane, it was the site of a major battle in 1764 between the EIC, led by Major Hector Munro (c. 1725–c. 1805), and the combined forces of the Nawab of Awadh Shujah-ud-Daulah, the Mughal Emperor Shah Allam II, and the Nawab of Bengal Mir Qasim. The Company's decisive victory over the indigenous allies ensured British dominance in eastern India. Consequently, in 1765, the Mughal Emperor granted the EIC *diwani*, or revenue collecting rights, in Bengal, Bihar, and Orissa.

126 *Colonel Commandant and his family*: Not identified.

127 a clergyman: Not identified

128 *Hamlet's ghost*: In William Shakespeare's play *Hamlet* (1599), the ghost of Hamlet's father frequently appears, initiating the play's tragic plot; see, for example, Act 1, scene 1.

129 Ghazipore: Now Ghazipur: a city in Uttar Pradesh and a manufacturing centre, famous for its cloth, as Deane goes on to discuss in the following paragraphs. However, it was also known for its opium factory, which was first established there by the EIC.
130 *Judge of* Ghazipore: Not identified.
131 *the General in command*: Not identified.
132 *the Judge of the district*: Not identified.
133 *Otta of roses*: Also *otto* or *attar*: an essential oil made from rose petals, mainly produced at Ghazipur.
134 *the General commanding*: Not identified
135 *Chief Judge of the Court of Appeal*: William Augustus Brooke (?–1833) was the Chief Judge of the Court of Appeal in Benares (1804–1829).
136 *It is a system of policy on the part of the English to protect . . . our possessions in the country*: Until 1813, the EIC held a policy of religious tolerance in the territories it controlled.
137 *Emperor* Aurungzebe: Muhi-ud-Din Muhammad or Aurangzeb (1618–1707) was the sixth Mughal Emperor (r. 1658–1707). During his reign, he greatly expanded the empire until it encompassed most of the subcontinent. As Deane alludes to in this paragraph, he was notorious for his lack of religious tolerance, destroying Hindu temples and erecting mosques in their place, notably in Benares, Mathura, and Rajasthan.
138 Musjeeds: Now *Musjid*: the Arabic word for mosque.
139 *In the month of November, 1809, so serious a dispute arose in consequence*: In 1809, conflict broke out when Holi celebrators clashed with a *Muharram* mourning procession. Subsequently, crowds of Hindus stormed the great mosque of Aurungzeb. This was seen as belated retaliation for the emperor's destruction of sacred Hindu sites.
140 *an old saying, "Do you cock your hat at me?" – "Sir, I cock my hat"*: This 'old saying' is reminiscent of an exchange in Shakespeare's *Romeo and Juliet* (1597), Act 1, Scene 1, ll. 42–3. The original reads: 'Abraham: Do you bite your thumb at us, sir? / Samson: I do bite my thumb, sir'.
141 bankas: In the nineteenth century, the Bankas were identified as a particularly quarrelsome sect. See, for example, J. F. Davis, *Vizier Ali Khan: Or, the Massacre of Benaras, a Chapter in British History* (London: John Murray, 1844), p. 67.
142 *Mahometans have four important periods in the year*: There are four sacred months in the Islamic calendar: *Muḥarram* (1), *Rajab* (7), *Dhū al-Qa'dah* (11), and *Dhu al-Ḥijjah* (12). These are set out by George Sale in his well-known translation of the Qur'an (London: C. Ackers, 1734), vol. 1, p. 197. However, these are not mentioned by Deane, who goes on to describe four selected times of Muslim celebration.
143 *First the birth of Mahomet*: Celebrations for the birth of the prophet Muhammad, called *Mawlid-un-Nabi*, take place in *Rabi' al-awwal*, the third month of the Islamic year.
144 Ramzaan, *or* Ramdaan: Now Ramadan: Deane claims that Ramadan takes place in September but it actually occurs in the ninth month of the Islamic calendar. During this time, there is strict fasting from sunrise to sunset.
145 Mecca: The birthplace of Muhammad, located in what is now Saudi Arabia.
146 Medina: The location of Muhammad's tomb, also now located in Saudi Arabia.
147 *The third is the commencement of their new year*: The Muslim New Year occurs on the first day of the month of *Muḥarram*.
148 *A fourth is called the* Moharum *to commemorate the deaths of* Hussan *and* Houssein: The first month of the Islamic year is *Muḥarram* and the first ten days of this month are a time of public and private mourning. It marks the death of the prophet's grandson, Husayn ibn Ali, and his supporters at the Battle of Karbala.
149 the plains of Kerbela: The grandson of Muhammad, Husayn ibn Ali, and his supporters were killed in Karbala (present-day Iraq) by the larger military force of Yazid I, the Umayyad caliph.

150 *bier*: A movable frame on which a coffin or a corpse is placed before burial or cremation, or on which the remains are carried to the grave.
151 *a festival of the Hindoos, sacred to the* God of Wealth: Deane is presumably referring to Diwali, the Hindu festival of lights that takes place in October/November to celebrate the new season after the monsoon. It is particularly associated with Lakshmi, the goddess of prosperity.
152 *carpets equal to those made at Wilton, in Wiltshire*: Since the seventeenth century, Wilton had been an important centre for weaving and in 1741 it began producing carpets.
153 *Judge of Allahabad*: William Towers Smith (1783–1826).
154 *"a burnt child dreads the fire"*: A common idiom.
155 Allahabad: A large city in Uttar Pradesh founded by Akbar I (1542–1605) and acquired by the British in 1801.
156 *a strong fortress and palace built by the Emperor* Acbar: The Mughal Emperor, Akbar I, established an imperial city with a fort at Allahabad in Uttar Pradesh in 1575. British troops were first stationed here after the Battle of Buxar and the Treaty of Allahabad, signed in 1765.
157 *A considerable revenue is derived from the* Mahrattas, *who come at particular seasons of the year to perform their ablutions*: According to Hindu mythology, the riverside of Allahabad is one of four places where Vishnu dropped *amrita*, the sacred nectar; these sites became the locations of the Kumbh Mela, a mass Hindu pilgrimage. In the nineteenth century the Mela was annual and Hindu pilgrims, especially those from Maratha territory, travelled to the site. The EIC imposed a tax of one rupee for anyone wanting to bathe there.
158 *a Hindoo woman had signified her intention to end her existence on the funeral pile of her husband*: Deane is referring to the practice of *sati* or *suttee*, which was still legal during Deane's time in India. It was banned by the British, with the support of many Indian reformers, in 1829 under the governance of Lord William Bentinck (1774–1839).
159 Futtehpore: Now Fatehpur: a city in Uttar Pradesh, located between the Ganges and the Yumuna rivers.
160 hookahs: Indian pipes for smoking through water.
161 zenanah: Also *zenana*: the apartments of a house in which the women of a family are secluded.
162 champoo: Shampoo.
163 bungalow: These one-storeyed thatched houses originated in Bengal as temporary dwellings for Officers of the EIC. Over time, these structures were replicated throughout the subcontinent and the word 'bungalow' evolved from the description 'Bengal-style'. See *Hobson-Jobson*, p. 128.
164 kooftas: *kofta*: a kind of Indian meatball.
165 tiffin: Usually luncheon for English households in India, although it could also refer to an early dinner. See *Hobson-Jobson*, p. 920.
166 *ayah*: An indigenous lady's maid, and often the only female employee in the home. She was responsible for the personal care of the women and children of the family.
167 Khanpore: See note 5.
168 *Bengal army*: The army of the Bengal Presidency. The three Presidencies each had separate armies until they merged in 1895 to form the Indian army.
169 *His Majesty's Light Dragoons*: A cavalry regiment in the British Army.
170 *Commander-in-Chief*: The supreme commander of the British Indian Army. During Deane's time in India, the position was held by General Gerard Lake (predominantly throughout 1801–1807); Sir George Hewett (1807); Lieutenant-General Forbes Champagné (1807–1811), Sir George Nugent (1811–1813), and Francis Rawdon-Hastings (1813–1823).

171 *at the Judges*: In 1805, William Leycester (1790–1831) was the Judge at Kanpur. See also note 362.
172 Lucknow: The capital of Uttar Pradesh, and formerly the capital of Awadh, part of the Mughal Empire. The British took control of the city in 1856.
173 dak: As previously noted, this was a system of mail transport via relays of bearers and horses. In this instance, the cargo is people not post.
174 *Nawaab* Sadut Alli: Saadat Ali Khan II, Nawab of Awadh: See note 37.
175 *Grand Vizier*: The principal leader of the Ottoman Empire.
176 *General Lord Lake*: Gerard Lake (1744–1808) was intermittently Commander-in-Chief of the British army in India from 1801–1807. His successes during the Second Anglo-Maratha War (1803–1804) were the highlight of his military career.
177 *Lebitt Ben Rabial, Alamary*: Lebid Ben Rabiat Alamary was a celebrated poet from Yemen at the time of Muhammad. Deane includes here one of his unnamed poems in an English translation by Joseph Dacre Carlyle. See *Specimens of Arabian Poetry from the Earliest Time to the Extinction of the Kaliphate, with Some Account of the Authors* (London: T. Cadell and W. Davies [1796] 1810), pp. 4–10.
178 *straight smooth reed*: Reed pens, usually made from bamboo, were extremely common for calligraphy.
179 Aliph: *Aleph* is the first letter of the Hebrew alphabet.
180 *Begum*: A title usually denoting an indigenous Indian woman of the upper classes or aristocracy.
181 *zephyrs*: Light breeze or wind.
182 *the lovely* Leila, *and made more frantic the enamoured* Mujnoon: *Layla and Majnun* is a narrative poem composed by the Persian poet Nezami in 1188. It was translated into English by the Orientalist Isaac Disraeli in 1797 and reprinted as *The Loves of Mejnoun and Leila, a celebrated Persian romance: With notes, Illustrative of the Manners and Customs of the Persians* (Calcutta, 1800).
183 *Worcestershire china*: The Royal Worcester China Company was established in 1751.
184 a la forchette: 'with a fork' (French). Also used to indicate a meal of such substance as to require cutlery; it often indicated a hearty breakfast, taken late morning or lunchtime.
185 Futty-ghur: Deane uses several different spellings for 'Fateghar', a cantonment town and an administrative centre for Furrukhabad.
186 Sudder *station*: The chief station of a district, where the Collector, Judge, and other officials reside.
187 Furrukabad: Farrukhabad: as Deane states, this was an important trade centre.
188 *Mahratta country*: Broadly refers to what is now the state of Maharashtra but Deane could also mean the Deccan plateau, from where the Marathas originated. See note 69.
189 *Scotch cambric*: Cambric is a light plain-weave cotton, originally from Cambrai in France. In the eighteenth century, England prohibited its importation because of its similarity to Indian materials, which became known as Scotch cambrics in order to distinguish them from the French originals.
190 *The Nawaab bearing the title of the city, resides within it*: The Nawab of Furrukhabad was Imdad Husain Khan (r. 1802–1813). In 1802, he ceded his entire territory to the Company in return for an annual pension.
191 *the family we quitted*: Not identified
192 Agra: A city in Uttar Pradesh, famous as the home of the Taj Mahal, as well as the Agra Fort. It came under British control during the Second Anglo-Maratha Wars.
193 Mynpoorie: Now Mainpuri: a city in Uttar Pradesh.
194 *the spectacle Noah must have witnessed when he took refuge in the ark*: Deane compares the scene here to the one witnessed by Noah as he escaped the Biblical flood. See Genesis: 6–12.

195 Shekoabad: Also Shikohabad: a town in Uttar Pradesh. As Deane goes on to describe, in 1803 during the Second Anglo-Maratha War a group of Maratha horsemen attacked the British detachment at Shekoabad. However, her report is rather sensationalist as records suggest that the Marathas actually negotiated with the British, allowing them safe passage in return for withdrawing from the campaign against Sindia, with the exception of Mrs Wilson, wife of EIC Captain Wilson, who was held hostage. See R. G. S. Cooper, *The Anglo-Maratha Campaigns and the Contest for India* (Cambridge: Cambridge University Press, 2003).

196 Pindarees: Pindaris: Originally a band of horsemen, attached to the Maratha Empire. They became notorious for their violence and rapacity during the Anglo-Maratha Wars.

197 *Our late operations, under the command of the Marquis of Hastings . . . this formidable enemy*: In 1818, after Deane's departure from India but prior to the publication of her book, Francis Edward Rawdon Hastings, 1st Marquess of Hastings, Commander-in-Chief of the Indian Army and Governor-General of India (1813–1823), defeated both the Pindaris and the Marathas in the third and final Anglo-Maratha War.

198 *war of 1818*: The Third Anglo-Maratha War was the final, decisive conflict between the British and the Marathas. It began when the British invaded Maratha territory to take action against the ongoing marauding violence of the Pindaris. In response, three of the Maratha leaders joined forces: Peshwa Baji Rao II, Appasaheb of Nagpur, and Tulsabai Holkar. They were defeated and the Maratha Empire collapsed.

199 *the river Indus*: Originates in Tibet and then runs through the length of what is now Pakistan.

200 *"The number of native servants . . . before the next hour"*: It has not been possible to trace the source of this quote.

201 *In 1812 they made an irruption into* Bengal . . . *into* Madras: Between 1812 and 1816, the Pindaris persistently invaded British territories. There were numerous reports of violent atrocities. Deane claims that these incursions, seemingly supported by the Marathas, were the motivation for the Third Anglo-Maratha War.

202 Scindia, Holkar: Deane is referring to the leaders of the Sindia and Holkar dynasties of the Maratha Confederacy: Daulat Rao Sindhia (1779–1827) and Malharrao Holkar III (1806–33) – although the latter's mother, Tulsabai, was largely in control of the Holkars due to Malharrao's young age.

203 Ameer Khan: Amir Khan (1769–1834) was a Pashtun who fought with the Maratha Empire against the EIC in the Third Anglo-Maratha War (1817–1818).

204 Peishwa: The hereditary leader of the Maratha Empire. At this time, it was Baji Rao II (1775–1851), who had been supported by the British during the Second Anglo-Maratha War. However, in 1817, he switched allegiances and joined forces with the other Maratha dynasties during the Third Anglo-Maratha War.

205 *Rajah of* Nagpore: Rajah Madhoji II Bhonsle, also known as Appasaheb, joined the Peshwa's forces during the Third Anglo-Maratha War.

206 *a treaty of peace in 1813*: Appasaheb actually formed an alliance with the British in 1816. However, he then went against the conditions of the treaty by engaging with Peshwa Baji Rao II a year later. This resulted in the Battle of Nagpur in 1817. Appasaheb and his troops were defeated and the British-installed Raghuji III in his place.

207 *One of these impregnable forts was* Huttrass, *near* Agra, *in possession of a Jaut chief, Diah Ram*: In the following pages Deane outlines the events of the siege of Hattrass, or Hathras, a city in Uttar Pradesh. In 1817, Raja Dayaram of Hathras resisted the British and subsequently escaped capture.

208 Rajpoots: Also Rajput: warrior clans based in northern and north-western India.

209 *Rajah of* Burtpore: Ranjit Singh was the Maharajah of Bharatpur (r. 1778–1805) and was succeeded by his son Randhir Singh (r. 1805–1823).

210 *The general*: Sir Dyson Marshall commanded the British regiment sent to capture the fortress at Hathras; see note 207.
211 Rohillah: Afghan warriors who settled in India in the second half of the eighteenth century in Rohilkhand, an area in Uttar Pradesh, on the upper Ganges.
212 *The unfortunate failure of our troops in their several attacks on this* Rajah of Burtpore: Ranjit Singh, the former ruler, resisted four attacks by the British, led by General Lake, during the siege of Bharatpur in 1805. Previously, he indicated his intention to join the British during the Second Anglo-Maratha War. Instead, however, he joined forces with Yashwantrao Holkar (1776–1811). Deane suggests his successful act of resistance at Bharatpur served as inspiration for further indigenous oppositions.
213 *The Jauts have repeatedly revolted against the Mogul government*: The Jats of Bharatpur fought many wars against the Mughal Empire in the seventeenth and eighteenth centuries.
214 *Within the last century . . . carried away plunder to an immense amount*: In the latter half of the eighteenth century, the Jats took advantage of the Maratha Empire's defeat of the Mughal Empire. They captured Delhi in 1771 and seized Agra in 1761, plundering the city.
215 Tadge: The Taj Mahal is a mausoleum erected between 1631–1648 by Shah Jahan (1592–1666), the fifth Mughal Emperor, for his favourite wife Mumtaz Mahal (1593–1631). Deane provides a lengthy description of the monument in Chapter 10.
216 *the tomb of the Emperor Acbar, situated at a place called* Secundra, *about 5 miles from* Agra: Akbar I's tomb remains at Sikandra, now a suburb of Agra. Akbar was the third Mughal Emperor (r. 1556–1605).
217 Koraan: The Qur'an is the principal religious text of Islam. As Deane states, verses and passages from the text are inscribed on the panels of the Taj Mahal.
218 Shaw Allum: Shah Allam II (1728–1806) became the Mughal Emperor in 1759 during a time of great conflict, and reigned until 1806, despite losing against the British at Buxar. Later he sought British protection and granted them the *diwani* of Bengal in exchange. See note 125.
219 *whose eyes were put out by one of his subjects*: Deane misidentifies the perpetrator of this incident. It was actually the Rohilla chief Ghulam Qadir Khan who captured Shah Allam II in Delhi in 1788 and then blinded him. Deane's contemporary, Lady Nugent, makes a similar mistake. See A. L. Cohen (ed.), *Lady Nugent's East India Journal* (Oxford: Oxford University Press, 2014), p. 194.
220 Ally Ghur: Aligarh is a city in Uttar Pradesh; in 1804 it was the site of a successful siege and battle led by General Lake during the Second Anglo-Maratha War.
221 Bhagwaut Singh, Diah Ram &c.: Rajah Dayaram was the ruler of the region but Deane's other references here are unclear. See also note 207.
222 *near the city of* Coel, *they placed a formidable garrison*: Coel or Koil was adjacent to the Aligarh fortress, and both were captured by the British under General Lake in 1803.
223 *August 1804:* Deane makes a mistake here regarding the date of the Siege at Aligarh. Lord Lake captured the fort from General Perron (see note 264) and the Maratha army in September 1803.
224 Ferozabad: Now Firozabad, a city in Uttar Pradesh.
225 Teeseldar: More commonly *tehsildar* or *tahsildar*: the chief indigenous revenue collector of a district.
226 dhye: This soured milk was a common ingredient in Indian cooking.
227 Ettamaadpore: Now Etmadpur: a town in Uttar Pradesh. It served as a *tehsil*, or administrative centre, during British rule.
228 *the collector of the district*: Not identified.
229 Jumna: The Yamuna river, the second largest tributary of the Ganges, flowing from the Himalayas and merging with the Ganges at Allahabad.

TOUR THROUGH HINDOSTAN.

230 *a man named* Ettamaad Dowlut, *meaning Ettamaad the Rich*: Deane refers to Mir Ghiyas Beg, also known as Itmad-ud-Daulah, a poor merchant who became the chief minister in the Mughal court of Jahangir (Akbar I's son). The tomb, mentioned by Deane, was commissioned by his daughter who had married Jahangir in 1611.

231 *Emperor of* Delhi: As Deane notes, the Mughal Emperor was now known as the Emperor of Delhi, signalling the diminishing extent of his power. For the majority of Deane's time in India, this position was held by Akbar Shah II (1760–1837). He reigned from 1806–1837.

232 *fort of* Agra: Agra fort and palace was commissioned by Akbar I in 1565. It remained the principal residence of the Mughal Emperor until 1638 when Delhi became the capital. The Marathas captured it in the eighteenth century and the British acquired it in 1803.

233 *predatory horsemen*: Pindaris, see note 196.

234 Moharum: See note 148.

235 *the commanding officer of Secundra*: Not identified.

236 Agra, *the fort and palace*: See note 232.

237 *the mausoleum of* Christie: The tomb of the Sufi saint Salim Chisti (1478–1572).

238 Futtypoor Siccra: Fatehpur Sikri is a town in Uttar Pradesh, near Agra, founded by Akbar I as the capital of the Mughal Empire. It contains a number of notable monuments and is now classified as a UNESCO World Heritage Site.

239 *a monastery*: I have found no mention of a monastery at Fatehpur Sikri; however, there is a Roman Catholic Church and Cemetery, in which Sumroo is buried.

240 Sumroo: See note 104.

241 *in this monastery he is buried*: Walter Reinhardt Sombre (or Sumroo; see Chapter 5, note 104) is buried in the Roman Catholic Cemetery in Fatehpur Sikri, one of the oldest Christian burial sites in India.

242 *Begum Sumroo*: See note 105.

243 Tadge Mahl: See note 215.

244 *Emperor* Shaw Jehaan: Shah Jahan was the Mughal Emperor (r. 1627–1658). He is often praised for his cultural achievements. He is especially remembered for commissioning the Taj Mahal in memory of his wife Mumtaz Mahal. See note 215.

245 *in the year 1719*: Deane is mistaken about the date of the Taj Mahal, which was largely completed by 1643.

246 Montaza Mhul: Mumtaz Mahal. See note 215.

247 *artificers arrived from England, France, Italy, Greece:* Reportedly, craftsmen from all over India, Persia, and Europe helped to complete the building.

248 *The Tomb of* Christie *at* Futty-poor Siccra: See notes 237 and 238.

249 *a magnificent palace built by Emperor* Acbar: Akbar I built a walled city and imperial palace complex at Fatehpur Sikri. Deane goes on to describe several of its features.

250 *The apartments we were shown as having belonged to* Tamoulah: Deane is surely referring to the Jodha Bai Palace built for Akbar I's chief wife, Mariam-uz-Zumani, also known as Jodha Bai. She was originally a Rajput princess and was the mother of Akbar's successor Jahangir. The Jodha Bai palace is made of red granite, just like the structure described here.

251 *A structure contiguous to the palace*: Deane is referring to Diwan-i-Khas or Hall of Private Audience, famed for its central pillar.

252 *the fort of* Bhurtpore, *before which our army were five times repulsed*: Lohagarh Fort at Bharatpur withstood the British army, led by Lord Lake, on four occasions in 1805.

253 *These provinces having been newly conquered by the British army*: In 1803, during the Second Anglo-Maratha War, the British gained control of Agra and Delhi and the surrounding areas.

254 *the Nile*: A major river in north-east Africa. It is widely regarded as the longest river in the world.
255 bauboool *tree*: The *Mimosaceae Acacia arabica*, also known as the babul or babool tree, is native to India and Africa. It has many uses, including those mentioned here.
256 *cotton plant*: Cotton comes from the *Gossypium* plants, a shrub native to tropical and subtropical regions.
257 bang: Also known as *bhang*: from Hindi, used to refer to the dried leaves of the Cannabis plant when used a narcotic.
258 palma christi: *Ricinus communis*, the castor bean plant, reportedly has medicinal qualities.
259 the fort of Alli Ghur: Aligarh: See note 220.
260 *Lisbon*: The capital city of Portugal.
261 *We encamped on this day near the field of battle on the memorable 11th September, 1803, when British forces under Lord Lake conquered the Mahratta army*: Putpore Gunge, or Patparganj, is where General Lake's army pitched their tents on 11 September 1803, after their victory at Aligarh. They were subsequently surprised by Maratha horsemen and the conflict that took place there became known as the Battle of Delhi because the Marathas surrendered the city soon after their defeat.
262 *the resident*: Sir Archibald Seton was the Resident at Delhi 1806–1811. The Resident was a British official stationed in Indian kingdoms. He largely controlled local policy while the Indian ruler was reduced to a symbolic figurehead.
263 *Monsieur L'Oiseaux*: More commonly recorded as Le Vassoult: Begum Sumroo's second husband. After Walter Reinhardt died, Begum Sumroo married a French nobleman who had joined her military force. However, he proved unable to lead her armies, and this provoked dissatisfaction and defections. Eventually the couple fled Sardhana but they were soon captured and Le Vassoult killed himself.
264 *General Perron*: Pierre Cuillier-Perron (c. 1755–1834) was a French adventurer in India. In 1795, he fought with the Maratha army and became Commander-in-Chief of Mahadji Sindhia's army, which was defeated by General Lake and Sir Arthur Wellesley (1769–1852).
265 Sirdanah: Sardhana: a small principality near Meerut, ruled by Begum Sumroo.
266 *During Lord Lake's sojourn at* Delhi, *he was her frequent guest*: After the battles of 1803, the Begum left the Marathas and joined the British. She frequently entertained prominent figures, such as Lord Lake and Reginald Heber (1783–1826), the Bishop of Calcutta.
267 *during the reign of the Emperor* Shaw Allum, *she is said to have saved the Mogul Empire by rallying and encouraging her troops*: Begum Sumroo helped Shah Allam II to quell a rebellion initiated by Najaf Quli Khan in 1787.
268 Zophany: Johan Joseph Zoffany (1733–1810) was a German neoclassical painter who had travelled in India between 1783–1790, and painted the altarpiece of the *Last Supper* for St. John's Church in Calcutta. His work was very popular in England.
269 *the* musnud: A large cushion used by native Princes in India instead of a throne.
270 *His Majesty*: Akbar II (1760–1837) was the Emperor of Delhi (1806–1837).
271 *crowds of eunuchs*: Eunuchs were frequently employed as the guards of women's living quarters in India.
272 *Queen Dowager, mother to the reigning Emperor*: Qudsia Begum, third wife of Shah Allam II and mother of Akbar II, the reigning Emperor.
273 betel nut: A palate cleanser and a mild stimulant made from wrapping the nut of the areca tree (*Areca catechu*) in the leaf of the betel vine (*Piper betle*).
274 *sat the Queen*: Begum Mumtaz-un-Nissa, mother of Mirza Jahangir (1791–1821).
275 *gold mohar*: Also mohur: the chief gold coin of British India.
276 *cornelian and lapis lazuli*: Semi-precious stones used in jewellery.

277 *Pitaan*: More commonly Pashtuns or Pathans: an ethnic group, mainly living today in Afghanistan and Pakistan.
278 *The Emperor, who is of Moghul extraction, of the house of Timoor, and a lineal descendent of the great Tamerlane*: Akbar II descended from Timur (1366–1405), also known as Tamerlane, who was known for his barbaric conquests from Russia through to his invasion of India in 1383. Christopher Marlowe (c. 1564–1593) wrote a two-part play about him, *Tamburlane the Great* (1587–1588).
279 *the wife of one of the princes, named* Jehanghier: Mirza Jahangir, Akbar II's son, had three wives: Halima-un-Nissa, Birj Bai, and Umrao Bai. It is unclear who Deane is describing here. Jahangir was exiled to Allahabad when he shot at Sir Archibald Seton, Resident at Delhi.
280 *Murza Selim*: Mirza Muhammad Salim Shah (1799–1836) was another son of Akbar II and Mumtaz-un-Nissa Begum.
281 *General O –* : Sir David Ochterlony (1758–1825) was previously the British Resident to the Mughal Court after the Battle of Delhi in 1803. Apparently, he had a *zenana* and would take evening walks with his thirteen Indian wives. See Cohen, *Lady Nugent's East India Journal*, p. 207.
282 *Kootub Minar*: The Qutub Minar dates from the twelfth or thirteenth century and forms part of a collection of buildings and monuments in Mehrauli. There are various theories as to the origin of the tower, but many historians believe it was built by Qutb al-Din Aibak the first Sultan of Delhi. See, for example, T. G. P. Spear, *Delhi: Its Monuments and History* (New Delhi: Oxford University Press, 1994).
283 *the adjmere gate*: The Adjmeri Gate, built in 1644, is one of the Gates of Delhi.
284 Meer Dahn Alli Khan: Not identified.
285 *the Royal Observatory*: Jantar Mantar, constructed in 1724 in Delhi, was one of the observatories built by Maharaja Jai Singh II of Jaipur.
286 *superb mausoleum of* Sufter Jung: Safdar Jang was the Nawab of Awadh (c. 1708–1754) and father of Shuja-ud-Daulah.
287 *late* Sadut Alli: Saadat Ali Kahn II died in 1814. See note 37.
288 *tomb of* Kootub ud Deen: The tomb of Qutbuddin Bakhtiar Kaki (1173–1235), a Sufi saint of the Chishti Order in Delhi, is the oldest shrine in Delhi. As Deane mentions, no women are allowed to enter the inner shrine.
289 *moolahs*: Also mullah: a Muslim learned in Islamic law and theology.
290 *tombs of* Bahadar Shaw *and* Shaw Allum *late Emperors of Delhi*: The graves of two Mughal emperors lie in the Qut'b complex: Bahadur Shah I (1643–1712) and Shah Allam II who, as Deane goes on to note, was the father of the reigning emperor, Akbar II. However, she mistakenly claims that Bahadur Shah was Akbar II's grandfather; this was, in fact, Alamgir II.
291 *"wonderful brazen pillar"*: Deane describes the Iron Pillar in the Qut'b complex. There is no definitive history for the pillar but it dates from third or fourth century AD.
292 Patowly, *the founder of* Delhi: Deane's reference here is not clear.
293 *the mausoleum of* Humayoon: Humayun, also known as Nasir-ud-Din Muhammad (r. 1530–1556), was the second emperor of the Mughal Empire, the son of Zahir ud-Din Muhammad Babur. The tomb was apparently commissioned by his first wife, Hamida Banu Begum in 1565.
294 Humayoon, *eldest son of* Timoor Shaw: Here Deane is mistaken. Humayun's father was Zahir ud-Din Muhammad Babur (1483–1530) the founder of the Mughal Empire in India. He was, however, a descendent of the conqueror Timur. See note 278.
295 *Candahar*: Kandahar is a city in Afghanistan.
296 *father of the renowned* Acbar: Humayun was the father of Akbar I (1542–1605) who succeeded him to become the third Mughal Emperor.

297 Humayoon *being the eldest son of* Timoor Shaw *ought . . . to have succeeded him on the throne*: As stated in note 294, Timoor Shaw was an ancestor of Humayun's but not his father. Deane also makes a further error here as Humayun did succeed his father, Babur, and subsequently assigned specific territories to his brothers.
298 Shaw Zemaan: Kamran Mirza (1509–1557), or Kamran, was Humayun's brother. He challenged Humayan's authority on a number of occasions until eventually, in 1553, Kamran was captured by his brother who blinded him and rendered him powerless.
299 Tippoo Sultaan: Tipu Sultan (1750–1799) was the ruler of the kingdom of Mysore. Clearly Deane's history here is chronologically inaccurate as he cannot have conspired with the brother of Humayun in the sixteenth century, or Timur Shaw's children.
300 *caused him to be seized and his eyes put out*: As stated in note 298, it was Prince Kamran, not Humayun who was blinded.
301 Begum Sumroo's *palace*: Bhagirath Palace was in Chandni Chowk, Delhi.
302 *a notch*: The *nautch* was a staged dance performed by women; however, the term often referred to any kind of stage entertainment.
303 *son of* Abdoulah Khan: Not identified
304 Cashmere: Kashmir is a large area in north-west India.
305 Jumna Musjeed: Constructed by Shah Jahan's daughter, Jahanara Begum, as the principal mosque of the city in 1648. It remains one of the largest mosques in India.
306 *the first verse of the Koran*: Deane provides the first verse of the Qur'an. Her source is not clear but her rendering is very close to that of George Sale's 1734 translation (see note 142).
307 Siads: Also Sayyids: Muslims who claim to be descendants of the prophet Muhammad.
308 Meratt: Another spelling of 'Meerut'. See note 84.
309 *The Judge . . . there encamped*: The members of this party have not been identified.
310 *Peton, a Frenchman*: Not identified.
311 *the* Dooab: Also doab: a tract of land between two rivers, most specifically, as is the case here, the Ganges and Yamuna.
312 Muzzuffer Nuggur: Also Muzaffanagar: a city in Uttar Pradesh.
313 Shah Naumeh: Also *Shahnameh or Shahname*: The *Shahnameh* or 'The Book of Kings' is a Persian epic by Abolqasem Ferdowsi. Ferdowsi brought together pre-Islamic narratives about the Persian Empire's mythical and historical past and recorded them in the form of a poem (c. 975–1010).
314 *the river* Hindon: A tributary of the Yamuna river.
315 Saharunpore: Also Saharanpur: a city in Uttar Pradesh. It came under British control in 1803 during the Second Anglo-Maratha War.
316 *the judge*: Roger Martin (1795–?).
317 Sieke *country*: Sikhs originated from the Punjab region of north-west India.
318 Runjeet Sing: Ranjit Singh (1780–1839), also known as the 'Lion of Lahore', ruled the Sikh empire in north-west India and stabilized the Punjab during his reign. Even though he signed a treaty with the British in 1806, he continued to expand his empire toward Afghanistan.
319 Fizabad: Also Faizabad: a city in Uttar Pradesh, and previously the capital of Awadh.
320 Ramdial Sing, *Rajah of* Hurdoar: Ramdayal Singh was a Gujar chief who ruled over the area of Landhaura, a city in the district of Haridwar that came under British occupation in 1803.
321 Blue Beard: The eponymous character from a French folk tale. He was a wealthy man who lived in castle and murdered several of his wives. The story was first recorded by Charles Perrault in *Histoires ou Contes du Temps Passé* (1697). Robert Samber is credited with the first English translation in 1729.
322 *Brobdingnags*: The giants in Jonathan Swift's satirical novel *Gulliver's Travels* (1726).

323 *jack-boots*: Large leather military boots often reaching to the knee.
324 Cabul: Kabul, now the capital of Afghanistan.
325 *Cape of Good Hope*: A vital stopping point in modern South Africa for ships on long voyages between Britain and India.
326 *Landowra*, a Palace belonging to Rajah of *Hurdwaar*: See note 320.
327 Bibbee Saheb: *Bibi* was often used as a respectful title for Indian women or to refer to the Indian mistresses of English men. *Sahib* more frequently referred to European men, but it is generally a polite form of address.
328 Umrutseer: Amritsar: A city in the north-west province of Punjab.
329 Tibett: Tibet: A country in Asia, on the north side of the Himalayas.
330 *Tartary*: A name given to an area of Asia and eastern Europe, which formed part of the Tartar Empire in the Middle Ages.
331 *Moradabad* district: In Uttar Pradesh.
332 *its judge and collector*: At this time, Charles Lloyd (1797–?) was the collector at Moradabad. Alexander Wright was the Judge until 1809, when William Leycester assumed the post. See also note 362.
333 *celebrated bathing-place of* Hurdoar: The city of Haridwar is located on the river Ganges and Hindus regard it as one of the seven holiest places in India. During the Haridwar Kumbh Mela, millions of pilgrims, devotees, and tourists congregate at the various ghats for ritualistic bathing in order to achieve *moksha*, i.e. self-realization.
334 Ranee Mutaab Kour, *wife of Rajah Rungeet Sing*: Mehtab Kaur (c. 1782–1813) was the first wife of Ranjit Singh and the mother of his son Sher Singh, who became ruler of the Sikh empire from 1841–1843. See note 318.
335 *Rajah* Sahib Sing *of* Patalia *and his wife*: Sahib Singh (1773–1813) was the Maharajah of Patiala, a princely state in the Punjab. His first wife was Ratan Kaur.
336 Bodge Sing: Rajah Bhag Singh (1760–1819), ruler of the princely state of Jind and Sangur.
337 Burgwaan Sing: Not identified.
338 *The name* Hurdoar: Also Hardwar and Haridwar. As Deane states, the name of the city derives from *doar*, or *dwar*, meaning gate or gateway in Sanskrit. However, the prefix Hari may refer to Lord Vishnu or the saint Bharthari mentioned by Deane. He apparently meditated here on the banks of the Ganges and bestowed his name on one of the ghats, Har Ki Pauri.
339 *Shanscrit*: Sanskrit is an ancient Indo-European language of India and the language of the Hindu scriptures and classical Indian poetry.
340 *annual fair held here to commemorate the anniversary of this man's birth*: Deane's reference here is unclear but there are various religious festivals at Haridwar, the most famous is the Kumbh Mela which now takes place every twelve years.
341 *Ahmed Shah*: Possibly a reference to Ahmad Shah Durrani, (1722–72), ruler of Afghanistan and founder of the Durrani empire.
342 *Rajah* Nyn Sing: Not identified.
343 Goorah Khan: Not identified.
344 Juggernaut: Deane is presumably referring to the Shree Jagannath Temple, Puri: an important pilgrimage site and famous for the annual Ratha Yatra, or chariot festival during which huge temple cars, or Juggernauts, pull representations of the principal deities through the town.
345 *bay of Bengal*: An area in the north-eastern part of the Indian ocean.
346 *New Forest at Hampshire*: An area of unenclosed pastureland and forest in the county of Hampshire in southern England.
347 Pungaab: Punjab: An area now encompassing part of eastern Pakistan and northern India. As Deane states, it means 'land of five rivers' in Persian.
348 Rohilcund: Rohilkhand: See note 211.
349 Nugeebabad: Najibabad: A town in Uttar Pradesh.

350 Sultan Khan: Zabita Khan (d. 1785), a Rohilla chief who fought alongside his father, Najib-ud-Daulah, during the third battle of Panipat in 1761 when the Afghan forces defeated the Marathas and prevented their expansion into the northern territories.
351 *Nawaab* Nugeeb ul Dowlah: Nawab Najib-ud-Daulah (d. 1770): a noted Rohilla warrior and tribal chief in the eighteenth century. His tomb, visited by Deane, lies in the city of Najibabad.
352 chunam: A powder made from prepared lime, which produces a polished plaster.
353 pice: A small copper coin worth very little at this time. The term, however, was also used to denote money in general.
354 *Chinese Tartar*: An ethnic group from China.
355 *a large fort*: The Patthargarh Fort outside Najibabad. It was built by Najib-ud-Daulah in 1755 and withstood a siege by Shah Alam II.
356 Nugeenah: Also Nugeena and Nagina: a town in Uttar Pradesh.
357 Arampore: Also Rampur, a city in Uttar Pradesh. It was established after the Rohilla War of 1774–1775 by Nawab Faizullah Khan. The incumbent Nawab of Rampur was Ahad Ali Khan Bahadur (1787–1840).
358 *These Rohillah chiefs are not very partial to the English*: In the First and Second Rohilla Wars (1773–1774 and 1794) the Rohillas had been driven from Rohilkhand and their capital of Bareilly by Shuja-ud-Daulah, Nawab of Awadh, who had the assistance of the EIC. There consequently remained much resistance to British rule.
359 bauble *tree*: Possibly the babool tree or the baobab tree, *Adansonia digitate*, which blooms with large sweetly scented flowers. See note 255.
360 *Moradabad*: Muradabad, a city in Uttar Pradesh. It came under British control in 1801.
361 *the culture of potatoes*: See note 42.
362 *attacked by the force under* Ameer Khan . . . *defended by Mr. Leicester*: Amir Khan (see note 203) attacked the house of the Collector William Leycester at Muradabad in 1805. However, the outbuildings had been fortified upon his arrival in the city and the British were able to defend it.
363 Ram Gonga: Ramganga West River is a tributary of the River Ganges.
364 Futteh Ghur: Also Futty Ghur, now Fatehgarh: a cantonment town in Uttar Pradesh.
365 zemeendar: Also *zemindar*, or *zamindar*. See note 58.
366 Rohillah *country*: Often referred to as Rohilkhand. See note 211.
367 jow jungle: Dense landscape of various species of shrubby tamarisk which abound in the low alluvials of India rivers and which were useful in many ways, such as making baskets.
368 Barreilli: Also Bareilly: the principal city of Rokhilkhand, situated on the banks of the Ramganga West River. As noted here, it was a centre of furniture making and has a significant history reaching back to the *Mahabharata* where it was said to be the birthplace of Draupadi, a key character in the Indian epic. In the following pages Deane gives a detailed description of the city.
369 Haffiz Ramut . . . *under the command of Colonel Champion*: Hafiz Rahmat Khan Barech (1723–1774) was a Rohilla chief remembered for his contribution to the Third Battle of Panipat in 1761. He entered into an alliance with Shuja-ud-Daulah, who assisted the Rohillas in their fight against the Marathas in exchange for money (see note 382). Hafiz later refused to pay his debt, and Shuja-ud-Daulah enlisted the help of the British, led by Colonel Alexander Champion, Commander-in Chief, to invade Rohilkhand. Hafiz Rahmut Khan was subsequently killed during the Battle of Kutterah in 1774.
370 *The city of* Bareilly *was founded by* Haffiz Ramut: During his reign, Hafiz Rehmat Khan made Bareilly the capital of Rohilkhand.
371 *Hamilton's Account of the Rohillah War*: Charles Hamilton (1752–1792) was an employee of the EIC. He took part in the campaign against the Rohilla tribes and

produced a history of them, *An Historical Relation of the Origin, Progress and Final Dissolution of the Government of the Rohilla Afghans in the Northern Provinces of Hindostan, Compiled from a Persian Manuscript and Other Original Papers* (London: Printed for G. Kearsley, 1787).
372 Pilibete: Also Pilibhit: a city in Uttar Pradesh. It is in an area dense with forest.
373 Gogra: Also the Ghaghara River: another tributary of the Ganges.
374 sissoo *trees*: *Dalbergia sissoo*, also known as the North Indian Rosewood, was a great source of timber and valuable for construction, joinery, boat and carriage building, and furniture.
375 Assafœtida: An extremely pungent gum frequently used in Indian and Middle Eastern cooking.
376 Young: Edward Young (1683–1765), an English poet best remembered for his poetic observations of the sublime in *Night Thoughts* (1742–1745).
377 Milton: John Milton. See note 73.
378 *Morpheus*: Greek god of dreams.
379 Mowattys: Robbers, something like gypsies, and very desperate.
380 ortolans: The ortolan bunting or *Emberiza hortulana* is a tiny songbird that was served as a delicacy, especially in France.
381 gram: Usually refers to chickpeas, which are legumes not grains. However, Deane may be referring to gram flour, which is made from the chickpea.
382 Kutterah: The battle of Kutterah took place in 1774 (see also note 369). It was the decisive battle in the First Rohilla War, a conflict between Hafiz Rahmut Khan and Shuja-ud-Daulah who had enlisted British support. After Colonel Alexander Champion claimed victory, the Rohillas retreated and Rohilkhand fell to the nawab.
383 banyan *trees*: The *Ficus benghalensis* is a common tree in India. It was often used as shaded meeting places in villages.
384 Jellalabad: The site of a siege and a battle between the Afghans and the British in 1842.
385 Umrutpore: Also Amritpur: a town in Uttar Pradesh.
386 banbool *trees*: Most likely the Babool tree.
387 *XIX*: This is clearly a misprint; it should read Chapter XV.
388 Poosa: Also Pusa: an estate in Bihar, used by the EIC for horse breeding.
389 pinnace: A small boat, typically with sails and/or oars that accompanies larger vessels for various purposes.
390 Khawnpore: Also Kanpur. See note 5.
391 seers: A varying Indian denomination of weight, roughly around one kilogram.
392 *Hindoos do not eat animal food at all*: Although Hinduism does not prohibit eating meat, many Hindus believe vegetarianism is the best way to observe their custom of respect for life.
393 *meat for Mussulmen must be prepared after the Jewish custom*: Deane is referring to the halal method of meat preparation in Islamic culture. It is similar to Judaism's kosher process. They both have specific ritualistic requirements for slaughtering permitted animals which involves draining the blood from the body.
394 Jehanabad: Also Kora Jahanabad: a city in the Fatehpur district of Uttar Pradesh.
395 *wherry*: Rowing boat, usually for carrying passengers.
396 legowing: See Deane's glossary.
397 Mirzapore: A city in Uttar Pradesh, known for its production of carpets but also renowned for its brassware.
398 *the fort of* Chunar: An ancient Fort in the Mirzapore district of Uttar Pradesh. Major Hector Munro seized it in 1764.
399 Chuperah: Also Chapra: a city in Bihar that from the eighteenth century thrived as a market town due to French, Portuguese, and English industries in the area.
400 *the river* Gunduk, *and soon reached* Soanepore: The Gandak River, one of Nepal's major rivers meets the Ganges at Sonpur, or Sonepur, in Bihar. As Deane goes on to

explain, it was the location of the annual Hajipur fair, now known as the Sonpur Cattle Fair.
401 *Mr Moorcroft . . . on the subject of his researches*: William Moorcroft (1767–1825) was an explorer employed by the EIC. He managed the company stud in Bengal and travelled extensively to Tibet and Nepal in order to find better breeding horses. Moorcroft published an extract of his account of the expedition in *Asiatick Researches; or Transactions of the Society Instituted in Bengal for Inquiring into the History and Antiquities, the Arts, Sciences and Literature, of Asia* (London: John Murray, 1818), vol. xii, p. 382.
402 Tirhoot: Also Tirhut: a division in the state of Bihar.
403 Hadjepore *fair*: Also Hajipur fair. See note 400.
404 traiteur: 'Caterer' (French).
405 Chobipore: Also Chaubepur: a village in the Kanpur district of Uttar Pradesh.
406 *a fort belonging to the Rajah of* Tutteah, *before which Colonel Guthrie, of the Company's service, lost his life in 1804*: Colonel Guthrie attempted to capture Rajah Chutter Saul, who was in possession of the fort of Tetteeah; but the Colonel died while trying to retreat.
407 Canoge: Also Kannauj: an ancient city in Uttar Pradesh, home to many ruins and artefacts.
408 *many curious coins have been dug up of as ancient a date as Alexander's conquest*: Alexander the Great (356–323 BC) led his army into India in 326 BC. He had coins minted to commemorate his Indian victories.
409 Rajah, *Bagoin Sing*: Not identified.
410 Bahadar Khan: Not identified.
411 *vetch*: A herbaceous plant of the pea family.
412 *that saying of St. Pauls, "When I was a man, I put away childish things"*: See 1 Corinthians 13:11. The full verse is as follows: 'When I was a child, I spoke as a child, I understood as a child, I thought as a child; but when I became a man, I put away childish things'.
413 *Chapter XV*: This should read XVI.
414 Jehanabad: Now Jahanabad: in the Pilibhit district of Uttar Pradesh.
415 Ghaut: Also *ghat*: the steps used in both river landings and mountain passes, although the British in India applied the word to mountains generally. In this case, Deane is referring to the landing place at the river.
416 Amrooah: Now Amroha: a city in Uttar Pradesh, north-west of Moradabad. It is known for its production of mangoes and textiles as well as the pottery industry mentioned by Deane.
417 *Bagshot-heath*: The borough and village of Bagshot are located in Surrey Heath.
418 *Mr. Wedgewood*: Josiah Wedgewood (1730–1795) was an English potter. He founded the Wedgewood Company, which is credited with industrializing the manufacture of pottery.
419 *"valleys filled with wavy corn"*: Deane slightly misquotes this line from 'O Lovely Peace' in Handel's oratorio *Judas Maccabaeus* (1746), based on the libretto by Thomas Morell. The correct line is: 'And vallies smile with wavy corn'. See 'O Lovely Peace, with Plenty Crown'd' in G. F. Handel, *Judas Maccabeus* (London: Printed for S. J. Button and J. Whitaker, 1809), p. 178.
420 *dropsy*: Now more commonly referred to as oedema, dropsy is a condition whereby watery fluid collects in the tissues or cavities of the body.
421 *calomel*: Mercurous chloride, is a white powder formerly used as a purgative.
422 *Epsom salts*: Or magnesium sulphate: used for medicinal purposes.
423 *Nawaab of* Rampoor: Ahmad Ali Khan (1787–1840) was the Nawab of Rampur, which became a princely state after the First Rohilla War of 1774.
424 *mango bird*: Presumably the Indian Golden Oriole which sucks the juice from the ripe mangoes.

425 Mrs. – : Not identified.
426 Don Juan's friends: Don Juan, or Don Giovanni, is a fictional libertine, first documented by Tirso de Molina in *El Burlada de Sevilla* (1630), but since immortalized in numerous fictional versions. Deane is presumably alluding to the sinful lifestyles depicted in the play.
427 *mosque, erected in memory of* Haffiz Ramut: Hafiz Rahmat Khan actually built a mosque here in 1769.
428 mullick: See Deane's glossary.
429 hakime: Also Hakim: usually refers to a native physician who uses traditional remedies. However, it can also refer to a judge or ruler.
430 *etymology of the word* paddy: See note 39: paddy is rice in the husk, not a different grain as stated here. Furthermore, Deane's etymology differs to that provided in *Hobson-Jobson*, which states that the word has a double origin, emerging from both the west of India and from Malay. See *Hobson-Jobson*, p. 650.
431 a la Turke: That is to say, reclining on the sofa.
432 Job: A biblical character known for his faith and patience while enduring many trials, as recounted in the Book of Job.
433 maunjie: See glossary entry for *Mhangy*.
434 *Messrs Barber and Co at Old Fort Ghaut*: An agency that hired boats with boatmen to new Company employees.
435 *clashee*: In this instance, an indigenous sailor who was in charge of work on the boat.
436 én passant: 'In passing' (French).
437 *milch goats*: A hardy animal that produces nutritious and sweet milk.
438 *the China Bazaar*: Since the early nineteenth century, Calcutta has had a large Chinese community. The Tiretta Bazaar and neighbourhood remain part of the old China Town.
439 *Ghur Moktasir Ghaut*: Now Garhmukteshwar: a town in Uttar Pradesh.
440 *cus cus*: Short, curly, and sweet-smelling grass. It is native to all tropical regions in Asia and can be used to make various products, such as mats, boxes, and baskets.
441 *Hadley's Grammar*: George Hadley's *A Compendious Grammar of the Current Corrupt Dialect of the Jargon of Hindostan, (Commonly Called Moors): With a Vocabulary, English and Moors, Moors and English* (7th edition, London: J. Asperne, [1796] 1809).
442 Bally Nuggur: Now Baranagar: a city in West Bengal, situated on the banks of the River Hoogly.
443 Jalingy *river*: A branch of the Ganges River.
444 Berhampore: A city in West Bengal.
445 Jungypoor: Now Jangipur: a city in West Bengal. As Deane mentions, it was an important trade centre for silk during British rule in the subcontinent.
446 *General Martine*: Major General Claude Martin (1735–1800) was an officer in the French, and then the English, EIC army. He later defected to the service of the Nawab of Lucknow.

JULIA MAITLAND, *LETTERS FROM MADRAS* (1846)

Julia Maitland (1808–1864), née Barrett, travelled to India in 1836, accompanying her first husband, James Thomas, who was a Judge in the Madras Presidency. Thomas was a widower with three children; during their time in India, the couple also had two further children. After seven months in Madras, Thomas was appointed Judge at Rajahmundry and the family relocated to this 'up country' station for the following 18 months, with the exception of brief sojourns in Samuldavee by the coast. In 1839, Thomas received two new postings, the first to Cuddapah and Bellary, and the second to Bangalore. However, by this time, their daughter Henrietta was sick and Julia had recently given birth to a son, James Cambridge Thomas. Thus, she was advised to return home with the children. Not long after she left, her husband died in India. Two years later, in 1842, Julia married the author and curate Charlies Maitland (1815–1866).

The following year, in 1843, Maitland's *Letters from Madras: During the Years 1836–1839* was published anonymously by John Murray. The volume received favourable reviews. The *Gentleman's Magazine* describing it as 'a good and evidently a genuine account of the manners and society of India, including not only the European portion of the inhabitants, but the native population also'.[1] In a long, anonymously written review-essay in the *Quarterly Review* in 1845, Elizabeth Eastlake judged it 'the very lightest work that has ever appeared from India, yet it tells us more of what everybody cares to know than any other'.[2] Maitland's successful blending of entertainment and information was presumably one reason why the publisher John Murray chose to reissue the volume, with very minor revisions, in 1846, as part of his Home and Colonial Library. This series ran from 1843–1849 and ultimately comprised 49 titles, mostly cheap reprints as well as some original works and translations. It was intended to help Murray acquire a greater share of the colonial writing market, and Maitland's inclusion in a predominantly male list indicates the contemporary perception of her text as authoritative and informative. This perception, and the volume's appeal, continued into the 1860s, with another edition appearing in 1861. A facsimile edition, with scholarly apparatus, has more recently been published by the Woodstock Press in 2003.[3]

JULIA MAITLAND, *LETTERS FROM MADRAS* (1846)

A prominent theme in *Letters from Madras* is Maitland's interest in education as a means of inculcating Christian morality in children. This interest continued once she returned home to Britain. Rather than become involved in philanthropic projects, however, she went on to write three moralistic children's novels: *Historical Acting Charades* (1847), *The Doll and her Friends, or Memoirs of the Lady Seraphina* (1852), and *Cat and Dog, or, Memoirs of Puss and the Captain* (1854). All were popular and went through several editions.

Julia Maitland died from phthisis in 1864.

Notes

1 'Review of *Letters from Madras:* By a Lady', *Gentleman's Magazine* (July 1843), p. 58.
2 E. Eastlake, 'Lady Travellers', *Quarterly Review* 76 (June 1845), p. 111.
3 J. Maitland, *Letters from Madras*, ed. A. Price (Otley: Woodstock Books, 2003).

LETTERS

FROM

MADRAS,

DURING THE YEARS 1836–1839.

BY A LADY.

———

LONDON:
JOHN MURRAY, ALBEMARLE STREET.
—
1846.

INTRODUCTION.

The public attention has of late been so much directed to our East Indian possessions, that any particulars concerning that portion of the globe may probably find a welcome from the general reader. It is under this impression that the following Letters are offered to the public. They were written during the years 1836, 37, 38, and 39, by a young married lady, who had accompanied her husband to Madras for the first time, and they are (with the necessary omission of family details) printed verbatim from the originals. This will account for some abruptness of transition, and also for a colloquial familiarity of style, which might easily have been remedied if it had not been thought more advisable to give the correspondence in its genuine unsophisticated state.

Those who open the volume with an expectation of finding details relative to the wars and vicissitudes[1] which have lately excited universal interest[a] will be disappointed, as the writer quitted India in 1840. Neither did she devote much attention to public affairs, though she occasionally notices the apprehensions and opinions that were prevalent at the time. But first impressions,[b] when they occur incidentally in a familiar narrative, are amusing, and may sometimes be useful: such, indeed, constitute the chief feature in these Letters. The reader will also find in them many traits[c] of national character; and some descriptions of the Author's intercourse with the natives of Hindostan, and of the endeavours[d] in which she shared to improve their condition.

It is proper to observe that, whenever European individuals are mentioned,[e] fictitious names have been assigned to them, and other precautions taken to prevent the personal application of such passages.

Note

1 *wars and vicissitudes*: The First Afghan War (1839–1842) took place directly after Maitland's departure from India and prior to the publication of her text.

CONTENTS.

LETTER THE FIRST.

Outward passage—Bay of Biscay—Combination of noises—Cure for sea-sickness—Passengers—Land at Madeira—Visit to a convent—Re-embarkation 188

LETTER THE SECOND.

Letters for England—Amusements on board—The Tropics—The "Wave" emigrant-vessel—Cape Verd—Fire-works—Slave-brig—Whales. . . . 190

LETTER THE THIRD.

A Triton—Letter from Neptune—Ceremonies on crossing the Line—Catching albatrosses 192

LETTER THE FOURTH.

Tristan d'Acunha—Governor Glass—Land at the Cape—Cape Town—Boa constrictor—English Church—Expenses—Society—Political Parties—Schools—View from the Kloof—Return on board 195

LETTER THE FIFTH.

Gales of wind—Passengers from the Cape—Landing at Madras—Catamarans—Witch of Fife's voyage—Curiosities—Snake-charmers—Native servants—"Griffins"—Visitors—A native's advice—Native servility—Treatment of servants—Jargon spoken by the English to the natives 199

LETTER THE SIXTH.

Bishop Corrie—Schools—A Moonshee—Lessons in Tamul—Dinner-parties—General laziness—Letters from Natives 203

CONTENTS.

LETTER THE SEVENTH.

Native entertainment—Mohammedan dancing-girls—Concert—Hindoo dancing-girl—Conjurer—Supper—Hindoo speech 206

LETTER THE EIGHTH.

Anxiety for despatches—Madras scenery—Moonshee's letter—Native ignorance—Religion—Death of the Bishop—Dishonesty of native servants—Trial of a thief—Reasons for submitting to a false charge 209

LETTER THE NINTH.

Entomologising—St. Thomé—Temperature—Wedding—Tamul translation—The tailor—Mohurrum—Excessive heat 213

LETTER THE TENTH.

Preparing for a journey—Sail for Coringa—Land at Vizagapatam—Arrive at Rajahmundry—Law-officers—Cholera—Domestic arrangements—Peons—A traveller 216

LETTER THE ELEVENTH.

Residents—Snakes—Hyænas—Thugs—Employment of time—Schemes—*Fishing* for wood—The Barrack-sergeant—Poor travellers—Visit from a Rajah—A Cobra capello—Snake-charmer. 221

LETTER THE TWELFTH.

Domestic expenses—An amah—The butler's bills—Indian mode of visiting—Religious service—Visit from "Penny-Whistle Row"—A dialogue. . . 225

LETTER THE THIRTEENTH.

Native school—Female education—Leopards—Hyænas—Letter from the Moonshee—M. d'Arzel—French adventures—An ensign and his pony—School opened—Utility of Schools 229

LETTER THE FOURTEENTH.

Visit to "Penny-Whistle"—Dratcharrum—The Rajah's palace—Method of dismissing visitors—Dinner—Procession—Pagoda—Amusements—The Rajah's Wife—A new tribe 233

CONTENTS.

LETTER THE FIFTEENTH.

Instance of faithfulness—Progress of the school—"Curry-and-rice" Christians—Want of missionaries—Topics of conversation—Visit to Narsapoor—The missionaries and their wives—Palanquin travelling—Return home 238

LETTER THE SIXTEENTH.

Discussion on divinity—Interruption to the school—Shore's 'Notes on Indian affairs'—English incivility to natives—Magazines and reviews—Pagoda service—Progress of the school—Snake-poison—Remedies for snake-bites—Dexterity of snake-charmers 244

LETTER THE SEVENTEENTH.

Indian toy—Rule against accepting presents—Dishonesty of rich natives—Company—Military and civilians—Hindoo tradition—A Moonshee translator—Lending-library—School lectures—Indian spring 248

LETTER THE EIGHTEENTH.

Religious discussion—Parables—Fondness of natives for metaphysical subtleties—Heads and tails—A native's notion of "charity"—Government circular—Salutes in honour of the native religions—Presents to idols by Government—Offerings to idols—Tricks of the Bramins—Idolatry encouraged by Government—School-prizes—Motives for learning English—A "tame boy"—Invitations to officers 252

LETTER THE NINETEENTH.

Samuldavee—Native dialects—Moonshee's method of reading the Church Prayer-book—"First-caste" monkeys—Jackals—Bramins' reasons for preserving idols—A dishonest Zemindar—"Don" and the monkey . . 257

LETTER THE TWENTIETH.

Filling of the rivers—Native indifference to truth on religious subjects—Progress of the school—Moonshee's definition of idolatry—Quaint translations—Land-wind—Moonshee's conscience—Boasting of natives—Notions of honesty—Devotedness to employers—A false alarm . . . 260

LETTER THE TWENTY-FIRST.

Snakes—Green bugs—Thugs—Trial of a Moonsiff—Dutch settlement—Black bugs—Return to Rajahmundry—A *cool* visitor—Captain and Mrs. C—— Exchange of presents—Instance of encouragement given to idolatry—Emigration of Hill Coolies—Proposed "Europe" shop—The Dussera—Prospect of war—Visitors—An eclipse—Importance attached to employment in a Government office—Indian "hospitality"—Misgovernment—Moonshee's account of the eclipse—Cause of superior progress of some of the scholars—National music—News from Europe 263

LETTER THE TWENTY-SECOND.

Delay of the post—Distress of natives—Sale of grain—Captain and Mrs. Kelly—Anxiety for letters—A lazy Moorman—The Hakeem and the idol—State of the country—Shipwreck—Female education—Robbers—Scarcity—Major C—'s drawings—Bone-stones—Method of teaching—Visit from "Penny-Whistle"—Progress of the school—Management of children 269

LETTER THE TWENTY-THIRD.

Decrease of the famine—Mode of distributing charity—Proposed native reading-room—Gentoo newspaper—A ball—Narsapoor missionaries—Reading-room opened—School-rewards—A Sunnyassee—Circulating library 274

LETTER THE TWENTY-FOURTH.

Arrive at Samuldavee—Magic lantern—Schools—The Collector and the Swamy—Christenings—A proxy—Abolition of the pilgrim-tax—Decline of idolatry—Want of elementary books—Schools—Letter to the editor of a Madras newspaper on native education—Return of plenty—Monsoon—A new school—Rajah Twelfth-cake—Society for protecting the natives—Native manner of ending letters 277

LETTER THE TWENTY-FIFTH.

Birthday feast—School at Samuldavee—Converts—Rule of promotion—Appointment—Chittoor—Masulipatam—Ramiahpatam—Arrive at Madras—Native love of finery—Female Orphan Asylum—Education—The "Caste" question—Addictedness of natives to perjury—Death of Runjeet Singh—Suttee—English encouragement of idolatry—Rebellions—"Chit"-writing—Etiquette of visiting 285

LETTER THE TWENTY-SIXTH.

Indian fever—Employment of a thorough Madras lady—Chittoor—An unwelcome arrival—Bangalore—The Pettah—Inhabitants—A Moorish

CONTENTS.

horseman—Architecture—Hindoo mythology—Reported conversion of a Hindoo tribe 291

LETTER THE TWENTY-SEVENTH.

Climate—European ladies in Bangalore—Conspiracy at Kurnool—Unjust proceeding at Rajahmundry—Storm on the coast—Poverty of the people—A "crack" Collector—End of the conspiracy—Return of the troops—Expectations of a war with China—Conclusion 295

LETTERS FROM MADRAS

LETTER THE FIRST.

Bay of Biscay, August 17th.

I BEGIN now, in hopes of meeting a ship, to tell you our histories. This is the first day I have been well enough to write; and I am not very steady yet, as you may perceive, but still we are all exceedingly well—*for the Bay of Biscay*.[1]

We have persuaded my brother Frank[2] to go with us as far as Madeira,[3] and take his chance of finding a homeward-bound ship.

The Captain[4] says he never had so smooth a passage, but there is a good deal of swell here. The wind allows of our passing outside the roughest part of this unfortunate Bay, which is a very great advantage.

Mrs. M—[5] was quite right in advising us to take the roundhouse. There is much more air than in the lower cabins, and the noises do not annoy me at all. We all go to bed at nine o'clock, so that it is no hardship to be awakened at five. Certainly, the first morning, when I woke, there did seem to be as quaint a combination and succession of noises as could well be imagined. Pigs, dogs, poultry, cow, cats, sheep, all in concert at sunrise. Then the nursery noises: Major O'Brien[6] twittering to his baby—the baby squealing—the nurse singing and squalling to it—the mamma cooing to it. Then the cuddy noises: all the servants quarrelling for their clothes, &c. &c. So on till breakfast-time.

I was too sick to laugh then, and I am used to it now. Then, when I was as sick and cross as possible, in came my Irish maid Freeman[7] with a great plate of beef-steak and potatoes. I exclaimed in despair at the very sight of it, "Oh, what *is* all that for? O dear me!"—"Sure, it's for you to ate, ma'am."—"Eat! I can't eat."—"Oh, you *must* ate it all, ma'am: you've no notion how well you would be if you would only ate hearty!" Her cramming was a great bore, but she cured me by it. Frank is nearly mad: he is in such raptures with everything on board, I think he will end by turning ship's surgeon. The first night his hammock was slung under the doctor's. The poor doctor complained to me in the morning how very odd it was he could not keep his cot steady,—he had been swinging about, he said, all night. Frank confided to me privately the reason, *viz.* that the doctor looked so tempting over his head, he could not resist swinging him at every opportunity. However, next night he was found out, for the doctor peeped over the top of his cot and caught him in the fact; and when Mr. Darke,[8] the second mate, came into the cabin, poor Dr. Lowe[9] exclaimed, "Here, Darke! I could not imagine why I could not keep my cot steady all night, and at last I looked over the top, when I found this precious fellow swinging me!"

Our passengers are Mr. and Mrs. Wilde[10] (he is going to St. Helena[11] as Chief Justice: they go with us to the Cape,[12] and there wait for a homeward-bound ship to take them to St. Helena);—the O'Briens;[13]—Miss Shields,[14] good humoured and lively, going out as a missionary;—Miss Knight,[15] sick and solemn;—several Irish girls apparently on their promotion;[16f]—Mr. Harvey,[17] who plays chess, and takes care of his flowers: he has them in an hermetically sealed glass case, which he is taking to the Cape;—a number of hitherto unnamed gentlemen, who sit down to eat and drink, and rise up to play;—one or two pretty boys, who saunter about with Lord Byron[18] in hand;—and Mr. Stevens,[19] the missionary, who is good and gentle, but so sick that we have not yet made much acquaintance: he is getting better, and talks of reading the service next Sunday.

August 23rd. FUNCHAL.[20]—Here we are on shore again, in this beautiful Madeira, and all excessively thankful and happy to be out of our ship, though it is very hot on shore, compared with the real sea air: it has been quite cold at sea. Our chief employment just now is eating figs and grapes, and planning our excursions for to-morrow. We have been landed about an hour, and are to remain here till Thursday. Frank is gone to the consul to get a passport, and inquire about a ship to take him home. We are grown pretty well used to the life on board ship. Everybody is good-natured and civil. Captain Faulkner[21] is our chief crony, but we are all good friends. I am beginning greatly to enjoy some parts of our sea-life, especially the bright blue water, and the bright yellow moonlight,—such colours as no shoregoing people ever saw.[g]

August 25th.—Madeira is very lively, very like Lucca:[22] the country, and the heat, and the people, are Italy over again. We have just been to visit a convent here.[23h] There is not much to be seen. The nuns spoke to us through a double grating and sold us flowers. Nobody is allowed to see the inside of the convent. They spoke nothing but Portuguese. They came to me, chirping, and asking me to talk to them, and to tell them something; but, unluckily, though I could understand what they said to me, I could not answer a word; so we were obliged to be content with nodding and bobbing, and looking friendly at each other. We have taken some beautiful rides and gathered nosegays of wild flowers—heliotropes, roses, fuchsias, and every variety of geraniums. To-night we go on board again, leaving Frank here to find his way home by the first ship. We shall be very anxious to hear his adventures: I am afraid he may be obliged to go round by Lisbon, for no English ship is expected just at present. The Captain has sent his summons for us, so I must say "Good-bye."

LETTER THE SECOND.

August 29th, Lat. 22° N., Lon. 23½° W.

THE Captain has just told us that he expects to pass a ship every day, so we are all setting to work getting our letters ready, as he only allows five minutes for sealing and sending off. I hope, by the time you receive this letter, Frank will have arrived safely at home, and not the worse for his journey. Pray make him write to me directly; I shall be quite uneasy till I hear from him, for we left him at Madeira quite ignorant of what his plans might be. Everybody on board was very sorry to lose him, and they all sing his praises with much good taste.

We are now entering the Tropics,[24] and the weather is still cool, owing to the constant breeze. We have had no calms, but on an average have made about one hundred and fifty miles in the twenty-four hours. I suspect I shall never get over the sea-sickness in rough weather, and I almost give up the hope of employing myself, for I really can do nothing; but as long as I keep quiet, and do not interrupt my idleness, I am much better. Towards evening, like all other sea-sick people, I grow very brisk, and can walk the quarter-deck, and chirp with anybody. Our chief adventures since we left Madeira have been the sight of flying-fish and porpoises. I made a good many sketches at Madeira, but cannot work much towards finishing them. I have learnt two or three Tamul[25] verbs, and read different bits of different books—made the Captain teach me now and then a little geography, and the first mate a little astronomy—finished Melville's 'University Sermons'[26]—chatted with our fellow-passengers—and that is all I have done; and in fact that is the way most of the ladies spend their time on board ship. We are too uncomfortable to be industrious, and too much interrupted and unsettled to be busy.

September 3rd.—We are beginning to be aware of our latitude. The trade-winds have left us, and we have a strong suspicion of a calm coming on; but, unluckily, *calm* does not mean *smooth*, for the rocking and rolling are just as bad as when we had plenty of wind. The thermometer now stands at 78° in the day, and higher, I should think, in the night; but our cabin is certainly the coolest of any, and I have not yet found the heat unbearable. The gentlemen are all "rigged Tropical," with their collars turned down, and small matters of neckcloths;—grisly Guys some of them turn out! The very sea looks tepid, and goes past with a lazy roll, as if it was too languid to carry us on.

We live in hopes of catching a shark: one was seen this morning, but he was too cunning for us. We are also on the look-out for an albatross. When we first sailed, all the gentlemen protested against the horror of ever shooting an albatross, and quoted the Ancient Mariner[27] at every opportunity; but since the 1st of September, the recollections of the shooting season have greatly softened down the sentiment, and they are now ready for all the albatrosses that may make their appearance. They say "they think that old fellow of Coleridge's[28] must have been a horrid bore." We passed the Cape de Verd Islands[29] the day before yesterday, but did not go on shore. They are not much of a sight.

September 9th.—Yesterday we overtook a ship going to New South Wales,[30] filled with settlers and live stock. A good many of our gentlemen went on board, and brought back miserable accounts of the discomforts of the ship compared with ours. This ship (the "Wave") left England before us, but we overtake all the ships. Mr. Kenrick,[31] our first mate, says he thinks *he* should feel quite mortified at being in a ship which let others pass her, but he supposes it is all habit! The "Wave" had felt a good deal of bad weather from going inside the Cape de Verd Islands, instead of outside, as we did. Captain—says he never settles his course till he sees how the weather promises; and this time he thought the outside would be best—which we all consider very clever of our skipper. At night we had a show of fireworks, that the two ships might know each other's places: it was really very pretty. We, being magnificent, sent up two blue-lights and two skyrockets: the blue-lights were the best; it looked as if the whole concern—ship, sails, and sea—were playing at snap-dragon:[32] altogether it was the best adventure we have had. I contrived to creep forward to see it, but I have been ill and keeping to my cabin lately. I sit with the door open, which gives me plenty of air: and if I spy any of the ladies looking neighbourly, as if they thought of "sitting with me," I just shut my eyes, which answers as well as "sporting my oak,"[33] and does not exclude the air; but they must think I get plenty of sleep!

September 24th.—Yesterday, at three o'clock in the morning, we came up with a French brig bound from Madagascar to Rio.[34] She was, as the sailors said, "A most beautiful little craft!" and looked to great advantage in the moonlight: I put my head out of the port to admire her and listen to the conversation, little suspecting her real character; but next morning the skipper told us there was no doubt she was a piratical slaver, and that, if we had been a ship of war, we should have stopped and examined her; but we are not strong enough for such adventures, so she and her poor slaves are gone on. Next morning we saw two whales playing in the waters, swimming, blowing, jumping, turning head over heels, and pleasuring themselves, as if they had been minnows.

October 1st.—News of a homeward-bound ship in the distance, so I must get ready.

LETTER THE THIRD.

TO HER YOUNGER BROTHER[35]

HEREWITH you will receive a full, true, and particular account of the ceremony of shaving on crossing the Line,[36] which you are requested to communicate to "Master Frank," whose absence was most particularly regretted on the occasion. The night before, we heard some one call out that a sail was in sight, upon which I scrambled out on deck in the greatest possible hurry, in hopes of an opportunity of sending a letter to Mamma.[37] When I got out, all the officers began to laugh at me, and I found that the announcement was merely some of the Tritons[38] informing Neptune[39] of the arrival of our ship. About an hour afterwards, a Triton suddenly appeared on the quarter-deck, dressed up in oil-cloth and rags, and bits of rope, &c. &c., bringing a letter from Neptune to the Captain, and waiting for an answer.

The Captain read the letter aloud: it was very civil, saying how happy Neptune was to see the Captain again, and that he would come on board at one o'clock next day, and have the pleasure of introducing any of the youngsters to his dominions: he condoled with the ladies who had been suffering from sea-sickness, and hoped to have the honour of seeing them all in the morning.

The Captain sent his compliments in return, with a cordial invitation to Neptune for the next day, only begging that he would use the youngsters very civilly.

Triton then took a glass of grog and made his bow. Then a lighted tar-barrel was sent off from the ship, supposed to be Triton's boat going off, and the first mate lighted him home with blue-lights and skyrockets. Altogether it had a very fine effect. Next morning the usual tricks were played on the novices. One young midshipman was up before light "to look out for the Line." Another *saw* it, as well he might, a hair having been put inside his telescope. Another declared he felt the bunt of the Line at the moment we crossed it. When I came out I beheld a great sail stretched across the deck, just in front of the main-mast, so that we could see nothing, except that on the other side of it there was an immense slop oozing out from something, and in front was written "Neptune's original easy shaving-shop." At the appointed time the sale was hauled away, and we saw all the contrivances. At the starboard gangway there was a sail hung across two masts, stretched from the bulwark to the long-boat, so as to make a great bag, filled about four or five feet deep with water: there was also a ladder by which to help the victims in on one side, but nothing to help them out on the other. On the other side of the ship were all Neptune's party, hallooing and bawling with speaking-trumpets. Neptune himself was not a bad figure. Face and legs painted black and white, and dressed up *à la* Guy,[40] with oil-cloth and bits of rope and yarn hanging on each side of his head. He sat in his car with his wife and daughter, who were merely dressed up in gowns and bonnets begged of the maids. The car was drawn by eight Tritons with painted legs, and black horns on their heads. Neptune was accompanied by his secretary, his doctor, and his *bear*, who was, by far, the best of the set, dressed in sheep-skins, and held by two Tritons.

We were all on the poop, to be out of the way of the mess; and all the gentlemen who had not crossed the Line before had taken care to dress conformably, in jerseys and trowsers, and no stockings. Presently all the party came aft, and Neptune and the Captain had a conversation[i] concerning the news of the ship and Neptune's own private history. "How are you off for fish, Mr. Neptune?" "Very badly, indeed, sir: I've had nothing these two months but a bit of an old soldier who was thrown overboard; and he was so tough I could not eat him." Bear began to growl. "Can't you keep that beast quiet?" said Neptune. Tritons tugged at bear. Bear sprawled and flounced, knocked down two men, all rolling in the slop together; at last Tritons tugged bear into order. The Captain desired Neptune to proceed to business: so the bear got into the sail, that being his domain, in order to duck the victims. The barber brought out his razor and shaving-pot, which were an old saw and a tar-brush, and established himself on the top of the ladder; the doctor at the bottom, with a box of tar-pills and a smelling-bottle, with the cork stuck full of pins; and all the Tritons with buckets of water in their hands. The two first mates went upon deck "*to see fair play*," as I was told. Of course, fair play is always a jewel, but in the present case it proved rather a rough diamond; for before many minutes were over Mr. Darke had a bucket of water in his hands, as hard at work as anybody; and Mr. Kenrick was mounted on the top of the hay, working[j] a water-pipe in full play. Then a Triton came on the poop to summon down the passengers, and began with Captain Faulkner.

As soon as he got on deck they received him with buckets of water, and hunted him up the ladder and into the bear's dominions. They had orders not to shave the gentlemen, only to duck them, which hurt nobody. Then came a scuffle between gentleman and bear, which ended by both going under water together. Then bear's work was done, and gentleman had to scramble out how he could, people being stationed on the other side with buckets of water, "a dissuading of the victim:" however, he got free at last, and was quite ready to help drown all the others, as their turn came round. Young Temple[41] managed best: he was so strong and active that the great bear (who was the most powerful man in the ship) could not get him under the water at all; but he kicked the barber down the ladder, and then, in spite of the water-pipe playing in his face, sprang on to the bear's back, like a monkey, and with one more leap cleared bear, bath, and buckets, and was in the midst of the liberated party, ready to take his share of the fun without having been touched by anybody. After they had settled all the stranger gentlemen, they took the midshipmen, and then the sailors. The gentlemen and midshipmen were all very good sport, but the sailors grew rather savage with each other, and especially when they came to shaving with tar and their rusty saw. The end of all was *Samson*:[42,k] Samson is a very little boy, who had a name of his own when he came on board, but it is quite forgotten now, and he is always called Samson, because he is so small and weak. They shaved him very gently and good-naturedly, holding him on their knees, as the monkey did Gulliver,[43] and then bathed him, and handed him over from one to another just like a baby: the poor little thing, partly frightened and partly amused, looked as if he scarcely knew whether to laugh or to cry; so he did both. This was the whole concern, I think.

We have seen plenty of whales and shoals of porpoises, and caught four albatrosses. They catch them by *fishing* with a line and a bait: the albatross comes peering at the bait in hopes of its being a fish, entangles himself in the line, and is drawn on deck quite easily, unhurt: when they are on deck they look about them and squall: they are rather stupid: they will not eat, but snap at anybody who is civil to them. They patter about with their great web feet, and seem to like to watch what is going on, but they are not really tame, only stupid: they are about the size of a large turkey, and have very long bills; some are all grey, but the largest are white and grey: they are rather handsome birds. Three of those we caught were set at liberty, but one was killed, to be stuffed. I am trying to get some of his feathers for Frank. Do not forget you promised to write to me. Be sure and send me off a letter as soon as ever you have taken your degree,[44] for I shall be most particularly anxious to hear of that grand event.

Tell me everything you can about all at home. The more trifles and the less worth telling they seem to you, the more valuable to me at such a distance.

LETTER THE FOURTH.

* * * * * *

October 6th.

YESTERDAY we arrived at Tristan d'Acunha:[45] very few ships touch there, on account of its being out of the way; but occasionally, as was the case with us, the wind allows of it, and good-natured skippers are glad when it so happens, on account of the poor Robinson Crusoes[46] who live there.

Tristan d'Acunha is an extinct volcano, so steep that it seems to rise perpendicularly from the sea: the Captain told me it was eight thousand feet high. It is almost a bare rock, but here and there are patches of ground which can be cultivated. In Bonaparte's time,[47] Lord Castlereagh[48] took a fancy that the French might make it useful as an intermediate point of communication with St. Helena: sailors say it was an absurd notion, for that the winds and currents make it impossible for any ship to sail from the one island to the other. However, Lord C. established a corporal and party of soldiers to take care of the island. When all fear of Boney was over, they were sent for home; but some of them had grown so fond of their desert island, that they begged leave to remain, and here they have been these twenty years—Corporal Glass,[49] now styled the Governor, and five of his men, with their six wives, and among them thirty-two children. It was not possible for us to go on shore, but Glass and four of his men came off to see us. They looked very healthy and comfortable—cared not a *sous*[50] for anything out of their island—and did not ask one question concerning anything outside their own little rock. The Captain gave them a good supper and plenty of valuable presents, and everybody made up a parcel of clothes or some little oddments. They said what they most wanted was nails, as the wind had lately blown down their houses. They have fifty head of cattle and a hundred sheep; a little corn, twelve acres of potatoes, plenty of apples and pears, and "*ecco tutto!*"[51] I was curious to know whether old Glass was master, and whether the others minded him; but he said no one was master; that the men never quarrel, but the women do; that they have no laws nor rules, and are all very happy together; and that no one ever interferes with another. Old Glass does a great deal of extra work; he is schoolmaster to the children, and says many of his scholars can read the Bible "quite pretty." He is also chaplain,—buries and christens, and reads the service every Sunday, "all according to the Church of England, Sir." They had only Blair's Sermons,[52] which they have read every Sunday for the last ten years, ever since they have possessed them; but the old man said, very innocently, "We do not understand them yet: I suppose they are too good for us." Of course they were well supplied with books before they left us. They make all their own clothes out of canvas given them by the whalers; they sew them with twine, and they looked very respectable: but they said it was not so easy to dress the ladies, and they were exceedingly glad of any old clothes we could rummage out for them. Their shoes are made of seal-skin: they put their feet into the skin while it is moist, and let it dry to the shape of the foot, and it turns out a very tidy shoe.

After they had collected all the "incoherent odds and ends" we could find for them, and finished their supper, they went off again in a beautiful little boat given them by a whaler. The Skipper gave the Governor a salute of one gun, two blue-lights, and two rockets; and they treated us with a bonfire from the shore. I was sorry for several things I had left behind, which would have been treasures to Mrs. Glass,[53] especially worsted for knitting.

These South Seas[54] are much worse than the Bay of Biscay; nothing but rolling by day and by night: but we are all looking forward to a week at the Cape to set us right again.

October 19*th*. CAPE OF GOOD HOPE.—We landed here on Sunday morning, and were very happy to find ourselves on shore. We are to stay a week, and have hired horses, and mean to ride every day.

Cape Town[55] is just like the Dutch toy-towns—straight streets; white houses of only two stories, with flat roofs; trees in almost every street. The place is filled with English, Dutch, Hottentots,[56] Malays,[57] Parsees,[58] fleas, and bugs; the last[l] appear to be the principal inhabitants and the oldest settlers. At first we got into a Dutch boarding-house, which Frank would have called the "Hotel de Bugs;"[m] now we are in an English lodging, much cleaner; only we have to wait on ourselves a good deal.

On leaving the ship we all divided into separate parties, as at Madeira: ours consists of ourselves, Misses Shields and Knight, Captain Faulkner, and Mr. Temple. Mr. Temple is a tame boy, whom Captain F. looks after, for fear he should get into scrapes on shore—going out as a cadet. He is very merry, good-natured, and hungry; and his company and pretty fresh face come very natural to me, and remind me of my brothers. I especially like him when he is very hungry.

We all went yesterday to see a live boa constrictor: he was the most horrible creature I ever saw; thirty-three feet long, greenish and brownish, and with a few silver scales, but the most detestable countenance you can imagine. If the Lady Geraldine's eyes were like his when they shrunk in her head, I do not wonder at anything that happened to Christabel.[59]

I hear there is a Hottentot infant-school here, which I mean to go and see; but we make all our distant excursions first; we have been about fifteen miles into the country. It is not so pretty as Madeira, but there are one or two magnificent views: the chief characteristics of the scenery are high rocks, green grass, and white sand, but the white sand is entirely covered with flowers—English hothouse flowers, growing wild.

We went to the English church twice on Sunday—a pretty church, built by the English residents, with a respectable High-church clergyman—somewhat dull. There is a Sunday-school belonging to the church, and taught principally by English ladies. Here are plenty of Methodist chapels;[60] the Wesleyans[61] are said to be the best.

There is a very poor museum; but I bought at it a couple of ugly shells for the C—s.[62] I hope they will not break in coming. Mr. Harvey, who is very scientific, says they are curious, and "right to have:" they are land-shells—Achatina.[63]

Papa always likes to know how a place would answer to live at; so tell him that here there are three prices: one cheap, for Dutch; one dear, for English; and one dearest, for visitors: we pay the dearest, of course; and we get six mutton-chops for fourpence halfpenny, and everything else in proportion. Houses are dear, and society baddish—second-rate—with a great deal of quarrelling concerning Colonial politics. Instead of Whigs and Tories, they have the Caffre party and the Government party,[64] who will scarcely speak to each other.

We dined yesterday with some people named Wilderspin[65]—queer, and good, and civil: they have been many years at the Cape, and are most curiously adrift as to English matters. They asked whether O'Connell[66] was still "celebrated in England?" whether he was received in good society? whether party-spirit ran high? whether there were many disputes among Church-people and Dissenters?[67] &c.

I saw at the Wilderspins' a Miss Bazacot,[68] who is here superintending the schools: she seems really clever, and minding her schools well. The Hottentots are very willing to come, both to week-day and Sunday schools. English, Malay, and Hottentot children are all taught together. At one of the schools there was a little Malay girl, who had learned to read, but was very dull at learning her tasks by heart, when suddenly she grew uncommonly bright, and knew all her texts, chapter and verse, better than any child in the school: when the mistress made inquiries into the cause of this great improvement, she found that the creature had taught her old Malay father to read, and he in return used to take immense pains in teaching the child her texts, till they were thoroughly driven into her head: she taught him to read and to pray; and now, every night before he goes to bed, he repeats his prayers and *the rules of the school!* I think the innocence of repeating the rules is very pretty.

I have got a Malay cap, for Frank's private admiration: they are high pointed things, made of straw and wicker-work, very uncouth, but picturesque-looking, especially on the boatmen.

We have been up the Kloof.[69] I long to go up Table Mountain,[70] but it is thought unsafe. When the cloud that they call the Table-cloth comes down, people are often lost in the fog. There is a magnificent view from the top of the Kloof—Cape Town, and the plain, and the hills on one side; and on the other only the sea and the rocks—but such sea, and such rocks, that anything else would be but an interruption, frittering away their grandeur. It is a sort of Chine,[71] as they call the openings between the hills in the Isle of Wight:[72] the side on which we stood, covered with the beautiful silver-tree; and, directly opposite, the immense rock of Table Mountain overhung by its cloud, and the sea at its base, so far below, that the roar of the breakers round Green Point[73] is only a murmur that just softens the silence. To-morrow we go on board again, leaving here our fellow-passengers, Mr. and Mrs. Wilde and Mr. Harvey. We shall all be sorry to part with them: their cabins are taken by people returning from the Cape to Madras,[74] and we shall think ourselves very fortunate if our new companions are as agreeable and friendly as those we lose.

LETTER THE FIFTH.

Madras, December 19th.

HERE we are at last, in our cousin Staunton's house,[75] safe and well. He and his wife very kind and friendly, and I like all that I have seen of the place and the people. We are most happy and thankful to be on shore. The latter part of our voyage was very wearisome. After leaving the Cape we had a constant succession of gales of wind, very often contrary, and what the sailors called "a chopping sea," pitching and tossing us every way at once; and whenever we asked whether there was any hope of a change, the sailors answered, "No, there seems a fresh hand at the bellows." Then we had calms where we did not expect them, and the Captain said there had been a hurricane somewhere, which had "upset all the winds." Then many of the passengers grew tired of one another, and squabbled a little for amusement, as it is said they always do after passing the Cape; and though the skipper used to harangue concerning the affecting scenes he always witnessed on the passengers leaving the ship, nobody seemed to agree with him. The passengers we took in at the Cape were chiefly officers in the Indian army, who went out as cadets before they had learnt much, and since that time had pretty well forgotten the little they knew. They might have been divided into two classes—those who knew their declensions, and those who did not. They were particularly fond of grammatical discussions, and quite eager about them,—such as whether any English words were really derived from the Latin; whether *regiment* is to be considered as a word of three syllables or two; whether *lunatic* comes from the French, because "*loon*" is French for moon, &c. They used also to extend their acquirements by the study of navigation. After breakfast the captain and officers always took an observation of the sun, technically called "taking a *sight*." Then the passengers all began doing the same, privately called "taking a *look*." They were a capital set in their attitudes,[n] with their glasses, all peering up into the sky, *à la chasse*[76] for the sun and moon. However, they were all very civil, and inoffensive, and unobjectionable; and I hope they are all as happy on shore as we are.

We had a beautiful day for landing—no surf at all. In England I have often bathed in a worse sea. It is very curious that the Madras surf should be so formidable: it generally looks nothing, not to compare to a Brighton[77] rough sea; but in reality its force is irresistible. I sometimes see the great lumbering Masoolah boats[78] as nearly as possible upset by waves which look so gentle and quiet that one longs to bathe in them. We landed in a great boat with twelve boatmen, all singing a queer kind of howl, and with very small matters of clothes on, but their black skins prevent them from looking so very uncomfortable as Europeans would in the same *minus* state.

The scene in the Madras Roads is the brightest and liveliest possible. The sea is completely studded with ships and boats of every size and shape, and the boats filled with crews even more quaint and picturesque than themselves. But none can compare to the catamarans,[79] and the wonderful people that manage them. Fancy a raft of only three logs of wood, tied together at each end when they go out to sea, and untied and left to dry on the beach when they come in again. Each catamaran has one, two, or three men to manage it: they sit crouched upon their heels, throwing their paddles about very dexterously, but remarkably unlike rowing. In one of the early Indian voyagers' log-books[80] there is an entry concerning a catamaran: "This morning, six A.M., saw distinctly two black devils playing at single-stick. We watched these infernal imps above an hour, when they were lost in the distance. Surely this doth portend some great tempest." It is very curious to watch these catamarans putting out to sea. They get through the fiercest surf, sometimes dancing at their ease on the top of the waves, sometimes hidden under the waters; sometimes the man completely washed off his catamaran, and man floating one way and catamaran another, till they seem to catch each other again by magic. They put me in mind of the witch of Fife's voyage in her cockle-shell: —[81]

> "And aye we mountit the sea-green hillis,
>   Till we brushed through the clouds of the hevin;
> Then sousit downright, like the star-shot light
>   Frae the liftis blue casement driven.
>
> But our taickil stood, and our bark was good,
>   And sae pang was our pearly prowe,
> Whan we could not climb the brow of the waves,
>   We needlit them through below."

December 27th.—I think I shall like Madras very much, and I am greatly amused with all I see and hear. The heat now is not at all oppressive, this being the cool season. The houses are so airy and large, and the air so light, that one does not feel the heat so much as one would in Italy when the temperature is the same. At present the thermometer is at 78°, but it feels so much cooler, from the thorough draughts they keep up in every room, that I would not believe it to be more than 70°, till I looked with my own eyes. The rooms are as large as chapels, and made up of doors and windows, open day and night. I have seen so many curiosities already, that I do not know which to describe to you first—jugglers, tumblers, snake-charmers, native visitors, &c. &c.; for the last few days we have been in a constant bustle. Those snake-charmers are most wonderful. One day we had eight cobras and three other snakes all dancing round us at once, and the snake-men singing and playing to them on a kind of bagpipes.[82] The venomous snakes they call *good* snakes: one, the Braminee cobra, they said was so good, his bite would kill a man in three hours; but of course all these had their fangs extracted.[83] I was told that they had their teeth drawn once a-month, but I suppose in fact they have the venom extracted from their teeth. The men bring them in covered baskets. They set the baskets on the ground, and play their bagpipes for a while; then they blow at the snakes through the baskets; then play a little more: at last they take off the lid of the basket, and the snake rises up very grand, arching his neck like a swan, and with his hood spread, looking very handsome, but very wicked.

There is one great convenience in visiting at an Indian house, viz.—every visitor keeps his own establishment of servants, so as to give no trouble to those of the house. The servants provide for themselves in a most curious way. They seem to me to sleep nowhere, and eat nothing,—that is to say, in our houses, or of our goods. They have mats on the steps, and live upon rice. But they do very little, and every one has his separate work. I have an ayah (or lady's maid), and a tailor (for the ayahs cannot work); and A—[84] has a boy: also two muddles—one to sweep my room, and another to bring water. There is one man to lay the cloth, another to bring in dinner, another to light the candles, and others to wait at table.[85] Every horse has a man and a maid to himself—the maid cuts grass for him; and every dog has a boy. I inquired whether the cat had any servants, but I found that she was allowed to wait upon herself; and, as she seemed the only person in the establishment capable of so doing, I respected her accordingly. Besides all these acknowledged and ostensible attendants, each servant has a kind of muddle or double of his own, who does all the work that can be put off upon him without being found out by the master and mistress. Notwithstanding their numbers, they are dreadfully slow. I often tire myself with doing things for myself rather than wait for their dawdling; but Mrs. Staunton laughs at me, and calls me a "griffin," and says I must learn to have patience and save my strength. (N.B. *Griffin* means a freshman or freshwoman in India.) The real Indian ladies lie on a sofa, and, if they drop their handkerchief, they just lower their voices and say, "Boy!" in a very gentle tone, and then creeps in, perhaps, some old wizen, skinny brownie, looking like a superannuated thread-paper, who twiddles after them for a little while, and then creeps out again as softly as a black cat, and sits down cross-legged in the verandah till "Mistress please to call again."

We have had a great many visits from natives to welcome A— back again, or, as they say, "to see the light of Master's countenance, and bless God for the honour!" One—a gentleman, in his black way—called at six in the morning: he left his carriage at the gate, and his slippers under a tree; and then, finding we were going out riding, he walked barefoot in the dust by the side of our horses till "our honours" were pleased to dismiss him. Another met us, got out of his carriage, kicked off his shoes, and stood bowing in the dirt while we passed; then drove on to the house, and waited humbly under the verandah for an hour and a half, till we were pleased to finish our ride. One paid me a visit alone, and took the opportunity to give me a great deal of friendly advice concerning managing A—. He especially counselled me to persuade him *to tell a few lies*." He said he had often advised "Master" to do so; but that he would not mind *him*, but "perhaps Mistress persuade Master. Master very good—very upright man; he always good: but Master say all same way that he think. Much better not! Mistress please tell Master. Anybody say wrong, Master's mind different: that quite right—Master keep his own mind; his mind always good: but let Master say all same what others say; that much better, and they give him fine appointment, and plenty much rupees!" I said that that was not English fashion, but my visitor assured me that there were "plenty many" Englishmen who told as many lies as the natives, and were all rich in consequence: so then I could only say it was very wrong, and not Master's fashion nor mine; to which he agreed, but thought it "plenty great pity!"

These natives are a cringing set, and behave to us English as if they were the dirt under our feet; and indeed we give them reason to suppose we consider them as such. Their servility is disagreeable, but the rudeness and contempt with which the English treat them are quite painful to witness. Civility to servants especially seems a complete characteristic of *griffinage*. One day I said to my ayah (a very elegant lady in white muslin), "Ayah, bring me a glass of toast-and-water, if you please." She crept to the door, and then came back again, looking extremely perplexed, and whined out, "What Mistress tell? I don't know." "I told you to bring me some toast-and-water." "Toast-water I know very well, but mistress tell *if you please;* I don't know *if you please.*" I believe the phrase had never before been addressed to her. Everything seems to be done by means of constantly finding fault: if one lets the people suppose they have given a moment's satisfaction, they begin to reason, "Master tell very good; try a little more than worse; perhaps Master like plenty as well." One day I gave some embroidery to be done by a Moorman[86] recommended by my tailor: the Moorman did not bring his work home in time; I asked Mrs. Staunton what was to be done. "Oh," she said, "of course stop the tailor's pay." "But it is no fault of the poor tailor's." "Oh, never mind that: he is the Moorman's particular friend, and he will go and beat him every day till he brings the work home."

They are like babies in their ways: fancy my great fat ayah, forty years old, amusing herself with puffing the wind in and out of my air-cushion till she has broken the screw! The jargon that the English speak to the natives is most absurd. I call it "John Company's English,"[87] which rather affronts Mrs. Staunton. It seems so silly and childish, that I really cannot yet bring myself to make use of it; but I fancy I must in time, for the King's English[88] is another characteristic of *griffinage*, and the servants seem unable to understand the commonest direction till it is translated into gibberish.

* * * * *

My letter is called for, as a ship sails this evening; so I must say Good-bye.

LETTER THE SIXTH.

* * * * *

January 11th, 1837.

BISHOP CORRIE[89] called on us the other day, to my great delight, for I had so long revered his character, that it was a very great pleasure to me to see and make acquaintance with him. He is a most noble-looking old man, with a very fine countenance, and a gentle, benevolent manner—a pattern for a bishop in appearance as well as everything else. On Sunday morning we went to the cathedral, but the good bishop did not preach, and we had but an indifferent sermon, on Virtue and Vice. In the evening we went to a chapel in Black Town,[90] some miles from the place where we live, and so crowded that we were obliged to be there three-quarters of an hour before the time, in order to secure seats; but we were well repaid for our labour and trouble. We heard a most delightful preacher:[91] his sermon was clear, and striking.º He is said to be doing an immense deal of good here. His chapel was originally intended for *half-castes*, but he is so popular that the Europeans will go there too. People complain, and perhaps justly, thatᵖ those for whom the chapel was built are kept out in consequence; but I do not see why the English should not have a good sermon once on a Sunday, as well as the blackies.

We went yesterday to the examination of a native school of *Caste* boys[92]—not Christians, but they learn to read the Bible for the sake of the education they receive in other respects. They looked very intelligent, and very picturesque in their turbans and jewels. They answered extremely well, in English, questions on Scripture, on geography, and history, and wrote English from dictation. However, they gave one or two queer, heathenish answers, such as: *Query*. "What is meant by God's *resting* from his work on the seventh day? Did God require rest?" *Answer*. "In the night time he did." This school was established by some English gentlemen for the more respectable classes of natives. Most of the English schools admit Caste boys and Pariahs[93] without any distinction, which is really almost like expecting young gentlemen and chimney-sweepers to learn together in England. The real Madras schools, which taught Dr. Bell[94] his system, are native hedge-schools,[95] held under a shed. The industry of the poor little scholars is wonderful: from six in the morning till eight at night (with the exception of a short time in the middle of the day to go to sleep and eat rice) they are hard at work, bawling their hearts out: our infant-school noise is nothing to theirs. It is very curious—such a lazy, inert race as the Hindoos are—what pains and trouble they will take for a little learning; and little enough they get (poor things!) with all their labour.

A *Moonshee*[96] seems to be a component part of most English establishments, so I have set up one also. He comes three times a-week to teach me Tamul. He is a very solemn sort of person, with long mustachios, and numbers of beautiful shawls which he twists round his waist till they stand out half a yard in front of him, and come into the room before his face appears. When we hired him he made many salams,[97] and said he preferred our friendship to any remuneration we could give; but he condescends to accept five pagodas[98] a month besides. He comes when I choose, and goes away when I bid him. If I am not ready, he sits on his heels in the verandah for a couple of hours doing nothing, till I call him. If I am tired in the course of my lesson, I walk away, and bid him write a little; and there he sits, scribbling very slowly, and very intently, till I please to come back again. He is President of a Hindoo Literary Society,[99] and at its first opening delivered a lecture in English, of which he is very proud. He brought it to me to-day to read. The whole was capital; and it concluded with a hope "that this respectable institution, so happily begun in smoke, might end in blaze!" This Tamul that he is to teach me is a fearfully ugly language—clattering, twittering, chirping, sputtering—like a whole poultry-yard let loose upon one, and not a singing-bird, not a melodious sound among them. I suspect I shall soon grow tired of it, but meanwhile it is a little amusement. I read stories to Moonshee, and then he writes down the roots of the words for me to learn by heart. One day I was reading about a "hero who ate kicks;" but Moonshee looked a little coy, and said he would not write down "kicks," because that was a word that would be of no use to me. A Tamul-writer came to-day to copy some document on cadjan-leaf[100] for Mr. Staunton. He held the leaf in one hand, and a sharp steel-pointed style for a pen in the other. He had the nail of his little finger as long as a bird's claw, which I thought was for untidiness, but I find it is for ornament. He wrote very fast, and seemed quite at his ease, though sitting on his heels, and writing on his hand in this inconvenient manner.

We have been to one or two large dinner-parties, rather grand, dull, and silent. The company are generally tired out with the heat and the office-work all day before they assemble at seven o'clock, and the houses are greatly infested by musquitos, which are in themselves enough to lower one's spirits and stop conversation. People talk a little in a very low voice to those next to them, but one scarcely ever hears any topic of general interest started except steam navigation. To be sure, "few changes can be rung on few bells;" but these good folks do ring on "the changes in the service," till I cannot help sometimes wishing all their appointments were permanent. At an Indian dinner all the guests bring their own servants to wait upon them, so there is a turbaned sultan-like creature behind every chair. A great fan is going over our heads the whole time, and every window and door open; so that, notwithstanding the number of people in the room, it is in reality cooler than an English dining-room. What would grandmamma say to the wastefulness of an Indian dinner? Everybody dines at luncheon, or, as it is here called, tiffin-time,[101] so that there is next to nothing eaten, but about four times as much food put upon the table as would serve for an English party. Geese and turkeys and joints of mutton for side-dishes, and everything else in proportion. All the fruit in India is not worth one visit to your strawberry-beds. The ingenious French at Pondicherry[102] have contrived to cultivate vines; but the English say nothing will grow, and they remain content to waste their substance and their stomach-aches on spongy shaddocks[103] and sour oranges, unless they send to Pondicherry for grapes, which the French are so obliging as to sell at a rupee a bunch. After dinner the company all sit round in the middle of the great gallery-like rooms, talk in whispers, and scratch their musquito-bites. Sometimes there is a little music, as languid as everything else. Concerning the company themselves, the ladies are all young and wizen, and the gentlemen are all old and wizen. Somebody says France is the paradise of married women, and England of girls: I am sure India is the paradise of middle-aged gentlemen. While they are young, they are thought nothing of—just supposed to be making or marring their fortunes, as the case may be; but at about forty, when they are "high in the service," rather yellow, and somewhat grey, they begin to be taken notice of, and called "young men." These respectable persons do all the flirtation too in a solemn sort of way, while the young ones sit by, looking on, and listening to the elderly gentlefolks discussing their livers instead of their hearts.

Every creature seems eaten up with laziness. Even my horse pretends he is too fine to switch off his own flies with his own long tail, but turns his head round to order the horse-keeper to wipe them off for him. Some old Anglo-Indians[104] think themselves too grand to walk in their gardens without servants behind them; and one may really see them, skinny and straw-coloured, and withered like old stubble, creeping along their gravel walks, with a couple of beautiful barefooted peons,[105] with handsome turbans, strutting behind them, and looking like bronze casts of the Apollo[106] in attendance upon Frank's caricatures of our old dancing-master.

Few things amuse me more than the letters we daily receive from natives, underlings in office, who knew A— before he went to England. One apologises for troubling him with "looking at the handwriting of such a remote individual," but begs leave humbly to congratulate him on the safe arrival in India of himself and "his respectable family," meaning me! Another hopes soon to have the honour of throwing himself "at your goodness's philanthropic feet." Is not this the true Fudge style?[107]

"——— The place where our Louis Dixhuit
Set the first of his own dear legitimate feet."

LETTER THE SEVENTH.

* * * * *

January 31st.

THE other day a very rich native, an old protégé of A—'s, came to say that he and his son wished to make a feast for me, if I would come to their house. I was extremely glad, for I was longing to get into one of their native houses; so last night we all went to him by appointment—Mr. and Mrs. Staunton, A—, and I. It was a most curious entertainment; but I was surprised to find that the Stauntons, who have been so long in the country, had never seen anything of the kind before. It is wonderful how little interested most of the English ladies seem by all the strange habits and ways of the natives; and it is not merely that they have grown used to it all, but that, by their own accounts, they never cared more about what goes on around them than they do now. I can only suppose they have forgotten their first impressions. But this makes me wish to try and see everything that I can while the bloom of my Orientalism[108] is fresh upon me, and before this apathy and listlessness have laid hold on me, as no doubt they will.

I asked one lady what she had seen of the country and the natives since she had been in India. "Oh, nothing!" said she: "thank goodness, I know nothing at all about them, nor I don't wish to: really I think the less one sees and knows of them the better!"

Armogum and Sooboo, our two entertainers, met us at their garden-gate, with numbers of lanterns, and rows of natives, some of them friends and some servants, all the way up to the house. The whole house was lighted up like a show, with chandeliers, lamps, and lustres in every possible corner, and hung from the ceiling and festooned to the walls besides: it looked very bright and pretty. The house consisted of one very large verandah, in which stood the native company; that opened into a large drawing-room, with a smaller room at each end, and sleeping-rooms beyond; and on the other side of the drawing-room another verandah leading into another garden. The house was furnished very much like a French lodging-house, only with more comfortable ottomans and sofas; but the general effect was very French: quantities of French nicknacks set out upon different tables, and the walls quite covered with looking-glasses.

We were led into the great drawing-room, and placed upon sofas, and servants stationed at our side to fan us: then Armagum and Sooboo brought us each a nosegay of roses, and poured rose-water over them and over our hands; and they gave me a queer kind of sprig made of rice and beads, like a twelfth-cake[109] ornament: then they gave us each a garland of scented flowers, so powerful that even now, at the end of the next day, I cannot get rid of the perfume on my hands and arms. Then the entertainment began: they had procured the musicians, dancers, and cooks belonging to the Nabob,[110] in order that I might see all the Mussulman[111] amusements, as well as those of the Hindoos. First, then, came in an old man with a long white beard, to play and sing to the vina,[112] an instrument like a large mandoline, very pretty and antique[q] to look at, but not much to hear. His music was miserable, just a mixture of twang and whine, and quite monotonous, without even a pretence to a tune. When we were quite tired of him, he was dismissed, and the Nabob's dancing-girls came in: most graceful creatures, walking, or rather sailing about, like queens, with long muslin robes from their throats to their feet. They were covered with gold and jewels, earrings, nose-rings, bracelets, armlets, anklets, bands round their heads, sévignés,[113] and rings on all their fingers and all their toes. Their dancing consisted of sailing about, waving their hands, turning slowly round and round, and bending from side to side: there were neither steps nor figure, as far as I could make out. The prettiest of their performances was their beautiful swan-like march. Then they sang, bawling like bad street-singers—a most fearful noise, and no tune. Then we had a concert of orchestra music, with different-looking instruments, but in tone like every modification of bagpipes—every variety of drone and squeak: you can form no idea of such sounds under the name of music: the chimney-sweepers' clatter on May-day[114] would be harmonious in comparison. Imagine a succession of unresolved discords, selected at random, and played on twenty or thirty loud instruments, all out of tune in themselves and with each other, and you will have a fair idea of Hindoo music and its effect on the nerves.

When my teeth had been set on edge till I could really bear it no longer, I was obliged to beg A— to give the musicians a hint to stop. Then there came in a man to imitate the notes of various birds: this sounded promising, but unfortunately the Madras birds are screaming, and not singing, birds; and my ears were assailed by screech-owls, crows, parrots, peacocks, &c., so well imitated that I was again obliged to beg relief from such torture. Then we had a Hindoo dancing-girl, with the most magnificent jewellery I ever saw: her dancing was very much like that of the Mahometans,[115] only a little more difficult. There was a good deal of running backwards and forwards upon her heels, and shaking her silver bangles or armlets, which jingled like bells: then glissading up to me, waving her pretty little hands, and making a number of graceful, unmeaning antics, with her eyes fixed on mine in a strange unnatural stare, like animal magnetism.[116] I think those magnetic actings and starings must first have been imitated from some Indian dancing-girl, and in fact the effect is much the same; for I defy any one to have watched this girl's dull, unvarying dance long, without going to sleep. The natives I believe can sit quite contented for hours without any more enlivening amusement; but then they are always half asleep by nature, and like to be quite asleep by choice at any opportunity.

After her performance was ended we had a conjuror, some of whose tricks were quite marvellous. He had on a turban and cummerbund (or piece of muslin wrapped round him), but no jacket, so that one could not imagine a possibility of his concealing any of his apparatus about him; but, among other tricks, he took a small twig of a tree, ran his fingers down it to strip the leaves off—small leaves, like those of a sensitive-plant—and showered down among us, with the leaves, five or six great live scorpions; not little things like Italian scorpions, but formidable animals, almost as long as my hand: I did not admire their company, creeping about the room, so he crumpled them up in his hand, and they disappeared; then he waved his bare arms in the air, and threw a live cobra into the midst of us. Most of his other tricks were juggling with cups and balls, &c., like any English conjuror; but the scorpions and cobra were quite beyond my comprehension.

Our gentlemen were surprised at seeing the string[117] which is always worn by Brahmins[118] round this man's neck, and said that twenty years ago no Brahmin could possibly have so degraded himself as to show off before us as a common juggler. After he was dismissed we had another gold and silver girl, to dance upon sharp swords, to music as sharp; then a fire-eater; and last of all a great supper laid out in the back verandah. The first course consisted of all the nabob's favourite dishes of meat, and curries and pillaws[119] set out in China plates; the second course, all Hindoo cookery, set out in cups and saucers. A— whispered to me that I must eat as much as I could, to please poor old Armagum; so I did my best, till I was almost choked with cayenne-pepper. The Moorman pillaws were very good; but among the Hindoo messes I at last came to something so queer, slimy, and oily, that I was obliged to stop.

After supper Armagum made me a speech, to inform me that he was aware that the Hindoos did not know how to treat ladies: that he had therefore been that morning to consult an English friend of his, Mr. Tracey,[120] concerning the proper mode of showing me the respect that was my due; and that Mr. Tracey had informed him that English ladies were accustomed to exactly the same respect as if they were gentlemen, and that he had better behave to me accordingly. He begged I would consider that, if there had been any deficiency, it was owing to ignorance, and not to want of affection; for that he looked upon me as his mother! Then he perfumed us all with attar of roses,[121] and we came away after thanking him very cordially for his hospitality and all the amusement he had given us. I was very curious to see the ladies of the family, but they could not appear before English gentlemen. I peeped about in hopes of catching a glimpse of them, and I did descry some black eyes and white dresses through one of the half-open doors, but I could not see them distinctly.

* * * *

LETTER THE EIGHTH.

Madras, February 9th.

WE have just received all your letters, which were more welcome than ever letters were before. In England, with your daily post, you little know the eagerness with which we poor Indians look out for our monthly despatch, nor the delight with which we receive it. For some days before the mail is expected all Madras is in a fever, speculating, calculating, hoping, almost praying, that it may arrive a few days, or even a few hours, before the usual time; and when it is known to be "in," the news travels like wildfire in all directions; peons are despatched from every compound to wait at the post-office and bring the letters the instant they are given out, in order to gain an hour upon the general postmen; all other interests and occupations are forgotten; and many people will receive no visits, if there should chance to be any unfortunate beings so letterless as to be able to pay them.

* * * * * *

You ask what kind of scenery we have round Madras. Flat plains of sandy ground, covered with a little harsh dry grass; half-cultivated gardens with high hedges; and large dilapidated-looking houses. Here and there we see very curious and picturesque native buildings, chiefly pagodas; but in general there is very little beauty either of architecture or scenery. Indian colouring is not for a moment to be compared with Italian for lightness, softness, or brilliancy. The sunsets are sometimes exceedingly beautiful, but in general I think the colouring is rather heavy and glaring. However, Madras is not considered a good specimen; people tell me that when I go up the country I shall be "surprised and delighted." The number of open fields and gardens must be healthy, but there is never any fresh feeling in the air: it is all as dead and close as the air of a street. The flowers have no perfume, except the pagoda-flowers, and those are sickly, like withered jessamine;[122] and at every turn in the road one meets with the smell of native cookery, fried cocoa-nut oil, and nasty messes of the same kind.

Moonshee has just sent me a plate of cakes, with a letter to say that he feels convinced I will not disdain the offer on account of its futility, but accept it as a token of the filial affection with which he regards my benignity; hoping I will foster him with the milk of my kindness, and regard him as my own son! This is really word for word his composition.[r]

This morning I had a visit from Armagum and Sooboo to ask leave to borrow Mrs. C—'s beautiful Landscape Annual,[123] which they had peeped into and admired as it lay on the drawing-room table. They promised to "make cover up, and plenty take care, if Mistress would lend," which of course Mistress was very happy to do. Armagum said that all the books about England were so long and big that it frightened anybody to look at them, and yet he wanted very much to know something about what Europe was like; and that this "little book, with very good yellow cover, plenty pictures, and very little read," was exactly what he wanted. So pray tell Mrs. C— that it is probably at this moment making grand show, with a party of natives solemnly looking over and wondering at it. They wonder at everything European, particularly children's toys. They admire our dolls so much, that they are almost ready to make Swamies[124,*] of them. At home we talk of ignorance and heathenism, but we have no idea of what the ignorance of heathenism really is. They think it a most marvellous piece of learning for a boy to be able to find Europe on a map of the world, and they are almost as ignorant of the history of their own country as of ours. They think they already know everything that is at all deep or dry and requires study.

A Mr. N—[125] has established a sort of conversazione once a-week at his own house, for the better class of natives to meet and discuss subjects of general interest and information, in hopes of leading them to think of something a little beyond their monthly salaries and diamond earrings. One of our visitors had been there last night, so we asked him how he liked it, and what was the subject of conversation. It was some branch of political economy connected with Indian government and taxation; but as to how he liked it, he said, "What use hear all that? I know everything master make talk. Now and then I look, just see other people there too, and then I make slumber!" And that is just the way with them in everything but money-getting; they seem awake and alive to nothing else. This man is a sort of half-heathen, half-deist, like most of those who have associated much with Europeans; but he declares that his religion is just the same as ours, only that there are four grades of religion, suited to different orders of minds—idolatry being the lowest, and proper for the common people, but more educated persons see what the idols are intended to represent, and they progress through all the different grades till they arrive at the highest, when they understand everything, and find all religions alike, and all true, only different ways of representing the same thing. A— says he has argued with him till he is tired, but that it is of no use: he always answers, "Yes, sar; that all same what I say."

February 12*th*.—Everybody in Madras has been in real sorrow of late for the death of Bishop Corrie.[126] They say he was the most useful person in all India, and

---

* Inferior gods.

the most beloved. He was thought to have more judgment, experience, and knowledge of the native character, than any one else. Everybody of every class looked up to his wisdom and firmness: yet he was so gentle, benevolent, and courteous, that it was impossible to know him without becoming really attached to him. I used always to think I had never seen such a pattern of "the meekness of wisdom." Like most good and active men here, he fell a victim to over-exertion of mind and body. He went on too long at the highest possible stretch, and was suddenly paralysed—carried home insensible from a public meeting at which he was presiding on Tuesday, and was buried on the Sunday following.

The weather is now fast changing and growing very oppressive: the thermometer stands at 87°. The other day we had a storm, which lowered it to 82°, and a native wrote us word that he was very sorry he could not keep an appointment with us, because the weather was so cold he was afraid to venture out!

As you say you like to hear all about our domestic economy, servants, &c., I must tell you of a thievery which took place last week. We lost a pair of sheets, and the loss was laid to the horse-keeper, who was fined two rupees, it being the custom to punish the servants for every misdemeanor just as if they were children.[127] But the purloiner of our sheets was in reality A——'s dress-boy, who had stolen them to make his own jackets. To avoid the expense of paying for making, he took them to a Coolie tailor,[128] which you may understand to mean a cobbling tailor, who sometimes cobbles for us, and is therefore obliged to do the servants' needle-work for nothing, for fear of having lies told of him to "Master," and so losing Master's favour. Coolie tailor lives near *my* tailor, who is a grandee in comparison; and Coolie, being very glad to have some good European materials to boast of, and extremely proud of his job, showed them off to my tailor. Grandee tailor was more used to the ways of Europeans, and knew that they did not give their good sheets for the servants to make jackets of; so he guessed they had been stolen, and told my ayah, and she told me, not out of any pretence of conscience or care of my goods, but because, as she said, Mrs. Staunton had told her, on hiring her, that she was to take care of my things, and that, if anything was lost, I would "take away her bread," meaning, dismiss her; and then she must "eat up her own money." It was hopeless for any of us to attempt to find out the truth, because the chances were even as to the dress-boy's being a thief, or the ayah and tailor liars; so the only way was to give orders that two of the other servants should search into the matter: one alone would have just told a lie on whichever side suited him, but two were supposed to be a check on each other. Accordingly, there was a regular form of trial held under a mango-tree in the compound:* I watched them from the window, and a capital group they made. The butler, as judge, waving his arms in the air like the leaves of a cocoa-nut tree; the criminal standing in the midst, looking more mean and crestfallen than any European could manage to look under any possible circumstances; the ayah, smoothing down her oily hair with her fingers

---

* Field, or garden, round the house.

as she told her story; and the rest of the servants standing round to make a kind of jury, assisted by all their retainers of hags and imps in the shape of old women and naked black children. A verdict of Guilty was brought in, and the thief, Chelapa by name, was of course dismissed from our service. Then followed a variety of queer scenes. Chelapa would not go, but remained on his knees in A—'s dressing-room, his turban in his hand, stroking his shaven poll, and kissing the floor, in hopes of being forgiven. When he was sent "out of that," the butler came back with him to bespeak compassion: "Sar! Master boy, cry Sar!" Chelapa took the hint and began to cry accordingly, till, finding nothing would do, he consoled himself by abusing the ayah, telling her he would "walk round the house" every day till he could find out some "rogue business" of her doing: to which, she says, she "made compliments;" but she was in reality so frightened at the threat, that she cried for three days. Then the tailor began to cry, for fear some harm should happen to him in the scuffle, and looked up in my face so piteously every time I went up and down stairs that I could not pass him without laughing. A— asked the horse-keeper why he had submitted to a false accusation, and to be fined for stealing, when he knew he had done no such thing; he answered, "What for make trouble? Master tell horse-keeper thief; what use horse-keeper tell? Horse-keeper make trouble, Master tell 'Go away!'" The probability is, that he was paid by the thief to take the blame. See what a set they are!

* * * * *

LETTER THE NINTH.

* * * * *

August 16th.

I HAVE been trying to entomologize,[129] as there are abundance of curious insects. Mr. Spence[130] himself told me, before I left home, that the insects of India were very little known; and that I could not fail to find many new specimens, especially among the smaller Coleoptera.[131] It is impossible to go "*à la chasse*" oneself, so I employed the beggar-boys, who at first liked the amusement and brought me a great many, but they gradually grew tired of it, and are now too lazy to find me any more at all. I raised my price, but all in vain. These naked imps prefer sitting on the grass all day with nothing to do, crumpled up and looking like tadpoles, and will not give themselves the trouble even to put out their paws to take an insect if he crosses their path. They are indeed a lazy race. The servants lie on their mats, strewing the floor like cats and dogs, and begin to puff and whine whenever one gives them any employment. The truest account of their occupations was given me in her blundering English by my muddle. I said, "Ellen, what are you doing? why don't you come when I call you?" "No, ma'am." "What are you doing, I say?" "Ma'am, I never do;" meaning, "I am doing nothing." However, sometimes they contrive to do mischief. I found my watch stopped: I said, "Ayah, how did you break my watch? did you knock it?"—"Ma'am, a little I knock, not too much!"

We are now living at St. Thomé,[132] a sort of suburb of Madras, close by the seaside, and comparatively cool. We are really now not oppressed by heat; I could not have supposed such a short distance could have made so much difference: the thermometer is at 84°, which is quite bearable after one has tried 92°. But St. Thomé is not thought healthy the whole year through, because the "long-shore winds," as they are called, are more felt here than inland. This long-shore wind is very disagreeable—a sort of sham sea-breeze blowing from the south; whereas the real sea-breeze blows from the east: it is a regular cheat upon the new-comers, feeling damp and fresh as if it were going to cool one, but in reality keeping up a constant cold perspiration, which is more weakening and relaxing than even the heat; and yet one cannot shut the wind out, for the moment one is out of its influence the heavy dead heat is insupportable. It only blows at particular times of the year, and is now going off.

This St. Thomé is said to be a thievish place: we have two Sepoys[133] to guard the house at night. When we first came we were awakened at intervals by a most horrible yelling and screaming: we thought it must be drunken men, and scolded the Sepoys for not keeping them off, but we found it was the Sepoys themselves, yelling for their own security, to frighten the hobgoblins. Yesterday I saw a slim young black creeping up my back-stairs outside the house, peering about in a sneaking, suspicious sort of a way; and as soon as he saw me he ran off and hid himself. I thought he might be a thief, so I turned out all the servants to catch him, but he proved to be nothing but the dog-boy looking for shoes to clean. I asked him why he ran away in that foolish fright, if he was only employed in his proper business; and I was told that he could not help it, for he had never seen the Mistress so close before, and she frightened him.

Mr. and Mrs. Staunton are gone to-day to the wedding of their young friend Miss L—.[134] She has married a lieutenant in the army with nothing but his pay, and I am afraid they will be very poor. It seems to me that in this country a small income must be wretched indeed, for what would be luxuries in England, such as large airy houses, carriages, plenty of servants, &c. &c., are here necessaries indispensable to the preservation of health, independently of comfort. The real luxury here, and for which one would gladly pay any price, would be the power of doing without such matters.

A— is busily employed in translating into Tamul a book which we hope may be useful. The Moonshee transcribes it for him, and is a complete baby about it. I think he must spend all his time in copying it over and over. One day he brings "to show Mistress a fair copy," and the next day "if Mistress please to look, a more fairer copy," and he will stand for a quarter of an hour at a time in the middle of the room, making salaam, and twirling his mustachios, and stroking his manuscript. A— works with the Moonshee while I scold the tailor. I scold him from the "best of motives," and here are my reasons: he is hired by the month, and paid a great deal more than he is worth,—dawdle that he is!—but it is the only way of getting needlework done at all here. He often asks for a day's leave of absence, and often takes it without asking. I used to be compassionate to him at first, believing his excuses; but when I repeated them to Mrs. Staunton, she said they were all lies. One day he told me that his mother was sick, and that she would soon be dead, and he would "put her out of the way;" but Mrs. Staunton said that this mother had already died three times to her certain knowledge, and that I must forbid her ever being sick again without my permission; so I gave my orders accordingly, and she has been quite well ever since. Sometimes he sits on his mat crying, and saying he is "plenty sick" himself, so then I send him away for half a day, with orders to come back quite well next morning, or I shall get another tailor; and this always cures him. One day he asked me for five days' leave "to paint his face:" this *did* puzzle me, but I found it was on account of the Mohurrum,[135] a kind of Mussulman carnival, when they all dress up, and paint not only their own faces, but those of all their animals. The cows' horns were all painted green and red, and sometimes one horn green and one red; and I met an elephant with his face painted in crimson and gold half way down his trunk, and his little cunning eyes peering through his finery, such an object that his own mother could not have known him; but he evidently thought himself dressed in a wonderfully becoming costume, and was floundering along, shaking his ears and waving his trunk, and never dreaming what a figure[s] they had made of him.

June 1st.—To-day we have the first specimen I have felt of real Indian heat; hitherto it has been an unusually cool season, but to-day there is a regular landwind, and plenty of it. I can only compare it to a blast from a furnace, withering one as it passes by. I have a tatt,[136] or thick mat, at my window, which excludes the sun, and men sit outside pouring water on it all day, so that the wind, which is extremely violent, blows always cooled through the water. This keeps the temperature of the room down at 90°, but it is dreadfully feverish, and far more distressing than a higher degree of the thermometer with the sea-breeze.

Just close under the tatt it is more tolerable, but the old Indians have a notion that it is unwholesome to sit in the damp: so it may be for them, but nothing will make me believe that I, just fresh from Europe, can catch cold with the thermometer at 90°: so I creep as close to the tatt as possible, and sit with my hands in a basin of water besides. This is a heat quite different from anything you ever felt in Europe, making one quite giddy; but they say it is only as bad as this for about ten days, after which the sea-breeze rises regularly at eleven or twelve o'clock, and restores one to life again. Now, the leaves of the trees are all curled up, and the grass crackles under our feet like snow, the sea is a dead yellow colour, and the air and light a sort of buff, as if the elements had the jaundice; and we are all *so* cross! creeping about and whining, and then lying down and growling—I hope it will not last long.

June 6th.—Weather better: the sea-breeze comes in the middle of the day, and one can breathe without crying; but the nights are hotter than the days. One contrives to sleep as well as one can, but Indian sleep is very unlike English—poor restless work! However, the musquitoes are not so bad here as in Italy: witness my sleeping without a musquito-net, rather than bear the additional heat of the gauze.

* * * * *

LETTER THE TENTH.

Madras, July 10th.

AT last I am able to resume my journal to you, and I hope to continue it regularly. A— wrote to you constantly and circumstantially during my confinement,[137] but till now I have not been able to sit up and write myself. How I long to show baby to you! She is a very fine creature, and as strong and healthy as if she had been born in Old England. She will be christened next week, and then, as soon as we are strong enough to travel, we are to set out on a long journey. A— has obtained the appointment of Zillah[138] (or District) Judge of Rajahmundry,[139] which makes us all very happy. He has never been in that part of the country before, and we are very busy, making all possible inquiries and preparations. Rajahmundry is in the Northern Circars (or Districts), and every one who has been there tells us that it is a pretty place, and has the grand recommendation of two months of really cool weather. They say the thermometer falls to 58°, and we are advised to take warm clothing with us. It is also a cheap place. There is very little European society, but that is a much less privation here than at home; for in this climate it is almost more trouble than pleasure to keep up the necessary civilities, and there will be plenty of amusement in seeing the really Indian part of India, which Rajahmundry will be.

We must take with us stores of everything that we are likely to want for six months,—furniture, clothes, and even great part of our food—for nothing is to be procured there, except meat, bread, and vegetables; and even our vegetables we must grow ourselves, and take the seeds with us from Madras. Anything we forget we must wait for till we can send to Madras. We have not yet decided whether to go by land or by sea, but I am afraid it will be wisest to go by sea, though I should much like to see the country; but a long land-journey at this time of the year would be very fatiguing, and perhaps dangerous, on account of the cholera, which is now very prevalent. At Rajahmundry they speak Gentoo,[140] or Teloogoo,[141] which is a much prettier language than Tamul. There is no Chaplain, nor even a Missionary, I am sorry to say; but that is the case at eight stations out of ten, and one cannot choose one's station.

RAJAHMUNDRY, *August 6th.*—I was prevented from finishing this letter at Madras, by take-leave visits, &c., so that I had not a moment to myself; but it was just as well, for now I can tell you of our safe arrival here. We embarked on Saturday night, July 29th, ourselves, baby, and servants, with almost a shipload of goods, on board a small Liverpool[142] vessel which happened to be in the roads, on its way to Calcutta.[143] We had a beautiful evening, and no surf. We found the Captain in a fume at our being rather later than he expected; but it did not really signify, for, after all his fretting, he could not get his anchor up, owing to his having bad tackle, so there we were detained at anchor till one o'clock on Sunday afternoon. It was a pretty specimen of sea comfort;—ship rolling, captain growling; sailors singing, or rather bawling, some chorus about being "Off in a hurry; fare ye well, for she must go!" while they were dragging up the anchor; tackle breaking, and chain cable all flying to the bottom of the sea, as soon as ever the song was done; things in our cabin not "cleated down," but all "fetching way" with every roll of the ship, shuffling about, and taking their pleasure, like the dancing furniture in Washington Irving's dream;[144] ayahs squatted on the floor, half-sick; baby squalling; A— turning round and round in the little cabin, like a tiger in his den, dancing her to keep her quiet, but quiet she would not be; I, ready to cry with sickness and despair, crouched up in a corner unable to move,—and all for nothing, during eighteen hours!

At last we were off. We had a pretty good voyage on the whole, but one violent storm on Sunday night; the thunder ringing like a gong, and the air all around us white with lightning. In the midst of it all, some Italian Capuchins[145] who were on board amused themselves with singing to their guitar. While the sea and wind together were roaring their loudest, twang, twang went that wretched guitar! The mixture was so absurd that I could not help laughing, in the midst of all my sickness and fright.

On Tuesday morning our stupid Captain passed by Coringa,[146] which was the port for which *we* were bound, and, when he took his observation at twelve o'clock, found himself half way to Vizagapatam.[147] It was extremely inconvenient. All our letters of introduction were for the Coringa people, and the land-journey from Vizagapatam to Rajahmundry three times as long as from Coringa. The other passengers were very good-natured and obliging, said the delay was of no consequence to them, and begged us to go back to Coringa, if we liked. Accordingly, we did have the ship put about, but there was a strong wind right in our teeth; we were likely to be five or six days putting back; and the pitching and tossing such, that every minute of it settled our minds as it unsettled our stomachs: so we determined to go on to Vizagapatam, where we arrived on Tuesday night.

Before we landed, a catamaran brought us off a note from Mr. R., the Assistant Judge[148] of the station, inviting us to his house. He has a little bungalow on the top of a rock, surrounded by bushes among which the hyænas walk about at their pleasure; but they never attack human beings, and the place is delightfully cool. Mr. R. received us most hospitably, supplied us with everything we wanted for our journey, and treated us just as if we had been old and intimate friends, though we had never seen nor heard of each other before. We spent Wednesday with him, and began our journey on Wednesday night, regular Indian fashion, in palanquins[149]—A—, baby, I, and the ayahs; leaving the other servants to follow at leisure, with the luggage, in carts. We had fifty-two men to carry us, our provisions, clothes, plates, knives and forks, &c., for all the accommodations prepared for travellers are public bungalows, containing one table and six chairs,—and sometimes not those, only bare walls for shelter. An old Sepoy lives at each bungalow, to fetch water, and cook curry and rice; so one can get on comfortably enough.

It is all pleasant to me: baby has borne the journey quite well, and I enjoyed it very much. We travelled sometimes all night, sometimes part of the night, according to my strength, and rested at the bungalows during the day, and arrived here on Saturday night. We passed through a great deal of pretty country, and some notorious tiger-jungles; but we saw no tigers—they are always afraid of the lights and noise of travellers. (N.B. A jungle is a tract of uncultivated ground, covered with thick brushwood, and trees here and there, and inhabited by tigers, hyænas, leopards—or cheetahs as they are called[150]—monkeys, wild hogs, snakes, and quantities of beautiful birds.) Rajahmundry itself is a most lovely spot, on the banks of a magnificent river, the Godavery,[151] with fine hills in the distance.

We have a good house, a capital garden, and are most uncommonly great grandees. I am very much amused with all the natives who come to pay their respects to the "Judge Doory." (Doory means gentleman.) My favourite, hitherto, is the Moofti, or principal Mahometan law expounder. He is one of the handsomest and most elegant creatures I ever saw,—somewhat dirty perhaps,—with beautiful Cashmere shawls[152] worn threadbare, and in his shabby magnificence looking like a beggarly king. Then there is the Pundit, or principal Hindoo law expounder—a Bramin,[153] very much of a mountebank, and something of a cheat, I should guess, by his face and manner. There are plenty of underlings, but these are the two principal men. They always come accompanied by their Vakeels,[154] a kind of secretaries, or interpreters, or flappers—their muddles,[155] in short: everybody here has a muddle, high or low. The Vakeels stand behind their masters during all the visit, and discuss with them all that A— says. Sometimes they tell him some barefaced lie, and, when they find he does not believe it, they turn to me grinning, and say, "Ma'am, the Doory plenty cunning gentlyman."

The cholera is raging here,—and no wonder! a hundred thousand people assembled twenty days ago, for a grand native festival which only takes place once in twelve years.[156] Many of them are too poor to afford to buy proper food, and most of them are dirty; and the accumulation of dirt and filth, with all the wretchedness and starvation to work upon, has bred a pestilence. When I arrived in the town I was fast asleep in my palanquin, and was literally awakened by the horrible stench. A—'s predecessor[157] was entirely occupied in making a road through the jungle to drive his tandem on, and never thought of taking any measures to lessen the sickness, which has gained ground fearfully. A— has set the prisoners at work immediately to clean the streets, and the heavy rains are to be expected soon, which always clear away diseases. There is little fear of cholera among Europeans, except in travelling. It is caused among the poor natives by bad feeding, dirt, and exposure to the climate. We always keep the cholera medicines in the house, in case any of the servants should be attacked; but that is very unlikely, as they are well fed and sheltered. The poor natives go on beating their tom-toms, or drums, all night, in hopes of driving it away; and the want of rest weakens them, and makes them still more liable to catch it.

August 11*th.*—We get on very comfortably, and are beginning to feel a little settled, though still rather in confusion. A— is excessively busy with his Court work, having to get through long arrears of his predecessors. Our furniture is not yet arrived, so we are dependent upon a table and six chairs lent to us for the present: however, a clear house at first arrival was rather a convenience with regard to cleaning the rooms, which I have been very busy about, as A— is in clearing out all the old "cases" accumulated in his Cutcherry. (N.B. Cutcherry means office.)

I fancy our predecessor was content with the same accommodation as the spiders, and thought sweeping unnecessary, so he kept no sweeper-woman, and, as may be supposed, the dirt crunched under our feet as we walked. I have had all the palanquin-boys, who are the best housemaids here, hard at work, taking away the old mats, hunting for scorpions and centipedes, dislodging the dirt-pies, disturbing the spiders, and clearing out every corner,—and now we are growing quite decent. We are planting vegetables, clipping hedges, and arranging all things to our own taste; and I think we shall soon be so comfortable, that when a better appointment offers, we shall not like to move.

Some of our arrangements are queer wild work. We have a hunting Peon, or "shoot-man," as he is called, who goes into the jungle every day to catch us half our dinner according to his taste or his luck. He brings hares, wild ducks, pigeons, &c., and yesterday he brought a magnificent peacock. It went to my heart to have such a beautiful creature cooked; but there was no help for it, and he was dead when he arrived. There are pretty spotted deer and antelopes wild about the country, and I am going to have some caught to keep in the compound: they soon grow quite tame, and come and eat out of one's hand.

"John Company" allows us nine Peons to look grand with. Their business is to stand about, go on messages, walk after us (which, by the bye, we, cannot endure), do odd jobs, and "help Bill" in various ways. The other day I sent the baby and nurse out for a walk in our garden, not supposing that she required any escort, but a great Peon immediately stepped forward to march after her. She crowed at his dagger and red belt, and much approved of his attendance. A— has given me two of the Peons for my particular service: I have nothing on earth for them to do, so I mean to set them collecting the pebbles found in the river here, which are very beautiful onyxes and agates.[1] When they have got over their surprise, and are a little broken in to the "Dooresany's" (lady's) ways, I mean to set them catching insects; but I must wait a little first, for fear they should think me mad.

We have had a travelling gentleman staying with us for the last two days: we never saw him before, but he asked for shelter on his arrival, so, India-fashion, we took him in to do the best we could for him. I am obliged to make him carry a chair about with him like a snail-shell—take it into his room at night, and bring it out again to breakfast the next morning. He is a good-humoured, simple sort of person, but most oddly fearful. He took such alarm at hearing the cholera was in one village at which he slept on his journey, that he lost his appetite, ate nothing for twenty-four hours, and came to us really ill with starvation and fright. Then he was exceedingly afraid of robbers on the road, and had a great mind to take a guard of Peons on with him to Vizagapatam, only we laughed him out of it. There was some excuse for his fears, because he was just come from a very wild part of the country, but here we are as quiet and safe as at home. *Home* always means England; nobody calls India home—not even those who have been here thirty years or more, and are never likely to return to Europe; even they still always speak of England as home.

* * * * *

LETTER THE ELEVENTH.

* * * * *

Rajahmundry, August 14th.

OUR goods arrived last week. They had all been wetted through in the journey, and very much spoiled, but, by dint of keeping the sun and the palanquin-boys at work upon them, they are coming round again.

Captain Price, the commanding officer[158] here, has just called. He seems very civil, nothing else particularly. He has a wife, whom I have not seen yet, as they were away till yesterday. The commanding officers are generally changed every three months. There is a Scotch Dr. Stewart,[159] and a Mr. Macdonald,[160] the sub-collector, but he is not here now. There will also be in time a Registrar, or, as they spell it here, "Register," but none is appointed yet. These and ourselves are all the residents; but there are continually travellers passing through, as this place is on the high road from the north to the south of Madras. I fancy the civilians all expect to come to us on their journey; and the militaries go to Captain Price: and whichever of us receives the visitor must make a dinner-party.

Last night I was awakened by a great uproar: I found it was on account of a snake who had crept into the house and hidden himself under a box. The maty[161] had found him out, and the servants were all hunting and fighting him with sticks. He was caught and killed. A— thought he was not of a venomous kind, but they are not pleasant visitors. I often hear the hyænas at night howling about the country. They are horrid spiteful-looking creatures, but so cowardly that they never attack any but weak animals. They do mischief in the poultry-yard, and sometimes carry off a small dog, and, if very hungry, now and then a young donkey; but one is no more afraid of them than of foxes in England.

Did you ever hear of the Thugs?[162] They are a tribe of Hindoos whose business and trade is murder. They are brought up to it from childhood, choose their victim by omen, consider themselves and their vocation under the especial patronage and direction of one of their goddesses, Kalee,[163] and set about their murdering work in the most cool and business-like manner. You will find a long account of them, and quite true, in Wolff's last volume of his Journal.[164] There is a great sensation about them just now, and we are hunting them out everywhere. One has been brought to A— for trial[165] to-day, and I am very curious to hear about him.

I left off writing just now for my "tiffin," and could not imagine what they were bringing me to eat. Some *bran*, which I had been boiling to season a new tin kettle, and which the maty supposed to be some particular Europe cookie I was making for myself; and, thinking I was provided for, he has eaten up all my meat!

August 15*th*.—The Thug turned out to be an accuser instead of a criminal. A Peon had caught him, and he pretended that the Peon had offered to release him on his paying a certain sum, and that he had paid it, but the Peon still kept him prisoner. On investigation it turned out to be all a lie from beginning to end; so the Peon is released and the Thug sent to prison.

I was hard at work to-day unpacking books, sitting on the ground all over dust, sorting and putting them on the shelves, when Mrs. Price called to pay her first devoirs with all her best clothes on, worked muslin and yellow gloves. I thought the only way to prevent her being ashamed of me was to make her as dirty and dusty as myself; therefore, under pretence that it would be so nice for her to have some new books to read, I made her sit down by me and look them over too, and we got on very well. She is very young, pretty, and unaffected, and I like the thoughts of having her for a neighbour. It is pleasant to have some Englishwoman within reach as a companion.

August 29*th*.—Your packet, sent by private opportunity, has just arrived, to my great delight. I had received, a fortnight ago, letters from home of a later date, but private-hand letters are always slow. People never seem to be able to lay their private hands upon them till after they have finished all their unpacking.

We like our station better and better; it is far pleasanter than Madras, which was like England in a perspiration: here we have fresh, sweet country air, and no troublesome company, yet always enough to prevent us from feeling lonely.

I thoroughly enjoy the quiet, and I have plenty to do, more than I can ever get through in the day, so that I am never dull. In fact, one has less time at one's command here than at home, although the very early rising seems to give so many hours. But we are obliged to go out in the early morning; it is indispensable to lie down for some time in the middle of the day; we go out again in the cool of the evening, and come home again too tired to employ ourselves much at night. One's time seems to be spent in tiring and resting oneself.

I have caught a number of most beautiful butterflies: Coleoptera are more scarce, as I cannot grub for them myself, for fear of centipedes. This morning, I took a fancy for gardening myself, and while I was removing some dry leaves a large centipede showed his horrid pincers within an inch of my hand. He did not hurt me, but he has cured me of gardening.[u] I have a number of schemes in hand; one is to make butter: the natives make it with rennet, shaking it in a bottle, and it is rather a nasty mess; but after a week's hard work and much scolding, the old carpenter has produced a churn: a fine, heavy, awkward concern it is, but the natives admire it greatly, and stand looking at it and calling it "Missis Dub" (meaning Mistress's tub). However, the butter is still waiting for pans to set the milk in, and they had to be made on purpose from description, and have not yet appeared. When I inquired for them this morning, I was told "Potman done fetch mud, chatties[166] done make, but mud not done dry yet."

The other day I wanted some book-shelves made, and I sent for the carpenter. They told me they thought I should be wanting wood, so he was gone *fishing*, which seemed rather, as Johnny M.[167] would say, a *"non sequitur;"*[168] but it was quite true, for they really do fish for all the wood they use. It is washed down by the river; and when any is wanted, they just swim out, and catch the first piece that suits them.

There is an old Englishman[169] living here as barrack-sergeant,—a sinecure for long service. He has been in the place these ten years, and is a very respectable old man. He has a half-caste, dropsical wife, and a sickly nigger-looking child, but seems quiet and contented. A— lends him books and the newspaper, and lets him come every Monday to change his books, and chat a little, which he likes best of all. He sits and proses for about half an hour, and is very happy at having a little intercourse with Europeans again. He takes particular interest in the young Queen,[170] thinking she has a troublesome life before her. Yesterday he said to me, "Only think, ma'am, of such a young person for to be Queen of the realm! And in these times too, when the oldest hand could hardly keep them in order. She'll have a tough job of it, poor young lady! I pity her from my heart, indeed I do! This paper says Lord Durham[171] is to be called to her Majesty's counsels. I hope his Lordship is a fatherly kind of gentleman, ma'am, who will help her Majesty in some of her difficulties."

A— is very kind in hunting out poor travellers who happen to be passing. The rich ones, who want for nothing, come to us as a matter of course, but the poor ones would pitch their tents under a tree during the hot hours, and go away again unnoticed, if he did not go and find them out. The other day he discovered seven English soldiers travelling to join their regiment: they were not in want of absolute necessaries, but, on his trying to find out what he could do for them, they told him at last, confidentially, that the greatest treat he could possibly give them would be a little tea and sugar to make themselves "a cup of English tea," which was a thing "they had not tasted they did not know when:" of course we sent them plenty, and books and tracts for the tea to wash down. They had a Bible among them, but they said "they set such store by it, they seldom let it see the light;" so we gave them another for use. A— is very anxious to set up an English school for the natives, if he can persuade Sergeant Keeling to be schoolmaster; but the Sergeant thinks himself "not scholar enough." *We* think he is, and he speaks Teloogoo very well.

To-day a great Zemindar,[172] or Rajah, came to pay us a visit: he is a proprietor of large estates in this district, and pays a rent to the Government of ten thousand a year,—quite a grandee; but he has some lawsuit going on at this court, so he said he was come to ask A— to "protect a poor little man." He stayed an immense time, and talked a great deal of nonsense, as they all do. It is very striking to see how completely want of education has blasted all their powers of intellect. They talk for hours and hours, without ever by any chance bringing out an original idea or a generous sentiment. Their conversation is never anything but wearisome twaddle. I suppose extremes meet. Do you remember Mr. J.[173] once telling us that some celebrated person was "too well informed"—that he had "lost his originality"? These people, from being too ill informed, have never found theirs.

September 16*th*.—A day or two ago the Maty bolted into the breakfast-room, exclaiming, "Sar! one snake, sar! One big snake in godown!"[174] He very good snake, sar!" They call the venomous snakes "good" by way of propitiating them: they consider them as a species of evil-disposed gods, and pay them some kind of worship, though they kill them too whenever they can. This brute was a large deadly cobra capello:[175] it had hidden itself behind some bottles in a recess under the steps where the water is cooled. A— went directly to load his gun, and I peeped out, but could not go near enough to see the creature on account of the sun, and I *calculate* I should not have gone any nearer if it had been ever so shady. There stood all the palanquin-boys with bamboos in their hands, ready to beat it if it came out, and all the Peons peeping over their shoulders, array enough to attack a tiger. A— forbade their killing it in that way, on account of the danger of their getting bitten if they missed a blow, and he shot it dead himself, after which they all dragged it out, and beat it to their hearts' content. Two days afterwards we were told of another cobra in a hole of a tree at the bottom of the garden; but while A— was preparing his gun, one of the snake-conjurers came and charmed it out of its hole, and brought it into the garden to show us: it was quite fresh, its teeth not extracted, and its bite certain death; but this man had it perfectly under command: he set it up and made it dance, and, when it tried to strike, he just whisked the tail of his gown in its face, and quieted it again. I offered to buy it, and pay him for killing and bottling it, but I could not persuade him to sell it at any price: he thought its possession would bring him good luck. In answer to my offers, the butler, who was interpreter, told me, "if Missis put snake in bottle of rack,[176] snake dead." "I know that," said I, "I like it dead." "Yes, ma'am, but that man like 'live." "What is the use of his keeping it alive? sometime snake bite." "No, ma'am, no can bite; that man make conjure." However, to-day the conjurer came to say that he had found another cobra, so he was willing to sell me one if I liked it. Accordingly, he took it with his bare hands out of a brass pan which he brought with him, set it up, made it show its hood and dance a little, and then put it into a bottle of spirits, which soon killed it, and I have it now on my table corked up. It is a magnificent specimen, four feet long, and quite uninjured.

The snakes have very much confirmed my belief in physiognomy.[177] They certainly have a great deal of countenance; a cunning, cruel, spiteful look that tells at once that they are capable of any mischief; in short, *"beaucoup de caractère,"*[178] and the more venomous the snake, the worse his expression. The harmless ones *look* harmless; I think I should almost know a "too much good snake" by his too much bad countenance. The Cobra is the worst, his eyes are quite hideous; and that boa constrictor at the Cape was very disgusting: but after all I do not know that there is anything more horrid in the way of physiognomy than a shark; there is a coldblooded, fishy malignity in his eyes that quite makes one shudder.[v]

September 26*th.*—There was a hyæna killed to-day about half a mile from the town: it had attacked a poor old Bramin, and wounded him severely, which is very extraordinary, as they almost always run away from men. I have ordered the tail to be kept as a trophy for Frank. Also I have a beautiful leopard's skin for him, to be sent by the first opportunity.

LETTER THE TWELFTH.

Rajahmundry, October 3rd.

IN your last letter you ask for particulars of living, servants, house-rent, and such-like domestic matters. We have a house unfurnished, and a garden of more than two acres, for which we pay about 60*l*.[179] per annum. Provisions are cheap, but there is great waste, because nothing will keep on account of the heat, and we are obliged to take much larger quantities of meat than we can consume, in order to make it worth the butcher's while to supply us at all. We send for potatoes from Madras, as they will not grow here; other vegetables we have from our own garden, and we keep our own poultry. Servants are expensive altogether, though cheap individually; but we are obliged to have such a number of them that their pay mounts up. We keep fewer than many people, because we wish to be economical. Here is our establishment:—one butler, one dress-boy,* one matee,† two ayahs, one amah,‡ one cook, one tunnicutchy,§ two gardeners, six bearers, one water-carrier, two horse-keepers, two grass-cutters, one dog-boy, one poultry-man, one washerman, one tailor, one hunter, and one amah's cook—altogether twenty-seven: and this is reckoned few;[180] and it is as much as ever they can do to get through their little work in their lazy dawdling way. If anybody comes to dinner, the cook sits down and cries for a cook's maty or helper, and I am obliged to hire one for him. They all find their own food themselves, and the caste people would not touch any of our food; but the maties and under-servants are generally Pariahs, and are very glad to eat up anything they can lay their hands on. The amah[181] is a caste woman, and her whims are the plague of my life: I am obliged to keep a cook on purpose for her, because her food must all be dressed by a person of her own caste; and even then she will sometimes starve all day rather than eat it, if she fancies anybody else has been near it: she has a house built of cocoa-nut leaves in the compound, on purpose to cook her food in. I am also obliged to keep

---

* Valet.
† The matee cleans plate, washes china, and lights candles.
‡ Wet-nurse.
§ Housemaid.

a separate nurse for her baby, and see after it regularly myself, because they are so careless about their own children when they are nursing other people's, that she and her husband would let the poor little creature die from neglect, and then curse us as the cause of it.

Think of the amah's being caught drinking rack and eating opium! She used to go out and howl so that the servants were afraid to come near her, saying she made "one pishashi[182] (devil) noise." When she had cleared the coast with her pishashi-ing, her own people crept out from their hiding-holes, and brought her rack and bang[183] (that is, spirits and opium).

You ask what shops we have. None at all: the butler buys everything in the bazaar or market, and brings in his bill every day. One of the Court native writers translates it into English, and very queer articles they concoct together! such as, "one beef of rump for biled;"—"one mutton of line beef for *alamoor estoo*," meaning *à-la-mode*[184] *stew;*—"mutton for curry pups" (puffs);—"durkey for stups" (stuffing for turkey);—"eggs for saps, snobs, tips, and pups" (chops, snipes, tipsycake,[185] and puffs);—"mediation (medicine) for ducks;"—and at the end "ghirand totell" (grand total), and "howl balance."

October 15*th*.—Of late I have been hindered from letter-writing and everything else by relays of stranger-company—true Indian-fashion. People say this custom of receiving everybody without previous notice, and being received in return, is "so very delightful," "hospitable," &c. &c.; and so it may be,—but it is also extremely inconvenient and disagreeable. I cannot get over the dislike to intrude myself upon people whom I never saw, and who *must* receive me whether they like it or not; neither do I enjoy being put out of my way and obliged to turn the house out of windows for chance travellers whom I never heard of before, and never shall see again. However, such is the mode here. One of our visitors, Mrs. S.,[186] was a very pleasing person, and I should have much liked to see more of her; but she was on her way to England, and only stayed with us two days. Two of our visitors are with us still, and will remain till they have found a bungalow to suit them, as they are coming to live here: they are Mr. and Mrs. Hamilton,[187] the new registrar and his wife.

We have had the English service now for the last month, and mean to continue it regularly; A— officiates, as is the custom when there is no clergyman: all the English residents attend very regularly, and some half-caste Protestants. There is a Roman Catholic half-caste dresser, or surgeon's assistant, named Rozer, father to Sergeant Keeling's wife: there is a little Roman Catholic chapel under his care, and he takes a great deal of pains about it, poor soul! keeping it clean, lighting the candles, and putting flowers before the images, though there is no priest living here, nor any one to notice him. When our service was announced, he sent a message to ask if he might be present at it, but when the day arrived he never appeared; and on making inquiry, we found from the Sergeant that poor Rozer himself was very anxious to attend, but was afraid of a reprimand from some distant priest who occasionally comes here in the course of his travels.

October 27th.—I continue to like "up country,"[188] as they call it, far better than the Presidency:[189] it is much more amusing. Of course everybody tried to make Madras as English as they could, though without much success, except doing away with everything curious; but this place is real India, and I am every day seeing something new and foreign. This is the country of the old Rajahs, and they are very sociable and fond of paying us visits. They think it a great incivility to appear without something in their hands as a present. It is contrary to regulation[190] to accept anything of value, so they bring limes, oranges, yams, &c. The other day we received a basket of oranges, with a message that a Rajah whom we had not before seen would come next day and pay us a visit. Accordingly next day, at the appointed hour, we heard a queer kind of twanging and piping, like a whistle and a Jew's-harp.[191] This was the Rajah's music, played before his palanquin: then came his guards,—men with halberds;[192] then his chief officer, carrying a silver mace; then his principal courtiers, running by the side of his palanquin to keep him "pleasant company." When they all arrived, the halberdiers grounded their arms, and the whole cortège stopped at the military word of command, "*Halt! Present! Fire!*" but the *firing* consisted of the old gentleman's getting out of his palanquin, and quietly shuffling into the house, between two rows of his own servants and ours, salaming him at every step. He was dressed in a clear muslin pelisse,[193] with his black skin showing through; the rims of his ears stuck full of jewels, gold bracelets on his arms, and a diamond locket hung round his neck. I call him "Penny Whistle Row:"[194] if that is not quite his real name, it is so like it, I am sure it must mean that. When he came into the drawing-room, he stopped at the entrance (N.B. we have no doors) to make us most profound salams, which we returned to the best of our ability: then he presented us with an orange each, and there were more salams on either side. At last, when we had all done all our "moppeing and moweing,"[195] he sat down and began his chirp. He paid a variety of set compliments, as they all do; but, those over, he was more curious about European matters than the natives in general are. In particular he wished to know whether it was true that our King[196] was dead, and that we had a woman to reign over us. This was quite beyond his comprehension—how she was to contrive to reign, and how *men* were to agree to obey her, he gave up in despair. He asked whether the King's death would make any difference to us: he was in hopes it might have given A— a step in the service. He invited us to come and spend a week with him, which we fully intend to do as soon as the weather allows. When he had sat about an hour, he took his leave with the same ceremonies as at his arrival: salams on all sides, pipe whistling, Jew's-harp twanging, guards recovering arms, courtiers putting on their shoes, and all marching off to the word of command as before. "*Halt! Present! Fire!*" At parting he shook hands to show how European his manners were, and he took leave of *me* in English: "My Lady, I now to your Excellency say farewell: I shall hope you to pay me one visit, and on one week go (meaning *hence*) I shall come again to see the face of your honour civilian."

Besides the Rajahs, there are a number of natives of lower rank who are very fond of calling to keep themselves in remembrance in case of an appointment falling vacant. Some only come as far as the gate, and stand there to make a salam when we go out. These never speak, but they put on some part of the dress belonging to the situation they want, in order that we may understand their meaning. A Court writer in expectance holds writing materials in his hand; a Peon sticks a dagger in his belt, &c. Others of rather higher pretensions come to the house and pay a visit. One of them calls regularly twice a-week, and the same dialogue takes place whenever he comes.

Visitor.—Salam, great chief!
A.—Salam to you.
Visitor.—Your Excellency is my father and my mother!
A.—I am much obliged to you.
Visitor.—Sar, I am come to behold your honourable face.
A.—Thank you. Have you anything to say to me?
Visitor.—Nothing, great chief!
A.—Neither have I anything to say, so good morning; enough for to-day.
Visitor.—Enough; good morning, sar: great chief, salam!

One has to dismiss one's own visitors, as they generally think it an impoliteness to go away of their own accord. We are obliged to appoint a particular hour at which they may come, else they would be hindering us the whole day.

* * * * *

LETTER THE THIRTEENTH.

* * * * *

Rajahmundry, October 31st.

WE are very eager about our intended Native School—writing, and planning, and preparing. The difficulty, as usual, has been to find a proper master. In this part of India there are no native Christians, and of course we did not wish to have a Heathen master. On Sunday there came unexpectedly to the service a half-caste stranger. As we had never seen him there before, A— made some inquiries about him afterwards, and heard that he was here only for a couple of days on some business of a lawsuit; that he understands English well, writes a good hand, and spells correctly; and it looked respectable and well-disposed his taking the opportunity of coming to church. He is now gone back to his own home; but, as he seemed promising, and we knew of no one better, A— has written to offer him the schoolmaster's post, if he understands Gentoo; and we are now waiting for his answer. Meanwhile we are busy giving it out among the natives, and collecting promises of scholars. To-day one of the upper Court servants (post-office head writer), called for a chat, so we documentized him, and he offered to look for scholars. A— asked whether, if we set up a girls' school, any girls would come; but Seenevasarow said, "No: what for girls learn?" We had a great discussion on the subject, but he ended by saying that if a girl learned to read, some misfortune was sure to happen to her relations—most likely her father or mother would die. We told him that *I* had learned both to read and to write, and my father and mother were alive and well, and that all European ladies learnt reading and writing, and yet no misfortune happened to any of their relations in consequence; but he said, "Ah! Europe people never mind—never hurt; only native people hurt." A— told him that it was a notion the Pishashi (devil) put into their heads in order to keep them from any good—and a great deal more besides; to which he answered, "Hum! sometime very true; but how can do? girl got no sense!" The consequence of this notion is, that the women, from being utterly neglected, are a hundred times worse than the men. As soon as European children are old enough to talk and understand, one is obliged to have bearers to attend upon them, because it is not safe to trust them with the women; they are so wicked, so lying, and so foolish.

The cool weather is coming on now: thermometer 86° and 84°. From having been completely *heated through* in the summer, I am now pretty well Indianized, and find the present temperature quite cool and pleasant. In the early mornings it is 74°, which feels so cold that I am glad of a cloak to go out with. The same degree of the thermometer certainly does not feel so hot here as it would at home.

There are so many changes in the service, that we shall probably not remain at this station very long, and we may be glad of a removal when the hot season returns; but, for the present, this place is so pleasant and so very pretty, that I should be quite sorry to leave it. Everybody says that the view from our windows is one of the most beautiful in all this part of India. We have just succeeded in putting the garden into nice order, and are are feeling quite settled and comfortable. I have three little deer tethered on the lawn: they are very pretty creatures, and quite tame and friendly. Also I am taming some fine jungle peacocks.

To-night the hunter brought in a superb leopard (dead); they had shot him in looking for game: his beauty was still perfect, and in my own heart I was almost sorry such a handsome creature should have been killed; but they are very mischievous among the cattle, and a price is paid by Government for every one killed. The skins all belong to the Collector;[197] but I mean to beg this one of him, as it was caught during our reign.

Now, in the cool nights, the hyænas and jackals come constantly into our garden, and howl under the windows: it is a most unpleasant noise, like a human being in agony. This morning I was told that "a cat had run away with a child." I was horror-struck, and thought it must have been a hyæna; but on inquiry I found the child was nothing but a young pigeon—"pigeon-child," as they explained it. The ducks laid a number of eggs, which were brought for us to see. "You must make little ducks," said the Master. "Sar, I shall do," said the butler. I laughed at the order; but a hen was caught, put into a basket with the eggs, and the lid shut down upon her; and in a little time I was told there were "four babies" in the poultry-yard.

I have just received a letter from the Madras Moonshee, who begs to express "the concern I have for your happiness as my matron, your state of health, and the state of my rising matron, your child." I suppose he thinks *matron* is the feminine of *patron*.

November 3rd.—One evening, while the Hamiltons and several other visitors were still with us, I had gone to my room to rest a little before tea, when I suddenly heard a queer familiar twang in the drawing-room, which, though I could not distinguish a word, I was sure could only come through a French nose. Presently Maty brought a note from the Collector to beg us to help his friend M. d'Arzel[198] on his journey; so I went into the drawing-room to receive him. There I found all my party of Englishmen working for their lives at French politesses, such as, "Permetty, Mushoo"—"Mushoo, je suis très aisy,"[199] &c. Monsieur himself was a true Frenchman, not at all *distingué* (an agent to one of the great French mercantile houses), but most completely at his ease, and ready for his company whatever it might be—keeping up conversation, and finding answers to English speeches in French, that I am sure it was impossible for him to understand. He addressed some remark to Mrs. Hamilton, which only meeting with a stare from her, Mr. Hamilton answered for her, "*Elle ne parle pas, Moseer!*"[200]—"A—h!" said the Frenchman, in a tone of most commiserating surprise. I believe he thought she was dumb.

He had contrived to travel from Madras, four hundred miles, without knowing one word of any of the native languages, or of English, making himself understood merely by signs. We gave him his supper, ordered his bearers, and sent him on. After he was gone, the Englishmen began talking over all the French adventures of their past lives, and I discovered that they were, as school-girls say, "very fond of French," not to say proud of it, and many Frenchmen had told them all—the innocent birds!—that they spoke it quite like natives. When Mr. Hamilton and some friend of his were travelling in France together, they took it in turn to give the orders at the inns, because "one man could not speak French every day:" but the friend often grew restive; he used to call to the waiter, "Gassor!"[201] "Monsieur." "Now, Hamilton, I wish you would tell him." "No, indeed; it is not my turn; I spoke French yesterday." "Well then, I won't. It is impossible to talk their nonsense: Gassor, ally vous or."[202]

One of our visitors at this time was a young ensign of seventeen, travelling in command of a company of Sepoys in charge of treasure, and it was quite a pleasure to see a creature so innocently important and happy. He travelled on horseback, and had a pony which he talked of just like a human being, and admired as much as any hero. He was attacked by some wild native horses at the entrance of the village—so, he said, "I took off my saddle and bridle, and set my pony at them; and if the people had not come and separated them, I know he would soon have licked them all. He is a capital fellow!" I saw his pony afterwards, the ugliest Pariah beast I ever set eyes on! You must know people here talk of high-caste and Pariah horses, Pariah dogs, &c. The native horses are Pariahs, the high-caste are Arabs. I have a high-caste horse, who is so excessively puffed up with pride that he will not bear the sight of a pony: I am obliged to make the horse-keeper run before me to clear the way of all ponies, or else this creature fights them, with me on his back.

November 23rd.—Our school is now opened with about twenty-five boys, and more coming. All caste boys. A— thinks it better to teach them whenever one can, as it is far more difficult to get at them than at the Pariahs, and also the education of the upper ranks has much more influence than that of the Pariahs. We have a Bramin to teach Gentoo, and David Gonsalves,[203] the half-caste, to teach English. I went to see them the other morning. (Tell your charity-school girls at home that they come at six o'clock, and are always in time!) The Bramins and merchant boys sat together; there was another row of the Moochy or workman caste;[204] another of Mussulman boys; and, behind all, a row of grown-up men, who come to amuse themselves by watching and picking up a little by listening: but they talk, and are very troublesome, so they are in future only to be admitted on examination days. We have but few books, as they are very expensive, and the whole cost of the school must devolve upon the Hamiltons and ourselves; therefore we mean to spend our money in good books, which will be useful for them to read, and not in mere spelling-books. I make great pasteboard columns, with alphabets, spelling and first lessons, in large printing hand. One column does for the whole school to learn from at once, and we mean to keep to these till the boys can read a little, so as really to make use of a book. I have printed a number of texts to hang round the school-room, and the first text I chose for my poor little heathens was Psalm cxv. 4–8.[205] I dare say by sending to Madras, by and by, we may be able to get printed sheets of lessons; but the wind has set in now the wrong way for ships coming from Madras, and parcels sent by land are a long while on the road, and, as our scholars are ready, we do not like to wait. You must understand that we have no immediate hope of making *Christians* of these boys by our teaching, but we wish to "do what we can:" this kind of school is all we can do for them, and I fully believe that, if schools were set up all over the country, it would go far towards shaking their Heathenism, by putting truth into their heads, at any rate, instead of falsehood.

LETTER THE FOURTEENTH.

December 15th.

WE are just returned from our long-promised visit to Penny-Whistle, after a very amusing excursion, though, if I had known what an undertaking the journey would be, I should never have attempted it, or rather A— never would have consented to it, however urgent my curiosity might have made me. However, we are safe at home again, and the journey has done us nothing but good. When the time came for us to start, according to appointment, A— said he thought it would be scarcely worth the trouble, and that we should be "more quiet and comfortable at home"—such a thorough John Bull![206]—but I made him go, as I wished to "see a little of life." The people had told us that the distance was fifteen miles; so we expected that, starting at half-past five in the afternoon, we should arrive about ten o'clock, in time for a good night's rest. But it turned out to be thirty miles, and no road; we had to grope our way over cotton-fields, a pouring rain during almost all the night coming down in such torrents that I could not hear the bearers' song, pitch-dark, and the ground almost all the way knee-deep in water. We were twelve hours splashing and wading through the mud, and "plenty tired" when we arrived. But a palanquin is much less fatiguing than a carriage, and an hour's sleep and a good breakfast soon set us to rights.

When we arrived at Dratcharrum,[207] the Rajah's town, we were taken to a choultry,[208,]* which he had prepared and ornamented with bits of old carpet for our first reception. I could not imagine why we did not go to his house at once, according to his invitation; but I found afterwards that he had arranged our going first to the choultry, in order that he might send for us in state to his mud palace. All his principal people came to pay their compliments, and he sent us a very good breakfast; and when we had eaten it, his Gomashta (a sort of secretary, at least more like that than anything else) came to say that all things were ready for our removal. I expected something of a row at starting, but I was quite unprepared for the uproar he had provided for us. As soon as our palanquins were taken into the street, a gang of musicians started up to play before us with all their might; a sort

---

* Building for the reception of native travellers. It is generally open to the air, and much less convenient than a 'Traveller's Bungalow.'

of performance much like an imitation of one of Rossini's most noisy overtures[209] played by bagpipes, hurdy-gurdies, penny trumpets and kettle-drums, all out of tune. Then came banners, swords, flags, and silver sticks; then heralds to proclaim our titles, but we could not make out what they were; and then dancing-girls. A— looked rather coy at being, as he said, "made such a fool of;" but when the dancing-girls began their antics, ankle-deep in the mud, the whole turn-out was so excessively absurd, that mortal gravity could stand it no longer, and he was obliged to resign himself to his fate, and laugh and be happy like me.

When we arrived at the palace, on entering the gateway, the first thing I saw was a very fine elephant making his salam; side by side with him a little wooden rocking-horse; the court filled with crowds of ragged retainers, and about fifty or more dancing-girls, all bobbing and bowing, salaming and anticking "nineteen to the dozen." At last we came to the Rajah's own hall, where we found him, the pink of Hindoo politeness, bestowing more flowers of speech upon us in a quarter of an hour than one could gather in all England in a twelvemonth. He ushered us to the rooms prepared for us, and stayed with us for some time to have a talk, surrounded by all his retinue. His palace consisted of a number of courts, walled in, unpaved, and literally ankle-deep in mud. We could not cross them, but all round there was a raised narrow pathway of hard earth, which we crept round, holding on by the wall for fear of slipping into the mud beneath. Our apartments consisted of one of these courts and the rooms belonging to it. At one end was a room, or rather gallery, which they call a hall, open to the court on one side, without any doors or windows; a small room at each end of the large one, and a sort of outer yard for the servants. The three other sides of the square communicated with other courts of the same kind, one opening into the Rajah's own hall. In the middle of our gallery there was a wooden alcove overhanging the street, in which Penny-Whistle sits and smokes when he is alone. The furniture was a table, a carpet, four chairs, two cane sofas, and a footstool. The room was hung with pictures of Swamies by native artists, two French looking-glasses in fine frames, fastened to the wall in their packing-cases, the lids being removed for the occasion, and two little shaving-glasses with the quicksilver rubbed off the back. Penny-Whistle was very fond of his pictures, and sent for some other great coloured prints of hares and foxes to show us. They had been given him by an Englishman long ago, and the colour was rubbed off in many places, so I offered to mend them for him, which greatly pleased him. While I was filling up the holes in his foxes' coats with a little Vandyke brown,[210] he stood by crossing his hands and exclaiming, "Ah! all same as new! wonderful skill!" and A— took the opportunity to put in his usual lecture concerning the advisableness of girls' education. Penny-Whistle said he thought it was a very fine thing to teach girls, but that his people were "too much stupid," and did not like it, and he would not go contrary to their prejudices, &c. When we were tired of him we dismissed him, as the natives think it a great impoliteness to go away till they are desired; so, when we had talked as long as we could, A— said that I was going to sleep, for that he (Penny-Whistle) "must be aware that sleep was a very good thing." That is the proper formula. When the peons come to report their going away to eat their rice, they always inform me that I "must be aware that eating is a very good thing, and necessary to a man's life."

After we were rested and brisk again, Penny sent us our dinner. We had brought with us, at his desire, plates, knives and forks, bread and beer, and he sent us, besides, all his own messes, native-fashion, brass trays lined with leaves, and a different little conundrum on each leaf; pillaws, quantities of pickles, ten or a dozen varieties of chutnies, different vegetables, and cakes made of grease, pepper, and sugar. The Bramins of Penny-Whistle's class always have their food served on the leaves of the banyan-tree.[211]

After dinner he took us out to see the town: we in our palanquins, and he in his tonjon,* and all his ragged robins piping and drumming before us. The whole town of course turned out to see the show: one of A—'s palanquin doors was shut, so Penny stopped his procession and came to beg that A— would do him the favour to keep it all open, and "show himself to the multitude." The town was all built of mud: the bettermost houses whitewashed, but the others not even that, and the streets ankle-deep in the mud washed off from the houses; but in the midst of all this dirt and discomfort, some little bit of tinsel would peep out at every opportunity: women covered with ornaments from head to foot, peeping out of the mud-hovels; men with superb Cashmere shawls looking quite beggarly from rags and dirt. This is "Eastern splendour;"—a compound of mud and magnificence, filth and finery. Penny-Whistle is a great Prince in his little way, one of the old hereditary Rajahs of the highest caste. In the course of our expedition he took us to see the pagoda.[212] I had never before been inside one, and was very curious to know what it really was. First, there was a high wall round a large square compound; in the middle of each wall an immensely high gateway. This gateway is the pyramid-like building[213] that one sees outside, and that I always supposed to be the pagoda, but I find it is only the portico. On entering the principal gateway, it was such a large place, that I thought we were inside the pagoda itself, but we went through to the compound, and inside that there was another very high wall round a square court, with one porch opposite the principal entrance: on going into this we found ourselves in the pagoda. It was a wonderful, dreamy, light-headed sort of a place, a low roof, and an interminable perspective of rows of massive, grotesque pillars, vanishing in darkness—I could not see the end of them—with many dark recesses in the walls, and here and there a strange, white-turbaned figure, just glancing out for a moment, and disappearing again in the darkness: altogether I never was in a place that gave me so much the feeling of a light-headed dream. In the middle of the court, round which these galleries of pillars ran, was the Swamy-house, or place in which the idol is enshrined. They brought us opposite to it, and by stooping a little I could have seen all the inside, but I thought that perhaps some of the lookers-on might fancy I was bowing down to the god, so I would not run the risk.

---

* A kind of open sedan-chair.

When we came back to Penny's house, we found it all lighted up with stinking torches, and the constant native amusement of nautch[214],* and fireworks, and crowds of spectators. We stayed with him as long as we could endure the heat, din, and glare, and then went to our own rooms. There we found everything such a complete contrast to the native taste, that we could scarcely fancy ourselves only a hundred yards from all the Rajah's row. Our matee had lighted the candles, and placed our tea things, books, and drawing materials on the table, all looking as quiet and comfortable as at home. I never saw anything so curiously different from the scene of the minute before: every feeling and idea was changed in an instant. But the next day we were to see, as the Hindoos say, "all things native" again; so I asked Puntooloo (that is his real name) to let me have a ride on his elephant. He had it brought out directly, but it was such an awful affair, such an awkward ladder to mount by, so many people in the way, such a bad howdah,[215] a present from some English gentleman of his own carpentering, and altogether so very inconvenient, that I was frightened and would not go; so I went out in my palanquin, and the elephant walked before me, to see Penny's garden, as he called it, a muddy swamp full of betel-nut[216] and cocoa-nut trees.

When we returned to the house, he introduced me to his wife: I had been longing to see her, but did not dare ask it for fear of distressing his feelings; however, he proposed it himself. They brought her when A— was out of the room. She was an immense creature, but young, with rather a good sphinx-like face,—altogether much like a handsome young feather bed,—dressed in green muslin embroidered with gold, and covered with jewels from top to toe, besides a belt of gold coins round her waist. All her attendant women came with her and stood at the door. The Rajah's Gomashta stood by, to order her about and teach her manners, and one of my peons acted as interpreter. When she first came in, she twirled, or rather rolled, round and round, and did not know what to do, so the Gomashta bid her make salaam, and sit down on a chair; and then I did the same.[w] We did not know much of each other's languages—she nothing of mine, and I only enough of Gentoo to be aware that the peon mistranslated every speech we made, and invented the conversation according to his own taste, making it consist entirely of most furious compliments on either side. She was very curious about my clothes, especially my bonnet, which she poised upon her forefinger, and spun round like a top. I showed her some pictures; she held them upside down, and admired them very much. She seemed well amused and comfortable till A— came accidentally into the room, when she jumped up, wheeled round so as to turn her broad back to him, and waddled off as fast as her fat sides would let her. Of course, he went away directly, not wishing to hurt her modesty; and as soon as he was gone she came mincing back again, reseated herself with all sorts of affected airs and graces, and sent him a condescending message to "beg he would not distress himself, for that he was her father and mother." She did not mind the peons and servants standing by.

---

* Dancing-girls.

While she remained with me, A— went and sat with Penny-Whistle, and took the opportunity of being alone with him to try to do him a little good. He was very ready to listen, unusually so for a Bramin, and did not refuse to take some books; so next day we sent him plenty, and I have written to Madras for a Gentoo Bible for him, well bound, that he may like it. I wish, when you have an opportunity, you would send me some of those twopenny "moral pocket-handkerchiefs"[217,x] with alphabets and pictures on them; also some children's penny pictures, especially anything of the Queen. They would be most acceptable presents to the natives. I took Penny some drawings I had made for him of subjects likely to suit his taste, particularly an eruption of Mount Vesuvius,[218] on account of the red flames. I put the drawings in a blue satin portfolio, embroidered with scarlet and gold, and poor Penny was enchanted with the whole concern.

We came home on a dry night, quite safely, and found all well; but another unexpected stranger visitor had arrived the night we were away, and was established in our house ready to receive us: however, he was an agreeable person, and we liked his company.

In your last letter you ask if we have been alarmed by an insurrection[219] of which the newspapers have spoken. I never heard of any one being frightened at it, and it is all quiet now. It was six hundred miles from Madras, and I never even heard any particulars of it till this gentleman passed through. He had been engaged in helping to quell it. He told me that a new tribe, hitherto unknown, had been discovered among the rebels: a fine, manly, but fierce race, showing many traces of Jewish origin, both in countenance and habits. They worshipped an invisible God, but had also one wretched image perched on a tree, which they seemed to look upon as a sort of devil to be propitiated. Unlike the other natives of India, they all lived in houses, boarded, floored, and ceiled with cedarwood.

LETTER THE FIFTEENTH.

December 21st.

I HAVE just despatched a letter to you, and I owe eight to other people, therefore I begin another to you; that, I perceive, is your method with regard to me, which I highly approve.

* * * * * *

To-day arrived the little parcel which you sent from England by the Hindoo servants. Poor things! the ship in which they sailed was wrecked off the Cape: no lives were lost, but the whole of the cargo was destroyed—all the little property of these two poor boys, the presents they had received in England, &c.; but in the midst of all their distress and alarm, they contrived to save my little package, and, to my very great surprise, brought it to me quite uninjured. Was it not a pretty instance of care and faithfulness?

Many thanks for the insect-box and pins, which are great treasures. I had been trying in vain to procure some, and had even sent to Calcutta, but they were unknown there. I wish we could have seen the friend you introduced to us, but he is at Madras, and we are four hundred miles off. It is very seldom that people introduced to each other from England really meet in this wide India. However, those young cadets are generally sent up the country soon after their arrival, and I hope Mr. M——[220] may come our way.

* * *

Our school is very pretty and satisfactory, the numbers daily increasing, and no objection made to the use of our books, which is in itself a great thing. Our boys learn such parts of the Bible as have been translated, and sensible lesson-books, instead of the rubbish they are taught in their own schools. The Hamiltons and ourselves take it in turn to examine the school every Saturday evening, when all the natives who choose to come are admitted to hear what goes on. Besides this, we pay private visits in the week; and as long as the "Doories" keep up this constant superintendence, I hope all will go on well. We have not many rules—the boys receive tickets for regular attendance, and forfeit them for non-attendance, and their rewards depend upon those tickets. When we examine them, I hear the English, and A— the Gentoo scholars. Their English learning at present only extends to B, A, Ba; but they read the Bible in Gentoo, and A— tries to make them understand it a little. We have a Gentoo master, a Bramin, at about 6*l*. per annum; an English master, at 30*l*.: house-rent, peon, and sweepers, about 6*l*. more; and the only other expenses will be books and rewards. The little half-caste English master is clever and willing, and does his work well. The Bramin is a solemn, stately creature, clever at teaching, but a mean old thing. He made all the boys give him a pice[221] (half a farthing) apiece whenever he obtained them a holiday, and he was always inventing excuses and pretences for holidays, till we found out the trick.

A— and Mr. Hamilton, who is a most kind and active coadjutor, are also establishing a Pariah school. This will be only for Gentoo. At first we had a great deal of consultation as to whether it would be best to make our scholars pay anything for admission; but, on talking it over with the natives themselves, we found it would not answer our purposes, as there were very few, even among the richest, who would be willing to pay, and we must have made the same rule for all, and our object was to teach as many as we could.

There is one little boy who comes dressed in the finest muslin, with a gold cap, and silver bangles, and emerald earrings, looking quite a little prince; but they all prefer a charity-school. They learn very quickly, and are in nice order; Mr. Hamilton says it is already superior to the N—school,[222] though that has been established nearly a year; but into that school they admit Pariahs, which always ruins a caste school. Even in England you could not expect a gentleman to send his son to the same school with the children of his footman, and here caste is a religious distinction, as well as a difference of rank. After any natives become Christians, it is doubtless highly desirable for the missionaries to do their utmost to induce them to give up caste, as far as it is a religious distinction; but while they are Heathens, it seems merely waste of time and trouble to attempt it, and only prevents any but Pariahs from coming under their influence. In Bengal[223] I hear that it is easier, as the natives there have associated more with Europeans, and their prejudices are less strong. This is strange, as their Heathenism is still worse: the suttees,[224] Juggernaut's sacrifices,[225] &c., were all peculiar to Bengal.

The castes are not now so unmixed as when first invented. Indeed I believe that some of the original divisions no longer exist; but they make up for it by subdividing the Sudra or merchant caste, and the common people call every different trade a caste. Ayah continually tells me "that man moochy (carpenter) caste;" or "bearer caste," &c. The shoemakers, I believe, are the lowest of any. The Pariahs are of no caste at all. Learned men think that the Sudras were the original inhabitants of the country, and the three higher castes the conquerors. Nobody seems to know much about the Pariahs; I suppose they were the refuse of all. The trades are as hereditary as the castes; every man follows his father's business, and seems to have no idea of raising himself in life, beyond making a little more money.[y]

I wish I could, as you ask, tell you any pretty stories for your schools; but I am sorry to say they are not at all plentiful: there are very few natives who are even nominal Christians, and still fewer whom we can reasonably believe to be anything but what is here called "curry-and-rice Christians."[226] In England, I think people have a very false impression of what is done in India. That is not the fault of the Missionaries, who write the real truth home; but the Committees seem to publish all the good and none of the bad, for fear of discouraging people. In fact, it is unreasonable to expect more to be done without more efficient means. Suppose thirty clergymen to the whole of England,—what could they do? and that is about the proportion of the Missionaries in Madras, and they have to work amongst Heathens. Perhaps about half of them know the language well, and the rest speak it like school-French. The chaplains are not Missionaries: their duties lie almost as completely amongst Europeans as if they had remained at home. Mr. C.,[227] for instance, is a very excellent, useful clergyman, with a large English and half-caste congregation, but no more a Missionary to the Heathen than your vicar.[228] There are thousands needed where one or two come; and schoolmasters are wanted as much as preachers.

There is great difference of opinion as to the class of men most wanted, and most likely to be useful as Missionaries. Some people have an idea that it is scarcely necessary to have persons of the birth and education of our English clergymen, but that a larger number of rather inferior men might be employed at a smaller salary, and be quite as efficient. Of course any Christian really working among the Heathen is likely to do some good; but I believe that the more educated and the more of a gentleman he is, the more influence he will have among the Hindoos. They are themselves most excellent judges of manners and standing in society, and invariably know a gentleman, and respect him accordingly. Their own priests are of the highest caste, and it lowers our religion in their eyes if they see that our *Padres*, as they call the Missionaries, are of what they consider low caste. Perhaps you will think this idea worldly, and too much like the proceedings of the Jesuits[229] when they pretended to be a new class of Bramins; but our home clergy are gentlemen and educated men, and I cannot see why we should send out Missionaries less qualified for a much more difficult work. An English University education, and the habit of *really* hard study, prove immense advantages in mastering these native languages.[z]

I am, as usual, expecting several visitors to-morrow, to stay till the end of next week. "Missis don't want, but no can help!" After all, perhaps, it is as well that we are obliged to have people come in this way, or we should grow quite *farouche*,[230] for we are both always so busy, and so fond of our own habits and occupations, that I am sure we should never invite interruptions. You ask what our visitors say, "if ever they say anything?" That, you know, depends upon taste; there is anything, and anything—"fagots et fagots."[231] However, some of them are very sensible and agreeable; and when I have them alone, they talk very well, and I like their company; but as soon as three or four of them get together they speak about nothing but "employment" and "promotion." Whatever subject may be started, they contrive to twist it, drag it, clip it, and pinch it, till they bring it round to that; and if left to themselves, they sit and conjugate the verb "to collect:" "I am a collector—He was a collector—We shall be collectors—You ought to be a collector—They might, could, should, or would have been collectors;" so, when it comes to that, while they *conjugate* "to collect," I *decline* listening.

January 18*th*.—A— and I have been out in the district, travelling about to see the world a little. He had a few days' holiday in his Court, and we took advantage of it to go and visit some of the places on the coast, in order to see which would be the best refuge in the hot season. Also A— wished to inspect the proceedings of some of the District Moonsiffs, or native judges, under his orders. We left the baby at home, as she was quite safe with the old ayah, who really deserves the character she gives herself, "I too much careful woman;" and baby would have been tired, and perhaps have caught cold, with a hurried journey at this time of the year. The nights are now really cold, and the days pleasant. First we went to Narsapoor,[232] a large native village about six miles from the sea. We did not expect to find that a good place for ourselves; but we had heard that two Missionaries were established there, and we wanted to see them, and learn how they went on, and whether there was anything we could do to make them more comfortable. They were English shoemakers, Mr. Bowden and Mr. Beer,[233] dissenters of Mr. Grove's[234] class, but good, zealous creatures, and in the way to be very useful. They have two pretty, young English wives, as simple as themselves. They are living completely among the natives, teaching and talking to them, and distributing books. One of them is a man of great natural talent, strong-headed, and clear and sensible in his arguments; if he had been educated, he would probably have turned out a very superior person. They complained much of the difficulties of the language; but A— says that the two men spoke it really much better than the general run of missionaries. One of the wives said to me very innocently, "It is pertickly difficult to us, ma'am, on account of our never having learnt any language at all. I don't know what to make of the grammar." I advised her not to trouble herself with the grammar, but only to try and learn to speak the language so as to converse with the natives—to learn it, in short, as a child learns to talk. At her age, and without any education, it was next to impossible for her to learn the grammar of an Oriental language; but I do not suppose she will follow my advice, as she had a great notion of studying, reading with Moonshees, and so on. They live almost like the natives, without either bread or meat, which in the long run is a great privation to Europeans; but they have rice, fish, fowls, and vegetables, and they say, "The Lord has brought down our appetites to what he gives us to feed them on." Though *they* could get no meat, we had our choice of all the sheep in the village, as I suppose the natives would kill themselves for the Judge if he would but eat them. We did not want mutton for ourselves, but we had a sheep killed in order to send it to the Missionaries, together with some bread, and a little supply of wine, to have by them in case of illness. They had not much of a school, only five or six boys; I do not think that schooling will ever be their vocation. They seem most likely to do good by conversing and associating familiarly with the natives. They said that the people in general were not only willing, but anxious, to talk with them and take their books, and to come and ask them questions; but one day Mr. Bowden went out with his tracts, and took his stand as usual in the bazaar, when a number of people, headed by some Bramins, came round him "a jeering and a hooting." The Bramins had nothing to say for themselves, but stood interrupting, mocking, and sneering, till they were tired, and then they said, "Now we have done laughing at you, you may go away—Go!" "No," said Bowden; "now you have done laughing at me, I shall stay here, and give away all my books;" and so he did, and the Bramins walked off, and left him the coast clear. One man said that it was of no use preaching to *him*, for that he was quite perfect and free from sin—he was sure he had no sin at all. Bowden gave him a sheet of paper, and told him to write down in black ink all the good things he did, and in red ink all the bad things he did, and to bring the paper to him at the end of a week. At the end of the week the man came, and said he still considered himself free from sin, but did not wish to show the paper! However, he seemed a little disconcerted, and will probably return before long with more inquiries.

After we left Narsapoor, we went round to several different villages on the coast, and have decided on establishing ourselves during the hot weather at Samuldavee. There is only one small bungalow, and no village near it;[aa] but it is close to the sea, and I hope will be cool. We returned home in one night's run of fifteen hours, which was "plenty long;" but a palanquin is much less fatiguing than a carriage. I find it the best way, instead of undressing and settling for the night at first starting, to begin the journey, all as usual, and to send on a Peon about twelve miles before us, to get ready fire and milk; and when we come up with him we have our palanquins put under trees, and remain there about half an hour, undress and take some coffee, and so settle for the night much more comfortably. Palanquin travelling pleases me very much: I can sleep a good part of the night, and, being able to sit up or lie down at pleasure, with plenty of room, I find it far less fatiguing than being cramped up all day in a carriage.

In passing through the villages, the head men, Moonsiffs,* Cutwalls,† &c., always turn out to come and make salaam while we are changing bearers, and we sit up and do our congées[235] in our dressing-gowns and nightcaps, quite agreeable. However, as we had seen them all in coming, and as it was a very long run, we did not want to be disturbed again in the middle of the night; so we sent a Peon on before to announce that the Judge certainly was to pass through, but that he would be fast asleep and could speak to nobody, and that he must be transferred from the shoulders of one set of bearers to the other without touching the ground, all of which was performed according to order. About three in the morning we were awakened by the silence and stillness: the bearers' song had stopped, and our palanquins were quietly set down on the ground, and no one near us. A— got out to see what was the matter, and he found that we were in a cocoa-nut tope,[236] the bearers all employed in stealing toddy,‡ and our palanquins completely laden with paddy,§ which they had stolen from the fields in coming along! It would have been a pretty story, if we had not found it out in time, the Judge returning to his

---

* Native judges.
† Head men of a village.
‡ Juice of the cocoa-nut leaves. It is collected in earthen vessels, and left to ferment, when it becomes very intoxicating.
§ Rice in the ear.

Zillah, with his palanquins laden with stolen paddy, and his bearers tipsy with stolen toddy!

We found all well at home, and a large packet of European letters waiting to greet us, which would in itself be enough to make all well.

LETTER THE SIXTEENTH.

WE have had a good deal of trouble with the school lately, which is very vexatious, because it really was going on beautifully; forty-five boys in constant attendance, reading and translating the Bible, using our books in school without the slightest objection, and asking for tracts to take home. But a little while ago there came a Mr. G.,[237] a Dissenting Missionary, to visit the Hamiltons: he was a conceited, show-off sort of person, and curiously ignorant. He dined with us one day, and also the Prices, who were staying with us, Mr. Lloyd,[238] Commander of the detachment, and our Scotch Doctor. The Hamiltons had headaches, and did not come, and I am sure I do not wonder, after their having had to attend to Mr. G.'s clatter for two days. At our house he chose, *à propos* of nothing, to begin a discussion concerning the evil of the Bishops being in the House of Lords,[239] and various other delinquencies and enormities of the Church, including the bigotry of supposing that ordination would make any one a minister, unless he was a godly man. Lloyd said nothing—he never does; the Scotch Doctor sided with Mr. G.; Captain Price thought the Church of England must be right, though he could not say why; A— quoted all the old divines, and I slipped in texts; Mr. G. quoted Mosheim[240] (that is to say, he did not quote him, but he mentioned him) as an authority, not in matters of history, but on points of divinity; and he declared that he did not know of any such text as "Not forsaking the assembling of yourselves together;"[241] and when it was proved by chapter and verse, he said one must consider such a text as that well before one could arrive at the real meaning, for that it never could mean us to meet for public worship with an indifferent minister, and that it would be much better to stay and read one's Bible at home. The Doctor said, "According to quhat ye're a saying then, ye must have got yer Church of England airdination from some o' the Pops." A—: "Very likely." Doctor S.: "Wall, and d'ye think it can be good for anything whan it's passed through all those rogs?" I suppose the end of the discussion might be, that Mr. G. thought us very bigoted, and we thought him very superficial and ignorant. After this, Mr. Hamilton took him to preach at the school, and ordered all the boys to attend. They did not tell A— what they were going to do, or he would not have allowed it; for although he is only too thankful to be able to help the Missionaries to preach on their own responsibility, when, where, and however they can, he thinks it both wrong and inexpedient for people in authority to accompany them, as it sets the natives on their guard directly, and persuades them that the Government are going to make them Christians by force, as the Moormans made them Mohammedans. In the present instance it raised a great disturbance. In addition to the preaching, Mr. G. got hold of a man's Lingum,[242] or badge of caste, and took it away; and though he was forced to return it, the whole town has been in a ferment at the insult, and our school is almost broken up in consequence. The boys brought back in a rage all the bags I had given them to put their tickets in, and said they never would come to school again. We have now only twenty boys, instead of forty-five, and they are all petitioning to use their own Heathen books, instead of ours, and we have no more requests for admittance. A little while ago, when we came in from our morning's ride, we used almost every day to find a pretty boy waiting at the gate, salaaming, and presenting his petition to be sent to school. I hope we shall be able to bring it round again in time, but it is very vexatious.

We are reading Shore's 'Notes on Indian Affairs,'[243]—very clever, true, and amusing. He complains much of the English incivility to the natives; and I quite agree with him: it is a great shame. A— says he exaggerates, but I really do not think so. A—, being an old Indian, is grown used to things that strike us griffins. The civilians behave better than the military, though all are bad enough. The other day an old Bramin of high caste called on us while the Prices were in the house; Captain Price, hearing his voice, sauntered out of the next room with his hands in his waistcoat-pockets, and planted himself directly before the poor old creature, without taking any other notice of all his salaams and compliments than "Well, old fellow, where are you going?" in a loud, rude voice. The Bramin answered with the utmost apparent respect, but I saw *such* an angry scowl pass over his face. A little politeness pleases them very much,[bb] and they have a good right to it. The upper classes are exceedingly well bred, and many of them are the descendants of native princes, and ought not to be treated like dirt.

A new magazine[244] is just advertised as coming out at Madras. It is to be conducted by some of the clergymen, in opposition to another periodical, conducted by some others of the clergymen. The first number is to contain strictures on a review which appeared last month in the other magazine. I grudge the waste of time and thought upon such useless work. The writers come out here, they themselves, and everybody else, believing they will work among the Heathen; and while the Idol services are going on all round them, they sit writing their reviews and anti-reviews to the sound of the Pagoda bell!

The other night I was sitting in my Tonjon sketching a pagoda, when I saw a long procession of Bramins go in, and suddenly the service began. I could hear it all, through the walls. The first part sounded exactly like a Roman Catholic mass. There was music, and the mumbling chant of the old priests who could not sing, and the shrill voices of the choir-boys, and at intervals a little bell tinkling; till it was all interrupted by violent screams from girls' voices—perhaps they were meant for singing, but they sounded very horrible: then came loud beating of drums and ringing of bells, and it was all finished.

February 3rd.—We are just come in from the school, the first time I have been there since Mr. G.'s unlucky visit. Some of the deserters have returned, but about fifteen are still obstinate. They all crowded round me, saying, "Good ivning, Sar!" I tried to teach them to say "Ma'am," and explained that "Sir" belonged to the "Doory;" but a Peon who understands a little English, and is extremely proud of his knowledge, would help, and teach them to say "Mammon:" so they got it perfect, "Good ivning, Mammon!" They are very boasting and confidential, and I am very sympathetic. "Sar! I larn very good; I am second man." "I am very glad to hear it—very good man." "And *I* larn too much good too! I am tree man." "That is right; you are a very good man too." Then they salaam and grin, and are very happy. I show them pictures, which makes me popular. The head boys are learning to write English: and to-day they made a petition to be allowed "Europe ink," as they could not write English words with Gentoo ink.

I have been trying to procure some of the cobra capello's poison for Frank to analyse; and also the native antidotes, the principal of which is a small, smooth, very light black stone[245] which they apply to the bite, and they say that it adheres till it has drawn out all the poison, and then falls off. To-day the snake-charmer brought three fresh caught cobras to give me their poison. He set them up, and made them dance as usual, but did not allow them to strike, as that exhausts the venom. When he had played with them as long as he liked, he shut up two of them in their baskets, and proceeded to catch the third by putting one hand on its tail, and slipping the other very quickly up to the nape of its neck, when he held it so tight as to force it to open its jaws, and then squeezed the poison into a tea-spoon. It is yellow at first, and turns red in about ten days. Each snake yielded only three drops; so think how powerful it must be! The cobra did not struggle or writhe at all while the man held it, but afterwards it seemed quite changed and subdued: it lost its spiteful look, and could not be made to stand up and strike, even when the man did his utmost to provoke it, but tried to slink quietly away, looking as if it knew it had lost its power, and was ashamed of not being able to do any mischief. I have put the poison into a little bottle, and keep it carefully covered up from the light. I shall send it home by the first opportunity. It will dry up, of course; but Dr. Stewart says it will not lose its virtue, or rather its vice, and that Frank must be careful what tricks he plays with it. The natives make pills of it, and take them for fever: I believe it is a strong narcotic. I know the bite of a cobra throws people into a stupor. General W.[246] told me that one of his servants was bitten, and wanted to lie down and go to sleep, but the General made him run before his horse for several miles till he was quite exhausted. No harm came of the bite; but, as the snake was not caught, it was impossible to be certain whether it actually was a cobra. The natives think their own remedies are much assisted by conjuring. Once, when we were travelling, my bearers stopped, and one of them began to cry and howl and writhe about, saying he was stung by a scorpion in the road, and could not go on. We gave him eau de luce[247] to rub the place with, but it did no good. One of the Peons then said he could conjure him: so he sat down before him, and began muttering, and sawing the air with his hand, making antics like animal magnetism; and in a few minutes the wounded man said he was quite well, put his shoulder under the palanquin-pole, and set off with his song again. In your last letter you ask me if the snake-charmers have any herb with them. I do not think they have anything but dexterity and presence of mind. They pretend to be conjurers, and play a number of antics, all quite absurd, but which impose upon the people. Their music seems to irritate the snakes and incite them to strike: but the snake-charmers know their distance exactly, and jump on one side. They take the snakes with perfect safety, as they know exactly where to seize them in the neck. The snakes grow very tame after a time, and the men extract the poison as fast as it collects. They begin their trade as children, so they grow up expert and fearless. The man who brought me the poison told me all his proceedings "for a consideration." He said his father was a snake-charmer before him, and used to take him out when he was quite a child, and teach him the manner of laying hold of the creatures, making him first practise upon harmless snakes; that there was no secret in it beyond dexterity: but that the people were so afraid of such "bad animals," that they "always tell conjure" when anybody was able to touch them.

LETTER THE SEVENTEENTH.

February 9th.

To-day the Narsapoor head of police sent me a present of a toy of his own invention. It was a representation of a justice-room. There sat the English Judge in his jacket, writing at a desk; round him all the native Gomashtas, squatted on the floor, writing at *their* desks; at the end of the room a wretched prisoner in the stocks; and, in front of the Judge, another prisoner being tried, with a great Peon by his side, holding a drawn sword in his hand to take care of him. The Englishmen and Court servants were made enormously fat, and when I asked the reason I was told it was to show how rich they were! It was a very droll performance; but I was obliged, much against my will, to refuse it. A— said it was too good to accept, for fear of that tiresome plague John Company's finding fault. However, I confess it is a good rule. If I had accepted that, some one else would soon have brought something of more value, and in a little while they would arrive at shawls and pearls, and expect injustice in Court in consequence. When A— is out, visitors often come to me privately, begging that I will persuade him to give them offices, or to excuse them fines and punishments, &c. Sometimes they go and make their petition to the baby if she is in another room, but she only sucks her thumb at them. When we are out in our tonjons without the "Master," the wives of the petitioners assail me, and their children the baby, screaming and throwing themselves on the ground before us. Baby likes the uproar extremely, and crows and dances in great glee. Then the petitioner comes to A— next day, and gravely tells him that "Missy" has promised him the post in question. This Court has been for some years past very badly managed;—idle men sent as Judges, nothing inquired into, cases neglected, and so on; and the consequence is, that some of the rich natives have quite got the upper hand of honesty. One very rich Zemindar's widow owed, and still owes, five thousand rupees to a man in this village. Instead of paying her debt, she took refuge with her son, the present Zemindar, and shut herself up in his house. One Judge after another has sent Peons with summonses to the old lady to make her pay the poor man his just due; but she cares for none of them, and the Zemindar's servants always beat the Peons, and send them away. One Judge summoned the Zemindar to account for the assault on the Peons, but he said it was no fault of his—it was the servants' pleasure: then the servants were summoned, but they ran away and hid themselves, and were not to be found all over the district. The same thing has just now happened again; but A— will not take the excuse, and has summoned the Zemindar to account for his servants' misdemeanors, as they are in the habit of taking their pleasure in that way. He has fined him two hundred rupees, and sent word that, unless his mother's debt is paid, he shall send a battalion to seize her jewels. It remains to be proved which will gain the day: I am curious to see how it ends. Another Zemindar, choosing to protect a man who had a notification sent to him, fought the peons who delivered it, and sent it and them back again: so A— then sent the notification to the Zemindar himself, with a polite request, or rather command, that he would himself see it served without delay. The Zemindar was frightened at this, and obeyed directly, as humbly as possible. All the Court histories and adventures amuse me very much.

The business is all taken down in writing, and translated into English. The trials, examination of the witnesses, sentences of the Judge, &c., all go under the general name of "Decrees," and every day a certain number of copies of these Decrees are brought in for the Judge to examine and verify. I often get hold of them to read, and very curious they are; but the lying and false witnessing are quite horrible. Sometimes the whole case is one great lie supported by innumerable forgeries. The other day a man laid claim to the house and land of another: the claim was well established; there were all the proper documents to show that the estate had been in his possession, witnesses in plenty to swear to the same, and a plausible story as to the manner in which the defendant had cheated him out of it; and, in short, everything to prove him a most ill-used man. But the defendant had just as good a story, as carefully arranged papers, and as many respectable witnesses on his side; but here and there different little things were allowed to transpire which weakened his cause, and gave the plaintiff rather the best of the story. A— made me guess how the matter had been decided; and, of course, I supposed that the land had been restored to the poor injured innocence who claimed it. No such thing: A— says, in the midst of such constant cheating, he is obliged often to judge by the manner and countenance of a witness rather than by his evidence, and in this case it struck him that there was a cunning under look that did not belong to a true man; he therefore set on foot a strict inquiry into the affair, and discovered that the whole was a concerted scheme between the two men; that neither the one nor the other had the property in his possession, nor the slightest claim upon it; and that it belonged altogether to another person, who knew nothing whatever about this lawsuit. The object of the two false claimants was to get a Decree passed in favour of one of them, it did not much signify which: the Court Peons must have seen it executed, and the real owner would have been turned out of his property, while the two cheats divided the spoil.

There seem to be very few cases that are not supported by *some* forgery or false evidence in the course of the trial. Even when the truth is on their side, and would be quite sufficient, they prefer trying to establish their cause by falsehood, though it discredits rather than helps them.[cc]

February 16*th*.—For the last few days we have been occupied with company again. A regiment passed through, and we had to dine all the officers, including a lady; now they are gone. I perceive the officers' ladies are curiously different from the civilians. The civil ladies are generally very quiet, rather languid, speaking in almost a whisper, simply dressed, almost always ladylike and *comme il faut*,[248] not pretty, but pleasant and nice-looking, rather dull, and give one very hard work in pumping for conversation. They talk of "the Governor," "the Presidency," the "Overland," and "girls' schools at home," and have daughters of about thirteen in England for education. The military ladies, on the contrary, are almost always quite young, pretty, noisy, affected, showily dressed, with a great many ornaments, and chatter incessantly from the moment they enter the house.[dd] While they are alone with me after dinner, they talk about suckling their babies, the disadvantages of scandal, "the Officers," and "the Regiment;" and when the gentlemen come into the drawing-room, they invariably flirt with them most furiously.

The military and civilians do not generally get on very well together. There is a great deal of very foolish envy and jealousy between them, and they are often downright ill-bred to each other, though in general the civilians behave much the best of the two. One day an officer who was dining here said to me, "Now I know very well, Mrs.—, you despise us all from the bottom of your heart; you think no one worth speaking to in reality but the Civil Service. Whatever people may really be, you just class them all as civil and military—civil and military; and you know no other distinction. Is it not so?" I could not resist saying, "No; I sometimes class them as civil and uncivil." He has made no more rude speeches to me since.

February 17*th*.—Yesterday the old Braminee post-office writer came to pay a visit and chat. He had been to a great Heathen feast at some distance—thirty thousand people present. He told us that the Narsapoor Missionaries and Mr. G. were there, preaching and giving away books, and that they said, "What use your feast? *arl* (all) too much nonsense! What for make noise,—tumtums,—washing?—arl that, what for do? pray to God, that *prarper* (proper)!" We asked if the people understood and listened, and if any of them believed the "padre's" words. He said, "Understand, very well;—listen, plenty;—believe, no, sar!" Then he went on to tell us that they could not believe now, no more could he, but that their children's children would all believe; that we were now in the ninth Avatar,[249] which would last sixty years longer; that then there would be "plenty too much great trouble," and everything "more worser" than it had ever been before; that all religion would be destroyed, and this state of confusion would last for some time, but that, within two hundred years from the present time, the tenth Avatar[250] would take place, and Vishnoo[251] would appear to put all in order; that he would not restore the Hindoo religion, but that caste would be done away with for ever, and all people be alike upon the earth, "just same Europe people tell." Then he went on with their usual story that all religions were alike in their beginning and would be alike in their end, and that all enlightened people believed the same thing, &c., &c.—just the nonsense they always talk; but I thought his tradition very curious.

I have taken a Moonshee to translate for me, and to teach me Gentoo. He is a tolerable translator, but a great booby. He was showing me some different forms of the same letter: I asked on what occasions each was to be employed. He said, "This one, carmon (common) letter, I teach boy;—arther (other) one, sublime letter, I teach hanner (honour) ma'am." Another time I was playing with the baby, and saying, "Talk, baby, talk!" when Moonshee rose from his chair and came to me very slowly and formally, holding his petticoats over his arm. After a solemn salaam, he told me, "I have one subject to inform your honour."—"Well?"—"I shall inform your honour that this baby cannot talk: it is not capable for her to talk until she shall have arrived at two years."—Did you ever know such an owl? They have no notion of anything in the shape of a joke, unless it is against the Collectors and the Board of Revenue. That touches their hearts and tickles their fancies directly.

So many people apply to us for books, that we are going to set up a lending library, to be kept in the school-room, for natives, half-castes, and travelling soldiers who may halt here. We cannot muster many volumes yet, and some of those are contrived by sewing tracts together. Tailor and I have been very busy making elegant covers out of bits of coloured paper. We greatly want some baby lectures on astronomy for our school. I am trying at them, but it is a tough job, because, first of all, I am a dunce myself, and next I have very few astronomical books, and those—such as Mrs. Somerville,[252] Herschel,[253] &c.—not suitable. All the elementary books are translated from English lesson-books, and are altogether out of the comprehension of the natives—not so much *above* them as *different* from them—expressed in terms which they cannot understand, from being completely unlike their own manner of thinking and explaining.

February 22*nd.*—This is now the Indian spring. The garden is in full flower, and the scent of the orange-blossoms and tube roses quite fills the room as I sit with the windows open; but it is beginning to grow very hot: the thermometer is at 90° in the middle of the day, but I do not find it so oppressive as at Madras; the air is much fresher and clearer. Dr. Stewart advises me not to remain here after the middle of the month, so on the 16th we are all to go to Samuldavee. A— will settle baby and me there, and then he must return by himself, I am sorry to say, to his hot Court. We shall probably be obliged to remain on the coast about four months, but he will be able to shut up the Court and come to us for one month, and occasionally at other times from Saturday till Monday.

LETTER THE EIGHTEENTH.

March 8th.

I AM very busy now, translating a story with my little squinny Moonshee. Moonshee chuckles over it, and enters into much conversation about it.

M.—Your honour has in this your handiwork taken much trouble to bring together *arl* things *prarper!*

I.—Because everybody ought to know those things, Moonshee.

M.—Those are from your honour's Shasters.[254,]* My people also have Shasters and Vedas;[255] are not those the true words of God?

I.—They are *not* true; they tell to worship idols. Now you know very well, Moonshee, that those idols are only wood and stone; you do not believe them to be really gods.

M.—I know very well—piece of stone—nothing at arl. What enlightened person thinks them to be God?—No Bramin, no Moonshee will think—but idols are of necessity for arl carmon people.

I.—Now you see we can know those Vedas to be lie, because, if they were words of truth, they would not tell you to make lie to anybody, common people or Bramins.

M.—Ah, ha! But if not the words of God, who did make write the Vedas? No man could write, therefore God write.

I.—Some Bramins, a great many years ago, wrote.

M.—No any Bramins; Vedas are written in the Devinagree[256]—the most holy Sanscrit—the language spoken by the planets. What man could write?

I.—*Now* could not write; but formerly the Devinagree was common language: Bramins could write very well.

M.—Will your honour tell me, is not Devinagree the language of the planets?

Upon this I gave him a touch of astronomy, and told him what astronomers could see with their telescopes, so as to know for certain that the astronomical legends in the Vedas are not true. Then he went off into a metaphysical disquisition on the nature of God, which I would not answer further than that man could

---
* Holy books.

know nothing of God but what he is pleased to reveal. Then he wanted to know why God had not taught all men to speak the same language, so that all might profit by each other's knowledge. I told him the history of the Tower of Babel,[257] which he liked very much, except that he was disappointed at my not knowing how many cubits high they had raised it. He had been educated at a Dissenting Mission school, but left it almost as ignorant as he entered it. He thought that the Bible had been written in English, and that that was an argument against it, English being a modern language. He was charmed at the sight of some Hebrew and Greek, which he had never heard of. He supposed that our Saviour had come to England about a hundred years ago, just when the English first came to India; and, when set right upon that, he argued that, if God had meant the Hindoos to receive the Bible, He would have sent some teachers to India when Jesus Christ came into the world. So then I told him about the first preachers, the Black Jews, the Syrian Christians,[258] &c. He said, "Will your honour not be angry if I ask one question, and will honour ma'am tell me that question?" "If I know I will tell, and I will not be angry." "Certainly no any anger upon me?" "Certainly not." "Then I would ask your honour, suppose any Europe lady or gentleman make much wickedness—never repent—never ask pardon of God—never think of Jesus Christ, but die in committing sin; what will become of them?" "They will go to hell." "What! Europe lady or gentleman?" "Certainly." Then he went on to tell me all about the transmigration of souls, which he said was a great advantage in his religion, for that going to hell was "very offensive." Then he told me a long story. "If your honour will listen to me, I shall make you sensible how it consists. One man had ten sons, and to his sons he gave rules. But those sons arl *ispeak* different languages; therefore he allow them take the rules every one in his own language, which may suit him best; is it not so?"

I.—Now, Moonshee, I will tell *you* how it consists. One man had ten sons, and to all he gave rules—*same* rules, understand. Those sons speak different languages, therefore he allowed them to translate the rules each into his own language, but always *same rules*. One son tell, "My father give too many rules; I don't want:" so that son throw away half his father's rules. Another son tell, "Don't like some of these rules; myself I shall make:" so that son change half his father's rules. Another son tell, "I will keep my father's rules; neither add nor take away." Which son best, Moonshee? He answered with his usual "Ah, ah!" and looked very cunning. I tried to persuade him to read the Bible, but he said it was too much trouble. I do not think these natives have the slightest notion of there being any beauty or advantage in *truth*. They think one way is good for them, and one way good for us. They are very fond of metaphysical subtleties, which at first makes one fancy them very acute, but one soon sees that they have no power of perceiving the real state of an argument. They are always caught and pleased with a cavil, when a reason has no effect upon them; but what they like best of all is any illustration or parable. That seems to be their own manner of reasoning.[ee] I do not suppose they ever have much real conversation with each other—mere chatter and gossip. They seem to have no pleasure in associating with each other on terms of equality. Everybody has a *tail*, consisting of poor followers, flappers, and flatterers. The head feeds the tail, and the tail flatters the head; and plenty of "soft sawder"[259] seems to be in use. When head walks abroad, tail walks after him at a respectful distance. If head stands still to smoke his cheroot,[260] tail, who has no cheroot, stands still and looks admiringly at him. If head condescends to make an observation, tail crosses his hands, bows, assents, and remarks what a wonderfully wise man head is!

The other day we happened to tell the post-office writer that the officers were coming to dine with us, and that we did not want him to go and peer out all the gossip concerning them, which he had offered to do, like an obliging jackal. "Sar," said he, "very great charity, indeed, sar!" "Charity!" exclaimed I, rather astonished. "Ma'am! too much great charity, indeed, ma'am!—but Master very charitable gentleman; always give bread to gentlemen passing through. Last Judge, when anybody pass by, Judge too much sick—gentlemen go 'way, Judge too much well again!"

A Government circular is just come to all the Zillah Judges, to inform them that "the Right Honourable the Governor in Council" has been considering the best means of facilitating the re-apprehension of prisoners who have escaped from confinement; and it has occurred to him that it would answer the purpose to make them always wear a dress of some particular colour or material, by which they might be easily identified.—The innocent bird! He must have kept his eyes in his pocket ever since he landed, not to know by this time that the natives strip off their clothes as soon as they are alone, or at work, or running; and, most certainly, runaway prisoners would not remain in full dress merely for the purpose of being identified.

To-day's Gazette[261] brings word that Government have just issued their orders that "*no salutes to idols be discontinued*, but that all respect be paid to the native religions as heretofore."[262] Is not this disgraceful? A fortnight ago,[ff] at a Mohammedan festival at Trichinopoly,[263] the European troops—Artillery-men—were kept exposed to the sun for nine hours, firing salutes, and "showing respect" to Mohammed.

The Government lately presented a shawl to a Hindoo idol, and the Government officer, Mr. D.,[264] with whom we are acquainted, was ordered to superintend the delivery of it. He does not pretend to be a religious man—a mere commonplace, hunting, card-playing dandy; but even *he* was disgusted at having such an office to perform; so he went with the shawl in his tonjon, and told the Bramins they might come and take it, for that he would not touch it with his own fingers, to present it to a Swamy. At the same place the Swamy was making a progress in its car, and the officiating Bramin came and told Mr. D. that it had stopped at a certain point for want of sufficient offerings; so Mr. D. went to see about it, and found that they had stuck a wedge under the wheel, which prevented its going on. He had the wedge knocked out, and gave orders that Swamy must arrive at his destination without delay, before all the poor offerers were ruined, or the cholera broke out, as generally happens at these horrid feasts, from the concourse of people, dirt, &c. In consequence of all this, Mr. D. was much blamed and reprehended at Madras, for having caused the feast to be hurried over more quickly than the Bramins liked. The cars are drawn by men, and very often these men are unwilling to leave their work for the service, and the Bramins cannot catch as many as they want; so the Government order the Collector to take unwilling men by force, and *make* them drag the car.

I believe that, if idolatry were merely tolerated and protected, the idol services would fall almost to nothing, from the indifference of the mass of the people; but our Christian Government not only support and encourage it, but force it down the people's throats. They have made a law that a Heathen Sepoy may not be flogged, but a Christian Sepoy may. If a Sepoy turns Christian, he is subject to a punishment which they are pleased to say would degrade a Heathen or a Mohammedan.

March 20th.—We are going to Samuldavee on Friday, and we had a grand giving away of prizes at the school, by way of taking leave. Every boy with a certain number of tickets had a prize, and they took their choice of the articles, according to their proficiency. First boy took first choice, and so on. The favourite goods were English books, particularly Grammars. Next, the tracts with woodcuts, which you sent me. I had had them bound, so that they looked very respectable, and those wretched woodcuts were wonderfully admired. I gave one tract to the butler's "volunteer," a Gomashta, who writes his accounts for him, in hopes "Master" will admire his talents and give him the next vacant post. The Peons admired the tract so much, that they intercepted it by the way, and they sit in a circle by the hour together, pawing and stroking the frontispiece, and Volunteer explaining the meaning to them.

There have been many more applications for admission to the school again, and one learned old Moonshee has sent two sons, which is a great compliment. The boys, in fact, only wish to learn English in hopes of making money by it, obtaining places in Court, &c.; but they have no love of knowledge for its own sake. A— gave them a 'History of the World'[265] in Gentoo, and desired them to read it, and answer questions from it; but they brought it back, saying they did not want to know anything that was in it, they only wanted to learn "vords." So then they were reproached with the attainments of parrots, minas, and such-like, till they looked very sheepish, and promised they would "get plenty sense."[gg]

We have a young officer staying with us now, who is to keep A— company while I am on the coast. He is a nice, innocent, good-natured boy, and as tame as can be. He has brought a cat and two kittens with him all the way from Bangalore,[266] upwards of four hundred miles, and in the evenings he brings them into the drawing-room to pay me a visit and drink some milk, and he sits quite contentedly with them crawling up his great knees, and sticking their claws into him, just like Frank and our old cat at home. He has had six jews'-harps sent him by a brother in England, and he performs Scotch jigs upon them by way of "a little music;" and in the morning, when I go to lie down before dinner, he sits with Moonshee, keeping him to his work, and explaining matters to him. I hope he will be a pleasant companion for the "Master," while I am obliged to be away.

A— has invited one or two other very young officers, but I do not know yet whether they will come or not. Those "boys" are very remiss about answering invitations; sometimes I do not know whether one of them means to accept an invitation or not, till he makes his appearance at the time appointed, bowing and smiling, with a ring and a gold chain, quite unconscious that he has not been the very pink of politeness.

LETTER THE NINETEENTH.

Samuldavee, March 26th.

HERE we are, safely arrived and established for the summer. The baby and I were beginning to be so ill with the heat at Rajahmundry, that A— brought us away in a hurry, and settled us here with Peons and servants, and is gone back himself this evening. He means to come every Saturday and stay till Monday, unless any particular business should prevent him. This is a most charming place—the thermometer eight degrees lower than at Rajahmundry, and at present a fine sea breeze from eleven in the morning till eleven at night, and a thick cocoa-nut tope between our house and the land-wind, so that I hope we never shall feel it in all its fury. I do not suppose there is a healthier or pleasanter summer place in all this part of India. Its only fault is its extreme loneliness. This is a solitary house on the shore of an estuary; not even a native village or hut near; forty miles from the nearest European station—Masulipatam;[267] and no English people at all within reach, except the two Missionaries at Narsapoor, ten miles off. I have no one ever to speak to, but my own Hindoo servants. I mean to amuse myself with learning Gentoo, and have brought a Moonshee with me. Gentoo is the language of this part of the country, and one of the prettiest of all the dialects, but there is nothing very fine or beautiful in any of them. The idioms are quite disagreeable; they have neither simplicity nor finesse. I believe the old Sanscrit is a very fine language, but it is excessively difficult, and would be of no use to me. The Moonshee I have brought with me is not the little talkative magpie who told me about the language of the planets, but a very slow, sober, solemn gentleman, with a great turn for reading and sententious observations. Whenever I keep him waiting, he reads my books. The other day he got hold of a Church Prayer Book, which he began to read straight through—Dedication, Calendar, and all. He told me that he perceived it was a very scarce and valuable work, but that he would take great care of it, if my honour would grant him permission to read it at his own house, which of course my honour was very willing to do. He admires it greatly, and says, "Ah! good words! very fine words!"—but he says he thinks a man must have "a very purified mind to be capable of using those prayers." He says he much wishes to read our Shasters, so I am going to give him a Gentoo Bible as soon as I can get one from Madras.

April 2nd.—To-day I have had a specimen of the kind of company I am likely to see at Samuldavee. Three wild monkeys came to take a walk round the house and peep in at the windows: they were the first I had seen, and very fine creatures—what the natives call "*first-caste* monkeys,"[268] not little wizen imps like live mummies, such as we see in England, but real handsome wild beasts. They were of a kind of greenish-grey colour, with black faces and long tails, and their coats as sleek as a race-horse's. They were as large as calves, and as slim as greyhounds. They bounded about most beautifully, and at last darted with one spring to the top of a rock ten feet high, and sat there like gentlemen taking the breeze and talking politics.

In the jungle behind our cocoa-nut tope there are clumps of prickly-pear, sixteen or eighteen feet high, and tribes of jackals sitting playing with their young ones on the turf—very pretty graceful creatures, like large foxes. I have found many shells on the beach, but I am afraid they are not good for much. They were, however, all alive, taking their evening walk, when I met them, taking mine. I set some boys to dig in the sand, but they brought me nothing but broken mussels and cockles.

April 23rd.—We are very comfortable here, and the Master pays us his visit once a-week. Moonshee comes every day, and I potter a little at my Gentoo; but I have not learnt much. I do not work very hard, and no Moonshee has any idea of teaching, but I just pick his brains a little by way of amusement. He is a Bramin, and, like all of them, very fond of questioning and discoursing. He has now read my Prayer Book straight through from beginning to end, and with great admiration; but he says the finest words in the book are "Maker of all things visible and invisible;" those, he says, are "very great words indeed." Now he is reading the Bible. He told me that a learned Bramin came to pay him a visit and to look over his new Bible. The Bramin said that all the words against graven images were "good and very true words," and that it was certainly a "senseless custom" for a man to bow down to a stone; but that still it was necessary to keep images for the Sudras (low-caste people), for fear they should not believe in any God at all. That is their constant argument. They never defend their idols, nor own that they worship them, any more than Roman Catholics will allow that *they* worship the saints. Moonshee says there is one particular tribe of Bramins who keep a sabbath, and it is on the same day as our Sunday; so it seems like a Christian tradition, as the Jews' sabbath was on a Saturday. He thinks it is kept in honour of Kistna,[269] but he says it is only a custom, and not commanded in the Shasters.

April 24th.—In one of my letters I told you about a bad Zemindar who would not pay his debts, and A— threatened to send a *battalion* against him. Upon this the Zemindar sent a very polite message with a tray-full of oranges, and a request that his honour the Judge would keep much favour upon him, and look upon him as his own son! But his Honour was extremely indignant, and returned the tray of oranges, with an answer, that he would hold no intercourse with him till the debt was paid. The returning a present which may be accepted is the greatest possible affront, and it hurt the Zemindar's feelings so much, that he immediately sent another message to say that, rather than in any way displease Master's honour, and have his oranges refused, he would pay his debt. Master's honour thought he had gained the day, but the cunning old fellow despatched a party of his ragamuffins to make an attack on the Government treasury in the next district, and seize money enough to pay his debts here. However, the thieves were detected and defeated, so there the matter rests for the present, and we do not yet know which will win.

In my tonjon yesterday I passed a large old tree, inhabited by a family of monkeys—father, mother, and children of all ages. Don, A—'s dog, who was with me, was in a perfect fury to get hold of them, sitting upon his hind legs, and whining with agony. The monkeys were in a rage too, but they were very clever. The old father hunted his wife and children up the tree, on to one of the high branches; and when he had seen them safe where they could only peep out and grin, he came down again himself, and stood at the edge of a dancing bough, chattering, grinning, and evidently trying to provoke Don—taking excellent care, however, to keep out of harm's way himself—and sneering, till poor Don was so wild with fury, that I was obliged to have him tied up and led away.

LETTER THE TWENTIETH.

June 22nd.

I HEAR that the river is come down at Rajahmundry, and I wish that, like Johnny Gilpin,[270] I had "been there to see," for the manner in which these Indian rivers come down is very grand. When I came away it was one bed of sand, except a narrow stream just in the middle.

A— had made the prisoners dig some channels for the convenience of the neighbourhood, but they had all gradually dried up, and the poor people had to go nearly a mile over the bed of the river to draw water from the middle stream, and the heat and glare from the sand were almost intolerable. But one morning last week he was looking out of the window, and he saw one of his little channels suddenly filled, and the water presently spread as if it was being poured into the channel. In the course of six hours the river was quite full from bank to bank, eighteen feet deep and two miles broad, and rushing along like the Rhone.[271] There will now be no more of the very hot weather. Here, at Samuldavee, there has been no really intolerable heat; but at Rajahmundry A— had the thermometer at 100° in our drawing-room, notwithstanding watered tatties[272] and every precaution. With us it has not been above 92°, and that only for a few days; generally 86° and a sea-breeze. I find the wind makes much more difference in one's feelings than the heat itself: 90°, with a sea-breeze, is far less oppressive than a much lower temperature with a land-wind.

Mr. and Mrs. Beer (one of the Narsapoor Missionaries and his wife) spent a day with me last week. He said they had been "very dull of late;" that the people seemed to have satisfied their curiosity, and now never came near them; and that they had not seen a single instance of a wish really to know or inquire into the truth—only mere curiosity. That is the great difficulty with these poor natives; they have not the slightest idea of the value and advantage of truth. No one in England knows the difficulty of making any impression upon them. The best means seems to be education, because false notions of science form one great part of their religion. Every belief of theirs is interwoven with some matter of religion; and if once their scientific absurdities are overthrown, a large portion of their religion goes with them, and there seems more likelihood of shaking their faith in the remainder.

Our school goes on nicely and keeps full. The children learn what we bid them, and read the Bible, and give an account of what they read, just as they might in England—but it makes no impression: they look upon it as a mere English lesson. They know that the Bible is our Shaster, and suppose it to be as good for *us*, as their own Shasters are for *them*. Moonshee reads and studies the Bible, and often brings it to have passages explained. He says he believes all the "good words" against idolatry, but that the worship of any of the superior invisible beings is not idolatry, only the worship of graven images and demons. He was reading the story of Cain,[273] and he supposed that the reprimand to Cain, "If thou doest well, shall it not be accepted,"[274] &c., was on account of his following "such a mean trade" as tilling the ground.

I have just been arranging some questions and answers for the school, and setting Moonshee to translate them. They were, of course, the most thorough *a, b, c* affairs possible; but Moonshee said they were "deep words," and his misunderstood translations were considerably quaint. For instance: "Water is a *fluid*," he translated so as to mean "Water is a *juice*." "Is it a *simple substance?*"—"Is it a *soft concern?*" "The sun is much larger than the earth;"—"Sun is a far greater man than earth:" &c., &c.

July 9th.—We have had some very bad weather for the last week; furious land-wind, very fatiguing and weakening. We were scarcely ever able to leave the house either morning or evening, as the wind lasted all the twenty-four hours. Everything was so dried up, that, when I attempted to walk a few yards towards the beach, the grass crunched under my feet like snow. I have taken a good many beautiful butterflies, and Moonshee often brings me insects. He will not kill them, being a man of too high caste to take away the life even of a flea; of which the fleas, *con rispetto*,[275] take great advantage, and hop about on his shawls and embroidery in a way that is apt to make me very uneasy. I told him, for fear he should hurt his caste or his conscience, that, if he collected insects for me, I should kill them and send them to Europe, and therefore he had better not bring them if he wished them to be preserved alive; but after a good deal of hesitation he came to the conclusion that it would be no sin in him to connive at taking away life, provided he himself did not commit murder.

I have a good many native visitors here. They like coming to me when A— is out of the way, in hopes that, when they can discourse to me alone, they will make me believe they are very clever, and that my private influence may persuade "Master" to think the same, and then perhaps he will turn out some one else to give them places. They sit and boast about themselves till they are enough to make anybody sick; and after having given me a catalogue of all their talents and virtues—which are all lies, or ought to be, for very often their boasts are of their own cleverness in cheating and oppressing their countrymen in order to obtain money for Government, squinnying cunningly at me the whole time, to see if I look as if I believe them—they put up their hands like the old knights on the monuments, and whine out, "Missis Honour, please recommend Master keep plenty favour upon me: I too much *clover* man!"

Moonshee asked me to-day whether the Governor of Madras[276] was really the wisest man in England. He supposed that the Governors were always picked out for being the wisest men that could be found in the country.

June 22*nd.*—The other day some of the villagers came to me to make a complaint that one of our Peons had taken up goods in our name, and never paid for them. Of course, I scolded the Peon. Yesterday he brought me a petition addressed to "Your worshipful Honour," setting forth that it was the poor petitioner's opinion that, "when any gentleman come to this place for cool breeze, it is the *duty* of the villagers to give the gentleman's servants everything they want, and he therefore hopes your charitable honour will look upon him for the future as a most innocent man." See what notions of honesty they have! This "injured innocence" had received the money from us to pay everybody. But with all their badness, and all their laziness, there is some good in them. If their master or mistress is in distress or difficulty, they do not grudge any trouble or fatigue to help them. Last Saturday I was in a great fright: A— did not come, as I expected, and I had not heard from him for two days. There is no regular post to this remote place, so we have messengers of our own to carry letters and parcels, and we send each other a note every day to say that all is well; for in a country like this, where all attacks of illness are so frightfully rapid, we could not be easy without hearing from day to day. But on Saturday evening, as he neither came nor sent, I was quite frightened, and thought he must certainly have the cholera and be too ill to write, and that I must go and see after him immediately. Accordingly I despatched messengers to post bearers for me all along the road, bade Moonshee write me a letter every day about the baby, and in the evening I set out in a great bustle for Rajahmundry, attended for some miles by all the inhabitants of the nearest villages, all shouting. I took the cheating Peon with me, and told him that he was to go half-way, and then stop, and send a chance village Peon on with me the other half, thinking twenty-five miles quite enough for a man to run in one night; but he said he would rather go all the fifty miles himself, for that he did not mind being tired, and should not be happy in trusting the Mistress to the care of a strange Peon. However, after I had gone about nine miles, I met the messengers with A—'s letters, which had only been delayed by the very common occurrence of the postmen being lazy;—they were fast asleep by the river-side when I met them: so, as A— was quite well, and only detained by some unfortunate visitor, I returned home again. The bearers, Peons, and people whom I had scuffled half out of their lives to get ready in time, all laughed very heartily; but I was glad enough that it was only a laughing matter, and laughed myself as they shouted with redoubled vigour all the way home.

LETTER THE TWENTY-FIRST.

Samuldavee, July 10th, 1838.

THERE are large snakes here, seven feet long, and as thick as my arm, not poisonous, but I always have them killed, nevertheless; for they are horrible creatures, and, even if they are not poisonous, no doubt they are something bad: I have no respect for any snakes. But, worse than snakes, scorpions, centipedes, and even land-wind, are the GREEN BUGS.[277] Fancy large flying bugs! they do not bite, but they scent the air for yards around. When there is no wind at night, they fly round and get into one's clothes and hair—horrible! there is nothing I dislike so much in India as those green bugs. The first time I was aware of their disgusting existence, one flew down my shoulders, and I, feeling myself tickled, and not knowing the danger, unwittingly crushed it. I shall never forget the stench as long as I live. The ayah undressed me as quickly as she could, almost without my knowing what she was doing, for I was nearly in a fit. You have no notion of anything so horrible! I call the land-wind, and the green bugs, the "Oriental luxuries."

You ask about the THUGS. They are a class of natives who live entirely by murder; they bring up their children to it, and initiate them by degrees—they feel no shame nor compunction; they strangle their victims and take all their property. They pretend that they look upon their horrid profession as commanded by some particular goddess,[278] as her service; but I do not believe it. I think they mystify people about their religious obligations in order to lessen the horror, and get off when examined.[hh] I believe their offerings and sacrifices are intended as expiations, not as propitiations: the worst of these heathens have sufficient light of natural conscience to understand and allow their duty to *man*.

COCANADA,[279] *August 10th*.—Finding the weather cool again, we started from Samuldavee about a fortnight ago, and made a little tour of five days along the coast in our way hither. It was "plenty hot" though, in some of the places we passed through. We went to one place, Amlapoor,[280] where A— had to settle a dispute between a Moonsiff, or native Judge, and some of his clerks. The clerks wanted to make out that the Moonsiff had taken bribes and committed other enormities. They came to our bungalow to tell their histories, and A— said that he must go to their Cutcherry (or office) to examine all the papers, and that he should bring with him *two ears*, and give one ear to the Moonsiff and the other to the clerks.

This obliging promise was quite satisfactory; but the result was that the clerks' ear heard nothing but falsehoods, and the poor Moonsiff was honourably acquitted, and the clerks pronounced to be rascals. I was glad of it, because I always thought the Moonsiff a very innocent pains-taking creature, and he has been worried quite thin by his clerks, and would have been dismissed from his post if A— had not sifted the stories. He came to see me after his trial was over, looking so pleased and so happy that for a minute I did not know him again, he had appeared so careworn a few hours before. I dare say, next time I see him he will be as fat as a porpoise.

We spent one day at a former Dutch settlement, *Nellapilly* and *Yanam*.[281] It was really quite a pleasure to see a place so neat: the poor Dutchmen had planted avenues, made tidy village greens, chopped the prickly-pears into shape, clipped the hedges, built white walls, and altogether changed the look of the country. They had raised their old-fashioned houses quite high above the ground, as if for fear of the Dutch fens, and made little brick walks and terraces in the gardens, with water-channels on each side to drain them! In short, they had contrived with great ingenuity every possible unappropriateness that could be devised.

We paid a pleasant visit of a few days to our friends the L—s,[282] whom we found comfortably established in their Collectorate, and objecting to nothing but the *black bugs*. These are not so horrible as the green ones, but bad enough, and in immense swarms. One very calm night the house was so full of them, that the dinner-table was literally covered with them. We were obliged to have all the servants fanning us with separate fans besides the punkah,[283] and one man to walk round the table with a dessert spoon[ii] and a napkin to take them off our shoulders. Except Mr. S—,[284] who contrived to be hungry, we gave up all idea of eating our dinner; we could not even stay in the house, but sat all the evening on the steps of the verandah, playing the guitar.

Rajahmundry, August 16th.—Here we are at home again; but on our arrival, instead of resting quietly, we found an uninvited visitor established in the house to be entertained for several days—altogether one of the coolest and least ceremonious persons I ever saw. He was lame; so A— one evening lent him his horse out of good nature, and always afterwards Mr.— took the horse without asking any leave, and A— was obliged to walk all the time he was pleased to stay. One day A— made, in his hearing, an appointment with another person to ride to a particular spot next day: "Oh, no," said our guest, "you can't go to-morrow, for I am going there myself, and I shall want the horse!" When at last, to my great joy, he took himself off, he left, without asking leave, all his luggage in our only spare room, to wait till he should like to come back again—without any invitation!

August 31st.—The present commanding officer here, and his wife, Captain and Mrs. C—,[285] are pleasant people, young and Irish, and well-mannered. *She* is *very* Irish, however—lets her tame goats run in and out of the house as they please, and break all the crockery. I sent her some fruit twice in plates, and both times she sent back the plates broken, with notes to say how shocked and confounded she was, but that "the goats had set their feet in them."

Our school is going on nicely; and while we were at Cocanada A— taught one of the Collector's assistants there how to set up a school, and supplied him with books; and I hope there will soon be a good one at that station also.

When we came home I found that all the time I was away the poor old sergeant was busy raising flowers for me. He sent me most beautiful balsams[286] and roses. Also the Mooftee sent me a present of a talc fan, in return for which I have sent Mrs. Mooftee some heart pincushions, which I hope she will admire.

We hear that the M—s[287] are going home overland in January. Everybody is very sorry to lose Sir P—.[288] Even those who do not care for religious matters have found the advantage of having an upright and just man over them.

Here is a story of the encouragement given to idolatry, which I know to be true; it took place about six weeks ago. A Collector happened to inquire the destination of a sum of money he was required to disburse. He found it was for a grand ceremony, performed by the order and at the expense of Government, in honour of a particular idol. On making further inquiries he found that the natives had requested to be allowed to take a part of the ceremony and the expense upon themselves, but Government said No, they would do it all. Besides this, he learned that some years ago this wicked feast was first established: it was afterwards discontinued for ten years without the slightest murmur or symptom of discontent from the natives; and within the last two or three years it has been revived by the Government, and entirely kept up by them.

The Collector represented all this at head-quarters (I saw a copy of his letter), petitioning that the natives might be allowed to conduct their feast without English interference, and showing how utterly gratuitous it was, from the proof that the ceremonies had gone on for ten years without the English having anything to do with the matter; but he was assured that Government thought it would be dangerous and inexpedient to make any alteration, and that the feast must be carried on in behalf of the English, as usual.

September 21*st*.—Have you heard of the Cooly Trade?[289] "Emigration of Hill Coolies to the Mauritius"[290] it is called, and divers other innocent-sounding names. In case you should ever hear anything said in its favour, this is the real state of the case. It is neither more nor less than an East Indian Slave-Trade—just as wicked as its predecessor, the African Slave-Trade. It is encouraged by Lord G—,[291] who ought to have inquired more before he gave his countenance to such horrors. These Coolies are shipped off by thousands from all parts of India to the colonies, instead of Negroes. Twenty-one thousand are said to have been sent from Pondicherry only; for though Pondicherry is a French settlement, the Coolies were shipped for our colonies. Numbers are kidnapped, and all are entrapped and persuaded under false pretences. They are "as ignorant as dirt," do not even know that they are quitting the Company's dominions, and meanwhile their families are left to starve. There is now danger of a famine, from the large number of cultivators who have been taken away. They are so ill-treated by their new masters that few even live to come back, and those who do bring with them the marks of the same cruelties and floggings that we used to hear of among the slaves. As the importation is legal, of course all the throwings overboard and atrocities of the Middle Passage[292] cannot take place; but there are great horrors from stowing numbers in too small a space on board ship. Many die, and many more have their health ruined. There is a great deal of verbiage in the Government newspapers about the Coolies "carrying their labour to the best market," and so on: but the fact is, these poor creatures are far too ignorant and stupid to have any sense or choice in the matter. Some slave-agent tells them they are to go—and they go: they know nothing about it. A Hindoo does not know how to *make a choice;*—it is an effort of mind quite beyond any but the very highest and most educated among them. Gentlemen's native servants are very superior in sense to those poor wild Coolies; but once or twice I have, quite innocently, puzzled and distressed some of our servants exceedingly, by giving them their choice about some affair that concerned only themselves: they have gone away and pined and cried for two or three hours, or sometimes days, and then come back and begged that "Missis Honour would please make order, for they did not know what to do."

I long to see my kaleidoscopes and all the school rewards you have sent me. A— has an idea that we might manage to set up a little *Europe shop* in the Rajahmundry bazaar, to be managed by a native who would be paid by us. He thinks they would be so pleased by books, pictures, and conundrums of various sorts, that one might thereby introduce useful things "*di nascosto;*"[293] but I fear it is impracticable, because they are so silly and so suspicious, that they would fancy we were trading and making money by it. We have the two first classes of our school now every Saturday evening at our own house, as A— finds he can instruct them better by that means. Our schoolmaster has taught them to read and write, but he is not capable of anything more; so now we send a Moonshee three times a-week to teach them some "sense." They are now busy upon a 'History of the World,' which is very good *learning* for them.

September 26th.—It is now a great native holiday for the *Dussera*,[294] a Hindoo feast. Here is a proof of how much they care about their feasts. There is always a holiday in the Courts for a week during the Dussera, and the Pundit, who is the principal Hindoo in the Court, and a Bramin of very high caste, sent to ask whether he might be excused from taking the holiday, because his work was in arrears, and he did not care for the feast. Of course, it would not be fair to let his underlings lose their holiday because he had been lazy and not done his work; but it shows how little stress they really lay upon these feasts, about which the Government makes so much ado.

The old postmaster Bramin is now come to make salaam, and inform us of an eclipse that will take place next week—a very frightful circumstance; and the people are preparing their drums, &c., "to frighten the giant, for who knows whether he may not eat up the moon entirely?" A— is trying to explain the matter to him, with the help of oranges and limes for the moon and earth. How charmed he will be to see the astronomical magic lantern!

September 29th.—A— thinks there is serious danger of a war.[295] The Russians have sent ten thousand men to help the Affghans against us, and we are at war with the Persians already.[296] Sir H. Fane,[297] the Commander-in-Chief in Bengal, says that thirty thousand men are necessary to conquer these combined Russians, Persians, and Affghans, and only five thousand are granted. All the Indian politicians declare that nothing but our obtaining a really sensible, energetic man as Governor-General can possibly save India to us—such a one as the Marquis of Wellesley[298] again. Since I have been in India, and have seen the traces of his wonderful wisdom, I have learnt to think him one of the first of human geniuses.

October 1st.—We have had two visits lately from Mr. S——,[299] the clergyman of L——. He is to come to Rajahmundry once a quarter. He is a good man, but has given offence[ij] by his punctiliousness about minor matters, such as *public* baptism, &c.

We have also been favoured with the company of a Mr. and Mrs. G——;[300] she is a bride, and as pretty and silly as any one I ever saw. S—— seems to be the principal topic of conversation in this division just now, so Mrs. G——, like everybody else, began to discuss him, and give her *piccolissimo parere*[301] about him. "I think Mr. S—— is very uncharitable—very much so. He thinks it wrong for Missionaries to preach to the natives." "Does he?" said I, somewhat astounded: "why, I understood that he particularly wished the Missionaries to confine their preaching to the natives, instead of employing themselves among the Europeans!" "Ah!" said Mrs. G——, "very likely that's it: I know he thinks something wrong—he's very uncharitable." She discoursed also a good deal on literature and science, chemistry and poetry, in a very innocent way, and I found she was, by way of being "blue." But, you know, ladies who are very *blue* are apt to be rather *green*.

October 5th.—Everybody had a holiday on the day of the eclipse; all the Bramins marched into the river to bathe and sing while it lasted; *such* a clatter they made!—An eclipse is a signal for particular purification. There was an old Bramin here in prison for debt; he would not eat anything for fear of defilement, and was literally starving himself to death. A—— found that he could allow him to live in a separate house guarded by Peons, and therefore removed him out of the jail, and now the poor old creature has taken again to his food. The post-office writer came to have a chat about the matter, as he generally does when there is any such trifle of news. I asked him whether he did not think the Dewan[302] a very foolish man to have run the risk of killing himself rather than eat in a prison.—"Yes," he said, "too much foolish; but that man all same one jungle beast—never been in one Government office, never read the regulations!" They look upon employment in a Government office as the height of human dignity, and strut to and from the Court-house like so many turkey-cocks.

I hope we shall soon have a respite from uninvited company, and be able to ask young Ch——,[303] whom we are both longing to see; but our house is a complete hotel for people we do not care to see, and I know not a greater bore than "Indian hospitality," as it is called by travellers. Some time ago there was an order given to build a public bungalow[304] at this place; but the Government changed their minds, and desired that none should be built at the *stations*, "as the residents can always receive travellers." This is mean enough, but all of a piece with the rest of their proceedings. In order to save money, Lord W. Bentinck reduced the army and sold the stores;[305] and now there is a war beginning, and not soldiers enough to carry it on. They are trying to raise regiments in a hurry, and find that all the able-bodied men, who ought to be soldiers, have been shipped off as slaves to the Mauritius. The Commanders-in-chief at the three Presidencies are all going home,[306] and the Governors can do nothing without them: India is, in fact, governed by the private secretaries, who are not responsible for the mischief they do, and are often intent only on feathering their own nests and promoting their young relations. Half the experienced men in the service who really understand matters are kept in subordinate situations, and young raw slips placed over their heads, to ride races and try fancies, whilst the country is in the most dangerous condition.

October 10*th*.—Moonshee has been telling me a long story about snakes and giants eating up the moon, to account for the eclipse: upon this he received a lecture about the shadow, and so forth; and he now informs me that he shall "*futurely* not believe that giant." When the schoolboys came for their examination last Saturday we found that three or four had learnt very well, and all the others nothing at all, for which Moonshee gave most excellent reasons: but upon a little cunning inquiry we discovered that all those who had learnt gave Moonshee a little extra private pay, and that those who paid him nothing were taught in proportion. The next process was, to reprimand Moonshee, which being done, he informed me that he should "*futurely* teach all the boys without *parturition*," meaning—partiality.

Yesterday I had an old Bramin to play the tamboura[307] and sing to me. I was in hopes, if I heard a solo performance, I might be able to make out some of their tunes undrowned by their horribly discordant accompaniments. He sang one tolerably pretty Hindostanee song, but was too stupid to sing it over again, therefore I could not catch it. The national airs of this country are remarkably ugly—like Spanish boleros,[308] with a profusion of caricature flourishes.

October 21*st*.—To-day I had the delight of receiving your most welcome packet of letters. You may imagine what raptures I am in at hearing that Frank has gained the T—scholarship![309] If I were but strong enough, I think I should dance, just by way of effervescence; as it is, I can only lie on the sofa and grin! I am exceedingly pleased. You are quite right, though, in thinking that you had betrayed his intention of trying for this scholarship. You tried to *un-betray* it afterwards, and make me think there was nothing in your hints,—but in vain; I was too cunning for you! I always knew he was going up for it, and calculated that this very mail would bring me the result.

LETTER THE TWENTY-SECOND.

Rajahmundry, October 31st, 1838.

EVERYTHING goes wrong—the overland post has been due this fortnight—all our letters are detained at Alexandria[310]—everybody in a fume—nobody more so than I. The steamers are sent to make war against the Persians[311] instead of doing their proper work—all the ships going on to China or Calcutta instead of to London—and when I shall be able to send this letter, *chi lo sa?*[312]

The Bishop[313,kk] is arrived at Bangalore, within two hundred miles of Madras, and is taken ill, so that he is detained there; but they say his illness is not dangerous. Every one who has seen him likes him very much. We are all well here, only in a fury for letters. There is a great deal of distress among the natives, owing to the failure of the Monsoon, and a prospect of great scarcity. Poor creatures! they are so screwed by taxes,[314] higher than the land will fairly bear, that they never have a farthing in hand. The natives and some of the European officers want the magistrates to force the sale of grain, and the grain-merchants want to hoard it. Some of the magistrates give way, and sell off all the hoarded grain: the consequence is, that the merchants decamp, there is no seed left for sowing, and what was a scarcity becomes a famine. Other magistrates, A— for one, will not interfere with the sale of the grain, because they have found, by much experience, that that method answers best; and it stands to reason that the merchants will bring the largest supplies wherever they find the freest sale and the best protection. Captain Kelly, the commanding officer here, wants to have the sale forced; A— will not allow it, and talks himself hoarse, all to no purpose, in trying to convince him that it does not answer, and that the merchants have as good a right to have their property in grain protected as in anything else. Kelly always ends with "I cannot see *that: I* think they ought to sell it;" and Mrs. Kelly puts in her little word in confirmation, "I think they certainly ought to be made to." She has a great idea of people being "made to." She is considerably affronted because A— will not fine or imprison the butcher and baker till they give their meat and their bread at the prices she thinks proper. He assures her in vain that he has no power over that class of crimes, and also that in such a small station it is not worth the people's while to serve us at the same prices as in a large town with a certain sale and plenty of competition. She still persists, "Hem! with all that, I am sure it *might* be done." There has been so much discussion about it all, that I quite dread to hear the subject mentioned, for fear of a quarrel, besides the wearisomeness: so now, when they dine here, I have invented having two large dishes of barley-sugar at dessert, which is the time when the arguing always takes place; and the barley-sugar being something new and very nice, it quite answers my purposes, and sweetens matters beautifully. They eat it all up, and are quite good-humoured.

November 6th.—To my greatest joy, the September steamer arrived the day before yesterday, and brought us a packet of letters. I go quite mad when the letters appear, and turn Moonshee out of the house without giving him time to make his salaams. But all the natives seem to understand and sympathise with our love of letters. They have plenty of queer notions about Europe letters, and think they add greatly to our respectability. One day I thought a letter from you had been lost, as it did not appear when I expected it; so I sent for the old post-office writer to ask if he was quite sure there were no more letters, as "Ma'am" wanted another. "Oh!" he said, "too much care arlways I take Ma'am's letters. Five letters this time come Ma'am!—Very high-caste lady indeed!—No any lady in this district so many Europe letters same as Ma'am!—No any lady such high caste!"

I am very glad you know Colonel B—y:[315] he was the cleverest man in India when he was here, and has left no one able to supply his place. You ask how I get the pebbles from our river polished. I keep an old Moorman, with a long white beard, cutting and polishing them all day. He is a most lazy old creature, and will do nothing unless he is teazed. Sometimes he does not bring me a stone for days together; then I send a Peon to ask whether he is *dead:* Peon brings back word, "Not dead, ma'am—that man 'live." Then I send to know how many more days he means to *sleep:* then they come back grinning and looking very cunning, with a pebble in their hands.

Here is a story for you and the national-school girls,[316] if you can make a moral to it. There was a Moorman Hakeem,[317] or doctor, at Calcutta, very anxious to cure one of his patients. The Moormans ought to know very well that idolatry is forbidden by their Koran,[318] but they are often very ignorant and heathenish. This Hakeem thought it would make matters surer with respect to his patient if he secured the aid of some of the Heathen gods as well as that of Mohammed; so he went to the temple of the idol Punchanund,[319] and promised him a large reward if he would help to cure the man, who was very rich, and had engaged to pay the Hakeem a considerable sum on his recovery. The patient died. The Hakeem went again to the temple and told Punchanund that he did not believe he had any power at all, and that, if he was a god, he must get up directly and eat the fruit and smell the flowers which the Hakeem had brought him out of goodnature, notwithstanding his disappointment. Punchanund, of course, sat still: the Hakeem, in a rage, broke off its head, and was found by the police walking about with the idol's head in his hand. On being asked why he had done it, he said, "What was the use of leaving a head on such a stupid fellow as that, who could not help either himself or me?"

November 26th.—The Bishop is well again, and arrived at Madras. The religious people at Madras are going to present an address to Sir P—M— before his departure, to express their respect for his conduct, and regret at losing him, &c., &c.

The country and the Government are in a shocking condition: it seems now to be doubtful whether we shall have a war with Affghanistan or not; plenty of preparations are making, but the Affghans have not decided whether they will attempt to stand against us; I think they would win. The Indian army is in a poor condition, especially the Bengal part of it, which would be sent. The Sepoys say they cannot go into the field without their *hookahs*.[320]

I very much fear I shall never see the letters you sent last. A ship was wrecked the other day off Cape l'Aguillas[321]—all lives saved, but most of the cargo lost: I am afraid two or three of my letters were in it. As is usual in shipwrecks, it was commanded by a young Captain making his first voyage: those young Captains almost always try some clever experiment, and lose their first ship.

November 19*th*, 1838.—Hindered till now by divers fellow-creatures. The other day we had a visit from a very intelligent native, a friend of Rammohun Roy's:[322] he came to ask A— to subscribe to a book he is going to publish. He told us he had three daughters and a son, and that he was determined not to be influenced by the Hindoo prejudices against female education, so he had taught his daughters to read and write their own language, English, and Sanscrit, and that he found they learnt just as well as their brother; but he had met with a great deal of trouble and opposition from his relations on account of his innovation—especially from his wife, who for a long time allowed no peace or quiet in the house. He says the natives much wish to see some of Rammohun Roy's suggestions adopted by the Government, and think them very useful and well adapted to their end. You could tell Mr. G—[323] this: Rammohun Roy's ideas were laid before Parliament, and Mr. G— will know what they were. There is great distress in our neighbourhood now, owing to the failure of the Monsoon. Whole gangs of robbers are going about, armed with sticks, waylaying the grain-merchants and breaking open the stores. A— is raising a subscription to buy grain and give it to those who will *work* for it—every man to have enough for himself, and his wife, and two children; and he intends that the workers shall dig a well, or deepen a tank, or do something of that kind which will be a benefit to the people. We have also sent for a quantity of potatoes,[324] in hopes of introducing their cultivation: the cultivators are willing to try them now, in this time of scarcity, and I hope they may succeed. I am to give the potatoes, and A— is to give a reward to the man who raises the best crop. Potatoes would be very good to cultivate here, because they require so little water. The tanks are all dried up, and people are beginning to grudge the trouble of drawing water from the wells for their bullocks. One man said to me, "Two pots water, whole family drink quite 'nough; and two pots water one bullock arl own hisself drink up: too much trouble that bullock!"

A— is just returned from Samulcottah[325] (the Military station), whither he went on occasion of a public dinner. Major C—[326] is very much given to drawing, and good-naturedly sent me two portfolios filled with his performances to look at: they are very clever and well done; but, like most amateur drawings, they have every merit except *beauty*. I do not know how it is we all contrive to avoid that!

I am just now deep in the *surface* of geology. Mantell[327] speaks of fine fossils in India, so I sent hunting about for some. One man brought word that he had found in the bed of the river a number of the "*bone-stones*" my honour desired: this put me in great glee; but when I came to see the "bone-stones" myself, they were nothing but common white flints, somewhat the colour and shape of bones.

Our school goes on but slowly, though we work a great deal at it. It requires time and patience to clear out their heads of nonsense. The old English school-books you have sent will be most valuable. We find the only way to teach these natives is by question and answer: they cannot take in anything of a prose, so we compose dialogues for them on what we want them to learn. The Narsapoor Missionaries go on zealously and sensibly, and I hope do the *beginning* of a little good. Bowden and his wife are here just now, that she may be under the Doctor's care during her confinement.

January 9th, 1839.—We had lately a long visit from poor Penny-Whistle. He came to tell us all his trouble on the loss of his wife. He said he was going to make a pilgrimage to Tripetty,[328] a very holy pagoda some hundred miles off, and to give many hundred rupees to the Swamy. It was an excellent opportunity for giving him a Christian exhortation, so A— discoursed a good deal to him, and he seemed to understand a little, and said they were "words of great wisdom:" but the difficulty of talking to natives is, that, instead of attending, they are all the time on the look-out for any loophole to insinuate some of their absurd provoking compliments, and one can never ascertain whether they really take in what is said to them. I gave him two of the Gospels bound in red satin with yellow flowers, and he seemed pleased, and promised to read them. Among other questions, he asked *where* our God was, that we could worship Him without making pilgrimages. He complained of being very dull for want of something to do, so A— advised him to set up a school in his town, and look to his estate, and employ people in cultivating the waste lands, which are all utterly neglected for miles around him.

We are now writing dialogues for the natives—to be printed in parallel columns of English, Tamul, and Teloogoo—on different subjects, just to give them a *soupçon*[329] of sense. Mr. Binning has made us a very good one on Grammar; A—is *doing* Ancient History; the Doctor is doing Anatomy; I am to do different ones. The school continues full, but does not advance much: the two first classes come to us every Saturday to read St. Luke's Gospel and repeat Scripture questions—I mean, questions and answers on Scripture History, which we prepare and they learn by heart. This they seem to like and enter into; but we are only as far as Abraham[330] yet. If we really get through the Scripture History we mean to publish it, as we think it might be useful.

Baby is very well and very intelligent. Every now and then she learns to pronounce some new word, which she thinks is very clever; but I intend, as much as possible, to prevent her learning the native languages: though it is rather difficult—most English children do learn them, and all sorts of mischief with them, and grow like little Hindoos. If my child were to stay long in the country, it would be worth while to send for an English nurse; but, as it is, I hope to bring her home before it becomes of any consequence, and meanwhile I keep her as much as possible with me. The native "system" of managing a child is to make it cry for everything. If "Missy," as they call her, asks for anything, Ayah is too lazy to give it, but argues, and tries to persuade her to do without it: then Missy whines—Ayah does not care for that, she whines too: then Missy roars—then, whether right or wrong, good or bad, Ayah gives her whatever she wants. She has nothing to do but to roar long enough and loud enough, and she is sure to get her own way—anything may be done by means of naughtiness.

LETTER THE TWENTY-THIRD.

Rajahmundry, January 19th, 1839.

THE famine is decreasing now,[331] but there has been much distress. A—collected about fifty pounds among the three or four English here, the Court writers, and the Rajahs; and the Government gave him fifty pounds more; with which he has fed daily about two hundred and fifty or three hundred people, giving them grain in payment for their work. The old sergeant gives out the tickets to the labourers, and superintends them, but he is somewhat slow,[ll] and cannot make them mind him. One day we asked him how he managed: he said, "Pretty well, sir, along with the men—they are pretty quiet; but the *women*, ma'am!" (turning to me with a very coy look)—"they are dreadful bad to be sure! I can't get on along with them at all!" Next day A— went himself to see how they got on: there he found the poor sergeant with the tickets tied up in the corner of his pocket-handkerchief, and about fifty able-bodied women, all fighting, pulling, and dragging at him; and as many more shut up in a sort of pen of prickly-pear, fighting, scratching, and tearing each other, till A— thought there would really be some serious mischief done, and some of the babies in arms killed; but the sergeant took it all very quietly:— "Lawk, sir, never mind 'em! they won't hurt theirselves!" A— goes now every morning to give the tickets away himself, and there is no trouble at all, but all the fighting ladies as quiet as mice. The women help to work as well as the men, but of course they only do a little of the easy part. They are all repairing the tanks and the roads, and the native subscribers are now much pleased with the plan of making the people work for their food. They are beginning to see the sense of it; but at first they tried hard to persuade A— to give it away in a sort of scramble to those that cried the loudest, which is the native way of giving charity.

We are just now very busy about a new plan, viz., to set up a native reading-room in the bazaar. A— thinks the people would often be induced to come and sit there and read, instead of spending all the day in gossiping and chewing betel[332] in the bazaar. He has consulted one or two of the most sensible of our native visitors, who like the thoughts of it very much, and say it would be sure to succeed. We mean to hire a good room in the middle of the bazaar, have it whitewashed and matted, and ornamented with some of the penny pictures which are coming from you, and which will be great attractions; and keep always there a supply of all the Gentoo books and tracts that are to be had, all the easy English ones we can muster, a Gentoo and an English newspaper. There is a Gentoo newspaper published at Madras, and A—takes it, in order to please some of the Court servants by lending it to them. It is very quaint: sometimes there are articles translated from the English papers, always the most uninteresting and frivolous that can possibly be selected: for instance, a description of the Queen's bed, with the very unexpected assertion that she always sleeps on a hard mat, with nothing over her! In the last number there was an account of a ball given by the Governor of Madras, to which many of the natives were invited. They say, "the Nabob entered with a grand *suwarree* (attendance) of a hundred guards, and a hundred lanterns all in one line, and appeared like a man of penetration. The English danced together pleasantly after their fashion, shaking each other's hands, and then proceeded to make their supper, when the respectable natives all retired." Of course, the "respectable natives" of caste could not remain to partake of our Pariah food! They always despise us very much for dancing to amuse ourselves; the proper grand thing would be to sit still, solemn and sleepy, smoking, or chewing betel, and have dancing-girls to dance to us.

That poor Mr. B—[333] I told you about, who was helping us to concoct dialogues, is going home ill. He had set up a native school at Cocanada with forty boys; it was going on very nicely, but I am afraid nobody will keep it up now. A Rajah who called here the other day promised to take it in hand, and pay the master, and keep it up himself; but I am afraid his promises will not come to much. He was rather a clever, intelligent man, and came to tell us of a book he is writing on revenue and judicial matters. Some of his notions and schemes were very good, and A— thought they really might be useful; but probably the performance will be so queer and rigmarole that nobody will read it. He wanted A— to write a public official letter to Government requesting that attention might be paid to the book: I think Government would be rather surprised.

Our Narsapoor Missionaries are now engaged in travelling through the district, preaching as they go along. It is a very good plan for exciting attention, and that is the chief benefit that is to be hoped for at present. These poor natives are a long time before they can even be roused from their apathy: as for their *opposition*, they are scarcely equal to making any—it is like the opposition of dormice. I believe they could sleep through a battle.

March 6th.—The reading-room is established and much approved. The doors are opened before six in the morning, but there are always people waiting outside, ready for the first moment they can get in. Always twenty or thirty at a time sit reading there, and about a hundred come in the course of the day. The wall is hung with divers of your penny pictures, which are much admired, especially that of the Queen on horseback. We have found plenty of suitable books, in English, Hindostanee, Tamul, and Gentoo; and I think it seems to be a very pretty invention, and likely to give great satisfaction.

The case of goods by the 'Argyle' arrived a little while ago, and we immediately selected a batch of rewards to give to our boys. There are sixty-five now in the school, but we only gave grand Europe presents to the twenty-four best, not to make them too cheap; and by way of a slight treat to the younger fry, they came to "point" at the presents, and scramble for *pice*. The penknives were more admired than anything; next the slates. We take a great deal of pains, but they learn very little; however, they just get the beginnings of notions.

The other day a Sunnyassee,[334] or Hindoo devotee, came to pray in the middle of the river, and, being a wonderful saint, a number of people made a subscription of fifty rupees that he might pray for them—*that* being the price he set upon his prayers. The Doctor happened to see the crowd in the middle of the river, and asked a boy what they were doing: the boy said they were going to be prayed for by a great saint like Jesus Christ. The Doctor asked where he had heard of Jesus Christ. He said at the Feringhees'[335] (Englishmen's) school, and that he thought Jesus Christ was a great saint, and that His prayers for any one would be granted. Miss L—'s[336] idea, which you mention, of translating 'Watts on Prejudices'[337] for the Hindoos, is just a hundred years in advance—they would not understand it. What they want is, 'des Catéchismes de six sous,' like Massillon's little infidel.[338]

At the Translation Committee at Madras,[339] some innocent Missionary sent in a proposal to translate Butler's 'Analogy'[340] into Tamul. One shrewd old German said, very quietly, "Perhaps he will first give us the Tamul word for *Analogy;*" and that was all the notice taken of the proposition.[mm]

We lately received a petition, signed by the principal people, chiefly Mussulmans, in several of the surrounding villages, begging us to supply them with books of the same kind as those in our reading-room, mentioning the names of several that they particularly wish to have, and saying that they will thankfully pay for them, if we will only procure them. Therefore we have now a sort of circulating library in the district. We consign a packet of books to the head man in one village, and he passes them on to the rest, and when they are all read, we send out a fresh supply.

* * * * * *

LETTER THE TWENTY-FOURTH.

Samuldavy, March 30th, 1839.

HERE we arrived this morning, and are enjoying ourselves, spreading our sails, and cooling delightfully. Rajahmundry was growing very hot, but this place is charming. Last night it was downright cold, and the colder and more uncomfortable it was the better I liked it. The babies and I shall stay here the next four months, and A— will come to us once a-week as before, if the Governor does not find it out; and in May he will have a lawful holiday. I had a little fever before I came away, and Henrietta[341] was grown pale and pining; but the sea-breeze has cleared my fever away in this one morning, and I dare say in a few days I shall see a great change in her too. We have built a new room here, which is very comfortable, and we are to pay no rent until we have repaid ourselves the expense of it, after which it is to belong to the landlord. This makes it a good bargain both for him and for us, and it only cost thirty pounds altogether.

I believe there is a Missionary coming to Rajahmundry at last—a Dissenter; but if the Church Mission can do nothing for all this immense district, of course we can only be glad that the Dissenters should take it up. He is a Mr. Johnston,[342] seemingly a very quiet, humble person; and I wish he may come, but it is not yet quite settled.

Before we came away we exhibited the astronomical magic lantern to the schoolboys. We sent for them unexpectedly, on a leisure evening, so all who were not at school were "caught out," and lost the show. They were enchanted with it, and understood it very prettily, considering they would not have been capable a year ago of understanding any one of the slides. They particularly admired the moon: I heard some whispering, "*Oh nulla chendroodoo!*"—"Oh good moon!" whenever it appeared. Mr. G. thinks our school is come on very nicely, and is much better than any of the others he has seen since he has been away: this pleases us, for we had been uneasy, thinking they learned nothing. One of the schools at which he has been teaching is an endowed school at Masulipatam, with a committee and a great deal of money; but very little really done, though much trouble taken in the committee-room: they think it necessary to write and ask the Archdeacon (of Madras)[343] permission for every book, and he allows of none but the English national-school books, which are quite useless to the natives, so they do not get on at all. Mr. Hamilton is going to have a *Pariah* school[344] at Rajahmundry, by way of a companion to ours, as we do not admit Pariahs.

The "reading-room" also answers very well, and is always full. Mr. H.[345] went to see it one morning early, and found people waiting for the doors to open.

Here is a story for you, but it did not happen lately.—There was a goddess carried in procession to one of the pagodas, and the Collector, as usual, had to supply the money: after the procession had advanced some way, the Bramins came and told the Collector that it had stopped because the goddess would not travel any farther with only twenty bullocks: the Collector gave ten more, and the Swamy went on another hundred yards; when the Bramins came back again and said she was still discontented and wanted more. This put the Collector in a passion: he said she was a "greedy devil," and various other little *politesses;* and if she could not be satisfied with thirty bullocks he would *chop her up.* So he sent his Peons to fetch her out of her car, and ordered them to chop her up on the spot: the Peons were afraid, and ran away: then he sent for the cook-boy, and made him chop her up before his eyes—and the Bramins just took it all quietly and went home. I believe this is quite true; and the moral of it is—that the people would not be so very ready to raise rebellions as is pretended on any deficiency of attention to the Swamies. The Collector was a very passionate man, but rather a favourite with the natives because he did not oppress them in money matters, which they care for much more than for Swamy. I must add, however, that A— says my story of the Collector chopping up the Swamy happened twenty years ago; and that no Collector in his senses would do such a thing now.

Our clerical friend, Mr.—, is always in some scrape about christenings: he refuses to admit any sponsors who are not regular communicants, and consequently many children under his jurisdiction are not christened at all. A little while ago he was absent from his station for three days, and D—, who is Judge there, took the opportunity to christen, himself, all the children Mr.—had refused; so when he returned he found it all done and registered, with the obnoxious godfathers and godmothers. Also, Master D— took upon himself to marry an English soldier to a Heathen woman, together with various other *scappate*[346] of less importance, but very provoking. Poor—felt himself uncommonly hurt, as he often does, and appealed to the Bishop. He showed us the Bishop's answer, which was really beautiful; condemning all D—'s misdemeanors, and at the same time giving—such good and wise advice about his own vagaries, and yet so kindly and delicately expressed, and the whole tone of the letter so humble and Christianlike, that it was quite a pattern. All the young hands are quite wild about these new ideas concerning baptism. A— asked young B—,[347] a slip of eighteen, to stand *proxy* for one of the godfathers at our baby's christening: B— said he could not possibly do it, because, if he were a proxy, he should feel called upon to remonstrate with the parents concerning their way of bringing up the child. A— explained that we by no means wished him to be godfather, and asked whether he knew the difference between that and proxy. No, he did not, but still "felt sure it must be wrong." Fancy a young chap like that thinking he *must* know best about education, and that his "remonstrances" would inevitably be wanted! He is a good lad too, only somewhat pragmatical and solemn. H——did not think it wrong to be proxy, but discoursed considerably on a variety of duties of a godfather, which being quite new to me, I ventured to inquire whether he found them in the Bible or the Prayer Book. "Why, neither," said he, "but I am sure they must be *somewhere!*"

April 16th.—Do you know that Government has abolished the pilgrim-tax?[348] It is a very good step towards leaving off their encouragement of idolatry. Mr. Hamilton received a letter from a Missionary who lives at one of the "Holy Shrines," giving an account of the last festival since the tax; and the compulsory attendance of the natives to drag the cars has been done away with. That part of his letter is so curious that I will copy it for you.

"I have just returned from a large Heathen festival held at the famous *Beejanuggur*.[349] It is pleasing to find that the Company have remitted the tax this year to visitors, and I hear they have had nothing to do with the usual expenses of decoration of the car, &c. No military were present as is usual; notwithstanding, the attendance was unprecedentedly small: I do not suppose there were above fifteen thousand persons present, when last year there were seventy thousand; the year before, near one hundred thousand; and when Mr. Hands,[350] twenty-five years ago, attended, the usual number was about two hundred thousand. This is a pleasing indication of the decline of idolatry. The scarcity of provisions and water, and the fear of cholera, no doubt kept many away; but the decrease of interest in the superstitions of the country, I hope, a larger number. I do hope that three or four years will shut up the festivities of Beejanuggur for ever. The Anagoondy Rajah[351] brought all his people, and used all his influence; but the large car could only be drawn a few yards on the first day, and, on the next day, instead of taking it to the end of the street, from which, had they conveyed it there, they never could have got it back, they brought it home to its place within about three yards, when, being quite exhausted, they left it there."

April 19th.—I have received a message from a Bramin, who sends word that he keeps a school in the village, but has no books, and would be very glad "if Mistress please to give some books to teach the boys." You see that is a very good thing, because we can introduce Christian books instead of the histories of their gods. The misfortune is, there are not above six or eight books published in Gentoo, and those are religious tracts and disquisitions that children cannot possibly understand. Nobody knows how much elementary books for the natives are wanted. There was once a School-book Society,[352] but it has dwindled to nothing; and once there was a sort of Native College at Madras for educating Moonshees, and Government was thinking of establishing schools up the country. Several were established; and though they were not Christian schools, they were much better than nothing; but they are all done away with now: there are neither schools nor college. Still, if every civilian up the country were to have a poor little school like ours, it would do something in time; but numbers of them disapprove, as they say, of everything of the kind. Mr. L——[353] set up a school at Cocanada: he had fifty boys and a capital master, much better than ours; but he was not here when we took ours, and now we do not like to turn ours away, as he does his best. L—'s school was going on very nicely when he was obliged to return to England on sick certificate: he asked the Collector to keep up his school, but the Collector thought the natives were better without education, and refused: so the school is broken up, for which I am very sorry.

The boys in our school take the trouble to copy for themselves all the question-and-answer lessons on Scripture History, &c., which we compose for them. A— and I write the English, Moonshee translates it, and the boys learn by heart and transcribe both the English and the Gentoo.

A— and I had been lamenting very much the breaking up of Mr. L—'s school, and if ever we leave Rajahmundry very likely our own will share the same fate: it depends entirely upon our successor. While we were thinking so much on the subject, A— made me write a letter to one of the Madras newspapers, with the results of our cogitations and calculations; and I will copy it for you, as I know you like to hear all our schemes and plans.

NATIVE EDUCATION.

To the Editor of 'The Spectator'[354]

SIR,—Your paper is so well known as a willing medium for the communication of any suggestions tending to the benefit of the native population, that I venture to request the insertion of a few remarks upon a plan for the more general diffusion of native education. At present all attempts for the improvement of the natives of this Presidency are confined to private, I might almost say to individual, exertions, which of course are capable of but very partial success. What is required is national education,[355] a boon far exceeding the limited means of a few individuals to bestow. Government only can confer it; but government can, and ought. I doubt not that there exists in the mind of our rulers the wish to improve by education the condition of their native subjects, if it could be accomplished without risk to our dominion, or too heavy an expenditure of public money.

The "auld warld" prejudice of "risk to our dominion" is, I suppose, exploded amongst all who are really acquainted with the native character. It still holds its sway among those whose knowledge of India is limited to the Presidency, and whose native acquaintance extends only to a few writers in government offices; but really experienced Europeans, who have been long *in* the country and *up* the country—who are conversant with the native languages, customs, habits of thought, wishes, and prejudices—know, beyond the possibility of doubt or mistake, how eager the natives are for education, and how grateful for its being in any way facilitated. A European in the provinces has but to open a school of any description in his district, and it is immediately filled beyond the power of one master to superintend. Even with regard to the books used, it is altogether a *presidency prejudice* that the natives are averse to being taught from books of our selecting. They never even consider the matter, but receive, without an idea of hesitating, whatever we may choose to direct. Their difficulties and objections have, I fully believe, been mainly elicited and encouraged by Europeans themselves. I can confidently appeal, for the accuracy of these statements, to any and every European who has himself fairly tried the establishment of native schools, in which truth should be taught, whether on religious subjects or on matters of general information.

Among some persons who are favourable in a general way to the establishment of schools, there still prevails the strange fallacy that we may venture to teach the natives truth on subjects of science, history, &c., but that we must use their own religious books in our schools, and, in fact, teach nothing but falsehood on matters connected with religion. Such arguers forget, or do not know, that what is physical science with us is religious doctrine with the Hindoos. We cannot teach them the most common known fact—such, for instance, as that the earth is suspended in space, instead of being perched upon an elephant, or that an eclipse is caused by a shadow instead of a snake—without overturning two or three dozen of their religious tenets: therefore, if we are to teach them nothing that is contrary to their own notions of religion, we must just leave them where they are on all other subjects; which procedure, or rather non-procedure, I believe few persons are quite prepared to advocate.

The expense of Government national education is, I conceive, greatly over-calculated, or rather over-estimated, for it is probably not calculated at all. A valuable and comprehensive Government general education might be given at a very moderate outlay, by the following plan.

Let there be four schools at Madras, one of which should be considered the central or model school; one at the principal station of every Zillah, and one in every Talook;* all, of course, free, unless it should be thought desirable to establish some payment at the Presidency central school, which might be rendered and considered superior to the rest, and would be chiefly attended by boys of the higher and richer classes. At the Presidency and station schools English should be taught, and a good substantial education given. In the Talook schools English would be unnecessary, but education should be carried on in the native languages to whatever extent the books published in those languages render possible. The Madras schools should be under the superintendence and direction of a Board of Education, and the provincial schools under that of the principal European residents at their respective stations. There should be a certain number of books authorized by government, and a fixed general plan, upon which all the schools should be conducted; but it appears to me expedient not to lay unnecessary restrictions upon the European superintendents' occasionally

---

* A smaller division of the district.

introducing additional books or trifling modifications of the system, according to their judgment. If they be too much fettered and restricted, they will naturally take less interest in the work, and their superintendence will be proportionably inefficient.

Now, let us calculate the expense. I believe one lac of rupees[†] per annum would amply cover the whole. There are twenty districts in the Madras Presidency, and altogether about two hundred and forty Talooks. Native teachers up the country may be engaged at from five to ten rupees per month. Houses in the villages may be bought, built, or hired for a few rupees per annum; and certainly the whole cost of the Talook schools, including cadjan, paper, pens, books, and sundries, need never exceed twenty rupees per month. This may even, in most cases, be reduced by the schoolmaster being paid by the grant of a small piece of land, free of taxes; and this land might be considered as an endowment, and always be the property of the schoolmaster for the time being. The expense of the station schools, where English should be taught, would be about fifty rupees per month; of the Madras three minor schools, one hundred and fifty rupees per month; and of the superior one, to which the scholars might contribute, three hundred and fifty rupees per month.

Now, let us sum up the whole: –

	Rupees
240 schools, at 20 rupees per month	4800
40, viz., 2 in each district—one under the collector and one under the Judge, at 50 rupees per month	2000
3 at Madras, at 150 rupees per month	450
1 do., at 350 rupees per month	350
Total	7600

or ninety-one thousand two hundred rupees per annum; and allowing the overplus for sundries and unforeseen expenses, I think there can be no doubt that education might be diffused over the Madras Presidency for the sum of one hundred thousand rupees per annum, even allowing for all being paid in hard money, which need not be the case if the system were adopted of attaching a piece of land to the situation of schoolmaster.

       I am, Sir,
        Yours obediently,
          MATTER OF FACT.

May 7th.—The scarcity is over now. Government gave a great deal of money to spend among the poor. Our Collector gave A— fifty pounds of it, all of which he laid out in grain for the workers, both men and women. They have made several

---

† Ten thousand pounds.

miles of beautiful high road, deepened tanks, and dug a well—the well is a very great acquisition to this place; you may suppose, in such a climate, how glad the people always are of additional water. A— was so pleased with his well that he sent all the way to it, a mile off, for water to christen our new baby!

SAMULDAVY, *May* 10*th*.—The Bombay monsoon has just set in, so there will probably be the same delay in the steamers as there was last year; wherefore I intend this letter to go by an old ship. It is very hot now—land-wind all day—very bad. However, I do not suppose it will last many days; and then, whatever sea-breeze there is we shall have in full perfection.

In your last you ask how our potato plan answered during the famine: we were unable even to try it, for, owing to the difficulties of carriage in India, the potatoes did not arrive at Rajahmundry till the season for planting them was completely over. There were contrary winds, which prevented ships from coming quickly, and there are no roads in our district—nor, indeed, scarcely anywhere to the north of Madras. People say that, if Government would spend money sufficient to make good roads, it would be repaid over and over again in the increased trade and traffic; but there are very few who care about the matter, so it dawdles on.[nn] Rich people travel four miles an hour on men's shoulders; poor people walk; and luggage waits for an opportunity by sea.

May 14*th*.—We are going to set up a school at Samuldavy for Gentoo only; we could not manage an English school here. The Missionary Beer came the other day, dined with me, and went to preach in the topes. A Bramin brought the tracts I had given, and asked Beer to explain them, as he said they were very fine, but nobody could understand them. He requested Beer to establish a school here, and said there would be plenty of boys glad to attend. So we are going to set one up, and Beer is to come now and then from Narsapoor to superintend it when we are at Rajahmundry. The head man of the village has offered to build a school-house himself;—you know their houses are only sheds.

We have just had a long visit from a young Rajah, whose ambition is to engraft the character of an English dandy on that of a native don; and the result is, a sort of king of twelfth-cake.[356] He goes about in an English palanquin with native penny flags by its side; and adds to his national muslin gown, and gold Rajah's cap, a pair of satin trousers, and a green satin waistcoat, embroidered with pearls. He wanted to show A— some papers, so one of his attendants brought in an English leather writing-desk, and Twelfth-Cake proceeded to twiddle at the lock, turning the key round the wrong way, clicking the bolt, and fumbling and fidgeting for full five minutes before he could get it open. By and by he produced an enormous silver watch, like a prize-turnip, with six chains, and begged to set it by our watches. He made a great fuss with the seal and key, but contrived it at last, and sat down again, looking as proud as an infant schoolboy—and almost as clever. He professed a wish to make his name famous, so A— advised him to educate the people in his Zemindary,[357] and especially to be the first to establish a girls' school. He promised that he would set up both a girls' and a boys' school; and looked at spelling-books, asked directions about building a school-house, and really seemed in earnest. I wish he may keep in the same mind, for he is a person of sufficient consequence to make the innovation, and to carry it through; but I fear it will all end in buying shaving-glasses and penny prints to stick up in his house.

Our last papers bring an account of a society in England for protecting the natives of India, with a very clever and true speech from a Mr. Thompson[358]—who is he? He puts a few tigers and boa constrictors into his speech, just to keep up attention, I suppose; but it is a capital speech; and his accounts of the shameful taxation, &c., &c., are not in the least exaggerated.

The troops have been short of food and water, owing to the bad arrangements of the Commissariat, and altogether the war is said to be grievously ill-managed.

There is now an opportunity for sending letters *viâ* Beyrout,[359] so I shall despatch this, as there is no ship now in the roads; but ten to one the Arabs or their dromedaries will eat up my letter.

"No more news to report, but I beg always to keep much regard upon me;—excuse me." That is the proper Native manner of ending a letter politely.

LETTER THE TWENTY-FIFTH.

Samuldavy, June 10th, 1839.

THE day before yesterday was Etta's birth day—two years old; so we had a feast in her honour. Feasts are cheap enough among these poor creatures; ours cost a guinea and a half, and fed five hundred people. We gave them rice, which is equivalent to roast beef and plum-pudding in England. They live on a cheaper sort of grain; and many of them cannot even get that, but live on such herbs and roots as they can pick up.

One cannot cook their dinners for them, and see them eat it, as one would at an English feast; but each person had a portion given to him enough for two meals, and took it home. They all sat down near the house, in rows; and Master, and servants, and Peons, measured out the rice, while Etta and I sat and looked on; but *she* soon grew tired of it. I noticed one old squinny man, with a long white beard, who sat a great way off from the rest, very solemn and dignified; a most grand grub, with his old wife at a respectable distance behind him. We found he was a decayed Rajah, who was thankful to come and receive his share of rice with the beggars! They were all very much pleased with their feast, and next morning many of them came back, to pick up, grain by grain, what little had been scattered on the ground in measuring it out.

A— has established a school here, at Samuldavy; and the schoolmaster is willing to teach with our books, so he and his boys have begun with St. Matthew.[360] They read, transcribe, and learn it by heart, and come once a-week to A— to be examined; the greatest difficulty in schools is, the want of school-books in the native languages.

A little while ago two young Parsees were baptized at Bombay,[361] and there is every reason to suppose they were real converts: their countrymen were furious, and assembled in crowds around them, as they left the church, using most violent menaces; and there were great apprehensions of a serious uproar, but the two young Christians were rescued. The Government have taken measures to protect them and keep the peace, and all is quiet again. I believe it never was anything more than the bluster of a mob, but the poor boys might have been hurt.

* * * * * *

There is just a chance of a move for us soon: two appointments are vacant, to either of which A— has the first claim:—*Sta a vedere*.[362]

What you say about Governors giving appointments, and people fitting themselves for them afterwards, is very true in England, but it is not the case here. There is a regular rule, established by Act of Parliament, that people of a certain standing are entitled to certain appointments,[363] and the Governor has no right to act contrary to it. He may very well choose among those of the *requisite standing*, and give the appointment to whichever may be his favourite; but he has no right to make "the lag of the school captain." *That* is the innovation complained of here: the natives say, "Lord E—[364] is fond of doing justice, but does not know how."

MASULIPATAM, *July 4th*.—"A change came o'er the spirit of my dream!"[365] I *now* look upon Lord E— as a most excellent Governor, and W—E— as an admirable Private Secretary.[366] A great many things have happened since I wrote last. A— is appointed "Acting First Judge of Circuit in the Centre Division," and with every prospect of being confirmed permanently, either as First or Second Judge, at the end of the year; the real holder of the appointment being expected to go home in January. It is not *quite* certain that we shall remain there, but very probable; and if we do, we can have nothing more to wish. It is a most capital appointment—high rank, high pay, good climate, and pretty country; at all events, we shall never return to Rajahmundry, and are now *en route* to our new station. The only drawback is, that A— is obliged to go on circuit directly, and to begin by two very hot places, Cuddapah[367] and Bellary,[368] to which he does not like to take the babies and me. We are therefore to stay at Madras with his brother, till he has finished all the Cuddapah and Bellary business; then we shall join him, and go the rest of the circuit with him, to Chingleput and Cuddalore,[369] which are both of them cool and pleasant. The name of the place we are to live at when stationary is Chittoor.[370] It is said to be healthy and pretty, with fine gardens and plenty of grapes; hot in summer; but there is a beautiful place, called Palmanair,[371] within twenty miles of it, very high and quite cool—a most delightful climate. We shall also be within two hundred miles of the Neilgherries,[372] so we *can* go thither if necessary, and within one hundred and twenty miles of Cuddalore, a good sea-coast.

We are both of us exceedingly pleased, and "quite content."

July 6th.—We are now fairly on our road.

Besides all our own attendants, in number a hundred and fifty, there are divers "camp followers," such as Amah's husband, Ayah's grub, &c., &c. We proceed, on an average, about twenty-five miles a-night, and rest every day, and on Sunday night, and any other night if we are fatigued. Masulipatam was an ugly place; a swamp, two miles broad, between the town and the sea; nothing to be seen but wide sandy roads, with prickly-pear hedges, enclosing black-looking Palmyra-trees,[373] and red-tiled houses peeping (no, not *peeping*, they are not coquette enough for that—*staring*) out from among them; altogether, a most *rapid* sort of place. The Twelfth-cake Rajah paid us a visit there, to ask all particulars about our school, as he thinks of keeping it up. We had plenty of curious farewell letters from the natives at Rajahmundry; one of them says "he depends entirely upon the protection of A—'s sublime feet, and Mistress Mama!"

RAMIAHPATAM, *July 15th.*—We have been halting here for two or three days, and were met by the best of all company, viz., nearly a dozen English letters brought by the two steamers of April and May, which arrived within three days of each other.

MADRAS, *July 31st.*—We arrived here, babies and I, on the 23rd, and A— on the same day at his destination, Cuddapah. He was able to come with us to within two nights' run of Madras; and we had servants and Peons, and made the rest of our journey without any difficulty. We are living about six or seven miles from Madras, on the very beach, and enjoy the sea-air much: this situation is cooler and drier than Samuldavy.

Miss T—[374] is very busy now with a school for half-caste young ladies, which seems likely to be very useful. Those half-caste girls are in the depths of ignorance, indolence, and worthlessness, and utterly neglected; they have no ideas but of dress and making love—one girl brought forty gowns to school! Our schoolmaster's sister at Rajahmundry (who was a half-caste) came very seldom to church; but, when she did, she used to be dressed in white shoes, gold chains, earrings, two or three brooches, and all such rubbish.

The poor Female Orphan Asylum[375] is as bad as ever: Lady N—,[376] the present Commander-in-Chief's lady, takes an interest in it, and is very sensible in her propositions, such as the teaching them washing, plain work, &c., &c., but the other ladies do not co-operate with her. If I come to live at Madras, I do not think I shall be likely to take a part in it, because A— has a great objection to the institution itself, though he would let me help if I wished to do so. But it is very bad:— professedly for orphans of European soldiers, while scarcely any of them really are orphans; and the half-caste young left-handed ladies look down upon the poor little honestly-born Europeans, and boast of being "gentlemen's children;" and they go out visiting their relatives without shame or ceremony.

There is always something doing in the way of schools, and certainly an increasing desire among the natives for instruction, and an increasing willingness to receive our books. Towards the south they are more bigoted, and their bigotry is greatly encouraged by timid or ungodly Europeans, who really put objections into their heads; but at Rajahmundry, where they had never heard of hesitations and difficulties, we used to receive applications for books from distant villages, and especially for any portions of Scripture; and the people used to sit in our reading-room for hours, copying our books on their own little cadjan-leaves. It is very remarkable that here, at Madras, people are declining to help the schools in which the Bible is taught, under the old pretence of its being "a dangerous interference with Native feelings," &c.; while, not two streets from the English school, which is dwindling away for want of support, there is a common native Braminee school, in which the Bramin master uses the Bible as a school-book, of his own accord, because he happens to like it; and no idea of difficulty enters his mind or those of his scholars, though they are all Heathens of a high and prejudiced caste. The Missionaries publish many tracts, of which some are very good, but the greater number are not sufficiently simple, and the natives cannot understand them; and the tracts which come from England are altogether *un-Indian*, and unfit to translate. We want an Indian Hannah More.[377]

I wish I could tell you anything satisfactory about the Tanjore Mission;[378] there is much talk of pruning and purifying it. The church at Tinnevelly[379] will very soon be begun; the plan and site are settled, and all is in progress.

You ask what news I can give you of the "caste question." It is all as undecided as ever. People, even religious people, take such very different views of the matter, that the discussions are never ended. A——, and his brother, and many others, look upon caste as a mixed usage, partly civil and partly religious; and they think it will only be broken down by education, and that many of the native Christians who still adhere to it are among the most satisfactory of the converts; but they think that those who do so should only be employed as schoolmasters or catechists, and not be considered fit for *Ordination*. The Bishop, however, looks upon caste as entirely a distinction of rank, and has lately ordained a native Christian who will not give it up;—others insist upon its being altogether a religious distinction, and will not even acknowledge as Christians those who do not renounce it. Mr. T——[380] was wishing lately to have a series of meetings for freely discussing the subject—the principal native Christians to take part in it, besides the English gentlemen who differ so much in their views. I, in my ignorance, thought it a very pretty plan and likely to be useful; but the wiser heads thought it would do no good, and I believe it is given up.

August 9th.—A—— is still on duty at Cuddapah, a place noted for fever, which can only be kept off by violent exercise. This *he* is able to take, so that his health does not suffer: he tells me he is quite well, notwithstanding very hard work. He is employed on criminal trials, most of them for life or death; and he says the incessant falsehood to which he is obliged to listen is most painful and wearing,— witnesses by scores coming forward to swear away the life of another, and often the only motive some petty spite,—and no shame or disgrace felt, even when detected! Certainly, the first characteristic of Heathenism is *lying!* A—— has met with a good painstaking Dissenting Missionary there—a Mr. Howell,[381] whom he is helping in his books, schools, &c., &c. Old civilians, like him and J——,[382] generally know much more of the people, and the languages and customs, than the Missionaries do, and can be of great use to them.

Have you heard yet in England of the horrors that took place at the funeral of that wretched old Runjeet Singh?[383] *Four* wives and *seven* slave-girls were burnt with him; and not a word even of remonstrance from the British Government! J—— says there cannot be a doubt that a word of disapprobation from the British Resident would have stopped it at once, for the whole power of the Punjaub depends on our will, and they profess to follow our wishes in everything. Is it not shocking? The four Ranees burnt themselves at their own desire, from pride of family and caste; but the poor slave-girls could have had no such motives, and must have been burnt by the wretches around them. One Grandee *man* pretended he meant to burn himself too, and could scarcely be persuaded against it; but I believe his was all sham: he knew very well they would not let him, because he was useful to the country. When poor old Runjeet Singh was dying, he gave away in charities and offerings to the Bramins, in order to propitiate the gods, treasure worth a million sterling. He was enormously rich, having never hesitated to steal anything he could lay his hands on. He wanted to give the immense diamond[384] he stole from Shah Soojah, but his courtiers persuaded him not.

Here is another disgraceful story of English ungodliness. When Shah Soojah[385] arrived at his capital, Candahar,[386] he and all his Mussulmans went directly to pay their devotions to a rag of Mohammed's shirt,[387] which is kept there as a precious relic. Of course, all the Mussulmans had a right to do so, and no one would think of preventing them; but think of *our Envoy* and the British troops and authorities all accompanying him in state on such an errand! I could scarcely believe it, but it is really true.

August 14*th*.—Preparations are making for a Burmese war,[388] and the Indian newspapers are full of Colonel Burney's wisdom,[389] and wishing they had followed his advice long ago. There has been a *"petite drôlerie"*[390] in the way of treason, headed by the Nizam's brother,[391] but it was found out and stopped long before it came to anything. The old experienced hands quiz it like the *"petits spectacles"*[392] in Paris, but some of the younger Collectors, who were not accustomed to such matters, were rather frightened, and one Collectress told me very solemnly that she understood it had been distinctly announced in the mosques that all the English ladies were to be seized and made slaves of. If you hear any frightful stories, *non pensi*,[393] for it is all fudge. There is another little Rajah trying at a little rebellion[394] fifty miles from the place at which A— now is; and a couple of regiments are sent to settle his mind. J— says as soon as he sees the red-coats[395] and Sepoys he will give in; but, poor man! I am rather sorry for him—he has been four or five years collecting arms and ammunition[396] and concocting his little rebellion, and of course his property will be confiscated, and his independent kingdom, such as it is, done away—and, after all, we shall only have *"conquered a green blight,"*[397] like Frank when he was a little boy.

I am very glad those insects I sent were so curious, and that you gave the new specimens to the British Museum.[398] No doubt I shall be able to send you plenty more: I do not at all recollect which they were, but in future I will keep numbered duplicates, that I may learn their names. Pray, ask Mr. Samouelle[399] what names were given to the five new species, and let me know.

I really believe the Madras ladies spend all their time in writing notes—"chits,"[400] as they are called. I do not know ten people now, and yet there never passes a day without my having one or two "chits" to answer:—what with writing them, composing them, finding my penknife, mending my pen, hunting for proper note-paper, which is always hidden in some scribbled foolscap beginnings of tracts, or such-like, all my morning is hindered;—and their chits are generally only to say "how sorry they are they have not been able to call lately, that I must have wondered at it, and *thought*," &c., &c. Now, I never *think* about it,—*"les absens*,"⁴⁰¹ &c.,°°—and I would always rather they did not call, because I must sit all day with my hair dressed and my best clothes on, waiting for them; and remember the thermometer is at 92°. I am going to-morrow to Mrs. W—E—.⁴⁰² I have not been able to call on her yet, because we live so far off that I quite dread going out for a *morning* visit according to this horrid Madras fashion. If I see her I shall say that I cannot come in the morning, and beg her to come to me in the evening; but for the first visit there is no help:—just now the weather is cloudy, so I shall take advantage of it before it clears up.

LETTER THE TWENTY-SIXTH.

Madras, September 24th, 1839.

HERE is the steamer going, and almost gone, and my letter for it not begun, though I have a whole steamer-load of things to say, and scarcely know where to begin; but I have been hindered by an attack of Indian fever, and the baby also has been ill, and the doctors talk very seriously of the desirableness of my sending her home. That is the grand Indian sorrow[403]—the necessity of parting with one's children. However, she is still so young that we hope change of air may possibly be sufficient for her; and therefore A— will fetch us, and leave us at Bangalore, a cool place in the table-land above the ghauts,[404] while he continues his circuit to Bellary, which he thinks too hot for us.

September 30th.—I have been paying a round of visits to all my Madras acquaintances: they seem just in the same state in which I left them, with nothing in this world to do. You can scarcely imagine such a life of inanity. A thorough Madras lady, in the course of the day, goes about a good deal to shops and auctions; buys a great many things she does not want, without inquiring the price; has plenty of books, but seldom reads—it is too hot, or she has not time—*liking to "have her time her own,"* I suppose, like old Lady Q—;[405] receives a number of morning visitors; takes up a little worsted work; goes to tiffin with Mrs. C.,[406] unless Miss D.[407] comes to tiffin[408] with her; and writes some dozen of *"chits."* Every inquiry after an acquaintance must be made in writing, as the servants can never understand or deliver a message, and would turn every "politesse" into an insult. These incessant *chits* are an immense trouble and interruption; but the ladies seem to like them, and sit at their desks with more zeal and perseverance than their husbands in their cutcherries. But when it comes to any really interesting occupation, it is pitiable to see the torpor of every faculty—worse than torpor: their minds seem to evaporate under this Indian sun, never to be condensed or concentrated again. The seven-years' sleep of the Beauty in the fairy-tale[409] was nothing to the seven-years' lethargy of a beauty's residence in Madras, for the fairy lady awoke to her former energies, which I should think they never can.

Chittoor, October 8th.—Here we are on our travels again in our way to Bangalore. This Chittoor is a very pretty place, with beautiful views all around, but the houses and gardens are so choked up with trees, that we can see nothing—I should like to cut down half of them. Our road lies through the most picturesque country I have yet seen in India, and I enjoy the scenery in the evenings and early mornings when I am not asleep. We are obliged to outrun all the servants, except the ayahs, who travel in palanquins like ourselves; so we manage rather, as Mr. Wilberforce[410] used to say, "in the wild-beast way"[411] in the daytime, but very comfortably notwithstanding. We have a towel for a table-cloth, plantain-leaves when dishes are not forthcoming, and we put the palanquin-cushions on the floor for sofas. Travelling by night, lying down in a palanquin, is much less fatiguing to me than sitting upright all day in an English carriage.

Bangalore, October 12th.—We arrived here yesterday safe and well, after a *pretty considerable* journey—seven nights travelling, with a rest of two days and nights half-way. We always stop on Sundays, but last Sunday night our rest did not do us much good, for in the middle of the night another travelling lady arrived at the bungalow. We had spread ourselves over all the rooms, thinking nobody else was likely to come at that time, and were very comfortably asleep, when I had to rise and scuffle my things out into the other half of the building, through the verandah, in a heavy rain, which was not at all pleasant; after which, some thieves came and ran away with a bundle of the bearers' clothes, so they were making an uproar, howling and yelling the whole night.

October 16th.—I am charmed with Bangalore, and hope it will do us all a great deal of good. The climate at this time of the year is delightful, equal to any in Europe. For the first two or three days there was a good deal of fog, but it has now cleared away, and all is so cool, clear, and bright, that it is quite a pleasure to feel oneself breathing. The early mornings especially are as pleasant as anything I can imagine: they have all the sweetness and freshness of an English summer. The air smells of hay and flowers, instead of ditches, dust, fried oil, curry, and onions, which are the *best* of the Madras smells. There are superb dahlias growing in the gardens, and to-day I saw a real staring full-blown hollyhock, which was like meeting an old friend from England, instead of the tuberoses, pomegranates, &c., I have been accustomed to see for the last two years. We have apples, pears, and peaches, and I really should know them one from the other, though it must be confessed there is a considerable family likeness, strongly reminding us of a potato; still they look like English fruit: and the boys bring baskets of raspberries for sale, which are very like blackberries indeed. The English children are quite fat and rosy, and wear shoes and stockings.

There are fire-places in most of the houses, and no punkahs in any of them. It is altogether very pleasant, but a queer place—a sort of cross-breed between the watering-places of every country in the world. Ladies going about dressed to every pitch of distraction they can invent, with long curls which the heat would not allow for an hour elsewhere, and warm close bonnets with flowers hanging in and out of them like queens of the May; black niggers, naked or not, as suits their taste; an English church, a Heathen pagoda, botanical garden, public ball-rooms, Dissenting meeting-house, circulating library, English shops, and Parsee merchants, all within sight of each other; elephants and horses walking together in pleasant company over a great green plain in front of our house, where the soldiers exercise; European soldiers and Sepoys meeting at every step; an evening promenade, where people take good brisk walks at an English pace, and chirp like English sparrows, while a band of blackies play "God save the Queen"[412] and call it the "General Salute." There is a fine old fort[413] here—Tippoo's stronghold; a most curious place, adjoining the old native town, surrounded with mud walls *to be strong!* The Pettah[414] it is called. The English ladies told me this Pettah was "a horrid place—quite native!" and advised me never to go into it; so I went next day, of course, and found it most curious—really "*quite native.*" It is *crammed* with inhabitants, and they bustle and hum like bees in a beehive. At first I thought my bearers would scarcely be able to make their way through the crowd of men, women, children, and monkeys, which thronged the street. The ground was covered with shops all spread out in the dirt; the monkeys were scrambling about in all directions, jumping, chattering, and climbing all over the roofs of the houses, and up and down the door-posts—hundreds of them; the children quarrelling, screaming, laughing, and rolling in the dust—hundreds of *them* too—in good imitation of the monkeys; the men smoking, quarrelling, chatting, and bargaining; the women covered with jewels, gossiping at their doors, with screams at each other that set my teeth on edge, and one or two that were very industrious, painting their door-steps instead of sweeping them; and native music to crown the whole. Such confusion was never seen! Landing at Naples[415] is nothing to it. As I came out of the gate I met some young Moorish dandies on horseback; one of them was evidently a "crack rider," and began to show off—as great a fool as Count P—. He reined up his ragged horse, facing me and dancing about till I had passed; then he dashed past me at full gallop, wheeled round and charged my tonjon, bending down to his saddle-bow, and pretending to throw a lance, showing his teeth, and uttering a loud quack! That quack was really too killing. I am busy now making a drawing of a very uncommon pagoda[416] inside the fort. It is a mixture of Hindoo and Moorish architecture,[417] very grotesque and curious indeed. I perceive there are regular styles and orders in the Hindoo architecture. Wild and confused as it seems, it is as determinate in its way as Grecian or Gothic. A— thinks it is all derived from Jewish or Egyptian traditions, and there is as much of *corruption* as of *invention* in their idolatry. Many of the stories in their mythology are most curiously like the Talmud,[418] and one sees numbers of idolatrous imitations of the Temple-service in every Indian pagoda. There are outer courts, and a Holy place, an altar of sacrifice, brazen bulls, &c. The Hindoos look upon both snakes and monkeys as sacred, but more like demons than gods; and do not you remember Adam Clarke's notion[419] among the quaint fancies of the world, that Satan tempted Eve in the form of a monkey?

In your last you ask whether there is any truth in the account of the conversion of a whole tribe of Hindoos in Bengal. I believe there *is* truth in it. I asked Mr. T—, and he said he had heard nothing to throw discredit on the story, but I could not learn any more details or particulars than what you seem to have heard already. One grows sadly suspicious here of all such histories. My mind is, as you say yours is, rather "poisoned;" still I believe it *is* poison, and must not be allowed to work. I do not think the failures, or even the faults, of the present Missionary system any reason at all for lessening exertion—quite the contrary; the less that has been done, the more remains to be done: but what we want are workmen—*schoolmasters* especially. I do not see any use in making the collections you mention for the *converts*—better not, unless it is to pay Missionaries or schoolmasters for them.

* * * * *

LETTER THE TWENTY-SEVENTH.

Bangalore, November 1st, 1839.

THIS place is not quite perfect as to climate, I see, pleasant as it is. I went a few days ago to call on some friends who live in a rather lower ground, in a very pretty English-looking house, with the compound sloping down towards a tank, to look like a villa on the banks of the Thames:[420] very pretty, but rather deadly—"horribly beautiful!" They walked me round their charming damp garden, and into their sweet shady walks, which all smelt of ague, till my feet were as cold as stones, and I felt myself inhaling fever with every breath I drew. I hurried home as soon as I civilly could, but I had a sharp fit of fever in the night, and was prevented from getting my letter ready for the last steamer.

The Europeans here are chiefly military, and the ladies are different from any I have seen yet. The climate does not tempt them to the dawdling kind of idleness, so they ride about in habits made according to the uniform of their husbands' regiments, and do various spirited things of that sort. Then there is another set—good-natured, housekeeper-like bodies, who talk only of ayahs and amahs, and bad nights and babies, and the advantages of Hodgson's ale[421] while they are nursing, and that sort of thing; seeming, in short, devoted to "suckling fools and chronicling small beer!" However, there are some of a very superior class—almost always the ladies of the colonels or principal officers in the European regiments. These seem never to become Indianized, and have the power of being exceedingly useful. Some of them keep up schools for the English soldiers' children, girls especially—superintend them, watch over the soldiers' wives, try to keep and encourage them in good ways, and are quite a blessing to their poor countrywomen.

We hear there has been a great deal of fighting at Kurnool.[422] Colonel D—[423] had the command of our troops, and has taken the country. The Rajah of Kurnool himself was an insignificant creature, but it turns out that he was in the pay of some higher power, supposed to be the Nizam's brother, who is trying to organize a conspiracy all over the country, but it is always discovered before it comes to anything. The Rajah of Kurnool, being unnoticed and out of the way, was chosen to collect and receive all the arms and ammunition; and when the English took his fort an enormous arsenal was found, and quantities of gunpowder kept in open chatties, under sheds made of dried leaves, and such queer contrivances, that it is a wonder the fort and the plot were not both blown up together long ago.

November 4th.—We have just heard news from Rajahmundry that has vexed us very much. Mr. X—,[424] who was appointed as A—'s temporary substitute, has taken the opportunity to turn out, by hook and by crook, under one pretence or another, a number of the native Court servants, writers, &c., just in order to put in his own dependants from another district. It is a shameful proceeding, for the poor people who are thus disgraced and deprived of their livelihood have committed no fault at all, and are among the most respectable and clever servants of the Court.

November 5th.—More bad news from poor Rajahmundry. A short time ago a violent storm[425]—such a storm as only occurs in the tropics—raged all along the coast from Narsapoor to Vizagapatam, and as far inland as Rajahmundry and Samulcottah. It must have been most awful. There was an irruption of the sea which drove all the shipping on shore, some of it four miles inland, and sloops are still fixed in gentlemen's gardens. It is computed that ten thousand people have been killed. All the little native huts at Samulcottah were blown down; all the European houses except two unroofed; our house at Rajahmundry all unroofed except one room; all X—'s furniture[pp] destroyed. We cannot be sufficiently thankful to the kind Providence which removed us before it took place, for with our two babies[qq] there is no saying what dreadful mischief might have happened. Neither we ourselves nor the children ever occupied the only room that remained safe, and the storm rose so suddenly in the night, that there would not have been time to escape from one part of the house to the other. The destruction of property has been enormous: all the goods in the merchants' storehouses at Coringa and Ingeram ruined; the crops destroyed; the tanks filled with salt water—till the irruption of the sea subsided, no fresh water was to be procured all along the coast. It has been a most fearful visitation. I am very sorry indeed for the poor people, already so impoverished by two years' scarcity and constant heavy taxation. The Collectors are chiefly bent upon keeping up the revenue, whatever may happen; and the people suffer terribly when they have any additional drawback. A "crack Collector," as the phrase goes, is one who makes a point of keeping up the usual revenue in defiance of impossibilities. There may be a famine, a hurricane; half the cultivators may take refuge in another district in despair; there may seem no possible means of obtaining the money: but still the Collector bullies, tyrannizes, starves the people—does what he pleases, in short,—and contrives to send in the usual sum to the Board of Revenue, and is said to be a "crack Collector."

December 12th.—All the fighting at Kurnool is now over. Colonel D— had the command of it. There were some European corps, dragoons and others, in the force. The fort which they went to besiege was given up to them directly, and they found it full of arms and gunpowder. But after they thought the whole affair was over, and that they had settled the matter without a shot, a party of Patans seized the Rajah, and our force was obliged to attack them. There was sharp fighting, and many killed; but it is all settled now. Colonel D——'s native regiment behaved so well, that, after the charge, the English dragoons went up and shook hands with them, and said they were as good soldiers as Englishmen, or "words to that effect." I saw the party of dragoons come home; poor things! they had lost the most men of any. Their band went out to meet them, with a large party of officers and civilians to welcome them home. The band had been practising the "Conquering Hero"[426] for a week, and they all marched in in great state and looking very grand. Then there was a break in the procession, and the led horses of the men who had been killed followed; and after that the widows, with their palanquins and bullock-carriages covered with black cloth. I think it was the most melancholy sight I ever saw, from the extreme contrast of all the music and gaiety preceding, and such a mournful change. A few days afterwards we saw Colonel D—— come in at the head of his Sepoys, very grand and proud, with all the colours and trophies they had taken. There seems no doubt but that there really *has* been a combination against us between all the Mohammedans in India; but, now they are put down, I suppose we are stronger than ever. It was remarkable that no Moormen came out to see the show of the regiments' return. In general they take such excessive delight in any military spectacle, that they will come from far and near to see it. This conspiracy seems like a last rise of the Mohammedan power: it is crumbling away everywhere. The English have now opened Affghanistan, and all that country will be under our orders. The Madras army is preparing for a Chinese war,[427] and expecting to be ordered to China very soon.

Vellore,[428] *December* 18*th*.—We are again on our road to Madras, and all our plans changed. This is the last letter you will receive from me, for I hope to be "over the surf" and on my way home to you all in another fortnight. We have been so strongly advised not to keep little Etta any longer in India, that we have at last made up our minds on the subject. A—— has applied for leave of absence, and will accompany her and me as far as the Cape, which he can do without losing his appointment; and I am then to proceed to England with her. Our passages are taken, and we expect to sail early next month.

THE END.

Editorial notes

Abbreviations

EIC	East India Company
Hobson-Jobson	H. Yule and A. C. Burnell, *Hobson-Jobson: The Anglo-Indian Dictionary* (Ware: Wordsworth, 1996)
Price	Alyson Price (ed.), *Julia Maitland: Letters from Madras During the Years 1836–1839* (Otley: Woodstock Books, 2003)

Notes

1. *Bay of Biscay*: A gulf in the Atlantic Ocean, along the west coast of France and the north coast of Spain.
2. *my brother Frank*: A pseudonym for Maitland's brother, Richard Francis Barrett.
3. *Madeira*: Now an autonomous Portuguese archipelago, off the north-west coast of Africa, Madeira was first occupied by the Portuguese in 1420. The British briefly took possession at the start of the nineteenth century, but it was returned to Portugal after the Napoleonic Wars.
4. *The Captain*: Captain Maitland. Not further identified. See Price, p. 8.
5. *Mrs M –* : Mrs. Mortlock. Not further identified. See Price, p. 10.
6. Major O'Brien: Not identified.
7. *Irish maid Freeman*: Not identified.
8. *Mr. Darke*: Not identified.
9. *Dr. Lowe*: Not identified.
10. *Mr. and Mrs. Wilde*: Mr. William Wilde was appointed Chief Justice of St Helena (see note 11) after control of the island passed from the EIC to the British Crown in 1833.
11. *St. Helena*: A tropical island in the south Atlantic Ocean. It was one of Britain's first colonies, governed by the EIC from 1657. It was also the location of Napoleon Bonaparte's exile from 1815 to 1821; see note 47.
12. *the Cape*: The Cape of Good Hope, in what is now South Africa, was a vital stopping point for ships on long voyages to and from India until the opening of the Suez Canal in 1869.
13. *the O'Briens*: Not identified.
14. *Miss Shields*: Miss Spiers; a missionary lady who went on to become assistant Governess of the Female Orphan Asylum in Madras. See Price, p. 10.
15. *Miss Knight*: Miss Craven. Not further identified. See Price, p. 10.
16. *promotion*: In the 1843 edition of her *Letters*, Maitland included here a description of a Captain Faulkner, the pseudonym for Captain Maitland. She wrote:

    > Captain Faulkner, very good humoured and civil, and rather original and clever, but the most incessant talker I ever did meet with in all my life: He can talk down the whole ship's company on every subject: I suspect he teaches the captain to sail.
    >
    > Price, p. 8.

17. *Mr. Harvey*: Not further identified.
18. *Lord Byron*: George Gordon Byron (1788–1824) was an English poet who travelled throughout the Mediterranean in his early twenties and who, for many, personified the figure of the Romantic traveller.
19. *Mr. Stevens*: Mr. Thomas. Not further identified. See Price, p. 10.
20. *Funchal*: The capital of Madeira.
21. *Captain Faulkner*: Captain Maitland; see note 16.
22. *Lucca*: A city in Tuscany, Italy. This is the first of several comparisons to Italy made by Maitland who had previously travelled there with her sister and her mother. Her time there also accounts for the various Italian phrases scattered throughout the text.
23. *a convent here*: The Santa Clara Covent, founded in Funchal in the sixteenth century.
24. *the Tropics*: The region surrounding the Equator.
25. *Tamul*: Tamil: Language spoken by the majority of people in Madras and the south Indian state of Tamil Nadu where Maitland spent the first eight months of her time in India.
26. *Melville's "University Sermons"*: Henry Melvill (1798–1871) was an evangelical preacher who published several collections of his sermons, including *Sermons Preached before the University of Cambridge, during the Month of February 1836* (Cambridge: Pitt Press, 1836).

27 *the Ancient Mariner*: 'The Rime of The Ancient Mariner' is a poem by Samuel Taylor Coleridge originally published in *Lyrical Ballads* (1798). In the poem, an albatross leads the mariner and his ship out of danger in the Antarctic. The crew applaud the albatross but the mariner shoots the bird and he is punished for this violent act.
28 *Coleridge's*: Samuel Taylor Coleridge (1772–1834), English Romantic poet and author of 'The Rime of The Ancient Mariner'; see note 27.
29 *Cape de Verd islands*: Cape Verde, an archipelago in the Atlantic Ocean and formerly a Portuguese colony. It was used as a depot during the transatlantic slave trade and as a stop for re-supplying ships.
30 *a ship going to New South Wales*: New South Wales was a British colony on the east coast of Australia. It was originally maintained as a penal colony, but by the 1830s there were growing efforts to encourage British settlers to the region.
31 *Mr Kenrick*: Not identified.
32 *snap-dragon*: A popular parlour game that consisted of placing raisins in a shallow bowl of brandy and setting it alight. Players then had to pick the raisins out of the bowl and eat them.
33 *"sporting my oak"*: Closing the door.
34 *Madagascar to Rio*: Madagascar is an island off the east coast of Africa. From the 1770s to 1820s, it gained prominence among pirates and European traders, particularly those involved in the transatlantic slave trade. In 1820 Radama I (1793–1828), its sovereign leader, pledged to end the export of slaves but, as seen here, the island continued to supply foreign markets, such as Rio de Janeiro in Brazil.
35 *To Her Younger Brother*: Maitland's brother Arthur.
36 *the ceremony of shaving on crossing the Line*: This ceremony originated as an initiation rite, usually involving some trials and hardships, to commemorate a sailor's first crossing of the equator. In the nineteenth century the ceremony also took place on passenger ships, largely for entertainment purposes, and it frequently featured King Neptune and his court as described in the following paragraphs.
37 *Mamma*: Charlotte Maitland, née Francis (1786–1870), a niece of the novelist Frances Burney (1752–1840).
38 *Tritons*: A race of sea gods and goddesses in Greek mythology. They were often depicted blowing into shells used as horns.
39 *Neptune*: Neptune was the Roman god of the sea, the equivalent to Poseidon and the father of Triton.
40 *à la Guy*: 'to the Guy' (French). Maitland is referring to the effigies of Guy Fawkes that are placed on the bonfire on 5 November and is perhaps denoting the quality of the costumes here.
41 *Young Temple*: Not identified.
42 Samson: A Biblical hero who possessed superhuman strength until Delilah cut his long hair. See Judges 13–16.
43 *as the monkey did Gulliver*: Gulliver is the protagonist of Jonathan Swift's novel *Gulliver's Travels* (1726). While in Brobdingnag, the land of giants, a huge monkey mistakes Gulliver for his son and carries him away.
44 *as soon as ever you have taken your degree*: Maitland's younger brother Arthur eventually graduated in 1838. See Price, p. 20.
45 *Tristan d'Acunha*: Also Tristan da Cunha: a remote island midway between Africa and South America that was uninhabited at the start of the nineteenth century. The first settler was Jonathan Lambert, an American, in 1810. In 1816 the United Kingdom annexed the islands and posted a garrison there. After the British withdrew in 1817, William Glass (see note 49), along with his wife and children, remained there and over time the settlement developed.

46 *Robinson Crusoes*: Maitland compares the residents of Tristan da Cunha to the eponymous protagonist of *Robinson Crusoe* (1719), a novel by Daniel Defoe (c. 1660–1731). Crusoe spent 28 years marooned on a remote island.
47 *In Bonaparte's time*: Napoleon Bonaparte (1769–1821) was a French military leader who built a large empire in Europe through a series of conflicts at the end of the eighteenth and start of the nineteenth century. He was eventually defeated by the British at Waterloo in 1815 and exiled on St Helena where he died in 1821. During his imprisonment, the British feared that French supporters would use the nearby island of Tristan da Cunha to rescue their former leader.
48 *Lord Castlereagh*: Robert Stewart (1769–1822), 2nd Marquess of Londonderry, and Viscount Castlereagh, was British Foreign Secretary from 1812. In this role, he was central to the defeat of Napoleon Bonaparte. He was, therefore, anxious to ensure the French did not rescue the military leader from nearby St Helena.
49 *Corporal Glass*: William Glass (1786–1853) was part of the garrison that took possession of Tristan da Cunha on behalf of the British. When the British withdrew troops in 1817, he remained on the island with his wife and two children. See note 45.
50 sous: A 'sou' was a French coin of little value.
51 "ecco tutto": 'That's all' (Italian).
52 *Blair's Sermons*: Hugh Blair (1718–1800) was a Scottish minister and university professor. He is best known for the five-volume compilation of his sermons; see H. Blair, *Sermons* (London: W. Strahan & T. Cadell, 1777–1801).
53 *Mrs. Glass*: The wife of Corporal Glass. See note 49.
54 *South Seas*: The South Pacific.
55 *Cape Town*: A city in South Africa first developed by the Dutch East India Company as a supply station for passing ships and then ceded to Britain in 1814. The colonial settlers along with the indigenous people and the earlier importation of slaves from Indonesia and Madagascar created a diverse population.
56 *Hottentots*: From the late-seventeenth century, white Europeans, especially the Dutch, derogatorily referred to the Khoikhoi people as Hottentots.
57 *Malays*: The people of Malaysia.
58 Parsees: During the seventh and eighth centuries, Zoroastrians from Persia migrated to India from modern-day Iran to avoid Muslim persecution; they became known as Parsees.
59 *If the Lady Geraldine's eyes . . . Christabel*: Maitland refers to Samuel Taylor Coleridge's narrative poem *Christabel*, in which Lady Geraldine transfixes and transforms the eponymous Christabel with her eyes. See S. T. Coleridge, *Christabel: Kubla Khan, a Vision: The Pains of Sleep* (London: John Murray, 1816).
60 *Methodist chapels*: The Methodists are a group of related Protestant Christian denominations that separated from the Established Church of England in 1784 in order to follow the evangelistic teachings of Charles Wesley (1707–1788) and John Wesley (1703–1791).
61 *Wesleyans*: A Methodist denomination that follows the methods and teachings of Charles and John Wesley.
62 *the C—s*: The Fieldings. Alyson Price suggests this could refer to Antony Vandyke Copley Fielding (1787–1855), Maitland's watercolour teacher, and his wife. See Price, p. 26.
63 *Achatina*: A genus of tropical land snail. Maitland's purchase of the shell reflects the popularity of conchology in the nineteenth century, particularly with women who took an increasing interest in the various branches of natural history.
64 *Instead of Whigs and Tories, they have the Caffre party and the Government party*: In Britain, in the first half of the nineteenth century, the political landscape was largely divided between two political parties: the Whigs, who went on to form the basis of the

Liberal party, and the Tories, who would eventually evolve into the modern Conservative party. In the Cape Colony at this time there were a number of conflicts between the European colonizers (who presumably Maitland refers to here when she talks of the 'Government party') and the Xhosa people (the 'Caffre party'); these gave rise to the Cape Frontier Wars or Kaffir Wars (1811–1858). Kaffir, or Caffre, was a term used by white Europeans to characterize South Africa's indigenous peoples.

65 *Wilderspin*: The Rutherfords. Not further identified. See Price, p. 26.
66 *O'Connell*: Daniel O'Connell (1775–1847): an Irish nationalist leader, who founded the Catholic Association in 1823 and worked with the Whig party during his campaigns for political reformism, specifically focusing on Catholic emancipation and the repeal of the Act of Union in Ireland.
67 *Dissenters*: Members of a non-established church, or nonconformists, in Britain.
68 *Miss Bazacot*: Not idenfitied.
69 *the Kloof*: A gorge in the greater Durban area of South Africa.
70 *Table Mountain*: A flat-topped mountain overlooking Cape Town in South Africa.
71 *Chine*: A deep narrow ravine or river valley.
72 *Isle of Wight*: Island off the south coast of England.
73 *Green Point*: Now a suburb of Cape Town.
74 *Madras*: Now Chennai: the capital city of the state of Tamil Nadu in south India. It developed around the site of the first major English settlement in India, Fort St. George.
75 *our cousin Staunton's house*: John and Diana Thomas, Maitland's brother-in-law and his wife. See Price, p. 33.
76 *à la chasse*: 'On the hunt' (French).
77 *Brighton*: A seaside resort, now part of the city of Brighton and Hove in East Sussex, England.
78 *Masoolah boats*: An Indian surfboat with many oars.
79 *catamarans*: A sea vessel with two parallel equal-sized hulls. The name derives from a Tamil word meaning 'logs bound together', although these boats were first developed by the Polynesians.
80 *early Indian voyagers' log books*: It has not been possible to identify Maitland's source here, although numerous subsequent publications used this passage and cited Maitland. See, for example, E. Thurston, *Castes and Tribes of Southern India* (Madras: Government Press, 1909), vol. 6, pp. 179–80.
81 *the witch of Fife's voyage in her cockle-shell*: 'The Witch of Fife' is a poem by James Hogg (1770–1835) published in the collection *The Queen's Wake* (1813). The eponymous witch sails across the sea in a cockle shell. Maitland then quotes lines 81–88.
82 *kind of bagpipes*: Probably *pungi*, a wind instrument made from a gourd and two reed-pipes that is often played by snake charmers in India.
83 *fangs extractcd*: Charmers removed the fangs or venal glands from poisonous snakes to ensure they were no longer dangerous.
84 *A –* : Maitland's husband, James Thomas Maitland, a judge.
85 *There is one man to lay my room, and another to bring in water . . . and others to wait at table*: This was a common assessment of how the caste system operated within the Anglo-Indian home. However, while caste undoubtedly dictated the division of household labour, many English men and women misrepresented it and took advantage of the affordability of Indian domestic workers.
86 *Moorman*: A synonym for Muslim.
87 *"John Company's English"*: The EIC was also known as John Company. Over time, employees and their families incorporated and adapted various Indian words into the English language; these words and phrases became known as Anglo-Indian. See Colonel Henry Yule and A. C. Burnell's comprehensive dictionary, *Hobson-Jobson: The Anglo-Indian Dictionary* (1886).

88 *the King's English*: Standardized English, complete with good grammar, proper usage of words, and correct pronunciation.
89 *Bishop Corrie*: Daniel Corrie (1777–1837) arrived as a missionary in India in 1806. He was appointed the first bishop of Madras in 1835. He was also a governor of the Church Missionary Society, founded various churches and schools, and fostered the growth of the Anglican Church in India. It is, therefore, unsurprising that Maitland enjoyed his visit, especially as he died a few weeks later. She records the news of his death in Letter 8.
90 *Black Town*: Originally the native quarter of Madras, situated just beyond the walls of Fort St. George. The term was also a generic one, used to denote indigenous areas as opposed to those occupied by Europeans in Indian cities.
91 *a most delightful preacher*: Reverend J. Tucker, secretary of the Church Missionary Society. See Price, p. 38.
92 Caste *boys*: Boys from the four established castes: Brahmins or the priestly caste; Kshatriya, the warrior caste; Vaisya, the merchant caste; and Sudra, the farmers and craftsmen.
93 *Pariahs*: Originally the name of the lowest caste in Indian society but the British used it more generally to refer to members of the lowest, or 'untouchable', castes in Indian society. These individuals were perceived as outcasts and they performed menial jobs. Maitland reveals here how British class prejudices were easily mapped onto the caste system.
94 *Dr. Bell*: Andrew Bell (1753–1832) was a priest and educationalist. In 1789, the EIC invited him to superintend the Madras Male Orphan Asylum, an institution for the orphaned, illegitimate and often half-caste sons of European officers. In this role, he focused as much on the development of a child's character as on their educational attainments and, in Madras, he devised a system of education based on mutual tuition whereby the older or brighter children in the class instructed the younger and less intelligent children.
95 *hedge-schools*: Small, informal schools. The term comes from the illegal, and therefore secret, Catholic schools that emerged in eighteenth- and nineteenth-century Ireland.
96 Moonshee: An indigenous secretary, reader, writer or, as is the case here, an interpreter and language instructor.
97 *salams*: See Deane, note 86.
98 *pagodas*: South Indian gold coins that, at this time, operated alongside the rupee. In 1818, a pagoda was worth 42 fanams, or three and a half rupees.
99 *Hindoo Literary Society*: It is unclear whether Maitland is referring to the Hindu Literary Society established by Lakshmaiah Kavali in 1834, or whether this is another similar society. Kavali modelled his scholarly venture on the Madras Literary Society and the work of Colin Mackenzie (1753–1821).
100 *cadjan-leaf*: Matted coconut palm leaf used in South India for thatching and as writing material.
101 *tiffin-time*: See Deane, note 165.
102 *Pondicherry*: The city of Pondicherry was a French colonial settlement in South India.
103 *shaddocks*: A citrus fruit, more commonly known as pomelo. It was named after Captain Philip Shaddock who apparently brought it from the east to the West Indies.
104 *Anglo-Indians*: Until the late nineteenth century, 'Anglo-Indian' referred to long-term English residents in India. Now, it more commonly refers to the mixed-race community, previously known as Eurasian. They won a legal battle in 1911 for sole ownership of the term.
105 *peons*: Foot soldiers, orderlies, or messengers. The term could also refer, more generally, to a low-ranking servant.
106 *bronze casts of the Apollo*: The Apollo Belvedere is a classical Roman marble sculpture of the god Apollo.

107 *true Fudge style*: *The Fudge Family in Paris* (London: Longman and Co., 1818) by the Irish poet Thomas Moore (1779–1852) is a comedic epistolary verse-novel. Maitland quotes, a little erroneously, from the text. The correct lines are: 'At the sight of that spot, where our darling Dixhuit / Set the first of his own dear legitimate feet' (ll. 23–4).
108 *Orientalism*: Maitland uses 'Orientalism' to refer to the scholarly pursuit of Indian languages and cultures. However, her approach to India is more Anglicist than Orientalist, influenced by Utilitarian thinkers who aimed to reform Indian culture and society.
109 *twelfth-cake*: Decorated cakes to celebrate the Epiphany.
110 *Nabob*: A corruption of *nawab* which, in this case refers to a Muslim gentlemen of distinction, an official or governor under the Mogul empire. However, it could also refer to European people who gained great wealth in India.
111 *Mussulman*: An archaic word for Muslim.
112 *vina*: Also *veena*: an Indian stringed instrument. It has seven strings and gourds at both ends.
113 *sévignés*: A type of brooch in the form of a bow. Named after the Marquise de Sévigné (1626–1696), it was particularly popular in the seventeenth and eighteenth centuries.
114 *the chimney-sweepers' clatter on May-day*: May Day was traditionally a holiday for chimney sweeps. They would parade through the streets banging their cleaning equipment and tools.
115 *Mahometans*: Another synonym for Muslims.
116 *animal magnetism*: During the 1830s and 1840s there was a craze for 'Mesmerism', a healing practice developed by Franz Anton Mesmer (1734–1815), whereby invisible flows of 'animal magnetism' or natural energy forces were supposedly channelled into the patient while they were in a trance-like state.
117 *the string*: A sacred white thread, sometimes known as the *Janeu* or *Yagyopaveet*, is worn by high-caste Hindus.
118 *Brahmins*: See Deane, note 90.
119 *pillaws*: Also pilau, pilaf: a rice dish often containing boiled meat or fowl, and spices.
120 *Mr. Tracey*: Not identified.
121 *attar of roses*: Usually *otta* of roses. See Deane, note 133.
122 *jessamine*: Jasmine flowers, from the genus *Jasminum*, are widely cultivated in India, partly due to their fragrance.
123 *Mrs. C – 's beautiful Landscape Annual*: Alyson Price claims this book belonged to Archdeacon George Owen Cambridge (1756–1841), a friend of the Burney and Barrett families. See Price, p. 53.
124 *Swamies*: Maitland includes a footnote defining *Swamies* as 'inferior gods', but this reflects her own personal biases. In actual fact, the term refers to a Hindu idol or it can be used as a respectful address or as an honorific title for a Hindu religious teacher.
125 *Mr N –* : Not identified.
126 *death of Bishop Corrie*: See note 89. As Maitland writes here, Bishop Corrie had impressed the English in Madras with his piety, devotion, and selflessness.
127 *the custom to punish the servants . . . as if they were children*: Nineteenth-century domestic advice manuals frequently advised Englishwomen to treat their Indian servants as they would their children. See, for example, F. A. Steel and G. Gardiner, *The Complete Indian Housekeeper and Cook . . . By Two Twenty Years' Residents* (London: Heinemann, 1888), p. 2.
128 *Coolie tailor*: A coolie was a hired or unskilled indigenous labourer in India.
129 *I have been trying to entomologize*: Entomology was a popular pastime for nineteenth-century middle-class women, and some sent their specimens to scientific establishments, such as Kew or the British Museum.

130 *Mr. Spence*: William Spence (c. 1782–1860) was a political economist and entomologist. He co-authored *Introduction to Entomology*, 4 vols (1815–1826), with William Kirby (1759–1850).
131 *Coleoptera*: An order of insects that includes beetles and weevils.
132 *St. Thomé*: Now a suburb in Madras, originally a Portuguese settlement named after Saint Thomas, one of Jesus's twelve disciples, who is interred on the site of the basilica there. Portuguese explorers built the church in the sixteenth century but it was rebuilt as a Gothic cathedral by the British in 1893.
133 *Sepoys*: Indigenous soldiers in the British Army.
134 *Miss L –* : Not identified.
135 *Mohurrum*: See Deane, note 148.
136 *a tatt*: Also tatty: see Deane, note 56.
137 *during my confinement*: Maitland gave birth to her daughter Henrietta on 8 June 1837.
138 *Zillah*: The name for the administrative districts of British India, each of which had a Collector and a Judge.
139 *Rajahmundry*: A city in the state of Andhra Pradesh. It was established by the British as an administrative district, or *Zillah*, in 1823.
140 *Gentoo*: In Madras, the Telugu-speaking Hindus and their language.
141 *Teloogoo*: Also Telugu: the primary language of the states of Andhra Pradesh and Telangana.
142 *Liverpool*: A city in the north-west of England.
143 *Calcutta*: Now Kolkata: see Deane, note 1.
144 *the dancing furniture in Washington Irving's dream*: Washington Irving (1783–1859) was an American writer. In his story 'The Bold Dragoon or The Adventure of my Grandfather', from *Tales of a Traveller* (1824), the furniture in an inn is bewitched and appears to dance.
145 *Italian Capuchins*: The Orders of Friars Minor Capuchin is an offshoot of the Franciscan Order, established by Francis of Assisi (c. 1181–1226).
146 *Coringa*: Korangi is a coastal village in Andhra Pradesh.
147 *Vizagapatam*: Visakhapatnam is a port city in Andhra Pradesh, approximately 175 km north of Korangi.
148 *Mr. R., the Assistant Judge*: Not identified.
149 palanquins: See Deane, note 9.
150 *leopards – or cheetahs as they are called*: Leopards and cheetahs are actually two different species: cheetahs have spots and leopards have rosettes. However, there is frequently some confusion about the two animals.
151 *the Godavery*: The Godavari River is India's second longest river, running from the state of Maharashtra to the Bay of Bengal.
152 *Cashmere shawls*: See Deane, note 82.
153 *Bramin*: See Deane, note 90.
154 *Vakeels*: Maitland defines Vakeel as a secretary or interpreter, but the term usually denoted an attorney or other authorized representative involved in political negotiations. See *Hobson-Jobson*, p. 961.
155 *muddles*: *Hobson-Jobson* casts doubt upon Maitland's usage of this term. The authors find no other instances of her definition and believe that it 'was probably a misapprehension'. See *Hobson-Jobson*, p. 593.
156 *a grand native festival which only takes place once in twelve years*: The Godavari Maha Pushkaram, a Hindu festival of spiritual purification that celebrates the river at Rajahmundry, takes place every twelve years, usually beginning in June.
157 *A – 's predecessor*: William Dowdeswell preceded and succeeded James Thomas Maitland in his post.
158 *Captain Price, the commanding officer*: Not further identified.

159 *Dr. Stewart*: Mr. Lyell, a relative of Sir Charles Lyell (1797–1875), the geologist. See Price, p. 75.
160 *Mr. McDonald*: Mr. Binning. Not further identified. See Price, p. 75.
161 *maty*: Also *matee*: an under-servant whose specific duties included cleaning crockery and attending to lighting.
162 *Thugs:* The Thugs were a gang of thieves who especially targeted travellers. They were notorious for their secrecy, their ritualistic strangling of travellers, and their worship of the goddess Kali. See Maitland's description in Letter 21. They became particularly noteworthy in the 1830s when William Sleeman (1788–1856) began his investigations and prosecutions as part of an extensive campaign to suppress the Thugs through law. This was supported by Governor-General William Bentinck and signalled his shift toward a more reformist policy.
163 Kalee: Kali: Hindu goddess, consort of Shiva. It was widely reported that the Thugs worshipped Kali and sacrificed their victims to her. However, there were some, like Maitland, who doubted the truth of this.
164 *Wolff's last volume of his Journal*: Joseph Wolff (1765–1862), a Church of England missionary who travelled extensively. He provided a long account of the Thugs in *Researches and Missionary Labours among the Jews, Mahommedans, and Other Sects*, where he defined them as 'a perfectly distinct class of persons who subsist almost entirely upon robbery and murder'. See J. Wolff, *Researches and Missionary Labours* (London: Nisbet, 1833), p. 438.
165 *One has been brought to A— for trial*: The British outlawed *Thuggee* through a series of legislations under the Thuggee and Dacoity Suppression Acts 1836–48.
166 *chatties*: A south Indian word denoting earthen pots. See *Hobson-Jobson*, p. 185.
167 *Johnny M*: This could be another reference to Maitland's husband.
168 "non sequitur": A Latin expression, meaning 'it does not follow' and usually used to signify a statement that does not seem logically connected to the previous one.
169 *an old Englishman*: Sergeant John Keeling. See Price, p. 77.
170 *the young Queen*: Queen Victoria (1819–1901) ascended to the throne in 1837 at the age of 18.
171 *Lord Durham*: John George Lambton (1792–1840), first Earl of Durham, politician and colonial administrator. He attempted to cultivate favour with the newly crowned Queen Victoria through his long-standing friendship with her uncle, King Leopold I of Belgium (1790–1865).
172 *Zemindar*: See Deane, note 58.
173 *Mr J.*: Not identified.
174 *godown*: A warehouse or outhouse for goods and stores.
175 *cobra capello*: See Deane, note 85.
176 *rack*: Arrack, a distilled spirit.
177 *physiognomy*: The theory that a person's facial features or expression are an indication of character.
178 "beaucoup de caractere": 'A lot of personality' (French).
179 *60l.*: 60 lakh: Indian currency. A lakh is the equivalent to 100,000 rupees.
180 *altogether twenty-seven: And this is reckoned few:* English households in India typically hired numerous servants, frequently blaming the caste system for the excess. However, a middle-class home could function with approximately ten indigenous employees. See É. Agnew, *Imperial Women Writers in Victorian India* (London: Palgrave, 2017), p. 63.
181 *amah*: Wet nurse. Although, according to Yule and Burnell, in Madras *amah* is frequently used instead of *ayah*; see *Hobson-Jobson*, p. 17.
182 "*pishashi*": In south India, the *pishachee* are devils or demons worshipped by ancient tribes.

183 *bang*: See Deane, note 257.
184 à-la-mode: 'fashionable' or 'of the moment' (French).
185 *tipsycake*: A cake made with sherry- and brandy-soaked sponge.
186 *Mrs. S.*: Not identified.
187 *Mr. and Mrs. Hamilton, the new registrar and his wife*: Mr. and Mrs. Jellicoe. Not further identified. See Price, p. 83.
188 *"up country"*: The interior regions of the country.
189 *the Presidency*: See Deane, note 7.
190 *contrary to regulation*: The Regulating Act of 1773 prohibited Company employees from receiving gifts, or bribes, from the indigenous people of India.
191 *a Jew's-harp*: Also known as the jaw or mouth harp.
192 *halberds*: The halberd was a weapon that combined a spear and a battle-axe.
193 *muslin pelisse*: Muslin is a type of cotton; a pelisse was a cloak with armholes or sleeves worn as part of a hussar's uniform, and also fashionable for English ladies in the early nineteenth century.
194 *Penny Whistle Row*: Not identified.
195 *"moppeing and moweing"*: The phrase 'mopping and mowing' meant pulling strange faces.
196 *our King*: William IV (1765–1837), who reigned from 1830 to 1837.
197 *the Collector*: Not identified.
198 *M. d'Arzel*: Not identified.
199 *"je suis trés aisy"*: Mock French for 'I am very easy'.
200 *"Elle ne parle pas, Moseer"*: 'She does not speak, Monsieur' (French).
201 *"Gassor"*: Mock French for *garçon*, the name for a waiter.
202 *"Gassor ally vous or"*: More mock French: 'Waiter, have you . . .?'
203 *David Gonsalves*: Not identified.
204 *Moochy or workman caste*: *Hobson-Jobson* states that members of the Moochy caste work in leather, either as shoemakers or sadlers. However, in south India, they might also be employed in painting, gilding, and upholstering. See *Hobson-Jobson*, p. 579.
205 *Psalm cxv 4–8*: This section of the Psalms reads:

> Their idols *are* silver and gold, / The work of men's hands. / They have mouths, but they do not speak; / Eyes they have, but they do not see; / They have ears, but they do not hear; / Noses they have, but they do not smell; / They have hands, but they do not handle; / Feet they have, but they do not walk; / Nor do they mutter through their throat.

206 *John Bull*: The name of John Arbuthnot's eighteenth-century personification of England as a stout, middle-aged, country-dwelling gentleman.
207 *Dratcharrum*: A Shaivite shrine and village.
208 *choultry*: According to *Hobson-Jobson*, the word *choultry* is specific to south India. As Maitland notes here, it is a simple dwelling where travellers can rest. See *Hobson-Jobson*, p. 211.
209 *Rossini's most noisy overtures*: Gioachino Antonio Rossini (1792–1868) was an Italian composer, known mainly for his operas and widely celebrated for his overtures.
210 *Vandyke brown*: An oil paint pigment named after Anthony Van Dyke (1599–1641), a Flemish painter who had great success in Italy and England, where he became the court painter.
211 *banyan-tree*: See Deane, note 383.
212 *the pagoda*: In this instance, an idol temple.
213 *pyramid-like building*: The *gopuram*, a heavily ornamented tower over the entrance of South Indian temples.
214 *nautch*: As previously stated (see Deane, note 302), the *nautch* was a staged dance performed by women; however, it could also refer to the girls themselves.

215 *howdah*: A travelling carriage, usually positioned on an elephant.
216 *betel-nut*: Betel nut is the fruit from the *areca* palm.
217 *"moral pocket-handkerchiefs"*: As the name suggests, these were handkerchiefs with moral maxims printed upon them and sold or donated to the poor.
218 *Mount Vesuvius*: A volcano located on the Gulf of Naples. It had recently erupted in 1834.
219 *insurrection*: The Coorg Rebellion. In 1837 the Gowdas, a hill tribe from the Western Ghats, attacked Mangalore in reaction to tax demands imposed by the Madras 'ryotwar' revenue system (see note 314).
220 *Mr. M –* : Mr. Montague Cholmeley; see Price, p. 109. Not further identified.
221 *pice*: See Deane, note 353.
222 *N – school*: Nellore, a town approximately 90 miles from Madras.
223 *Bengal*: See Deane, note 2.
224 *suttees*: The widows who joined their husband's corpse on the funeral pyre, thereby engaging in *sati*. See Deane, note 158.
225 *Juggernaut's sacrifices*: Annually in the town of Puri, Orissa, massive temple chariots, juggernauts, drag images of Jagannatha, a form of Krishna, through the streets. It was often alleged that devotees cast themselves under the wheels so that they might be crushed to death. See also Deane, note 344.
226 *"curry-and-rice Christians"*: People who convert to Christianity in order to obtain food or other material benefits from the missionaries.
227 *Mr. C.*: Mr. Cotterill; see Price, p. 109. Not further identified.
228 *your vicar*: Langdon, one of Maitland's suitors; see Price, p. 109.
229 *Jesuits*: Members of the Society of Jesus, a scholarly Catholic organization founded by St. Francis Xavier in 1534 to do missionary work. The Jesuits work primarily in education and other intellectual activities.
230 *farouche*: 'shy in company' (French).
231 *"fagots et fagots"*: Quotation from Moliere's play *Le Médecin Malgré Lui* or *The Doctor in Spite of Himself* (1666), Act 1, scene 6; its meaning is that all things of the same sort are not equal in quality.
232 *Narsapoor*: Narsapur is a town in the West Godavari district of Andhra Pradesh, and the site of one of the earliest Christian missions in Andhra Pradesh
233 *Mr. Bowden and Mr. Beer*: Edwin Skinner Bowden and Charles Henry Beer established an independent mission at Narasapur in 1837.
234 *Mr. Grove's*: Henry Grove (1684–1738) a dissenting tutor; see Price, p. 110.
235 *congées*: Maitland may mean *congé*, French for 'permission to leave'.
236 *cocoa-nut tope*: Coconut grove.
237 *Mr. G.*: Mr. Gordon; see Price, p. 116. Not further identified.
238 Mr. Lloyd: Not identified.
239 *Bishops being in the House of Lords*: As senior members of the Church of England, some Bishops are entitled to sit in the House of Lords, the upper house of the British Parliament.
240 *Mosheim*: Johann Lorenz von Mosheim (1693–1755) was an ecclesiastical historian.
241 *"Not forsaking the assembling of yourselves together"*: From Hebrews 10:25.
242 *Lingum*: Also *lingam*: a symbol representing the Hindu deity Shiva worn by Shaivite devotees, such as the Lingáyats (who were not a caste, as Maitland suggests here, but a Hindu sect).
243 *Shore's "Notes on Indian Affairs"*: Frederick John Shore (1799–1837) was a judge in the Civil Court in Furrukhabad, and the author of *Notes on Indian Affairs* (London: John W. Parker, 1837). The book was critical of British attitudes to, and governance of, the indigenous people of India.
244 *new magazine*: Maitland is referring to *Christian Knowledge*, a magazine set up in opposition to Cotterill's *Christian Repository*; see Price, p. 116. See also note 227.

245 *light black stone*: Snake stone, or viper's stone, is used in folk medicine to treat snake bites in various parts of the world.
246 *General W.*: Not identified.
247 *eau de luce*: A strong solution used in India as an antidote to venomous snake bites and insect stings; the main components are alcohol, ammonia, and oil of amber.
248 comme il faut: 'As required' (French).
249 *ninth Avatar*: In Hinduism, an avatar refers to the alternative forms, manifestations, incarnations, and personae of a deity, especially of Vishnu, who had ten primary avatars, each appearing at moments of conflict or crisis in order to restore order in the world. In his ninth avatar, he appeared as Buddha.
250 *tenth Avatar*: Vishnu's tenth and final avatar is Kalki. He appears when chaos prevails and ends the *kali yuga* cycle, or era, in order to restart the cycle of existence. Each *yuga* is understood to last for many thousands of years.
251 *Vishnoo*: The Hindu god Vishnu, the preserver and protector, and one of the Hindu trinity along with Brahma and Shiva.
252 *Mrs. Somerville*: Mary Somerville (1780–1872), Scottish scientist and astronomer. She wrote a number of highly influential texts, including *The Mechanism of the Heavens* (1831), and in 1835 the Royal Academy elected her and Caroline Herschel as their first women members.
253 *Herschel*: Frederick William Herschel (1738–1822) was a British astronomer (although born in Germany) who discovered the planet Uranus and constructed one of the most powerful telescopes of the time.
254 *Shasters*: Or *Shastras* or *Sutras*: the law books, or teaching texts, explicating Hindu scriptures such as the Vedas; see note 255.
255 *Vedas*: The ancient Hindu scriptures, written in Sanskrit. There are four vedas: the *Rigveda*, the *Yajurveda*, the *Sameveda*, and the *Artharvaveda*.
256 *Devinagree*: Devanāgarī is a script used to write many Indian languages such as Hindi, Konkani, Sanskrit, Marathi, and Nepali.
257 *Tower of Babel*: An origin myth, found in Genesis 11:1–9, to explain why people speak different languages.
258 *Syrian Christians*: The Saint Thomas Christians are a Christian community in south India that trace their origins back to St. Thomas the Apostle, who travelled to India in the first century AD. They use Eastern Christian traditions that employ the Syriac language in their liturgy.
259 *"soft sawder"*: A phrase meaning soft-soaping, blarney, or flattery.
260 *cheroot*: A cigar, especially those that have been cut at both ends, as they are in India.
261 *Gazette*: The Fort St. George Gazette printed official notices from the Government.
262 "*no salutes to idols be discontinued, but that all respect be paid to the native religions as heretofore*": The EIC Court of Directors issued a letter on 18 October 1837 stating:

> We now desire that no customary salutes, or marks of respect to native festivals be discontinued at any of the presidencies, that no protection hitherto given be withdrawn, and that no change whatever be made in any matter relating to the native religion except under the authority of the Supreme Government.

It came in response to a memorial submitted to the Madras Government from 203 members of the Christian community seeking exemption from compulsory attendance at indigenous worship. See Price, p. 151.
263 *Trichinopoly*: Now Tiruchirappalli: one of the major cities in Tamil Nadu. It was annexed by the British during the Fourth Anglo-Mysore War (1798–1799).
264 *Mr. D.*: Mr. Dowdeswell. See note 157.
265 *a 'History of the World'*: A text produced for the Indian students.

266 *Bangalore*: Now the capital city of the state of Karnataka. It was captured by the British during the Fourth Anglo-Mysore War (1799).
267 *Masulipatam*: Also Masulipatnam: a city in Andhra Pradesh. Since the early seventeenth century, it had been used by various European countries as a trading port, until the British took control in 1759.
268 *"first-caste monkeys"*: Maitland possibly means the Gray Langur monkey, commonly found throughout the Indian subcontinent.
269 Kistna: Another name for Krishna, usually used in reference to the river Kistna in southern India. It is the fourth-largest river in India.
270 *Johnny Gilpin*: *The Diverting History of John Gilpin* (1782) is a well-known comic ballad by William Cowper (1731–1800). In the final line, the speaker declares his wish to bear witness to Gilpin's future escapades, crying 'May I be there to see!'
271 *the Rhone*: The Rhône is a major European river, running from the Swiss Alps.
272 *tatties*: See Deane, note 56.
273 *the story of Cain*: The Biblical story of Cain and Abel appears in Genesis 4: 1–15. In these verses, Cain murders his brother and is punished by God.
274 *"If thou doest well, shall it not be accepted"*: Maitland refers specifically to Genesis 4:7, which states: 'If you do well, will you not be accepted? And if you do not do well, sin lies at the door. And its desire *is* for you, but you should rule over it'.
275 con rispetto: 'With all due respect' (Italian).
276 *Governor of Madras*: John Elphinstone (1807–1860) was the Governor of Madras 1837–1842.
277 *GREEN BUGS*: Maitland possibly means the *Chrysocoris stollii*, a green jewel bug from India that produces a pungent odour when disturbed.
278 *some particular goddess*: It was widely reported that the Thugs worshipped Kali and sacrificed their victims to her. See note 163.
279 *Cocanada*: Kakinada, now one of the largest cities in Andhra Pradesh.
280 *Amalpoor*: Amalpurum, a town in Andhra Pradesh.
281 Nellapilly *and* Yanam: A Dutch colony until 1720 when the French took control. From then until 1840 it went back and forth between Britain and France, when the latter assumed ownership. It was returned to India in 1954.
282 *the L – s*: Not identified.
283 *punkah*: A large cloth fan on a frame suspended from the ceiling, moved back and forth by pulling on a cord.
284 *Mr. S –* : Not identified.
285 *The present commanding officer here . . . Captain and Mrs. C–*: Captain Kelly and his wife: Not further identified.
286 *baslams*: Himalayan basalms, *Impatiens*, are native to the Himalayas but now grow across much of the northern hemisphere.
287 *the M – s*: Sir Peregrine Maitland (1777–1854) resigned as Commander-in-Chief in 1838 because the EIC would not enforce the Charter Act of 1833 which stated that Company employees no longer had to attend indigenous religious gatherings.
288 *Sir P –* : Sir Peregrine Maitland; see note 287.
289 *Cooly Trade*: For much of the nineteenth century, after the abolition of the slave trade, many low-caste Hindus travelled as indentured labour from south India to Mauritius to work on sugar and rubber plantations. As Maitland goes on to explain in this paragraph, many former slave plantations were in need of cheap and plentiful labour and, because the anti-slave legislation did not extend to the EIC's possessions, Indians were recruited to work in these colonial outposts. There were regulations and penalties for abuse but reports of the harsh conditions suggest their employment was merely another form of slavery.

290 *"Emigration of the Hill Coolies to the Mauritius"*: Indian emigration to Mauritius, an island in the Indian Ocean, started around 1830. There were particularly high numbers of Indians from the poorer rural and hill regions of the subcontinent.
291 *Lord G –* : Sir John Gladstone (1764–1851), Scottish MP and slave trader. He initially complied with the Abolition Act of 1833, but then imported large numbers of Indian workers to his plantations in Jamaica and Guyana.
292 *Middle Passage*: The Middle Passage was one stage on the trade route through which Europeans shipped millions of enslaved Africans to the Americas and the West Indies to work on plantations. Conditions on board the ships were notoriously awful and many died during the journey.
293 "di nacosto": 'Out of sight' (Italian).
294 Dussera: Also Vijayadashami: a ten-day Hindu festival in October. It generally celebrates the triumph of good over evil, although the focus of the festivities depends upon the region.
295 *A – thinks there is serious danger of a war*: James Thomas Maitland was fearful of an outbreak of war between Britain and Russia as both countries attempted to establish control of Afghanistan. His anxiety became more pronounced when Dost Mohammad Khan (1793–1863) reached out to Russia for support against Ranjit Singh. The British prepared to invade Kabul and remove Dost Mohammad Khan from the throne, an act which led to the First Anglo-Afghan War (1839–1842).
296 *we are at war with the Persians already*: The Persian dynasty, led by Shah Mohammed Miraz, attempted to capture Herat from the Afghans in 1837 with the help of a Russian envoy. They laid the city under siege and, in July 1838, the British retaliated by occupying Iranian territory. Consequently, the Persian Shah gave up his siege of Herat.
297 *Sir H. Fane*: Sir Henry Fane (1778–1840) was an army officer, and from 1835, he served as Commander-in-Chief in India. He quelled the siege of Herat (see note 296) and subsequently retired.
298 *Marquis of Wellesley*: Richard, Marquess Wellesley (1760–1842) was Governor-General of India 1798–1805. He greatly expanded British imperial reach during his rule and Maitland's praise of him here clearly indicates her opposition to the current Governor-General, George Eden (1784–1849), Earl of Auckland, whose actions against Afghanistan led to the First Anglo-Afghan War. Many in Britain viewed the war as unnecessary, rash, and without benefit, and it ultimately damaged Lord Auckland's reputation.
299 *Mr. S –* : Reverend Vincent Shortland (1803–1880) was an Anglican Archdeacon in India; see Price, p. 152.
300 *Mr. and Mrs. G –* : The Butlers; see Price, p. 152. Not further identified.
301 piccolissimo parere: 'Humble opinion' (Italian).
302 *Dewan*: Also *diwan*: title denoting an indigenous official, or person in charge of an establishment.
303 *young Ch –* : Not identified.
304 *a public bungalow*: Usually referred to as a *dak* or *dawk* bungalow. These structures were maintained by the EIC, and later the British Government, in order to house travellers as they moved through the country. See Deane, note 163.
305 *In order to save money, Lord W. Bentinck reduced the army and sold the stores*: Lord William Bentinck (1774–1839) was Governor-General of India 1828–1835. He is remembered for his social, political, and economic reforms. During his reign, the EIC was under financial pressure and he gained a reputation for dramatic cost-cutting in many areas, including the military.
306 *The Commanders-in-chief at the three Presidencies are all going home*: Sir Peregrine Maitland was the Commander-in-Chief at Madras and, as stated in note 287,

he retired in 1838. Sir Henry Fane, of the Bengal army, retired in 1839 after the siege of Herat. Lieutenant-General John Keane, Commander-in-Chief of the Bombay Army also departed in 1839.

307 *tamboura*: Large four-stringed lute used in Indian music.
308 *Spanish boleros*: A genre of slow-tempo Latin music and the associated dance.
309 *Frank has gained the T – scholarship!*: Maitland's brother Richard was named Tyrwhitt Hebrew Scholar at King's College, Cambridge.
310 *Alexandria*: A port city in Egypt, on the route to India prior to the Suez Canal.
311 *war against the Persians*: Another reference to the siege of Herat. See note 296.
312 chi lo sa: 'Who knows?' (Italian).
313 *The Bishop*: In November 1837, following Bishop Corrie's death, George Trevor Spencer (1799–1866) was consecrated as the second Bishop of Madras.
314 *Poor creatures! they are so screwed by taxes*: There were two main tax systems in place throughout British India: The *ryotwari* and the *zamindar* systems. The former was introduced to the Madras Presidency in 1820 by Sir Thomas Munro, Governor of Madras (1820–7) and Captain Alexander Reed. In this system, the government directly imposed land revenues on individual peasants. According to critics, taxes were routinely set too high.
315 *Colonel B – y*: Henry Burney (1792–1845), Frances Burney's nephew, worked for the EIC. See also note 389.
316 *national-school girls*: The National Society for Promoting Religious Education is an organization that promotes Christian education. In the nineteenth century, they provided funding for so-called National Schools.
317 Hakeem: Also *hakim*; see Deane, note 429.
318 *Idolatry is forbidden by their Koran*: In Islam, practicing idolatry or polytheism is forbidden because it deifies something other than the singular God, i.e. Allah.
319 *temple of the idol Punchanund*: The temple is situated near the Kidderpore Bridge in Calcutta.
320 hookahs: See Deane, note 160.
321 *Cape l'Aguillas*: Cape Agulhas is the southernmost point of the African continent, and where the African and Indian Oceans clash. It is known for its violent waves and the danger it posed to ships; there were many shipwrecks along this coast.
322 *a friend of Rammohun Roy's*: It has not been possible to identify the friend but Rammohun Roy (1772–1833) was an Indian religious, social, and educational reformer. He founded the Brahmo Samaj, a rationalist Hindu movement that challenged aspects of traditional Hindu culture and which sought progress for Indian society under British rule.
323 *Mr. G –* : Mr. Garrett; see Price, p. 161. Not further identified.
324 *a quantity of potatoes*: The Portuguese first introduced potatoes to India, and the British continued planting them in the late eighteenth century, in the north of India, as a cheap and durable crop. Later, they tried to introduce them throughout the subcontinent.
325 *Samulcottah*: Samalkota is a town in Andhra Pradesh.
326 *Major C –* : Major McCurdy; see Price, p. 161. Not further identified.
327 *Mantell*: Gideon Mantell (1790–1852) was a geologist and palaeontologist. He wrote a number of books on these subjects and was assisted in his work by his wife Mary Ann Woodhouse.
328 *Tripetty*: The temple devoted to Lord Venkatesa on the hill of Tirumala in Tripetty, or Tirupathi, is one of the most popular pilgrimage sites in India.
329 soupçon: 'A hint of' (French).
330 *Abraham*: The story of Abraham appears in Genesis 12–25.

331 *'The famine is decreasing now'*: Under the British Raj, India suffered countless famines. The EIC, through its crushing of the textile industry, had pushed people into agriculture. As a consequence, the economy was much more dependent on the weather and subject to the difficult seasonal issues, such as the monsoon. Furthermore, Britain exported large proportions of crops leaving insubstantial supplies for the indigenous population. In 1837–1838, there was a major famine in the north-west of India; however, there were also many localized instances such as this at Rajahmundry.
332 *chewing betel*: See Deane, note 273.
333 *Mr. B –* : Not identified.
334 *a Sunnyassee*: A Hindu mendicant who resigns or abandons worldly affairs.
335 *Feringhees*: A *feringhee* is a foreigner, especially one with white skin.
336 *Miss L – 's*: Mary Elliot; see Price, p. 166. Not further identified.
337 *"Watts on Prejudices"*: Isaac Watts (1674–1748) was a non-conformist writer. In *Logic: or, the right use of Reason in the Enquiry after Truth* (1724) there was a section entitled, 'The Springs of False Judgement' or 'The Doctrine of Prejudice'.
338 *"des Catechismes de six sous" like Massillon's little infidel*: From the sermons of Jean Baptiste Massillon (1663–1742), a Catholic bishop and famous preacher.
339 *Translation Committee at Madras*: Maitland may be referring to the Oriental Translation Committee, which had recently become attached to the Royal Asiatic Society for the purpose of selecting and superintending the translation and printing of Oriental Works. However, this was mostly concerned with translating works into English.
340 *Butler's "Analogy"*: Joseph Butler, bishop of Durham (1692–1752) was a religious and moral philosopher. He wrote *The Analogy of Religion, Natural and Revealed, to the Constitution and Course of Nature* (1736), which was greatly respected at this time.
341 *Henrietta*: Maitland's daughter. Also referred to as Etta.
342 *Mr. Johnston*: Not identified.
343 *Archdeacon (of Madras)*: Thomas Robinson (1790–1873) was Archdeacon of Madras from 1826.
344 *Pariah school*: A school for members of the lowest castes. See note 93.
345 *Mr. H.*: Mr Hamilton; not further identified.
346 *scappate*: Possibly 'runaways' (in Italian).
347 *young B –* : Boswell; see Price, p. 178. Not further identified.
348 *pilgrim tax:* The EIC collected taxes at various temples and religious festivals throughout the country. The tax had been put in place by previous rulers and afforded protection or toleration of religious sites, but it also provided revenue for the Company. Many perceived this as evidence of the Company's support of indigenous religions. It was abolished in 1839.
349 *Beejanuggur*: Also Vijayanagara: a city in Karnataka, which was once the capital city of the historic Vijayanagara Empire. The ruins, called Hampi, have now been designated as a UNESCO Word Heritage Site.
350 *Mr. Hands*: Possibly John Hands, a missionary with the London Missionary Society. He was sent to India in 1810, whereupon he founded a mission station at Bellary and was the first to translate the Bible into Kannada.
351 *Anagoondy Rajah*: Not identified.
352 *School-book Society:* The Madras School Book Society was a voluntary organization formed in 1820.
353 *Mr. L –* : Mr. Binning; see Price, p. 178. Not further identified.
354 *"The Spectator"*: An English-language newspaper published in Madras 1836–1859. It was the first daily newspaper to be published from the city.
355 *national education*: In this letter, Maitland sets out her detailed plan for a widespread government-supported education system in the Presidency of Madras.

356 *king of twelfth-cake*: Twelfth-cakes were frequently decorated with royal wax figurines or crowns; see also note 109.
357 *Zemindary*: Office or territory held or administered by a *zemindar* (see Deane, note 58).
358 *Mr. Thompson*: George Dunisthorpe Thompson (1804–1878) was an orator, abolitionist, and political reformer. He became involved with Joseph Pease (1772–1846), a Quaker activist and founding member of the British India Society in 1839.
359 *Beyrout*: Now Beirut, the capital city of Lebanon.
360 *St. Matthew*: One of Jesus Christ's twelve apostles and author of one of the four gospels of the New Testament.
361 *two young Parsees were baptized 'at Bombay'*: Maitland refers to the controversial case of Dhanjibhai Nauroji, a 16-year-old Parsee convert. In 1839 his uncle, Heerjeebhoy Dadabhoy, filed a case against Dr. John Wilson, an evangelical missionary, citing forced conversion of Dhanjibhai and a friend, and the case went to trial. It was extremely high profile and there were violent scenes reported from the courthouse. See J. S. Palsetia, *The Parsis of India: Preservation of Identity in Bombay City* (Leiden: Brill, 2001), p. 114.
362 Sta a vedere: 'You'll see' (Italian).
363 *Act of Parliament, that people of a certain standing are entitled to certain appointments*: Commissioned officers could obtain promotion by buying the next senior rank from an officer who was either himself being promoted, or else leaving the army. See A. Sattin (ed.), *An Englishwoman in India: The Memoirs of Harriet Tytler 1828–1858* (Oxford: Oxford University Press, 1986), p. 198.
364 *Lord E—*: Lord Elphinstone, Governor of Madras (1837–1842). See note 276.
365 *"A change came o'er the spirit of my dream"*: Quotation from Lord Byron's poem 'The Dream' (1816), l. 79.
366 *W—E—as an admirable Private Secretary*: Walter Elliot (1803–1887) was Private Secretary to his cousin Lord Elphinstone, the Governor of Madras. Maitland's praise here is surely due to Elliot's and Elphinstone's support for educational projects in south India.
367 *Cuddapah*: Now Kadapa, a city in Andhra Pradesh. It came under British control in 1800 and the London Missionary Society established a mission there in 1822.
368 *Bellary*: Also Ballari: a city in the state of Karnataka.
369 *Chingleput and Cuddalore*: Districts in the Madras Presidency.
370 *Chittoor*: A city in Andhra Pradesh.
371 *Palmanair*: Also Palmaner: a plateau near Chittoor.
372 *Neilgherries*: From the 1820s, the Nilgiri hills became an increasingly popular retreat area for the British.
373 *Palmyra-trees*: The *Borassus* or Palmyra palm is the official tree of Tamil Nadu. It is highly regarded because all parts of the tree can be used.
374 *Miss T—*: Miss Tucker; see Price, p. 187.
375 *Female Orphan Asylum*: The Madras Military Female Orphan Asylum, established in 1787 by Lady Archibald Campbell, catered for the children of British Army soldiers.
376 *Lady N—, the present Commander-in-Chief's lady*: Lady Nicolls, wife of Lieutenant General Sir Jasper Nicolls, who became Commander-in-Chief of the Madras Army in 1839.
377 *Hannah More*: Hannah More (1745–1833) was an English writer and philanthropist. She was particularly concerned with moral and religious subjects and called for increased intellectual, religious, and sentimental education for girls. She wrote a famous tract on the issue, *Strictures on the Modern System of Female Education*, 2 vols (1799).

378 *the Tanjore Mission*: Carl Theophilus Ewald Rhenius (1790–1838) was a Prussian missionary who worked with Church Missionary Society in Tirunelveli (1820–1835) before establishing the German Evangelical Mission due to disagreements with the CMS committee.
379 *Tinnevelly*: Tirunelveli: a city in the state of Tamil Nadu.
380 *Mr. T –* : Not identified.
381 *Mr. Howell*: Not further identified.
382 *J –* : Maitland's brother-in-law John Thomas; see Price, p. 187.
383 *at the funeral of that wretched old RUNJEET SINGH*: It was widely reported that four wives and seven slave girls died on the funeral pyre of Ranjit Singh (see Deane, note 318), despite recent legislation against the practice of *sati*.
384 *the immense diamond*: Maitland refers here to the Koh-i-noor diamond, one of the largest cut diamonds in the world, now part of the British crown jewels. Previously, Ranjit Singh had procured it as payment for sheltering Shah Shuja Durrani after he was overthrown (see note 385), and he bequeathed the diamond to the Jagannath Temple, Puri. However, the British later acquired it after the Second Anglo-Sikh War (1848–1849) when they annexed the Kingdom of Punjab and gained control of its assets.
385 *Shah Soojah:* Shah Shuja Durrani (1785–1842) was the ruler of the Durrani Empire and the self-proclaimed King of Afghanistan 1803–1809. However, he was overthrown by his predecessor and remained in exile until 1838. At this time, with the help of the British and Ranjit Singh, he ousted Dost Mohammad Khan and reclaimed control of Afghanistan.
386 Candahar: See Deane, note 295.
387 *to pay their devotions to a rag of Mohammed's shirt:* The Shrine of the Cloak in Kandahar contains a piece of cloth allegedly worn by Muhammad. Shah Shuja apparently visited the shrine when he returned to Kandahar, accompanied by a British escort that included William Hay Macnaghten (1793–1841) and Alexander Burnes (1805–1841).
388 *a Burmese war*: The First Anglo-Burmese War took place in 1824–1826. It concluded with the Burney, or Yandabo Peace Treaty, brokered by Henry Burney; see note 315. Then in 1837 Prince Tharrawaddy (1787–1846) ousted King Bagyidaw (1784–1846) of Burma, and rejected the terms of the Treaty. Although this renewed tensions between Burma and England, the next outbreak of war did not occur until 1852–1853.
389 *Colonel Burney's wisdom*: During the First Anglo-Burmese War, Henry Burney collected much information about Burma and Siam for England. When Prince Thayawaddy assumed the throne and rejected the Peace Treaty, Burney withdrew his residency.
390 "petite drolerie": 'Little trickery' (French).
391 *the Nizam's brother*: Prince Mubarez-ud-Daulah was the younger brother of the Nizam of Hyderabad. He opposed British presence in Hyderabad and in 1830 gathered an army to rebel against them but his plans were discovered and he was quickly imprisoned.
392 'petits spectacles': 'Small shows' (French).
393 non pensi: 'Don't you think?' (Italian).
394 *another little Rajah trying at a rebellion:* Rasool Khan, Nawab of Kurnool, also opposed the British and entered into a secret alliance with Prince Mubarez; see note 391. The British soon discovered this plot and prevented the insurrection.
395 *the red coats*: Military clothing worn by the Presidency armies of the EIC and British India.
396 *four or five years collecting arms and ammunition*: The Nawab of Kurnool had collected a huge arsenal in preparation for his rebellion against the British.
397 *"conquered a green blight"*: Not identified.

398 *British Museum*: The British Museum in London was established in 1753, largely based on the collections of Sir Hans Sloane (1660–1753). Maitland's donations are recorded by the Natural History Museum although the specimens are missing; see Price, p. 188.
399 *Mr Samouelle*: George Samouelle (c. 1790–1846) was a curator in the British Museum with an interest in Lepidoptera. He also wrote *A Nomenclature of British Entomology, or a Catalogue of above 4000 Species of the Classes Crustacea, Myriapoda, Spiders, Mites and Insects Intended as Labels for Cabinets of Insects, etc., Alphabetically Arranged* (London, 1819).
400 *chits*: In Anglo-Indian, a letter or note.
401 *les absens*: 'Those absent' (French).
402 *Mrs. W – E –* : Mrs Walter Elliot: Maria Dorothea Hunter Elliot (c. 1816–1890), the Private Secretary's wife.
403 *That is the grand Indian sorrow – the necessity of parting with one's children:* It was the custom for British children born in India to be sent home around the age of six or seven due to concerns about acquiring poor health and bad habits.
404 *the ghauts*: Two converging mountain ranges in south-east India, the eastern and western Ghats.
405 *Lady Q –* : Not identified.
406 *Mrs. C.*: Not identified.
407 *Miss D.*: Not identified.
408 *tiffin*: See Deane, note 165.
409 *seven-years' sleep of the Beauty in the fairy tale*: The reference here is surely to Charles Perrault's 'Sleeping Beauty in the Forest', from his collection, *Histoires ou contes temps passé* (1697). However, in Perrault's tale, the beauty slept for a hundred years.
410 *Mr. Wilberforce*: William Wilberforce (1759–1833), English politician and philanthropist, who played a key part in the abolition of the slave trade.
411 *"in the wild-beast way"*: It has not been possible to identify Wilberforce's connection to this common phrase.
412 *"God save the Queen"*: The British national anthem.
413 *fine old fort*: Bangalore Fort, a stronghold for Tipu Sultan which was captured by the British in 1791 during the Third Mysore War (1790–1792).
414 *The Pettah*: Bangalore Fort had a fortified town, or pettah, outside it.
415 *Naples*: Italian city in the region of Campagna.
416 *uncommon pagoda*: Inside Bangalore Fort there is a temple dedicated to Lord Ganapathy, also known as Ganesha.
417 *Moorish architecture*: Islamic architecture originating in north Africa and parts of Spain.
418 *the Talmud*: The book of Jewish law.
419 *Adam Clarke's notion*: Adam Clarke (1762–1832) was a British Methodist theologian and Biblical scholar. He is chiefly remembered for writing a commentary on the Bible in which he argued the serpent that tempted Eve was actually an ape-like creature. He believed the error had been caused by mistranslation. See A. Clarke, *The Holy Bible: Containing the Old and New Testaments: The Text Carefully Printed from the Most Correct Copies of the Present Authorized Version, Including the Marginal Readings and Parallel Texts: With a Commentary and Critical Notes*, 6 vols (1810–1826).
420 *Thames*: River running through London.
421 *Hodgons's ale*: An Indian Pale Ale (IPA), i.e. an ale that is brewed from pale malt. Among the first brewers known to export beer to India was George Hodgson of the Bow Brewery, located near the East India Docks. His beers were popular among the Company traders from the late eighteenth century.

422 *fighting at Kurnool:* The British attacked the Kurnool fort in Andhra Pradesh in October 1839, after learning about the conspiracies between Nawab Rasool Khan and Prince Mubarez-ud-Daulah and gleaning knowledge of the vast armoury stored there. They defeated the Nawab after six days of conflict.
423 *Colonel D –* : Colonel Dyce of the Twenty-Seventh Native Cavalry.
424 *Mr. X –* : Mr Dowdeswell. See Price, p. 199. Also see note 157.
425 *a violent storm*: A hurricane occurred along the coast north of Madras in November 1839. As Maitland notes, the death toll neared 10,000. See Price, p. 199.
426 *"Conquering Hero"*: A reference to the victorious chorus 'See the Conquering Hero Comes' from *Judas Maccabeus* (1746), Handel's tribute to the Duke of Cumberland after he had defeated the Jacobite army of Bonnie Prince Charlie at Culloden.
427 *a Chinese war*: In the late 1830s, Chinese officials grew increasingly uncomfortable with the misuse of opium in the wider Chinese. In 1839 they destroyed a storehouse and forbid the merchants to trade the product. The British took this as an attack on free trade and sent out troops to reinstate trading. This was the beginning of the Opium War (1839–1842).
428 Vellore: A city in the state of Tamil Nadu. It was the location of a brief but violent mutiny by Indian sepoys against their EIC officers in July 1806.

TEXTUAL VARIANTS

Three editions of *Letters of Madras* were published, *1843*, *1846*, and *1861*. There are some small amendments and additions in the second edition (our source text), as detailed below. The second and third editions are identical.

a. have lately excited universal interest] have excited such universal interest *1843*
b. first impressions] first impressions such as these *1843*
c. many traits] many graphic traits *1843*
d. the endeavours] the earnest endeavours *1843*
e. mentioned] mentioned in terms not altogether commendatory *1843*
f. promotion] promotion: – Captain Faulkner, very good humoured and civil, and rather original and clever, but the most incessant talker I ever did meet with in all my life: he can talk down the whole ship's company, and be quite as fresh to begin his rounds again: he is the universal adviser to the whole company on every subject: I suspect he teaches the captain to sail; *1843*
g. ever saw.] Madeira is very lively, very like Lucca: the country, and the heat, and the people, are Italy over again *1843*
h. *August 25th.-* Madeira is very lively, very like Lucca: the country, and the heat, and the people, are Italy over again. We have just been to visit a convent here.] *August 25th.-* We have just been to visit a convent here. *1843*
i. a conversation] a chirp *1843*
j. working] waging *1843*
k. *Samson*] *Sampson 1843*
l. and bugs; the last] and bugs, but the bugs *1843*
m. a Dutch boarding house, which Frank would have called the "Hotel de Bugs;"] a Dutch boarding house, where we were eaten up alive *1843*
n. a capital set in their attitudes] a capital set, poor things! in their attitudes *1843*
o. clear, and striking] clear, true, and striking *1843*
p. People complain, and perhaps justly, that] People complain that *1843*

q.	very pretty and antique] very pretty, graceful, and antique *1843*	
r.	composition.] composition. Is it not absurd? *1843*	
s.	what a figure] what a Guy *1843*	
t.	onyxes and agates] onyxes. *1843*	
u.	This morning . . . cured me of gardening] *1843 omit*	
v.	The snakes have . . . quite makes one shudder] *1843 omit*	
w.	I did the same.] I did the same, and we had a chirp *1843*	
x.	twopenny "moral pocket-handkerchiefs"] twopenny handkerchiefs *1843*	
y.	The castes . . . making a little more money] *1843 omit*	
z.	There is great difference . . . these native languages] *1843 omit*	
aa.	no village near it] no village even, near it *1843*	
bb.	very much] very much, poor things! *1843*	
cc.	The business . . . rather than helps them] *1843 omit*	
dd.	a great many ornaments, and chatter incessantly from the moment they enter the house] a great many ornaments, *mauvais ton*, chatter incessantly from the moment they enter the house, twist their curls, shake their bustles, and are altogether what you may call "Low Toss." *1843*	
ee.	manner of reasoning] manner of thinking *1843*.	
ff.	A fortnight ago] Accordingly, a fortnight ago *1843*	
gg.	I believe . . . promised they would get "plenty sense".] *1843 omit*	
hh.	get off when examined] when examined, and get off *1843*	
ii.	with a dessert spoon] with a spoon *1843*	
jj.	a good man, but has given offence] a good man, but gives great offence *1843*	
kk.	The Bishop] The poor Bishop *1843*	
ll.	Slow] dunny *1843*	
mm.	At the Translation Committee . . . the proposition.] *1843 this paragraph included as footnote rather than main text*	
nn.	it dawdles on] it just dawdles on *1843*	
oo.	"*les absens*," &c,] *footnote included here 1843, reading*: 'Alluding to the recorded speech of a French lady, who exclaimed, "Je ne sais d'oú cela vient, mais les absens me passent toujours de l'âme!"'.	
pp.	All X – 's furniture] all D's – 's furniture *1843*	
qq.	our two babies] our two poor babies *1843*	